Routledge Revivals

Trade Union Growth, Structure and Policy

First published in 1962, *Trade Union Growth, Structure and Policy starts* with the long history of the textile unions and their remarkable structures and techniques. By comparing these unions to each other and to other key unions, Professor Turner explores those major problems in the development and contemporary position of trade unionism which are of public interest. He reappraises the general theory of the labour movement's evolution and is able to show that, what are essentially modern unions have existed longer than has been realized and also that 'unofficial' movements often repeat the pattern of very early unionism. A detailed comparison and contrast of modern unions reveals that they fall into a greater number of different types and are subject to a greater diversity of influences than is generally supposed both in formal government and in effective democracy. The author assesses the factors which have in the past have brought about a major change in trade unions and the likelihood of major changes in the future. This book is an important historical document for scholars and researchers of labour movement, labour economics and political economy.

Trade Union Growth, Structure and Policy

A Comparative Study of the Cotton Unions

H. A. Turner

Routledge
Taylor & Francis Group
Routledge Revivals

First published in 1962
by George Allen & Unwin Ltd.

This edition first published in 2022 by Routledge
4 Park Square, Milton Park, Abingdon, Oxon, OX14 4RN

and by Routledge
605 Third Avenue, New York, NY 10017

Routledge is an imprint of the Taylor & Francis Group, an informa business

Publisher's Note
The publisher has gone to great lengths to ensure the quality of this reprint but points out that some imperfections in the original copies may be apparent.

Disclaimer
The publisher has made every effort to trace copyright holders and welcomes correspondence from those they have been unable to contact.

A Library of Congress record exists under LCCN: 63004474

ISBN: 978-1-032-25505-7 (hbk)
ISBN: 978-1-003-28359-1 (ebk)
ISBN: 978-1-032-25506-4 (pbk)

Book DOI 10.4324/9781003283591

(*Courtesy of City of Salford Art Gallery*)

Coming from The Mill—by L. S. LOWRY

TRADE UNION GROWTH STRUCTURE AND POLICY

A Comparative study
of the Cotton Unions

BY H. A. TURNER

Montague Burton Professor of Industrial Relations
in the University of Leeds

LONDON

GEORGE ALLEN & UNWIN LTD

RUSKIN HOUSE MUSEUM STREET

FIRST PUBLISHED IN 1962

DEDICATION

The J's, R's and various

Lancastrians

This book has been set in Times type face. It has been printed in Great Britain by Taylor Garnett Evans & Co. Ltd., Watford, Herts, and bound by them

CONTENTS

IV. SOME COMPARISONS

V. UNION STRUCTURE AND UNION GOVERNMENT

GRAPHS AND CHARTS

I

INTRODUCTORY

1

Preface

Just over two centuries ago as this is written, eighteen Lancashire weavers were prosecuted for their part in what was probably the first substantial and substantiated strike in the industrial history of Britain—or for that matter, of any other country. That stoppage was provoked by a refusal of the weavers' employers to recognize a 'combination' of their workers. Two hundred years later, during 1959 and 1960, the British textile workers' leaders presided, as joint members of a legally-empowered Board with the leaders of textile employers' organizations, over a state-supported and subsidized re-organization of the United Kingdom's cotton industries themselves.

Despite the historical contrast, some of the demands of the striking weavers of 1758—for increased pay and the control of labour recruitment—would not seem at all unintelligible to wage-earners today. But in other respects the modern trade union's situation is clearly very different. Indeed, it is just this addition to the traditional functions of trade unions of others imposed by the latters' contemporary status and influence to which the modern problems of trade unionism itself can be largely traced.

Many contemporary labour issues seem, in fact, the product of success. Just how far the present century's—and particularly the last generation's—advance in the condition and status of wage-earners is due to the growth of union power to extract direct concessions from employers may be argued. But certainly the economic and social order with which that advance was most associated—the 'full employment', 'welfare state', and 'guided' (if not quite 'controlled') economy—owes its existence largely to the pressure or presence of a movement to which organized labour has both given the continuing force and indicated the main direction.

Of that movement, the trade unions are the solid core. And to many this seems inevitably to involve the unions in some responsibility (if one necessarily hard to define in exact terms) for the functioning of the system that has emerged from their pressure. As a result, one major problem of organized labour is how to adapt its policies to a 'mixed economy'—one in which employment is still largely provided by profit-making employers, but which is also subject to a significant degree of social restraint and guidance. But to this problem, the character of the unions themselves is clearly central. They have evolved mainly (some would say inevitably) as organized sectional interests, only loosely federated in a recognizable class interest or in broader social movements. The trade union's prime function is to protect and improve its *own* members' conditions. And its ability to do so has been strengthened by its growth of membership, its recognition by employers and the state, and by a recently-continuing prosperity.

This problem of reconciling effective general policy with continuing sectional action is exhibited in such contrasts as that between the labour movement's principle of equitable income distribution and the unions' practice of catch-as-catch-can wage-bargaining, or between labour's insistence on full employment and its preservation of sectional barriers to unemployed workers' adopting new jobs. But the problem is also complicated by British trade unionism's own structure. Individual unions appear to have evolved separately, according to no common principle, and accepting no general pattern of membership-allocation or of internal organization. And in trade unionism at large, such central authority as the TUC embodies is still weak. Overt competition for members between unions is perhaps much limited by the willingness of now long-established organizations to compromise with each other. And it is rarely that co-operation between unions is nowadays imposed—as it once sometimes was—by employers embarrassed by incompatible claims. But inter-union disputes are still not infrequent; while such things as the existing centralization of collective bargaining, and its accompanying need for unions to formulate and pursue policies in relation to whole industries, continue to raise many difficulties of inter-union co-ordination. And these difficulties have been necessarily—not to say obviously—the greater where the issue concerns the unions' role in the economy as a whole.

The development of trade unionism's functions has nevertheless drawn its leaders into a complex machinery of wage-fixing and social-economic administration. And this has combined with the mere growth of union membership and its concentration in an ever smaller number of organizations to raise another problem, of the relation between the union and the workers whose interest it was erected to present. The problem is described in ways which differ according to the beholder's viewpoint. But practically, it has been expressed in a public concern for the rights of individual workers in relation to unions, and especially in an impression of indifference as the normal quality of trade union membership. If valid, however, this impression contrasts strangely with the contemporary frequency of direct but 'unofficial' action by workers—a tendency perhaps most marked in just those industries, like the mines and docks, where labour's political pressure has achieved the greatest transformation. So while the unfortunate union leaderships have been pressed to apply more central direction to trade union policy and greater discipline to its implementation, they have been alternately (or even at the same time) urged to become 'less remote' from the workers and to allow the latter more freedom of individual or group action.

We have, at any rate, two sets of trade union problems. On the one hand, there are problems, in a sense, of form. This includes the relation between trade unionism and the general labour movement, between individual trade unions themselves, and between the individual union and its members. On the other hand, there are problems of policy—in effect, of what unions do, should do, or of why they do it. In any organization, form and function condition, if they do not quite determine, each other. So the two groups of problems cannot really be separated.

*

There are several ways in which such questions can be studied. Since the Webbs, nobody has attempted (or at least, succeeded in) an emulation of their classic study of trade unionism's history and character at large. But particular aspects of trade unionism as a broad institution—strikes, wages, internal government, and so on—have been taken up by specialists of various kinds. Then, particular unions have been separated as objects of description or enquiry—a line especially developed by labour historians,[1] and to some extent encouraged by the desire of individual unions to commemmorate themselves. A more recently developed interest concerns the smaller group of workers, in a particular workplace for instance, from whom it is hoped to establish some general conclusion.

As between these approaches, the present study has no overwhelming preference. Its main subject is a *group* of unions which, though of great importance in the British labour movement's general development, has been relatively neglected by its students.

[1] So far as the writer is aware, H. A. Clegg's study of the NUGMW, *General Union* (Blackwell, Oxford, 1954), is the only British attempt to apply this technique from a mainly contemporary angle to a single union in the round.

However, these unions' relations with their membership, in the locality and workplace, have a rather unusual character. And some attempt will also be made to compare them with other major unions, and to examine certain general questions of union development and structure in the comparison's light. So that this study will have at least one prejudice. Methodologically, it favours comparison. The purpose of social enquiry is to suggest useful and general conclusions about the behaviour of people and organizations. And conclusions drawn from even a quite wide sector of experience may mislead if untested against related experience outside that sector. A second prejudice of this study, however, is that, though not a historian's study, it favours history. The character of organizations, like that of people, is very much a product of their ancestry and the circumstances of their early growth. Once these things are set, only a rather radical change in an organism's environment can usually disturb its character; and sometimes the disturbance is fatal. In people, the quality these things impart is called personality. In organizations it is called (to the extent that it is recognized) tradition. But British trade unions, more than those of most countries perhaps, are historical deposits and repositories of history. And anyone with close experience of trade unionism will be aware of the extent to which every union possesses a personality of its own.

The cotton textile unions are perhaps peculiarly suited to a study with this comparative and historical bias because they not only have (in one form or another) one of the longest continuing histories among trade union groups, but from the nature of their industry's role and priority in industrial development, their experience is also one of the most complete. For that very reason, however, this study cannot pretend to include a definitive history of the textile unions, although it follows a (very) roughly chronological arrangement. Many incidents in the crowded record of more than two centuries' collective activity by textile operatives will inevitably be passed over; and even the most important events may be treated rather briefly, without the full detail they would deserve in a different context. While the evolution of wages, wage-systems and labour conditions in the cotton trade would provide material enough for a substantial study in itself, and is neglected here except in so far as reference to these things seems essential to the main theme. This study contains what is hoped may be found a not too inadequate account of the cotton unions' general development. But of that development, the main intention is to select those features which seem most relevant to the understanding of trade unionism in general, and particularly of those contemporary problems already referred to.

For instance, perhaps the strongest interest of recent trade union studies has been in the union's relation to its members. This interest is natural: the unions embody an immense social force, and people want to how how it is controlled. But students of the unions' internal democracy have given rather conflicting answers. Some have described an almost random variety of governmental forms.[1] Others have selected a single tendency towards centralization or bureaucracy as most significant.[2] Here this study will suggest that the very real diversity of union governmental systems mostly arises from variation upon two or three historical themes. And one of those themes is centralization; but others run contrary to it. These themes embody the distinct traditions that major groups of unions derive from their origins. However, they have also been modified by changes in the functioning of individual unions—which returns to the earlier proposition, that function conditions form.

On the other hand—and for instance again—from the trend of the British cotton trade since the 1920s (and particularly from the seeming failure as yet of the recent publicly-organized 'concentration' of the industry to bring about any stability in its prospects) some might suppose this study to be a sort of anticipatory post-mortem on the cotton unions. That is not the writer's view: other considerations apart, there seems to him to be still room for union policy itself to help in reaching a viable base of employment and production in the cotton industry. But in any case, the problems the cotton unions have faced in this period are not so different, in essence, from those of other organized labour groups—including those in industries still expanding. So that a discussion of the cotton unions' reaction to these problems is relevant to contemporary union policy in general.

*

History then, is treated here as a starting point, with the history of the cotton trade unions as a continuing core of reference. Because of this there follows an introductory chapter which sketches briefly the development and structure of the cotton trades, and outlines in a preliminary way the recent state of trade unionism amongst the cotton workers. Thereafter, this study is divided into five short

[1] For instance, the most systematic of recent discussions of trade union government, B. C. Roberts' *Trade Union Government and Administration in Great Britain* (Bell, London, 1956) which covers the eighteen larger unions.

[2] This theme is exhibited alike by V. L. Allen's *Power in Trade Unions* (Longmans, London, 1954) which surveys a very wide field of union constitutional practice, and Joseph Goldstein's *Government of British Trade* (Allen and Unwin, London, 1952) which examined in detail this aspect of the largest union only.

books of two chapters apiece—but to which is added (since the study's historical narrative is to some large extent not merely of necessity incomplete but also intermittent, being frequently interrupted by discussion or comparison) an Appendix of which one part is a straightforward chronology of cotton unionism's development. And in the first book, which traces the early record of trade unionism among the cotton operatives, it is suggested that the collective organization of workers has even deeper roots, and greater historical continuity, than has often been supposed. But this book also asks why labour organization took a particular path, in which narrow occupational associations predominated over broader labour movements—and granted that it did so, what distinguishes early trade unionism from its modern forms. To this last question it finds the answer in the institutional organization of modern trade unions. Which leads to the suggestion that there are continuing and important analogies to early unionism in certain contemporary labour phenomena.

The second book traces the development of modern textile unionism itself—by which is meant the techniques of action and the institutional forms by which trade unionism is now identified. The usual picture of trade union growth is one of a persistent struggle against employers and employing interests, in which the skilled workers were the first to achieve a stable organization because they had the advantage that '. . . in the economic and technical process they occupied strategic positions.'[1] This book's two chapters, however, propose an alternative interpretation of trade union development as equally valid—one of a conflict between the interests of different groups among workers themselves, in which it was by no means inevitable that skilled workers should be the first to organize effectively. They suggest that such workers rather owed their early supremacy to historical factors; indeed, that some workers should have become (or remained) 'skilled' was partly attributable to their superior organization. It is again usual to distinguish between the exclusive 'Old Unions' of the nineteenth century and the mass 'New Unions' of the twentieth. But this book will also suggest that stable and strong unions which were essentially of the 'New' type existed from the mid-nineteenth century on—and that, had not the labour movement been dominated by more exclusive organizations, mass unionism might have become general much earlier.

These first two books are pretty closely concerned with the cotton unions' development, and carry the story up to the point at which

[1] John T. Dunlop, in *U.S. Industrial Relations: The Next Twenty Years* (J. Stieber, ed., Michigan State University Press, 1958) p. 50.

they reached approximately their modern form. The third book widens the area of enquiry. It first tests the foregoing propositions by comparing the evolution of trade unionism among the cotton operatives with that in other major occupations. There are the relative failures of labour organization, until quite recently, in the industry most closely related to cotton—the wool and worsted trades, together with the textile finishing industry. There is a not dissimilar pattern of collective evolution among the miners, whose organization nearest resembles that of the cotton unions. And there is the effect of nineteenth-century craft unionism in the industries which it influenced. But this book's second chapter goes on to consider the character of such organizations and of the newer mass unions more closely, and (again by comparison between the cotton unions and others) to trace the impact of different traditions and, especially, of different policies on the institutional forms that unions adopted.

This comparative preoccupation extends particularly into the fourth book, of which the first chapter contrasts the shape of the cotton unions, as they ultimately emerged from their long evolution, with that of modern unions at large. In the recent concern with trade unions' internal management the general structure of trade unionism has been somewhat neglected. So this chapter first considers the things that determine the sorts of union to which workers may belong—its size and external shape, its operative technique, the variety of its interests and membership, and so on. This chapter argues the usual classification of unions to be unsatisfactory, and puts forward an alternative one which perhaps may be more usefully related to such things as their attitudes to compulsory membership (which the fourth book also discusses). But then the book's second chapter returns to the issue of internal union government. It suggests, from some detailed analysis of the cotton unions' actual working, that the popular contrast between trade unionism's formal democracy and the habitual non-participation of most of its members is too simple, and that there are very considerable differences between unions in their actual government, which are not necessarily related to their particular constitutional type, but which derive mainly from the differing character of their separate memberships.

But there is some point in a body's formal system of organization; and the fifth book's first chapter here returns more particularly to the cotton unions by remarking on some advantages of their now rather unusual structure by comparison with more typical trade union forms. It also notes, however, certain 'extra-constitutional' pressures that may influence the response of union leaderships in general to their members' desires. The chapter then goes on to examine some disadvantages of the cotton union's organizational system, considering these in relation to the industrial policies with which the unions confronted their inter-war and post-war situations —a discussion which leads to some general comments on union policy in a 'mixed economy'.

That discussion also leads, however, to the question with which the study's last chapter deals—of why union organization in general has been so little modified in response to recent industrial, social and economic developments. One answer to this is given by examining the cotton unions' political policies since the 1920s—which (apart from confirming some prior hints about the attitude of trade unions to politics) are suggested to have been partly a substitute for institutional change in the unions themselves. So that since changed circumstances have not produced major changes in trade unionism, the study concludes by considering what factors have done and may do so. But because the growth of collective organization among workers has been closely inter-related with that among employers, one part of the final Appendix considers the development of cotton employers' organization and its impact on trade unionism.

*

As regard the material of this study, no particular credit may be claimed for that on which the first book is based. Apart from one or two gaps that seemed to need filling, this consists largely of a re-arrangement of the incidental work of historians of general social events into a consecutive sequence, and the relation of that sequence to known economic data. The second book's material is drawn from many sources, including the records of various unions, official reports, and material collected by previous students. But the help of several union officers who have been interested by their own societies' past should be acknowledged, and particularly that of Mr Edwin Hopwood, until recently Assistant General Secretary of the Weavers' Amalgamation, who has assembled a deal of data on that body's history. Where the third book refers to the cotton unions, it derives from similar sources. And some help on the history of the wool unions, and of those in the textile finishing trades, has also come from local union officials. Other material, however, is drawn from the published histories of non-textile unions. The fourth and fifth books draw partly on union and official reports, and similar more contemporary material. But they are also the product of many conversations and some correspondence with people in the cotton trade, of the writer's own (contrasting) former experience as a union member and officer, and of some subsequent general study of contemporary trade unionism (as well as of the cotton trade in particular).

The writer should especially acknowledge the help of those who gave their time to reading the whole or part of his draft, and without whose many comments this study's present deficiencies would have been multiplied intolerably. They include Professor Ely Devons, now of the London School of Economics, Mr A. E. Musson of Manchester University's Economic History Department, Mr Ernest Thornton, M.P. for Farnworth and former Secretary of the United Textile Factory Workers' Association, and particularly (for their repeated assistance) Mr H. A. Clegg of Nuffield College, Oxford and Mr Edwin Hopwood of the Weavers' Amalgamation again.

But here perhaps the writer should also especially refer to what he has learnt from participation in not a few discussions of trade union policy at the annual summer course for cotton trade unionists organized by Manchester University, at the occasional week-end schools of the Weavers' Amalgamation, and in the annual seminar of Legislative Council members of the United Textile Factory Workers' Association. This reference has the incidental merit that those many officers and members of the cotton unions who have extended the writer a friendly patience, and who might otherwise have felt certain critical notes in this study's later chapters to be a poor return, would anyway have a pretty shrewd idea what to expect!

I

INTRODUCTORY

2

The Cotton Trades and Textile Unions

I

The British cotton textile trades form the classic case of industrial development. The textile industry's expansion was central to the general growth of the British economy—as, more recently, to that of other economies the first industrial development of which was natural and undirected. The cotton manufacture's demand for materials and its search for markets stimulated revolutions in transport and trade. Its technical demands provoked a great wave of extractive, engineering and chemical innovation which drew many other industries into the stream of change. Its demand for capital, and the profits of its first violent but risky growth, created a new social group, of great manufacturing entrepreneurs and employers. And its demand for labour drew together the first massed, industrial and urbanized wage-earning class. If it did not invent the factory, it created that social symbol of the modern industrial order, the factory town.

Of all the great factory industries, cotton has the longest history and displays the most complete evolutionary record. The mediaeval city's productive foundation, the corporately-controlled handicraft, was definitively undermined by the competing spread of commercial textile manufacture as a cottage and village industry. That trade dissolved the subsistence communities of whole countrysides, and laid a base on which the factory order erected itself, first as a supplier of semi-finished materials to the domestic hand-workers, then as their mechanized supplanter. As it emerged from this transitional phase, the new machine-industry of Lancashire made an impact on the human imagination perhaps more dramatic than any subsequent technical event up to the release of nuclear power. 'The tens of millions of revolving bobbins, the hundred of thousands of shuttles passing to and fro . . . Manchester in 1820 left a more dazzling impression on visitors than did Detroit in 1920: for this was the first time that a vast array of machines serving the whole world had ever been seen.'[1] Other impressions were more sinister. The contrast between this immense achievement of technique and organization, and its carelessness of human material—the rigours of the new industrial labour, the swarming, spreading filth of the new industrial cities—is still vivid, and a continuing source of historians' controversy. But the cotton trade was by then already well launched upon that headlong course which was to carry it, though often stumbling from the violence of its own pace, within a century to a place of apparently unchallengeable eminence. On the eve of the First World War, and despite the imitation (sometimes, improvement) of its technique in other countries, Lancashire alone possessed half the world's factory equipment for manufacturing cotton goods, while British mills, exporting seven-eighths of their output, supplied 70 per cent of international trade in cotton fabrics. In retrospect, the ensuing collapse now seems inevitable. The British industry was to pay the price of its own originality. Competition, first from countries inferior in their technical competence but much lower in their living standards and therefore costs, later from industries less hampered by now out-dated plant and driven by high wages to develop techniques that British mills had not found worth elaborating, was already advanced before the British industry's peak. The First World War gave this rivalry a double stimulus, economic from its drastic interruption of Lancashire supplies, political from its encouragement of national independencies. There followed what one manufacturer himself called 'the most terrible retreat in the history of industry . . .'[2]

This course, in both its grand movement and frequent subsidiary fluctuations, is dramatically sketched by the U.K.'s annual record of raw cotton fibre consumption, which is charted[3] in Graph I.

[1] De Jouvenel in *Problems of Socialist England* (Batchworth, London, 1947) p. 101.

[2] Godfrey Armitage in *The Cotton Trade from the Great Inventions to The Great Depression* (Manchester Literary & Philosophical Society, 1951) p. 15. This paper is one of the most vivid accounts of the industry's fall, and especially of the bafflement its inter-War collapse induced in those who lived by the cotton trade.

[3] *Sources* for Graph I: for 1780–99, *McCulloch's Dictionary of Commerce and Navigation* (London, 1832); for 1800 to 1955, Dr R. Robson's *The Cotton Industry in Britain* (Macmillan, London, 1957, Appendix); and for 1955 to 1960, Cotton Board. The very deep fall in the 1860s is, of course, the Cotton Famine. Before 1780 (when the Graph begins) mixed fibres were used, but between 1700 and that date cotton consumption rose from about 2 to about 6 million.

We cannot trace the industry's employment in such detail. But by the 1770s, before the great spinning inventions transformed the trade, there were already some 30,000 people engaged in the cotton manufacture around Manchester. At the 1851 Census, it was the biggest source of occupation in Britain after agriculture, with nearly half a million operatives—more than were engaged in the coal, metal, and engineering industries together, and twice as many as in the next biggest manufacturing trade, wool textiles. In 1913, the industry employed over 700,000 workers. But by 1924, its employment had fallen back to half a million, and by 1939 to a third of a million.

For advanced trading economies, this progression is so much the type of industrial history—if the most starkly delineated—that it may well claim to be the most studied of industrial transformations. For economists, and for economic and social historians, its various stages have provided both a mine of material and a continuing provocation. All the problems are there. Where labour alone is concerned, for instance, it illustrates the whole formation of an industrial working force, its induction to the disciplinary demands of mechanical production, the impact on it of what is now called 'automation',[1] as well as of the dissolution of established skills before technical innovation and new sub-divisions of labour. And, to an extent that no other modern industry has yet encountered, the cotton trades demonstrate the problems involved by labour's exposure and adjustment to a permanently-contracted demand.

The industry's documentation has more recently been enlarged by a post-war bout of public and self-criticism.[2] Under the Labour

---

lbs. From the 1930s, 'man-made' fibres become increasingly important, but even by the 1950s only increased the material consumption shown by a quarter. (It is not intended to quote references for other statistics in this introductory chapter where round figures will suffice. In cotton, there is often such a proliferation of statistical data that any more detail usually involves discussion of many definitional problems as well as of the reason for selecting, say, one apparently precise figure instead of a rival statistic. There is, for instance, a substantial difference between the recent employment statistics of the Cotton Board and the Ministry of Labour.)

[1] The first automatic control device, the steam governor, was designed at a cotton-spinning firm's request to secure a greater constancy of engine speeds than the stokers could produce. While the first system of automatic machine-guidance was embodied in the Jacquard loom, which operated on a principle similar to that of the modern 'punched card' technique to produce elaborately patterned cloths.

[2] There is a convenient partial summary of several official or semi-official Reports, from those of the 1944 Cotton Textile Mission to the United States (the Platt Report) and of the 'Cotton Working Party' of 1945/46 onwards, in *The British Cotton Industry* (Anglo-American Productivity Council, 1952).

ANNUAL CONSUMPTION OF RAW COTTON IN THE U.K.
1780-1960
HUNDREDS of MILLIONS of LBS.
0
1
2
3
4
5
6
7
8
9
10
11
12
13
14
15
16
17
18
19
20
21
22
1780
1790
1800
1810
1820
1830
1840
1850
1860
1870
1880
1890
1900
1910
1920
1930
1940
1950
1960

Graph I

government of 1945–51, it was pressed to a production drive that restored its employment, which had been much further reduced in the Second World War, to near its pre-war figure. While in the resumed contraction that followed the world textile recession of 1951–2, the process of public and self-questioning was revived.

II

Curiously, in all this material, the cotton operatives' own organization has received, at least in its later development, comparatively little attention. The history of the unions, for instance, has lacked a systematic recording, although it extends over more than two centuries and occupies a massive place in the British labour movement's story. The present cotton unions descend from the world's first substantial organizations of machine-minders and machine-servers—of those workers without traditional craft who were the Industrial Revolution's most obvious human product. Nevertheless, some of these unions are contemporary with the famous 'New Models,' the amalgamated nineteenth-century associations of apprenticed craftsmen the formation of which has generally been regarded as marking the end of British labour's period of unsatisfactory organizational experiment. The cotton unions' membership, even in the New Models' early days, rivalled the latters'. Some of them, again, were already developing forms of employment control at least equal to those of the mid-nineteenth century craft unions' in effectiveness. And they by far outdistanced those unions in their development of collective bargaining. By the 1880s, their methods of wage-fixing were already so advanced as to induce the British Association for the Advancement of Science to appoint a special committee to record and examine them. And twenty years later the Webbs confessed themselves impressed, if baffled by some aspects of their wage-systems' technical elaboration. The Webbs, too, held the cotton-spinners' system of union government as a model of representative perfection, described their procedure agreement with the employers as '. . . the first great treaty between Capital and Labour', and considered the Weavers' method of selecting their officers to be close to the ideal. R. H. Tawney has called the cotton unions of that time '. . . the most powerful and best-disciplined labour organizations the world had yet seen.' And this, while the miners had established a secure organization in only one district, and that on a restricted basis, and while other unions of non-craft workers were still fighting for an initial foothold. Until the First World War, indeed—and this is perhaps one of their most significant achievements—the cotton unions remained the only ones to organize women workers effectively. And that they did in a large way. The first Board of Trade *Report on Trade Unions*, for 1896, gives them over 90,000 female members—five-sixths of all organized women workers in Britain. And by that Report's last issue, for 1910, the cotton unions' female membership of over 150,000 still comprised 70 per cent of all unionized women.

It is not, of course, that the cotton operatives' history is quite unrecorded. To their early organizations, indeed, there is a mass of reference scattered through the social and economic histories of the Industrial Revolution. The more dramatic incidents of the cotton workers' early struggles are so much part of that time's texture that they recur again and again in the diverse accounts of it[1] —so much so that it is often impossible to attribute their recording to individual students. The problem in tracing the early story of the cotton unions is rather that of assembling a jigsaw of historians' statements—a jigsaw of which many pieces have differently-coloured duplicates, others are missing, and some just do not quite fit. It is the unions' later history—covering roughly the past century—that has been more sparsely dealt with. Rather little attention has been paid to them in general accounts of trades unionism after the Webbs, though as late as 1914 they still commanded nearly a sixth of the U.K.'s total union membership, at their peak immediately after the First World War had some 400,000 members, and remain one of the most strongly-organized groups of wage-earners. But the fashion for individual union histories that set in during the inter-war period did not touch them. There is a brilliant but very incomplete commentary on their development in Chapman's *Lancashire Cotton Industry*[2] of 1904. Beyond that, we have only Jewkes' and Gray's inter-war study of labour conditions in cotton-spinning as of any substance.[3] The mule-spinners' organization and methods seem, indeed, to have exercised a special fascination on students: Chapman himself appears especially preoccupied with them, and even the Webbs referred only to the Weavers among the other unions. Certainly, in the nineteenth-century's last decade the Spinners were

[1] One index to the cotton workers' early importance is that in A. Aspinall's invaluable selection of Home Office documents, *The Early English Trade Unions* (Batchworth, London, 1949), which covers only the period 1791–1825, their activity claims twenty of his seventy-one classificatory sub-heads.

[2] S. J. Chapman, *The Lancashire Cotton Industry: A Study in Economic Development* (Manchester University Press, 1904).

[3] J. Jewkes and E. M. Gray, *Wages and Labour in the Cotton Spinning Industry* (Manchester University Press, 1935). This, of course, confines itself to spinning proper, and does not deal with the cardroom and preparatory workers. Another short study by Gray, *The Weavers' Wage* (Manchester University Press, 1937), includes a brief discussion of the state of the weavers' unionism in the 1930s.

probably the most completely organized of all the major groups of British labour, with over 90 per cent of spinners in membership. But meanwhile the cardroom operatives' Amalgamation—now the second biggest union in the industry—has gone largely unnoticed, to say nothing of the dozen or so smaller groupings that operate or have operated there. And it is of the nature of the cotton trades' labour situation that workers' organization or bargaining practice in one or two sections only—admirable as the studies referred to are—cannot be taken as representative of the whole.

The sparseness of this later material is not fully explained by the writing of trade union histories having become more common only after the unions in cotton had passed their membership peak. Nor by the great 'general' and 'industrial' unions' growth eclipsing the cotton unions' significance from the First World War on. The industry represented, in fact, one of the great 'problem sectors' of the British social economy in the inter-war period, and has continued in that role—though in differing senses—in more recent years. Partly, no doubt, the explanation is the extreme concentration of the cotton trade in a single region, which made the unions much less omnipresent than those of other industries and thus less stimulating to the more remote enquirer. And he may well have been deterred also by their highly technical systems of regulating wages and conditions, and elaborately specific trade jargon. The former are well-known to be complex. But they are also sometimes misleading in their trade documentation; there is one section of the weavers' 'Uniform List' of piece-prices, for instance, which still appears to the writer to say the opposite to what all those practically concerned with it assume (and, presumably intended) it to mean. While the trade's language is not merely exotic: it is frequently confusing. No sooner has the innocent outsider discovered that such barbarous-sounding pursuits as 'slashing' are in fact relatively gentle occupations, than he is likely to be stopped short by such quite local descriptions as 'devil-feeder', or by local appropriations of what he had thought to be generally-valid terms to some other use ('twisters', for instance, is largely used to describe the followers of a respectably-skilled trade connected with cotton-weaving, but in some places and times has applied to a sort of cotton-yarn spinners or doublers). Or he may be finally confounded by the apparently universal occupation of 'tenting', which in fact can only be described in some one of several specific contexts. Anyone who ventures on a general study of the cotton industry, in fact, is advised to apologize in advance for such misunderstandings or errors as may arise from a lack of sectional or local expertise.

But the major obstacle to the labour historian has apparently been the unions' system of organization. This is much less centralized than in the case of most other British labour groups, so that what one is dealing with is to a large extent the separate histories, not merely of some dozen 'Amalgamations', but of upwards of two hundred local units, on which superstructures of a sectional, trade and political character have been at different times—and sometimes incompletely—constructed. The autonomy of these local associations is quite real, as may appear at various points in this study. And some of them—the Bolton Spinners or Blackburn Weavers, for instance—could well claim to be made subjects of respectable histories in their own right.[1] It would really be unsatisfactory, of course, to examine the growth of any one cotton union—or even of a connected group such as the cardroom and ring-spinners' unions—in isolation, because the various societies have not only been subject to the common circumstances of the cotton trade; they have considerably influenced each other. By contrast, Raymond Postgate's monumental *Builders' History* covers what is now a group of six centralized trade unions, while R. Page Arnot's multi-volume history of the miners has to deal with only the score or so associations that existed before their merger in the modern National Union of Mineworkers. Most other union histories each concern the growth of a single contemporary association.

The difficulties occasioned by the cotton unions' dispersed form of organization, however, are multiplied by two other factors. One, that this organization has itself been conducted with a shrewd and special economy of professional administration and hence of systematic record. And this is particularly true of such central bodies as the unions possess: the United Textile Factory Workers' Association, for instance, which has for certain common purposes linked most of the unions during three-quarters of a century, has not even accumulated a complete set of its own Reports. Two, that half-way through its history, trade unionism in the cotton industry experienced a revolution that followed on the revolution in textile techniques, so that many organizations disappeared, and others took their place. Yet again, the later unions were so clearly influenced by their predecessors that one cannot satisfactorily shorten matters by starting, as it were, in the middle.

[1] One or two such local histories actually exist. There is an *Origin and Progress of the Nelson Weavers' Association*, 1870–1920 (Burnley, 1922). A brief history of the now extinct Manchester & Salford Weavers' Association is contained in a thesis presented for the degree of B.A. (Econ.) at Manchester University in 1953, by Lloyd Jones.

III

Whatever its reason (and these things may at least somewhat extenuate the present study's deficiencies) the cotton operatives' lack of a historian has not only led to a certain neglect of their achievements in collective organization and action; it also seems to have promoted a picture of them which is not wholly accurate. They are, for instance, commonly thought to have been lacking in militancy. And it is true that, during the past century at least, their leaders have never looked upon industrial conflict as an instrument of broad social or political change, or upon the strike as anything else than an expensive occasional necessity of bread-and-butter policy. But the cotton industry has nevertheless witnessed some of the most formidable labour battles, from that first major strike of the eighteenth century when the several thousand check-weavers around Manchester concerted to cease work for some months, to what was the last great strike in twentieth-century British unionism's phase of general industrial conflict, the four-week stoppage of the weaving unions in 1932. In the old Board of Trade Labour Correspondent's Reports, the annual record of disputes in cotton is only slightly less than in mining, accounting for nearly a sixth of reported incidents. Knowles, for a later period (1911–47), found more workers had been locked-out in cotton than in any other industry.[1] The TUC's Annual Report of 1934 declared that more working days had been lost there from disputes than in any other trade since the end of the First World War. While from the 'Great Strike' of 1878 to the events of 1932, some dozen cotton stoppages were close to general in character.

Another common impression of the cotton operatives is of an especial dependence on full-time officials, a lack of direct drive and initiative from the generality of union members. G. D. H. Cole, for instance, once commented on an apparently negligible level of workshop disputes, such as are characteristic of the engineering industry, among cotton workers.[2] In fact, in several of their associations one might argue the reverse tendency—of an excessive dependence of officials upon the members. But others, in recent times, have certainly assumed the characteristics of 'business unionism'. 'Unofficial' movements have never achieved much significance among the cotton workers—certainly nothing like that attained by

[1] K. G. J. C. Knowles, *Strikes: A Study in Industrial Conflict* (Blackwell, Oxford, 1952) pp. 168 et seq.

[2] In *Workshop Organization* (Oxford University Press, 1923) pp. 105–6. Though Cole himself pointed out that issues of the kind that promoted workshop militancy in engineering were much less likely to arise in cotton ('*Chaos and Order in Industry*,' London 1920, p. 161).

oppositionist movements of engineering operatives and dockers. While both union leaders and major groups of employers in cotton have persistently sought to limit occasions for factory disputes by elaborating a general code of principles for their resolution. Nevertheless, this code's achievement, enforcement and continued acceptance depended largely, in its earlier days at least, on direct initiative by the operatives themselves.

In the decade before the great 'Brooklands' lock-out of 1893, for example, the Oldham Spinners' and Cardroom Associations alone were each reporting two to three hundred mill disputes a year. And if the tendency to workshop disputes has subsided, this may partly reflect its earlier success. Industrial conflict in cotton has thus concentrated in the occasional major stoppage, rather than in frequent minor strikes. That workplace militancy has not altogether disappeared in the cotton operatives, despite their discouraging experience of the past two generations, is illustrated by the remarkable six-months' stoppage of a Rochdale mill in 1958. This—famous locally as the 'Black-eye Strike'—was carried to the extraordinary point of achieving, not merely the reinstatement of the union representative whose discharge had first occasioned it, but also the dismissal of the managing director responsible and the re-organization of the firm.

In cotton, the ability of the union leaders to direct rank-and-file action into considered channels of policy has largely rested on a mutual relationship rather different from that of most non-cotton unions. While in major cases the absence of rival 'official' and 'workshop' tendencies there is to be explained by the parallel absence of any organizational dichotomy such as, in engineering for instance, supplies a basis for internal conflicts between the operatives' national and workplace leaderships. In such respects as these, indeed, there are considerable differences between the various cotton unions themselves—and this again is contrary to some common impressions. The TUC's own Report on 'Trade Union Structure and Closer Unity' of 1944, for example, appears to treat them as a group of essentially similar organizations.

But perhaps the impression of the cotton operatives and their organizations most widespread in other sections of the labour movement is of a prevailing industrial and political conservatism, a relative isolation from that movement's more general trends. There are, in fact, centres of radical activity and opinion in the cotton unions to which this study will refer. But it is generally the case that the modern unions' development was largely uninfluenced by the Socialist ideas that played a formative part in the construction of other mass unions of non-craft workers. They have, since their affiliation with the Labour Party, generally been identified with its more cautious tendencies. While the operatives themselves remain apparently less affected by Labour political sentiment than do other well-organized groups. The Lancashire constituencies, despite their predominantly industrial character, currently include a greater proportion that are 'marginal' from the viewpoint of the two great political parties than any other county.[1]

But against these things the unions had already developed an effective technique of limited political action long before the formation of the Labour Party: and if some of them appeared at first lukewarm to the broader social ideas associated with the latter, they had previously taken a leading part in the promotion of concerted general action by labour for specific ends. Up to the introduction of block-voting and stricter numerical representation in the TUC, for instance, they sent by far the largest delegation to its annual Congress, which with the miners they then almost dominated; while their foremost leaders continued to play a major part in that body's early Parliamentary Committee and later in its modern General Council. They displayed an early interest in the international association of workers for industrial purposes. And if they were comparatively slow to absorb what is at present virtually British trade unionism's official ideology, they played a critical part in the formation of the Labour Party itself. A recent student has remarked of the unopposed election to Parliament in 1902 of the Weavers' official David Shackleton, as the candidate of the new Labour Representation Committee, that 'Clitheroe rather than Woolwich portends that upsurge in Labour strength which was in 1906 to sweep thirty Labour M.P.'s into the House.'[2] While the cotton unions' affiliation to the LRC in 1903 led the conversion of the established major unions to the new political body.

It may well be, however, that their particular political quality constitutes yet another reason for the cotton unions' lack of a historian. Socialist thought inspired not merely later developments in mass unionization, but several of the latter's most noted students —and it is quite possible that these found the cotton unions an unsympathetic subject. Postgate, for instance, described the inceptive moves in the modern cotton unions' formation as reinforcing the 'pacific forces' in trades unionism—a judgement so curious in the

[1] The Labour Party's North-West Regional organizer classified 38 of the 80 Lancashire and Cheshire constituencies as 'marginal' in 1957.

[2] F. Bealey. 'The Northern Weavers, Independent Labour Representation, and Clitheroe; 1902' (*Manchester School*, Jan. 1957). The Woolwich reference is, of course, to Will Crooks' election in the following year. The significance of the Clitheroe by-election was probably obscured by contemporary press and public pre-occupation with the King's illness and the following coronation.

light of their stormy industrial history that it can only refer to their political character.[1] But is likely that this view has influenced interpretation of the cotton unions' less political aspects.

However, this study does not intend an apologia for the cotton unions—indeed, their methods' appropriateness to the more recent situations that have confronted them may be somewhat criticized in its concluding part. And it has been said that it is neither the study's main purpose to present a history. But the cotton operatives' story contains much of great human interest and colour. The early cotton industry might well be thought to have invented, not merely the technique of factory civilization, but new forms of human cruelty. The record of the cotton unions includes many incidents of a near-heroic loyalty and stubbornness. At one point, the Lancashire cotton workers could certainly claim to have influenced the course of world history. The attitude of this then key group of industrial producers to the American Civil War was one factor that withheld the British government from intervening for the South; and Abraham Lincoln, at least, recognized the contribution that the British cotton operatives' stoicism in face of the resultant Cotton Famine made to the North's success. That story is imaginatively told in Armstrong's novel *King Cotton*. And the suffering of the cotton workers between the two World Wars has inspired several fine works of that sort, like Greenwood's play *Love on the Dole*, or Hodson's novel *Harvest in the North*. In the rise of the cotton unions themselves, moreover, many remarkable individuals have played a part which deserves more notice than such passing reference—if that—as the following pages give them. It is inevitable, from this study's main interest, that such things as these are neglected by it. But they have contributed to the distinctive psychology of the cotton trade, and to the 'personalities' of its unions, and should not be forgotten by the reader.

IV

It is probable that between three-quarters and four-fifths of the operatives at present employed in the cotton industry—restricting the latter term to its narrower traditional sense of spinning, weaving and those related processes usually carried on by the same factories or firms—are trade union members. The picture, as nearly always with a British trade union structure, blurs at the edges. Two or three of the Lancashire-based labour organizations—again, the

[1] Raymond Postgate, *A Pocket History of the British Working Class* (NCLC Publishing Society, Tillicoultry, Scotland 1947).

traditional 'cotton unions' proper—concern themselves in other textile industries. Some few cotton workers, particularly outside the 'cotton area' proper, belong to one of the two great general labour unions (the Transport & General Workers' Union or the National Union of General & Municipal Workers) or to the Yorkshire-based 'Textile Workers' Union' (the National Union of Dyers, Bleachers & Textile Workers) which is primarily interested in the wool trades. The NUGMW also has a more extensive organization among certain operatives in cotton yarn-doubling, where (as in one locality) this process is carried on by specialist factories instead of in the spinning mills proper. A handful of very small independent local unions of cotton operatives survives in Scotland. The generality of textile finishing workers—although some of these in Lancashire were once briefly associated with the main cotton unions—are now also organized by the Textile Workers' Union, but of these operatives again a number of small independent unions survive, operating from Manchester. That city also houses an extraordinary group of minute associations of cotton warehouse workers, distinguished by mysterious names—The Society of Female Workers in the Shipping Industry, for instance: and here a major woodworkers' union is also concerned.

Inside the cotton mills themselves, one or two organized groups lead an existence detached from that of the operatives' unions. There are some local associations of mill managers, officials and supervisors which have quite recently federated together. And some mechanics will, as in almost any industry, be found as members of the Amalgamated Engineering Union or Electrical Trade Union. The cotton industry, in fact, played a great part in the rise of engineering trade unionism itself. The early Lancashire mills drew engineers; and a movement of textile machinery workers was critical to the formation of the modern AEU's predecessor. Even today, however, there survive several independent local unions originally of mechanical specialists in the mills' service or supply—of enginemen, for instance, of Jacquard loom fitters, or (quite disproportionately powerful) of shuttlemakers. One or two such societies have associated with the main cotton unions. But one that has not, the National Engineers' Association, after leading a modestly sober existence for over a century, recently achieved the sudden and rare distinction of expulsion from the TUC.

However, for present purposes all these other groups constitute 'fringe' organizations, with which this study will only concern itself in so far as their relation with the main cotton operatives' associations illustrates certain general questions of trade union structure, or their history demonstrates a contrasting path of union development. The cotton unions proper are grouped into several so-called 'Amalgamations'. These are really more or less close federations, but it will suffice for the moment to describe the unions at that organizational level alone. These may be conveniently depicted in the order of the successive operations upon the fibre—cotton or some man-made alternative to it—that each Amalgamation's principal membership performs. As in the following page's Table.

The centre column there by no means comprises a full list of the occupations each union organizes, and thus materially over-simplifies the picture. There is, for instance, a very large number of workers engaged in various mechanical processes of re-winding yarn off the package in which it is delivered by one operation (spinning or doubling, for instance) on to packages of a more convenient type for some subsequent process. And these operatives are mainly (but not entirely) organized by either the Cardroom or Weavers' Amalgamation, depending upon whether the job is done in a spinning or weaving plant. However, the classifications will again suffice for the present, although such inter-union overlaps will be found important at a later stage.

One variation among the unions will be immediately apparent. Though certainly not among the giants of contemporary trade unionism, the Cardroom and Weavers' Amalgamations are still sizeable organizations, being each well above the current average union size.[1] The Weavers' Amalgamation, especially, was at its 1921 peak among the biggest unions of that time, with nearly a quarter-million members. At the other extreme, the Warpdressers' and Tapesizers' Amalgamations are no bigger than some major unions' individual branches—the average size of the Weavers' local societies in 1956, for instance, was nearly 3,000. However, the power of these organizations is by no means mathematically proportionate to their membership. Despite their minuteness, the Warpdressers' and Tapesizers' unions have been singularly effective agents of their members' interests, because of the solidity with which they organize a selected group of 'key men'. In any case, recent studies of trades unionism have been much concerned with the very big organization. A contrast with some of the very small union's qualities may prove

[1] This, for all trade unions known to the Ministry of Labour, was in 1959/60 some 15,000 members, and for unions affiliated to the T.U.C. only, 45,000 members. Cotton union membership was, of course, declining during the period of the writer's enquiries even before the formal 'concentration' of the trade. In the latter's interval of post-war re-expansion, the Weavers', Cardroom and Spinners' Amalgamations had memberships above 80,000, 50,000 and 20,000 respectively. The peak figures of cotton union membership are given in the Chart 'Formation of Modern Cotton Unions' in Chapter III, 1, section I—where the Warehousemen's Amalgamation is described by its earlier title, as the 'Clothlookers'.

Table: COTTON UNION MEMBERSHIPS AND JURISDICTIONS

	Amalgamation	*Organizes Workers:*	*Approximate membership* 1959/60 and short description*
Spinning Industry	1 National Association of Card, Blowing and Ring Room Operatives	in the preparatory stages to yarn-spinning, on the ring-spinning, process, and in certain auxiliary trades	42,000 'The Cardroom Amalgamation'
	2 Amalgamated Association of Operative Cotton-Spinners and Twiners	on the mule-spinning process (spinners and assistants, or 'minders' and 'piecers')	10,500 'The Spinners' Amalgamation'
Weaving (or 'Manufacturing') Industry	1 (a) Lancashire Amalgamated Tapesizers' Association (b) Amalgamated Tapesizers' Friendly Protective Society	in the process of sizing (or 'slashing') yarn for weaving	1,000 'The Tapesizers' Amalgamations' 120
	2 General Union of Lancashire and Yorkshire Warpdressers' Associations	in the process of setting up coloured warps for patterned weaving†	2,000 'The Warpdressers' Amalgamation'
	3 Amalgamated Association of Beamers, Twisters and Drawers (Hand and Machine)	in the process of fixing and arranging warps for use in the weaver's loom	3,200 'The Twisters' Amalgamation'
	4 General Union of Associations of Loom Overlookers	who set up and maintain the looms ('tackling') and supervise weavers	5,400 'The Overlookers' Amalgamation'
	5 Amalgamated Weavers' Association	in weaving and ancillary occupations	57,000 'The Weavers' Amalgamation'
	6 Amalgamated Textile Warehousemen's Association	workers in the inspection and storage of cloth and its preparation for despatch	6,000 'The Warehousemen's Amalgamation'

* *Source:* Annual Report of United Textile Factory Workers' Association (the UTFWA) and of the TUC, except for Warpdressers (which includes Yorkshire affiliated membership) and Tapesizers whose membership is estimated from earlier figures supplied by the unions concerned. Since union membership returns were made up at various times during this period, which is that of the cotton trade 'concentration' scheme, they do not necessarily record the full effect of that adjustment.

† The warp is the lengthwise run of yarns in cloth. The normal loom weaves by thrusting a crosswise thread, or weft yarn, through the warps in a predetermined alternation.

enlightening: and to ask why some unions are big and others small is itself not quite as pointless as it may seem.

Other differences between the cotton Amalgamations will appear in due time. One that may be noted here, however, is the diverse sex-ratios of their memberships. Of the Weavers' members 87 per cent, and of the Cardroom's 90 per cent, were female at the time of the writer's enquiries. The Overlookers' Union and the Tapesizers' Amalgamations, however, are entirely male in their composition. The other four Amalgamations have varying, but in no case substantial, minorities of women and girls—in the case of the Warehousemen about a sixth of its membership, but only a hundred or two apiece in the rest. It should not be assumed from this, however —and though some two-thirds of the cotton trades' labour force are female—that only the two bigger unions have the qualities of mass organizations. The Spinners' Amalgamation, for example, outnumbered the Cardroom Amalgamation until the First World War, but has suffered an especial decline (to only a sixth of its former strength) because of the substitution of ring- for mule-spinning.

The experience of the unions during the cotton trades' phases of contraction have in fact differed substantially. The Warehousemen, for instance, have maintained their membership rather better than have most other cotton unions. The total number of trade union members in cotton has probably fallen less rapidly than the total employment of operatives since 1921, but this particular Amalgamation has been especially successful in recruiting previously-unorganized workers. The Overlookers, though already virtually 100 per cent organized, declined much less proportionately than the other unions in the inter-war period, and have at present a membership still close to their pre-war figure. This organization has been favoured by technical changes that have increased the demand for its members' skill. Within the bigger unions, there are similarly particular groups of operatives—automatic-loom weavers, for instance—whose number is rising, against the general ebb. Moreover, differences may occur between the economic situations of the spinning and weaving sections as a whole. A simple illustration is that a sizeable part of spinning output is not taken by the weaving trade but is directly exported or is consumed by other industries—like hosiery. On the other hand, a growing proportion of the yarn used by weaving firms comes direct from the chemical plants as continuous man-made filaments. The two sections of the cotton trade may thus experience independent trends and fluctuations, as well as *inter*-dependent ones. While after the Second World War, particularly, price-fixing associations developed among the spinning employers which the much less concentrated weaving firms were unable to emulate. So that even when the whole trade was subjected to a common depression, the weavers felt (correctly from some viewpoints, if not from others) that their section had been made to bear the brunt of it.

The cotton workers' Amalgamations are sufficiently related in their interests, structure and problems to constitute a traditionally self-conscious group. They nevertheless differ in their size, composition, strategic position and economic circumstance—as well as in their methods and internal working. In labour's attempt to adjust its organization and policy to recent social and economic trends, we have noted the problem of co-operation between unions the interests of whose members are here related and there diverge as a major one. To this extent, the cotton unions are a microcosm of the trade union movement itself.

V

It would be as well here to have a general picture of the cotton textile trades and their development. At the time of the writer's enquiries[1] the U.K.'s cotton industry employed nearly a quarter-million workers in the firms performing the main spinning and weaving processes, between which two main branches of the trade these workers are about equally divided. Up to a further hundred thousand (depending upon definitions) were employed in various directly related or dependent trades—in the production of artificial and synthetic fibres used by the spinning or weaving firms, in the finishing (dyeing, bleaching, printing and so on) of their products, or in the warehouses of the merchants that handle the latter. But with workers outside the main spinning and weaving trades we shall not be very much concerned. The cotton industry is, in the main, 'horizontally' organized, each major process (spinning, weaving, finishing) being performed by different groups of firms: and of these, there were some four hundred in spinning, and near twice that number in weaving. However, about a quarter of the plant in these two branches was in the hands of firms that conduct both, but the number of firms thus 'vertically' integrated was less than a tenth of the total, so that such concerns are also unusually large. Such firms, moreover, may operate more than one mill, and mav

[1] These, again, antedated the 1960 'concentration' of the industry, and full information of its effects was not available at the time of writing—though the number of workers in spinning and weaving was certainly reduced to around 200,000—and the number of mills operating in and about Lancashire cut by some 300, from about 1,000 in 1959 (and 1,250 in 1950).

continue to separate their spinning and weaving plants, as well as to buy or sell yarn.

Between 85 and 90 per cent of the spinning and weaving workers are employed in Lancashire or in the immediately adjoining parts

THE 'COTTON REGION', AND OTHER DISTRICTS

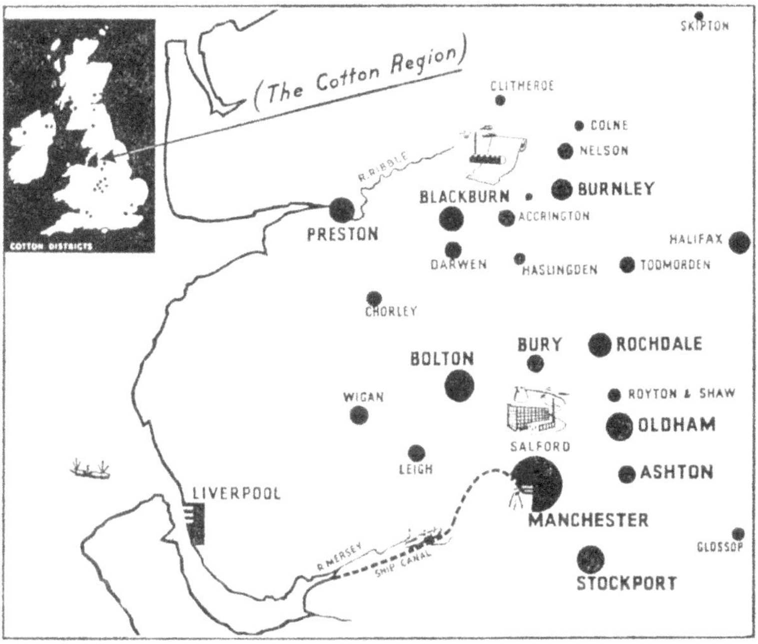

(*Courtesy of the Cotton Board*)

of neighbouring counties—Yorkshire, Cheshire, and Derbyshire.[1] The rest—mostly weavers—are widely scattered. But there is a marked geographical division inside this 'cotton area' itself. The spinning of cotton and its alternative fibres has concentrated in the industrial towns—particularly Bolton and Oldham—that form an arc north and east round Manchester. The weaving trade is now more widely spread, but is again heavily concentrated in another, more distant arc of towns that form the northern and eastern bastions of the Lancashire industrial complex. Some of these towns —particularly the smaller ones and those in the extreme north-east —are still in large measure 'cotton towns' proper, the greatest part of their people depending on the trade for their livelihood.

Similarly, the mercantile warehousing of fabrics is concentrated

[1] I am greatly obliged to the Cotton Board for the accompanying pictorial map.

in Manchester itself, and their finishing and printing both there and in Derbyshire and Yorkshire. But even if the term 'the cotton industry' is applied only to spinning and weaving, it thus really embraces two separate industries, related but economically and geographically distinct. The significance of this division has been, and continues to be, considerable. We have already noted that the spinning and weaving industries may experience different economic circumstances, and that the former is much more concentrated, both in its structure and geographical distribution. The distinction between them is, however, particularly important for labour relations. There are, for instance, two separate major employers' organizations. The Federation of Master Cotton Spinners' Associations for many years included the great majority of firms, in turn representing the overwhelming bulk of the plant, in spinning and doubling; while the Cotton Spinners' & Manufacturers' Association has been almost as strongly representative of firms in the weaving industry—though it originally included many with strong spinning interests as well.[1] Similarly, the two groups of employers have their own agreements with the various unions that cover their employees, and the two industries have separate negotiating procedures. The weaving trade has since 1932 had its own Conciliation Committee, which includes an independent chairman and other outside nominees. But an almost identical arrangement established at the same time for the spinning industry was abandoned after only three years because the unions were dissatisfied with its working, and there has since been no special provision for arbitration in disputes that concern spinning operatives. The division between the two industries is specially important to this study because it permits some contrasts in the evolution of trade unionism, and in its forms and policies.

It will be useful to sketch briefly the development of this industrial structure. One can distinguish several distinct phases in the history of the cotton trades. Their development first began in what was already an established textile-working area. 'Manchester Cottones', a rather coarse cloth of mixed fibres distinct from the pure 'calicos' imported from India, were a British export in the sixteenth century. These, and other textiles, were first manufactured largely by independent domestic producers—though it is probable that the latters'

[1] Since the 1960 'concentration' several other trade associations have merged with the Master Spinners, which is now re-named the British Spinners' & Doublers' Association (Cotton & Allied Industries); the Master Manufacturers has similarly become the United Kingdom Textile Manufacturers' Association (Cotton, Man-made & Allied Fibres). But see the *Appendix*, Part 1, on the employers' organization.

status had already been much modified by a growing dependence on the credit extended by merchants of material and cloth before the eighteenth-century's industrial expansion. Of this expansion, the first phase began when the woollen manufacturers' corporate monopoly engineered a prohibition of 'calico' import or production. The Lancashire interests in turn secured (by the Manchester Act of 1736) exemption from this ban for their particular mixed product. A rapid increase of their trade followed, culminating, in the generation before the French Wars that closed the century, with a glittering boom induced by the brilliant mechanical inventions in spinning. This phase of accelerating growth can be simply illustrated:[1]

Percentage change in Production of Cotton Textiles in each decade
1721–90

1721–30	+2½
1731–40	+14
1741–50	+20
1751–60	+29
1761–70	+34
1771–80	+37
1781–90	+80

And quite early in this phase the domestic workers' transition to a wage-earning status was largely completed.

The second phase is one of violent transition. The water-powered spinning factory had only strengthened the domestic manufacturing structure, enabling it to dispense with the linen yarns previously imported from Ireland for warps and to produce pure cotton cloth, as well as much extending its productive potentiality. The steam-powered mill undermined that structure, first by undercutting the domestic spinners of cotton, later by competing with the hand-weavers themselves. And these handworkers were further reduced in condition by the economic crises the French Wars set off, and by the flood of new labour released by the latters' conclusion. This phase—running roughly from the 1790s to the 1840s—is one of competition between older and newer systems and workers, of

[1] Calculated from A. P. Wadsworth and Julia de L. Mann: *The Cotton Trade & Industrial Lancashire 1600–1780* (Manchester University Press, 1931), p. 170—table of retained imports of cotton wool and yarn; and for 1781–90, from McCulloch's figures (loc. cit.) of raw cotton imports retained, but allowing for the substitution of linen yarns by cotton. A fairly continuous series is available for the whole eighteenth century, but in its first decade trade was interrupted by wars. Only scattered statistics are available for earlier times: such as there are (e.g. in R. Burn, *Statistics of the Cotton Trade*, Manchester, 1847) suggest little change in production between the late seventeenth century and the 1720s.

upheaval and conflict, of Industrial Revolution in its generally-understood sense. But in it, the rate of expansion set in the preceding period's climax was consistently maintained or exceeded—apart from a forced interruption, for a few years from 1811, by Napoleon's Continental blockade, by war with America and by the aftermath of these things[1]:

Percentage change in Production of Cotton Textiles in each decade
1791–1840

1791–1800	+86
1801–10	+84
1811–20	+62
1821–30	+93
1831–40	+91

In the third phase what was now almost entirely a powered-machine, factory industry took on a shape recognizably similar to its present one. Its mechanical techniques were perfected and stabilized. The spinning and weaving branches separated out again into distinct economic units. Within the cotton districts, new local specializations—in coarse or in fine yarns, or in different types of cloth—developed. While a balance of employment was struck with other industries: mining in this district, engineering in that, and so on. And expansion continued, if at a less revolutionary pace:

Percentage change in Production of Cotton Textiles in each decade[2]
1841–80

1841–50	+60
1851–60	+57
1861–70	−4½
1871–80	+52½

But after the universal depression of the later 1870s, there follows a fourth phase. In this, the cotton trade's growth, though it continued up to the First World War itself, slackened in the face of gathering competition. Production abroad of the coarser cotton textiles took hold and grew, in turn imposing a fiercer competition at home of which new forms of economic combination—first the impersonal

[1] Calculated from Robson's Appendix (op. cit.) as for Graph I.

[2] The *decline* in production over 1861–70 is, of course, due to the American Civil War and consequent Cotton Famine. So the 1871–80 increase has been calculated on 1851–60.

joint stock company and then the merged industrial trust—were the agents:

Percentage changes in Production o,
Cotton Textiles in each decade
1881–1920

1881–90	+16
1891–1900	+11½
1901–10	+11
1911–20	+ 4

The fifth phase is that of collapse and retreat, in an inter-War context of general economic and social crisis. And this movement was extended by the deliberate and systematic reduction of textile output during the Second World War:

Percentage change in Production of
Cotton Textiles in each decade[1]
1921–45

1921–30	–24
1931–40	–11
1941–45	–35

While the sixth phase is the present one, in which the industry, after a brief and to some degree artificial post-war re-expansion, struggles to re-adjust itself to a renewal of its inter-war trend:

Percentage change in output of cotton
industry by five-year periods,[2] 1946–60

1946–50	+14
1951–55	+11
1956–60	–20

But in this phase, the industry's circumstances are now modified by a general situation of high employment and of a pressure for social control reflected, in the industry itself, in various attempts at purposive guidance. Indeed, from the late 1930s on, the industry has provided the outstanding British example of a 'tripartite' attempt—that is, one involving co-operation between private employers, organized labour and the government—at industrial modernization.

[1] Except, of course, that the five years 1941–5 are compared with the previous five.

[2] Taking here Cotton Board figures of total output of cloth woven from cotton, man-made and mixture fibres, contrasted with the previous five years in each case.

In each of these six phases, there were changes not only in the technique and economic organization of the cotton trade, but in its location. Thus in the first phase—from the 1730s to the 1790s—when cotton was still struggling to establish itself against competing textile industries, there was an early tendency for weaving to concentrate in and immediately around Manchester, while spinning was still given out to handworkers in the further country districts of Lancashire. But the introduction of water-power gave the trade a strong centrifugal impulse. The new mills drew cotton textile production not only into the upland valleys of the Northern counties, but into other regions of the Kingdom. In 1787 (according to Baines[1]) less than a third of them were in Lancashire itself. In particular, a thriving Scottish industry developed, based on the tributaries of the Clyde, which fostered some of the most formidable of the early trade unions. Steam-power—the introduction of which marks our second phase—reversed this tendency. The Lancashire branch outpaced its rivals, possessing by the 1830s over half the powered mills, and nearly two-thirds of all the U.K.'s textile factory workers. But this growth again was heavily concentrated in and immediately around the area's leading city. However, in the third phase—from the 1840s—Manchester itself declined as a productive centre. Its trade had developed 'horizontally', on a combination of steam-factory spinning with domestic weaving, and gave way before a growth of new 'vertically-integrated' mills on the area's Northern fringe—especially in Preston, but also in and about Blackburn. The rise of these new factory centres seems to have sealed the Scottish industry's defeat. But they in turn lagged as the still newer specialized spinning mills thrived in the inner ring of towns near Manchester. They fell back on factory weaving, which itself spread, booming, up the north-eastern valleys towards the Yorkshire passes—a growth which continued into the fourth phase, of gathering foreign competition; during which, however, the Oldham and Bolton centres became quite dominant in spinning. And in the fifth and sixth phases—of inter-war crisis, brief post-war prosperity and renewed contraction—spinning continued to fall into its focal towns of South Lancashire. But the more flexible weaving trade became more dispersed, not only in the county proper but to a significant extent outside it.

But each of these six phases is also critically related to a stage in the evolution of the cotton unions. Active combinations first appeared among the handworkers, quite early in the cotton trade's phase of growth as a domestic manufacture. There is evidence of a continuing activity by such bodies well into the period of Industrial

[1] *History of the Cotton Manufacture in Great Britain* (London, 1835) p. 219.

Revolution proper; and the methods the handworkers evolved or attempted of controlling their conditions were to influence the factory operatives who then flocked into such organizations as—most notably, perhaps—the Spinners' 'Grand Union' of 1829–30. Trade unionism crystallized into a shape not essentially dissimilar, in either its structure or its method, from that of the modern unions after a flurry of conflict around the middle of the nineteenth century—just as the cotton trade itself then settled into an approximately modern form. The phase of decelerating industrial growth and intensified competition that closed the century witnessed several most extensive or obstinate labour conflicts, of which the great weaving strike of 1878 and the 'Brooklands' spinning lockout of 1893 were only the most remarkable. And this phase also saw the consolidating of the cotton operatives' organization, the recruitment to it of several classes of workers among whom it had previously little hold, and a general hardening of union controls over labour conditions. Indeed, the unions reached the peak of their strength, if not of their general influence, in the present century's second decade, when the slowing trend of the cotton trade's economic growth was very near to consummation, and the main policies on which they had formed themselves were by then almost fully developed. But in the inter-war phase of industrial contraction the unions and employers virtually fought each other to a standstill by the mid-1930s. And around this time, some quite significant modifications in union policy began to emerge. Nevertheless, it is one of the problems of the cotton unions' development that they should have kept their forms of organization unchanged throughout the inter-war economic retreat and that period's labour upheavals. And how their methods stand the test of the industry's post-war phase is one question for this study's later chapters.

II

TRADE UNION ORIGINS

1

The Early Unions: Did They Exist?

I

When the history of the cotton operatives is assembled, one marked discontinuity appears. The 'Hungry Forties', the decade between the great depressions of 1837 and 1847—the decade of Chartism and the attempted revolutionary general strike in the north—seem to form a natural divide. Till then, and although the preceding century includes both the cotton trade's phase of infant growth and its Industrial Revolution proper, the record is dominated by organizations of handworkers—or of workers who, if they had already moved into the factory, were still not completely subjected to the machine.

The break is sharply marked by the trial of the Glasgow spinners in 1838, which initiates an interval of confusion, of conflicting (if often forceful) trends. In the century between the 1736 Act's release of Lancashire textile production from legal restraints and this divide, there were brief movements among operatives (like the jenny-spinners) whose career in the industry was to prove ephemeral; and there were occasional outbreaks of trade unionism among other cotton workers who only later were to become important. But only two groups, the mule-spinners and handloom weavers, have histories that significantly antedate the 1840s. And only the weavers' antecedents reach back into the earliest phase of the cotton industry's expansion. Until the 1780s, of course, yarn was either imported (mostly of Irish linen for warps) or hand-spun in the home. The spinners, as a distinct and stable class, appeared only a few years before the powered factory became dominant in their branch.

But the confused decade that ran into the 1840s is only the last, if the most outstanding, of several seeming discontinuities in the early history of cotton trade unionism. And here, one finds a certain contrast between the views of past students of the subject. General historians of the labour movement have regarded trade unionism as only sporadic among the early cotton operatives. The Webbs speak of their 'ephemeral combinations', of their 'passionate struggles to maintain a bare subsistence wage' alternating with 'intervals of abject submission'.[1] While Cole identifies the textile workers with the miners as 'latecomers to trade unionism'.[2] On the other hand, specialist historians of the cotton trade itself—like Wadsworth (whose work will be referred to later)—refer to collective organization amongst its workers as if that reached back to quite early days. Chapman, for instance, says that among the weavers 'continuous associations certainly existed . . . as early as the middle of the eighteenth century.'[3]

At first sight, conditions in this first century of the cotton industry's development hardly appear favourable to trade unionism. And labour itself presents an impression of increasing heterogeneity. The domestic system of manufacture itself went through three phases, which considerably overlapped. Before cotton became a major material in Lancashire, cloths of linen and wool, as well as the mixed cotton-linen 'fustians', were largely produced by home-working 'small masters', buying in their own materials, employing little assistance to work them up beyond that of their families and neighbours, and selling their own product again. Then, merchants began to supply materials on credit against the returned cloth; and this practice seems particularly likely to have developed when these materials—linen yarn for warps and cotton-wool for domestic hand-spinning into weft—were imported, especially for cotton irregular in supply, and therefore a somewhat speculative purchase. Fairly early in the eighteenth century, moreover, looms that were beyond the independent weaver's power to construct or purchase—the 'Dutch loom' for smallwares (narrow fabrics) and the 'harness loom' for figured fabrics—were coming into use.[4] So that many domestic weavers became involved in a dual debt dependence—for both materials and equipment. But very early in the first marked

[1] *The History of Trade Unionism*, 1920 edition, p. 87.

[2] G. D. H. Cole, *An Introduction to Trade Unionism* (Allen & Unwin, London, 1953) p. 53.

[3] *Lancashire Cotton Industry* (op. cit.), p. 180.

[4] Dutch or 'swivel' looms were quite elaborate machines which produced several strips of cloth at once, and could be worked by horse or water power. The 'harness' looms or 'drawboys' were predecessors of the Jacquards. Their principle was a 'harness' attachment by which the warp threads' arrangement could be varied to produce a pattern as the weft shuttle passed through.

uprush of the cotton trade, these arrangements mainly gave way —if they had not already to some degree done so—to their logical end-form, the 'putting-out' system. Manchester fustian merchants were already employing a sort of sub-contracting piece-master (the 'cruel fustian masters' of Rowbottom's diary[1]) in the country weaving districts, and the renting of looms had already appeared in the smallwares trade.[2] The generality of producers continued to work in their own homes; but by the 1750s 'they were certainly the workpeople of capitalist employers.'[3]

However, among these workers there was nevertheless a considerable diversity. There were differences in economic status. Some groups for a while remained more independent of the merchant-employers than was general. Some domestic weavers themselves employed journeymen or apprentice-labour. And there was a significant group of 'shop-weavers', employed in workshops attached to the 'putting-out' merchants' warehouses.[4] Among the domestic weavers, there were variations in the extent of their dependence upon weaving as such. Many had a smallholding, and though the enclosures of common land later reduced its contribution to their subsistence, in earlier days there were some who could live off their land if need be; and even later on, their position still differed from that of the increasingly numerous town-weavers.

There were also divisions of skill. The general adoption of Kay's 'spring' or 'fly' shuttle in the 1760s made weaving easier to learn, as did the 'drop-box' (which avoided shuttle-changes with multi-coloured cloths). But the skill demanded of the handloom weaver was also being reduced in ways that have attracted less notice. About 1750 the warping mill, which could be worked by a horse and enabled warps to be sent to the weaver ready wound on a beam, began to be used by merchants, and probably facilitated the 'putting-out' system. Then, it became common for the beams to be fixed in the loom by a specialist 'beamer' or 'gaiter-up'—a practice which one trade union was afterwards able to exploit for its own purposes. Later, simple winding machines became available, so that weft yarn could be supplied already packed for insertion in the weaver's

[1] In 'The Annals of Oldham' (S. Andrew, ed., *Oldham Standard* series from January 1, 1887).

[2] Chapman (op. cit.) p. 20 footnote 2.

[3] Daniels, *The Early English Cotton Industry* (Manchester University Press, 1920) p. 39.

[4] It is interesting to note, in the period's documentation, the way in which the term 'master' (or 'manufacturer') itself shifts from the producer proper—the initiate of the trade's occupational mysteries—to the merchant-entrepreneur; becoming at last firmly attached, quite early in the nineteenth century, to the factory employers themselves.

shuttle.[1] The uneven introduction of such devices naturally widened the differences of skill and economic status between weavers.

And there were, of course, also demarcations by product. Weavers specialized in one of the main types of cloth in which cotton was used, like smallwares, 'checks' (including a variety of patterned cloths), 'printers', or fustians—the early expansion of which branch was especially instrumental in expelling the established wool and linen trades from Lancashire. Varieties of cotton cloth, however, might also compete with each other. Their specialist weavers certainly competed for material in times when expanding trade pressed upon a still irregular supply of the latter. But they might also have differing market prospects—a very large proportion of 'checks' for instance, went for export.

When, in the 1770s and '80s, the outbreak of spinning inventions struck the trade, these diversities—several of which involved conflicts of interest among the workers themselves—were naturally multiplied, and this not merely by a greatly intensified division of labour, but by rival systems of production. The handloom weavers at first benefited: it was not until the last stages of the industry's transitional period, nearly half a century on, that power-looms were produced that could compete with them (at least on the minimal wages to which they were later reduced). But in the 1760s, weavers had been sometimes unemployed from a thread shortage because the simpler weaving improvements had virtually doubled their potential output. The spinning-jenny—which duplicated the hand-spinner's motions mechanically—thus secured full employment to the weavers, and drew more of the agricultural population into the work of supplying their needs. And the water-frame, a factory instrument from the first, produced a thread that, replacing imported linen warps, permitted cloths to be woven wholly of cotton and so induced a fantastic expansion in trade: between the 1770s and '80s, output roughly doubled.[2]

But the spinning-jennies themselves were improved, became too expensive for the domestic producer, and moved into merchants' workshops and the water-mills. Factory machinery for preparing (carding and roving) the fibres for spinning was perfected: and that most elegant of all the spinning inventions, the mule, was rapidly adapted to a partial application of steam-power. Technically, the

[1] These machines, of course, became useful only with the availability of factory yarn, which was of a more consistent quality than the domestic product. In the 1760s and '70s, the weaver was usually made responsible for arranging his own spinning because the 'putter-out' found it difficult to protect himself against bad work or fraud by domestic spinners.

[2] See Tables of Chapter I, 2, section v.

period then seems one of immense confusion, with almost complete factory and hand production systems existing side-by-side, and with all sorts of intermediate compromises. But in the course of it, the handloom weavers were early deprived of their families' earnings from the spinning and preparation of fibre at home.

However, perhaps the most potent influence in this stage of the cotton workers' history—certainly the most direct factor in the hand-weavers' later decline—was the vast influx of new labour. Mechanics and artisans from all kinds of trades, colliers and numbers of farm labourers, came in to run the new factory machines. Paupers—particularly children—were brought up in masses from London and the agricultural south to provide their assistants. Of children, the mere upsurge of population growth created a new supply. The factories were at first absolutely dependent on child labour, and as late as 1833, when the supply of 'parish apprentices' had for some years been restricted and so-called 'free children' were the source, a fifth of the workers in Manchester's biggest factory[1] were aged under fourteen. And there were, perhaps above all among the adult recruits, the Irish. Into cotton weaving came first those displaced or drawn from other weaving trades, and small farmers who mortgaged their land to put up loom-lofts and buy appliances. But as the flood grew, and the factories filled up, the Irish immigrants—many at first driven by the collapse of their own linen industry—spilled over into the handloom weaving of the towns. The Irish are continually referred to as a source of riot and violence among the cotton operatives. They were sometimes prominent among strikers, particularly in the more brutal disputes: they were equally likely to turn up as strikebreakers. Quite late in the nineteenth century, one or two local unions in south-east Lancashire still refused to admit them.[2] And as early as 1791, Lancashire magistrates report warily of '. . . a very numerous and *foreign* population, estranged, unconnected, and in general composed of persons who are a species of exile.'[3]

[1] R. Smith, 'Manchester as a Centre for the Manufacture and Merchanting of Cotton Goods, 1820–30' (*Birmingham Historical Journal, No. 1, 1953*). The account refers to McConnell's Long Mill, which still stands within sight of the Operative Spinners' Amalgamation Office.

[2] Before the South-East Lancashire Province of the present Cardroom Amalgamation was formed, there were rival cardroom unions in the district. Another and once most powerfully-organized textile trade, the Woolcombers, added this note to its *Rules* of 1821: 'N.B. No Irishman to be admitted to Society, after the date of these articles.'

[3] Letter to the Home Secretary, No. 2 in Aspinall's documentary collection (op. cit.). The Hammonds say there were between 30,000 and 40,000 Irish weavers in Manchester in the 1820s (*The Town Labourer*, Longmans, London, 1919, p. 13). Smith (loc. cit.) gives a more conservative figure of 30,000 in 1841.

Within this new mass, the rise and fall of particular occupational groups was accelerated by the intenser pace of industrial advance. On the eve of the French Revolutionary Wars, contemporary accounts of the cambric and muslin weavers, the mule-spinners, the calico-printers all speak in the same tone: they dressed in a gentlemanly style, exercised a convivial and select leisure, furnished themselves well. Within a generation, however, the calico-printers were to be committed to a rearguard action against the advance of machinery, the mule-spinners embroiled in a violent technical transition, the fine-weavers driven near a desperate poverty. But the latter had already seized much of the older fustian-weavers' trade, while the mule-spinners' competition was undercutting the cottage jenny-spinners—as it was later to make factory spinning on jennies and water-frames obsolete. And there are other classes which must once have been both numerous and prosperous—the winders and warpers of yarn for handloom weaving, for instance—whose career was so brief that we know little of them.

On the other hand there was the possibility, open to anyone who would (in the Hammonds' phrase) 'work like a slave and live like a slave-master'—as well as to some who (like Fielden, Hanson, and Robert Owen himself)[1] combined sensibility with a shrewd intelligence—of rapid rise to the status of capitalist employer. If many came to the rising cotton towns driven by loss of livelihood or as a species of transported serf, others came to seek their fortune. The new industrial towns in any case '. . . split men into separate self-seeking atoms'. Many of the ablest rose quickly from the operatives' ranks; others, equally venturesome but less successful, were forced by debt to continue producing under unprofitable conditions and thus to undercut the employed workers.

These apparent social and occupational instabilities were finally aggravated by the economic instability of the industry itself.[2] Dramatic bursts of expansion were interrupted by severe depressions, brought on by the booming export trade's exposure to wars, by the highly speculative character of much of the industry's investment—particularly in stocks—occasionally, by plain overproduction.

[1] Fielden and Hanson, of course, were also both 'self-made men' who retained radical and popular sympathies.

[2] These chapters were written before Neil J. Smelser's *Social Change in the Industrial Revolution: An Application of Theory to the Lancashire Cotton Industry, 1770–1840* (International Library of Sociology and Social Reconstruction, 1959) came to hand. One need not subscribe to this monolithic study's sociological categories, but they frame an immense assembly of material on the economic transition's detailed social implications.

From the data collected by Gayer, Rostow and Schwartz[1] one can reckon that in the sixty years from 1790 the British cotton industry, despite (or perhaps because of) its exceptional growth, experienced nine major depressions and nearly as many minor ones—a fluctuation much above the general frequency.

Over the 'century of unrest'[2] that the Seven Years' War initiated in 1756, it is by no means conclusively established that the working population at large gained or lost in real terms. How one strikes the balance of the Industrial Revolution seems to depend largely on whether one thinks it to the worse that it entailed so much suffering, or to the better that it permitted so many more people to survive and suffer. What *is* certain is that workpeople in general experienced large variations in their conditions, and that particular sections and individuals among them were greatly elevated or cast down—and sometimes both in succession.

II

Add to all these circumstances the persistent hostility of the state, the law and usually of the local governing class to workers' organizations, the existence throughout the industry's early history until 1824 of laws against combination which were repeatedly strengthened and in several cases (as in the Act of 1800) specifically directed against textile workers' unions,[3] the frequently-supposed identification of those unions, from the outbreak of the French wars to the 1820s, with sedition and insurrection, and the consequent employment against them of a paraphernalia of suppression, with spies, agent-provocateurs, imprisonments and transportations. And the supposition of labour historians, that no significantly continuing trade unionism existed among the cotton operatives before the mid-nineteenth century, seems reasonably founded.

Such views must command respect—though the reasons advanced to explain them are not always really convincing. Cole, for instance, regarded the 'many attempts' at workers' organization under the domestic system as inevitably doomed because . . . such movements were powerless unless organized over quite large areas; for it was easy for . . . the (merchant) employers . . . to withdraw work from any one place, and combinations extending over a large area were

[1] *The Growth and Fluctuation of the British Economy, 1790–1850* (Oxford University Press, 1953).

[2] Postgate's phrase, I think.

[3] According to the Webbs (*History*, p. 81) the main weight of the Combination Acts in any case fell on the textile workers. They note particularly (p. 86) a difference in the law's application to the 'aristocracy' of the old London crafts.

difficult to maintain because of bad communications, and were also more likely to be broken up by the strong hand of the law.'[1] But this neglects the fact that local specialization has been a recurrent feature of the cotton industry. Before factory spinning developed, the weavers' combinations were of distinct trades which were usually congregated in a particular district—fustian weavers round Oldham, smallware weavers in and about Manchester, muslin weavers round Bolton, and so on. It is, in fact, very relevant to some later conclusions of this study that *general* weavers' unions were only proposed when *sectional* conditions deteriorated; while some sectional associations still continued a detached existence thereafter, and even survived when the mass combinations of handloom weavers had long distintegrated. The Bolton Handloom Counterpane Weavers' Association, for instance, which officers of the present Bolton Weavers' Union suggest may have had early eighteenth-century antecedents,[2] was apparently still active in 1846; and a handloom association was actually re-formed in the town as late as 1880.

Nevertheless, if one thinks of trade unions in terms of formally-constituted organizations—with documentary constitutions, formally-appointed officers, formally-stated agreements, trade regulations and so on—most of the surviving evidence is of intermittent eruptions only. But a 'continuous association' (the Webbs' term) is not necessarily the same thing as a formal organization: people of the same occupation, who are regularly brought together in the same workplace or town, may acknowledge regular leaders, develop customs of work-regulation and systematic 'trade practices', and produce a disciplined observance of the latter, without embedding these procedures in any formal records—just as (and this was certainly true of the handloom weavers' general unions) a formally-constituted organization may have small control over its members' conduct. In any case, it will be suggested later that organization among the early cotton operatives was generally of a kind that could readily submerge in time of trouble.

Most of the evidence of the early unions' activity is indirect: few records of their own survive (probably, not many were kept anyway —the initial records of many modern local unions are of the most primitive and fragmentary kind). They left an imprint on history mainly when they came into conflict with employers or with

[1] *An Introduction to Trade Unionism* (op. cit.) p. 53.

[2] This is perhaps not impossible, since its speciality presumably involved weaving on 'drawboys' which came in around 1730–40. But some relics in the present Bolton Union's possession are probably from the early nineteenth century association.

authority. True, these conflicts occasionally turn up evidence of formal (or at least, regularly-conducted) association over a number of years. Thus it is only in connection with the struggles of 1756–8 that the rules of the very earliest union which can be considered one of cotton operatives, the Smallware Weavers' Association, are publicized—with certain articles dated 1747 and referring to a preceding organization.[1] The Bolton Spinners' committee-men are arrested in 1823 and their books seized—and these last include the subscription returns from 1812.[2] The Glasgow Spinners in 1838 are tried on evidence adducing 'a twenty years' reign of terror'. Otherwise, however, the record is of the incidents to the operatives' surges of activity—sequences of strikes, phases of agitation and riot, and so on. But what happened in between these surges? The intervals may have been ones of exhaustion or suppression: but there is an occasional suggestion of mere normality as predominant.

Thus, the weavers' unions make no notable mark on the historians' record for twenty years from 1760 (when their leaders publicly renounced their combinations). But in 1769 an elaborate wage-list appeared for 'those branches of the weaving manufacture called the Strong Plain, Foot, Figured and Flowered Branches . . . Prices agreed between a number of Masters and Journeymen."[3] In 1798, in a lull between the outburst of combination and radicalism that followed the French Revolution and the surge of weavers' activity with which the Combination Act itself was associated, two enterprising Manchester Welshmen and another manufacturer issued 'The Ready Numberer, or Cotton Spinners' Calculator' as an aid to wage-calculation, 'since masters and men have agreed that the fairest way of reckoning sets is by the whole weight and length.'[4]

Around 1818, a few years after 300,000 signatures had been collected for a petition for legal enforcement of the collapsing apprenticeship system, with insurrection in the air and muslin weavers, spinners and several other groups about to fling themselves into a crescendo of strikes, the Manchester Smallware Weavers are peaceably issuing certificates of completed indentures and enforcing

[1] The Rules adopted in 1755 are set out in *The Worsted Smallware Weavers' Apology*, issued in Manchester in 1756 (copy in the Manchester Reference Library)

[2] Aspinall (op. cit.), document No. 393.

[3] The discovery of the List was reported in the *Manchester Evening Chronicle* of January 10, 1938, with a photograph. The Weavers' Amalgamation's former Assistant General Secretary says it actually included five separate lists, and thirty pages of prices—as well as a retort to objectors to price-lists! The list's preamble described it as having been printed at the expense of 'subscribers for the work' (of drawing it up).

[4] In the Manchester Reference Library. A 'set' is an archaic output unit of yarn, the different grades of which would correspond to piece-prices in a wage-list.

a standard wage-list.[1] There are quite a few other reports of agreements which had at least a few years' currency in the cotton or closely-associated Lancashire textile trades—the extreme case, of course, being that of the Rochdale flannel workers' union (which may later have become a mixed wool-cotton association). This, in 1819, drew up a wage-list with a group of the more important employers, who then subscribed to the union's strikes against non-complying masters: and this agreement apparently ran through the years between Peterloo and the industrial outbreaks of 1826—until, in fact, it was condemned by the 1825 Committee on the Combination Laws and discontinued.[2]

The 'surges' of workers' activity, moreover, are themselves sometimes quite long. The record of weavers' activities, for instance, is almost continuous from 1799 to 1819, and it is difficult to study it without concluding that some form of general combination existed over the whole period. And when unions become prominent again after intervals of apparent quiescence, they often bear a striking resemblance of form to their local predecessors. A peculiarity of internal organization may appear and re-appear (some instances, at a later stage). Names are similar—'The Association of Weavers' is formed and disappears from view; a lag, and 'The Associated Weavers' appears. The Smallware Weavers' appearances are scattered over the whole period: between their very early combination of the mid-eighteenth century and the evidence of their later activity cited above, for instance, they are found in the 1760s prosecuting unapprenticed weavers, are thanked in 1779 by the Manchester silk-weavers (who had formed an association a few years previously) for their help in a trade dispute,[3] and are involved in another strike in 1781. At a still later stage, they re-appear as an affiliate of the 1830 National Association for the Protection of Labour. And it seems in fact not unlikely that their association was close to continuous over nearly a century. However, by its end they had probably become a relatively isolated group, since their very early exposure to technical and economic change by the 'Dutch' looms somewhat insulated them against its later developments.

And there are also some more general suggestions that collective regulation of some kind was effective over substantial periods. For instance, the delayed introduction of the 'fly-shuttle' in the eighteenth

[1] Copies in the Manchester Reference Library—unindexed, but bound, oddly enough, with 'Tracts on Labour and Capital'.

[2] This case is referred to by the Hammonds in *The Skilled Labourer* (Longmans, London, 1919) p. 164.

[3] See Ch. XVIII of Wadsworth & Mann (op. cit.) for these two incidents. There is an account of the early Smallware Weavers' trade regulations, etc., in Daniels (op. cit.) p. 40 et seq.

century: although patented in the 1730s, and certainly known of in Lancashire in the 1740s (since there was a riot against it), this device did not come into general use for another twenty years, under pressure, apparently—but still amid some controversy—of the boom that closed the Seven Years' War. Again, a major object of the early mule-spinners' unions was to control entry into their trade: the Factory Commissioners in 1833 received witness[1] from Bolton that, although power-spinning was rapidly expanding in the district, the entry of 'grown-up men' to the occupation had ceased between 1815 and 1820 (only a few years after the first evidence of a union's existence in the town)—and this, despite the mass return of soldiers after Waterloo. And again, there is the curious stability of cotton factory wages in the early decades of the nineteenth century. Despite the violent fluctuations in the industry and the appalling collapse of the handloom workers' wages (which fell by at least two-thirds in the same time) wages of factory operatives in 1846 were apparently within two or three pence of their figure of forty years before, and did not vary more than 5 or 6 per cent of it over the intervening period.[2] And this stability was, apparently, particularly marked in Glasgow—where the most formidable of the early Spinners' unions was entrenched. By contrast, wages in the wool and worsted industries—in which the pace of economic and technical development was slower and less staccato, but where the handworkers' organizations were distintegrating without successors in the factories—were much more fluctuating.

III

For any group of workers, common standards and traditions are among the most powerful of cohesive forces. And the Webbs considered the absence of such traditions to be a factor in the supposedly-sporadic character of trade unionism among the early cotton operatives.[3] But there were certainly groups among them that cherished historical standards they thought defensible, as well as near models of workers' organization which stimulated other groups to combine in emulation. From the Middle Ages, of course, many European textile industries operated with a large sector of wage-earning employment. And from the fourteenth century on, unrecognized guilds of journeymen are found in conflict with their

[1] Quoted by the Hammonds '*Town Labourer*', p. 12.

[2] See G. H. Wood's *History of Wages in the Cotton Trade during the past Hundred years* (Sherratt & Hughes, London, 1910) Table 41 for this; the following comments deduced from his final section.

[3] *The History*, p. 78.

employers. A powerful federation of journeymen weavers existed in the Low Countries in the fifteenth century (it actually blacklisted the whole of England.[1] And although the Continental journeymen's activities had subsided by the time of the Huguenot exodus, it is not impossible that many of the immigrants who then carried textile skills to England also brought memories of this primitive trade unionism: many of them at least possessed traditions of collective organization derived from their guilds. The origin of the Lancashire cotton manufacture is often attributed to a settlement of several hundred 'Flemmings' in the mid-sixteenth century. And Flemish names still appear among the signatories of the Lancashire weavers' wage-list of 1769.

Again, forms of capitalist employment were early advanced in the English woollen trades, and combinations of woollen and worsted workers existed in the eighteenth century's first half (an Act against them was passed in 1749) and extended into Yorkshire. There is no early record of any Lancashire activity on their part, but movements of wool workers over the Pennines and into the expanding cotton trades have also occurred—the north-east Lancashire valleys, especially, formed an uncertain frontier between the two industries—and the Manchester Smallware Weavers themselves were originally worsted workers. Certainly, it is suggestive that the appearance of weavers' combinations follows quite promptly upon the first marked expansion that the 1736 Manchester Act induced in the cotton trade—and upon the introduction to that trade of capital-demanding looms.

However, there is no need to rely heavily on such external influences. The early growth of the cotton industry was stimulated by its relative freedom from the elaborate legal regulation that bound the older textile manufactures, and one reason for its selection of Lancashire as a major field was the absence there of guild-ridden corporate towns. But of the legal and corporate monopolies of previous industrial eras, one tradition survived in the region. A. P. Wadsworth, in the best account of trade unionism's beginnings among the handloom cotton weavers, remarked that '. . . two threads stand out conspicuously in the fabric of working-class organization in the eighteenth century. One is the tradition of the incorporated monopoly of the legally-apprenticed small master, inherited from the close regulation of Tudor and Stuart times. The other is the tradition of widespread organization among journeymen, which combined friendly society purposes with the

[1] G. Unwin's Introduction to Daniels' *Early English Cotton Industry* (op. cit.) p. xxiii.

tramping ticket, the house of call, and the "blank".'[1] Wadsworth regarded (as, of course, have other writers[2]) the first influence as more important among the weavers. When in 1557 Lancashire was excluded from the main scope of the Tudor Weavers' Act (which intended to restrict country weaving in the interest of corporate towns) the Act's apprenticeship requirements still applied: as did the apprenticeship and wage-regulation clauses of the 1563 Statute of Apprentices. The original intent of these measures had been to keep apprentice-labour tied and hold down wages. Nevertheless, the domestic weavers of the eighteenth century read into them an ideal system of trade protection, to defend and be defended against the disturbances of change.

But the second tradition—the incipient craft unionism of journeymen—also played a part. Early weavers' societies occasionally adopted, not merely 'friendly' functions (which were not unique to trade unions) but the device of the trade 'blank'—a sort of certificate of the worker's good standing. Of this second tradition, however, it is probable that the special influence was rather on the early spinners' gropings for a method of collective action. The technical development of the mule-spinning process was extremely rapid, but in its first years it too was a domestic occupation. Many of the first spinners (like the inventor Crompton himself) were former hand-weavers: some of these were quite skilled mechanics (at this time weavers often built their own looms) who readily mastered the primitive mule's construction and set up as 'little spinners'. The first mule-spinners' societies appeared while the mule was still being adapted to power—the union in Oldham, for example, antedating by two years the town's first steam factory.[3] The entry of weavers into spinning was soon cut off; but it very likely sufficed to transmit at least a germ of collective organization. And there is some indirect evidence of a link between the first spinners' societies and the already-existing weavers' unions in certain similar local variations in their organizational methods. The first Oldham spinners' union seems to have had essentially the same 'village association' structure as the district's prior combination of fustian weavers.

[1] In Wadsworth & Mann (op. cit.) Ch. 11, 'The Beginnings of Trade Unionism'.

[2] See, for instance, Daniels (op. cit.) p. 48.

[3] Some combination of Stockport spinners was actually instructing its adherents not to work 'below the usual prices' in 1785 (Unwin, *Samuel Oldknow and the Arkwrights*, MUP, 1924 p. 33)—before a metal mule was available or even water-power had been applied to the wooden machine. It is possible, however, that these were jenny- rather than mule-spinners. The last factory jennies were too big to be worked by women and children. Some Stockport factories seem to have adopted the jenny rather than the new and still little-developed mule, and a strike of jenny-spinners occurred there more than twenty years later.

But the early Manchester spinners' union was based on the 'shop'—like the smallware weavers' organization that antedated it.

As the factories grew, however, and the mule-frames moved into them, their operatives must soon have found the weavers' associative concepts inadequate. And it was here that the second tradition offered itself. Despite the absence of a preceding corporate organization in the new textile towns, one group of workers came into them with an established system of combination—the calico-printers. Their trade had crystallized as a capitalist industry in London at the end of the seventeenth century, and they had what was virtually a journeymen's guild from these times on.[1] Firms that set up in the north—where textile-printing early became a factory trade—to pattern the first English 'calicos' had to bring these skilled workmen in. These brought their association with them, and it rapidly took on all the characteristics of a militantly-restrictive trade union. Just before the first spinners' societies were formed, the calico-printers had already fought two major strikes—one, in 1790, a 'general turnout' lasting three months to reinforce their apprenticeship restrictions. For nearly thirty years after, and despite the Combination Acts, they remained 'one of the strongest and most complete of unions'.[2] And by 1814 their association was a national one . . . 'pervading the greater part of the three kingdoms . . .'[3]

To a similar model the early spinners' unions turned, to such effect that in 1816 the Home Office's special commissioner in Lancashire could write: 'The classes . . . that have been most formidable are the calico printers and cotton spinners who, labouring in large numbers together in print works or cotton factories under the same employers respectively, have for many years past been almost every year in some place or other in a state of combination against their employers.'[4] In at least one respect, indeed, the spinners improved upon the calico-printers' technique. Their remarkable 'rolling strike' tactic—the method of striking selected groups of operatives in turn, so that those on strike can be supported from the contributions of those still at work—the spinners' unions applied first between the mills within a district, then between districts, and finally between different sections of mule-spinners spread over the whole region (selecting 'long-wheel' from 'small-wheel' spinners, or coarse spinners from fine). The calico-printers had not carried

[1] See Turnbull's *History of the Calico Printing Industry* (Sherratt, Altrincham, 1951) Ch. 6.

[2] Webbs, *History*, p. 75, referring to the *Considerations addressed to the Journeymen Calico-printers by one of their Masters*, of 1815.

[3] Aspinall, Document No. 172 (see also Nos. 164–8).

[4] Aspinall's No. 185.

the tactic beyond the workshop level, although its invention was enshrined in their rules.[1] In its upshot, the spinners' other (and also perhaps imitative) attempt, to mould their organization like the printers' into a national craft, was to fail. But from it a quite different, and in some ways more typically modern technique of restrictive regulation emerged. Meanwhile, that ambition represented a cohesive ideal, essentially different from, but as effective as, the handloom weavers' appeal to a supposed pre-established and legally-supported status.

IV

To the early spinners' and weavers' contrasting objects, their surges of recorded activity are themselves a major clue. And these surges are in fact such as to suggest an underlying continuity. It is not merely that they occur in circumstances that are, for each group, distinct but consistent. The conditions that provoke them are also very different—indeed, almost opposite—as between the spinners and weavers respectively; so that when the spinners are active the weavers are passive, and vice-versa.

These surges in any case provide a convenient way to trace the early unions' history: and for that purpose, the century this history embraces can be roughly divided into three sequences. The first practically coincides with the cotton industry's own phase of infant growth, and is terminated by the outbreak of the French Revolutionary Wars. The industry's phase of transition to the factory system is divided, from the viewpoint of the labour movement's development, by the Peterloo Massacre of 1819: so that the second sequence of trade union activity covers the great French wars and their aftermath. While the third sequence of early union history extends from Peterloo to the 'Hungry 'Forties'.

Here—and though this involves compressing a long course of fascinating and complex incidents—this record is set out fairly cryptically, partly to limit the tedium of chronological recital, but particularly so that the connection of labour activity with economic events may be the clearer. However, the account that follows at least summarizes (in one or two cases, attempts to reconcile) nearly every reference the writer has been able to trace to the early cotton unions' activities that has not been employed elsewhere in this study![2]

[1] *Rules for the Conducting of the Union Society of Printers, Cutters and Drawers in Lancashire, Cheshire, Derbyshire, etc.*, 1813 (in the Manchester Reference Library, but not indexed). The technique, of course, is essentially that revived by the ETU's 'guerrilla strike' campaign of 1953/54.

[2] Most of the basic material has been well worked over by social and economic historians for other purposes than the present one, and since certain standard

In the first and earliest sequence, no dramatic symptoms of trade unionism appear before the 1750s. Until the outbreak of the Seven Years' War in 1756, the workpeople's general condition was comparatively prosperous. And such weavers' associations as existed were probably little more than informal village and neighbourhood friendly societies—or public house clubs—at which trade conditions and disputes with merchants or masters about such things as the prices, specification or quality of work might be discussed, but of which no more militant activity seemed required. There is no evidence, for instance, that the early weavers' opposition to the adoption of the 'fly-shuttle' or other mechanical improvements (a 'cotton reel' was attacked in 1753) represented a co-ordinated movement. The smallware weavers' priority in more systematic organization—the men the Manchester constable arrested for 'combination' in 1754 were probably smallware weavers, and their rules of 1747 were revised in 1755—seems sufficiently explained by their fear of the 'Dutch' looms' labour-saving effects, and of a consequential flood of apprentices into their specialized trade.

But the first years of the Seven Years' War were ones of bad harvest, as well as bad trade, and there was widespread distress. The smallware weavers moved first, with a wage demand in 1757; but by the following year a combination of the much more numerous check weavers had appeared, demanding that wage-rates be increased, that the length of cloth according to which weaving prices were paid be specified (apparently 'putting out' masters were surreptitiously reducing actual wages by *increasing* the length of the warps issued), and that 'unfair weavers' (i.e. weavers who were not properly apprenticed or who would accept work under conditions inferior to the customary ones) be not employed. When the masters threatened prosecution, the weavers retaliated with a general stoppage of work lasting four months, which compelled their employers to accept mediation. The employers were apparently induced to accept several proposals, including the establishment of an arbitration procedure for price-disputes, but jibbed at recognizing a permanent

---

works which have resulted from their efforts have already been noted, direct reference here will be mainly confined to points of supposition, statistics, or quotation, to little-known sources or to fuller accounts of certain highlights. Otherwise there would be more footnotes than script!

The economic information to which this material has been related can be partly derived from Gayer, Rostow and Schwartz (op. cit). and from Smart's *Economic Annals of the Nineteenth Century* (Macmillan, London, 2 vols., 1910 and 1917), as well as various studies of particular periods. However, many of the economic fluctuations to be referred to can also be picked out in the Graph 'Annual Consumption of Raw Cotton in the U.K., 1780–1960' of Ch. I, 2, section I.

weavers' combination.[1] What the weavers finally achieved is unclear, but they later announced that the dispute had been settled and that their combination had dissolved. Nevertheless, eighteen of their leaders were brought up at the Lancashire Assizes in 1759 and fined nominal amounts, after hearing a judicial lecture and making an apology for their illegal action. And in 1760, some smallware weavers were similarly prosecuted on account of their stoppage of three years previously: in their case, the action was dropped on a promise of future good behaviour. Despite these renunciations, however, it appears that minor weavers' strikes occurred in outlying districts—Wigan and Kendal—the same year.

In 1758, too, a combination of weavers in Oldham—a fustian centre—conducted an interchange of protest and threat with their Mancunian merchant employers, while the Manchester silk-weavers announced their intention to limit apprentices; so that 1757-8 marks the first extensive and organized militancy among the Lancashire weavers. But the weavers' agitation subsided in the Seven Years' War's closing boom. And for the cotton workers—though not for others—the next twenty years were ones of continued trade expansion, apparently of relative comfort, and of quiescence. There is a hint of generally-heightened activity around 1768-9: years of riots against dear food and the new spinning-jenny, and of some bad trade. The formulation of the weavers' wage-list of 1769, already referred to, suggests some more organized dispute; and about this time the silk-weavers' society was certainly active in Manchester. But the following decade was undoubtedly one of relative prosperity, for the cotton workers at least. Then, in the midst of the American War (which, though for Independence, had also the usual effect of wars on food prices) came a trade recession, which was particularly severe over 1779–81. And with this, new signs of militancy appeared.

This time, the movement was more vigorous. Several Lancashire weavers' societies united in 1779 to present an address to the Home Office requesting legal enforcement of wage-rates. The domestic jenny-spinners—who were closely associated with the handloom weavers in their villages—made a brief appearance with a petition against 'patent machines'. There were riots in north Lancashire, attacks on Arkwright's new water-powered factories, a brief but widespread outbreak of smashing 'work-shop jennies'—spinning machines that were not in the hands of the workpeople themselves. And amidst these events, the first proposal for an all-Lancashire federation of weavers' societies was published by the weavers of

[1] There are accounts of these negotiations—or rather conciliation proceedings —in Wadsworth (loc. cit.) and Daniels (op. cit, p. 45 et seq).

Chowbent—a centre of the now increasingly-insecure fustian trade. A new Combination Act was hurried through Parliament, largely it seems because of the increase of trade unionism among the northern textile workers.[1] It is at this time, too, that we first hear of the Scottish operatives: by 1778, a number of weavers' clubs were in existence around Glasgow, and in 1780 these united in an attempt to secure a uniform scale of weaving prices. They did not succeed, apparently; but in Lancashire in 1781, the Oldham weavers issued a manifesto demanding trade regulations, and the smallware weavers 'swore out of the trade' (blacklisted) two masters, and attempted to enforce their own list of prices by a lengthy 'turn-out' —which actually succeeded to the extent of achieving a negotiated agreement.

But the domestic operatives' movement again subsided with a trade recovery—this time merging in the 'fever of production' that followed the release of Arkwright's mechanical spinning patents over 1783–5. In this last year, however, the first known strike of spinners is reported from Stockport. And at this time, the cotton trade was launched on some years of immense prosperity. Then, a recession in 1787–8, and the Clyde valley weavers' general association was re-formed to withstand wage-reductions: a defence that ended in violence. This recession marked the beginning of the fustian manufacture's decline; from then on, the weavers' condition in the textile trade's coarser branches decayed. In 1790 the first power-loom mill was attacked and burnt by weavers in Manchester. In 1791 there was '. . . a very general spirit of combination.'[2] The weavers of finer cotton fabrics were as yet less affected, and their economic advancement was temporarily renewed. But the weaving trade was now entering uncertain times. In 1792 a dispute between the fine-weavers, centred on Bolton and Bury, and their masters ended in mutual concession: an indirect wage-reduction (by way of lengthening the customary 'stint' of cloth) was exchanged for guarantees as to the future method of fixing piece-prices. The handloom weavers' wages, which had risen fast in the preceding decade of violently-accelerated industrial growth, had now reached their historical peak and begun to turn.

V

The lesson of this first phase in the early unions' development is fairly clear. Only a deterioration in their conditions could stimulate the handloom weavers to any strong collective action. And this is

[1] Webbs' *History*, p. 62.
[2] Aspinall, Letter No. 2.

also true of the phase that now followed on. But in this phase, the weavers' activity changes its character. Not only does it become more continuous—the period is for them one of persistent, if irregular decline. But as the weavers' various specialist groups are forced into a common economic regression, their former sectional associations appear to merge into general ones; and these are less directed towards trade action than to securing state support (a point, incidentally of some relevance to our later consideration of trade unions and politics). This period, however, is also particularly marked by the rise of militant unions among the spinning-factory operatives—unions of a kind distinctly different from the societies which had already appeared among the domestic workers.

For the weavers, this second phase of development appears to have been initiated by the major slump that the French Wars' outbreak set off in 1793. At this time, any immediate growth of workers' associations was largely inhibited by the repression of popular movements in general which had, in Britain, followed the Jacobins' seizure of power in France. Nevertheless, agitation for a legal minimum wage in weaving became significant; Whitbread's Bill to provide legal wage-enforcement was presented to Parliament —and by the latter rejected in 1795. By then, however, any reaction among the weavers was doubtless muffled by a temporary improvement in their condition. The situation of the now dominant fine-weavers, at least, had again recovered: by 1796, the trade was at the peak of a renewed prosperity.

But in 1797 depression returned: in 1798, apparently, the Bolton/Bury weavers' collective agreement became ineffective[1] when 'manufacturers began to multiply, and every new hand found out some new invention to reduce the price of weaving'. At the same time, food prices were rising fast. And in 1799 The Association of Weavers, federating fourteen local unions of Lancashire and about, was formed with a General Committee announcing itself from Bolton, and the largest representation from that town.[2] While 23,000 signatures were collected to a petition for wage and apprenticeship regulation by law.

In these times, too, the earliest systematic societies of mule-spinners appeared. The first had already been formed at Stockport during the boom of 1792, followed in the same year by an initial regular organization at Manchester: and these were now joined by

[1] Mantoux, *The Industrial Revolution in the Eighteenth Century* (Cape, London, 1928, p. 453), quoting the Select Committee on the Handloom Weavers' Petitions of 1835.

[2] The Committee's manifesto is reproduced as Aspinall's No. 25, together with a list of the districts represented.

another union at Oldham, which in 1796 adopted definitive rules.[1] It is significant of the contrast with the weavers' unions that these years, too, were ones of good or improving trade. The newly-passed Combination Act perhaps restrained the spinners from exploiting the brief boom that closed the century. But we next hear directly of the spinners in 1801–2—the year of brief peace with France, and one of heightened prosperity—when they struck successfully in Manchester for a wage-advance, and their Stockport union's activity attracted official wrath: it was dissolved and its leaders imprisoned under the Combination Act.

From the first, the spinners' organization seems to have been regarded by employers and authority as the more menacing affair. Despite its infancy, it was apparently already conducting wage-disputes efficiently; indeed, as early as 1795, the year of their revised Rules' publication, the Manchester spinners had already conducted two strikes for wage-increases—the second achieving success after a month.[2] And by 1803, when the war's resumption brought a trade crisis, the employers were driven to counter-attack. The master-spinners in and about Manchester associated to raise a fighting-fund of £20,000 to defeat '. . . this dangerous and unjust combination'[3]: apparently with a certain success, since the spinners appear to have been rather subdued for the next three or four years. The new weavers' federation was certainly more massive than the spinners' organization. The Home Secretary actually advised Lancashire magistrates to employ '. . . some confidential persons' in towns from which delegates were sent to its monthly General Committee—the first recorded use of spies against trade unions[4]; and publicans were forbidden to accommodate weavers' meetings. But the Association of Weavers itself was apparently tolerated by the authorities as being mainly concerned to seek Parliamentary help. Many masters, in any case, supported the weavers' petition for a legal minimum wage. And though Parliament refused this demand, it at least responded

[1] Mantoux (op. cit., p. 461) takes the Webbs to task for giving 1786 (actually, 1796—*History*, p. 41) as the Stockport Society's date but himself, like them, gives 1792 for Oldham. The Stockport Spinners' *Rules* were certainly promulgated (as for a friendly society) in 1792, though there is a report of some preceding combination there as early as 1785 (see section iii, above, however). Similarly, the Oldham union's *Rules* were adopted in 1796: it is not impossible that some informal association existed there beforehand, of course, but the writer knows of no evidence to that effect. Perhaps both the Webbs and Mantoux got the two societies' dates a little mixed?

[2] Daniels: 'The Cotton Trade during the Revolutionary and Napoleonic Wars', *Transactions, Manchester Statistical Society*, 1915.

[3] Circular of October 7, 1803, quoted by Daniels (*Early English Cotton Industry*, p. 144).

[4] According to Aspinall (op. cit., *Introduction*).

so far as to pass, in 1800, the Cotton Arbitration Act, which provided for the settlement of wage-disputes between 'arbitrators' nominated by the parties, or by final reference to Justices of the Peace.

The Association of Weavers seems, moreover, to have been astutely conducted. The Association may, indeed, have formally dissolved itself by 1800—late in 1799 Lancashire magistrates met together to stimulate enforcement of the Combination Acts against the weavers. But if so, its affairs continued to be efficiently prosecuted, and contact between the weaving districts maintained, by its secretary, James Holcroft of Bolton. In 1801, for instance, a new weavers' petition was organized and presented, for improvements in the Arbitration Act. But if the weavers were dissatisfied with the latter, they nevertheless used it extensively, taking legal advice for this purpose. In 1803, the new trade difficulties apparently led to such a flood of applications that the magistrates ruled that the Act was being improperly used (one employer received 108 arbitration notices in a single day, and after a wage reduction in Whitefield 900 applications were submitted to the justices).[1] By then, however, some 1,500 cases had been dealt with under the Act's procedure, most settlements favouring the weavers.[2] Over 300 of these applications were presented through Holcroft, who is also reported about this time as being in correspondence with the Scottish weavers, and appears as an active witness before Parliamentary committees.[3]

In 1804, Parliament itself amended the Arbitration Act, to restrict its application to individual disputes about payment for work actually done, and thus cut off its use by the weavers as a means of collective wage-fixing. There was, however, no strong and immediate reaction on the workers' part: trade was recovering, and continued to expand for two or three years. In such times, despite the continued poverty of many weavers, it seems likely that others of them were too prosperous to enthuse for united action. Although weavers' leaders moved to re-organize their federation and sent deputations to Ministers, and although a group of the biggest Bolton employers themselves took the initiative in proposing a joint approach with the weavers, it was not until 1807 that Holcroft succeeded in presenting a new minimum wage petition—this time, however, with 130,000 signatures. Trade was then turning again; by 1808 there was a severe slump; and a renewed 'Monster' petition was rejected by Parliament although it was supported independently

[1] *Cotton Factory Times*. 'The Road We Have Travelled', historical article of May 12, 1933.

[2] I. C. Sharp, *Industrial Conciliation and Arbitration in Great Britain* (Allen & Unwin, London, 1950).

[3] *C.F.T.*, loc. cit.

by petitions from certain masters. The weavers turned to a direct demand for an increase in wage-rates, and called a strike on its refusal. There followed 'the most brutal industrial conflict in British history'[1]: some 60,000 looms were stopped, there were riots and street fighting—even the Guards were called in to patrol the streets of Manchester.

The weavers' peaceable mien had dissolved: to such effect that when their Blackburn committee, two years later, issued a manifesto proposing a joint association with the masters to regulate trade instead of cutting wages,[2] the local magistrates requested that troops be sent as a safeguard. But although the weavers' gains from the strike (they had demanded an increase of one-third in weaving prices, and apparently secured most of it after rejecting an employers' offer of one-fifth) were quickly lost again—and although too the trial and imprisonment in 1809 of the Radical manufacturer Colonel Joseph Hanson, for publicly encouraging the strikers at a weavers' meeting, occasioned general indignation (40,000 subscribed to present him with a silver cup)—the weavers were quiet for a while. They drew up another petition in 1809, but 1810 was marked by a speculative boom in the cotton trade; even for the weavers it was a year of some prosperity. But it closed with a slump even worse than that of 1807–8, and there was a renewed wave of activity. Weavers' committees in other towns, apparently acting in concert, issued proposals for joint restriction of output, like that of the Blackburn club. In 1811, new petitions for legal regulation of weaving were organized from Manchester, Stockport and Bolton, with 55,000 signatures. The recession of 1811-12, however, demonstrated the existence of a growing element among the weavers that was dissatisfied with this relatively moderate approach to their problems—while some Luddite influence was suggested by attacks 'on steam looms' in Stockport and other towns.

But at this point the Scottish weavers, of whom little had been heard for twenty years—although they had apparently been associated over most of that time—made a dramatic reappearance on the scene. They sent their own petition up to Westminster with 30,000 signatures. They also, however, prosecuted a successful litigation in Edinburgh to have their magistrates fix a minimum wage-list. But when the list was put to employers, the weavers discovered that no order for its enforcement had been made, and struck to enforce it themselves. The strike lasted three weeks, involved 40,000 weavers 'from Carlisle to Aberdeen', and was on

[1] The description of Gayer, Rostow and Schwartz. The Hammonds give a quite detailed account (*Skilled Labourer*, pp. 78–81).

[2] Reproduced with Aspinall's No. 110.

the point of success when the Committee was arrested under the Combination Acts.[1] At this time, the weavers' federation apparently extended throughout the country: delegates from Nottingham, Carlisle and Glasgow were in Manchester late in 1812, reportedly[2] urging a national strike. But, although there were food riots in Manchester, the Lancashire weavers' organized response was limited to yet another petition from Bolton. In 1813 trade was recovering, and towards the year's end the workers' condition was helped by a fall in food prices. Other attempts were made, in Scotland and Carlisle, to get wage-enforcement through the magistrates (before Parliament, embarrassed by the discovery that this power still existed, repealed in 1813 the Elizabethan statutes on which it depended). However, 1814 was a year of prosperity that, though very relative, the weavers were to recall within a short time as a golden interlude; it invited no further militancy from them.

Then came Waterloo and demobilization: 400,000 men were turned on to the labour market. By 1816—although the cotton industry was regathering the impetus lost a few years before through the continental blockade and the American entry into the war—handloom weavers' wages were down by nearly half, and still falling: there was very widespread unemployment. But the weavers, their numbers inflated to nearly 250,000 (against a probable 100,000 at the French Wars' outbreak) by the new labour influx, were losing their capacity for collective action. They were also now apparently suffering from divided counsel. A renewed petition for legal minimum wages produced only 20,000 signatures. There were local strikes in Preston and other places, but the main leadership could not agree on a general stoppage: many were persuaded that hope now lay only in political Reform. A number of weavers were arrested in Manchester for political agitation—and handloom weavers, of course, were mainly concerned in the tragi-fiasco of the Blanketeers' March of the following year.

The handloom weavers were to produce one more disciplined effort. But to this they were apparently stimulated by other groups. Over this period of recurrent and deepening distress for the weavers, the mule-spinners had apparently been continuously active in a small way, and had already achieved an almost complete organization in most Lancashire factory towns.[3] But they had mounted only one major operation—and this in 1810, when production abruptly

[1] According to the Webbs (*History*, p. 58) this was '. . . the most extensive strike the trade has ever known'.

[2] See Aspinall's No. 119.

[3] See Colonel Fletcher's report (Aspinall's No. 185) and the account of 'The Character, Objects and Effects of Trade Unions, London", 1834.

rose by half, to a level not to be reached again for at least another decade. At this time, the spinners formed a county-wide federation in Lancashire, and proceeded to organize a systematic 'rolling strike' beginning in Stalybridge, to bring the 'country' spinners' rates up to those paid in Manchester. Support was organized from spinners outside the county, but the Manchester society itself was the major contributor—raising £600 a week for the strike—and their new 'General Union' directed the affair from that centre. The employers retaliated with a lock-out of the mills; the whole county became involved, from Preston to Stockport. The resulting stoppage lasted four months (during which the spinners' federation distributed £17,000 in strike pay) and probably involved some 30,000 workers of whom, however, only a small proportion (perhaps a tenth) were actually spinners.[1] The strike was defeated by the spinners' exhaustion and the 1810 boom's collapse. But from then on, and although their federation disintegrated temporarily, the spinners are heard of more frequently, and their actions assume a larger scale than before.

The discouragement of their 1810 defeat was aggravated by the imprisonment, in 1811, of several spinners for 'combination'. And some few of their more extreme spirits were apparently attracted to Luddism by the 1810 strike's failure—just as some of the weavers' leaders were at this time persuaded to the Reform agitation by the Parliamentary treatment of the 1811 petitions for wage-regulation. For the cotton operatives of Lancashire generally, 1811–12 was apparently a period of despair. But the lull in the spinners' trade activity was only temporary. By the end of 1811 they were already calling mill strikes in Manchester against wage-reductions. In 1813, with trade recovering, the first district wage-list for factory spinning of which record survives appeared in Bolton. In the new boom of 1814, the spinners achieved some kind of joint agreement with Stockport employers, their Preston society was re-organized, and a general revival of the mule-spinners' combination was noted.[2]

The post-war unemployment of 1816 compelled even the Manchester spinners to accept wage reductions. But by 1817 they had not merely re-forged their links with other societies in the Lancashire cotton districts, but were resuming their correspondence with spinners' unions in other regions.[3] In a burst of production, the cotton trade's growth resumed by 1818 the impetus it had lost in the decade's

[1] The Hammonds (*Skilled Labourer*, p. 93) give only 8,000 to 10,000: but the figure taken here is quoted not only by Chapman, but in Sydney Webb's manuscript notes on the Spinners' Amalgamation's history, and corrected by Fielding, a famous Secretary of the Bolton Spinners' Union (in the Webb Collection). It also seems more consistent with contemporary employment figures.

[2] According to the Webb-Fielding MS. (ibid.).

[3] Aspinall's No. 221 presumably refers to this activity.

earlier years. The Manchester spinners promptly took advantage of this recovery to demand the return of their 1814 wages: the local manufacturers put their mills on short-time to forestall the movement; and the spinners retaliated with a large-scale strike, which ultimately stopped some 20,000 operatives. The Manchester spinners' action was only the most forceful in a major wave of such events: building workers, dyers, hatters, struck in and about the city; in Stockport there were two remarkable strikes—of factory jenny-spinners (the sole such action recorded of this class of workers) and the first recorded strike of power-loom factory workers. Mule-spinners also struck in Wigan (though presumably out of turn, since this conflicted with the general tactic of the spinners' federations): the colliers in the Lancashire pits joined the movement and cut off the mills' coal supply. And finally, the handloom weavers themselves were drawn in—their only major action during a time of good trade; in this case, however, the weavers had hardly benefited from the latter.

The Manchester spinners' strike was, by all accounts, extremely well-organized. The Manchester committee were clearly again acting in concert with the other local spinners' societies, so that '. . . if they thought it conducive to their ends, the whole neighbourhood might be in the same condition.'[1] The spinners' financial support was, in fact, organized '. . . to an amazing extent', some £4,500 being raised by outside contributions. And although the strike extended over two months, its conduct apparently remained systematic until near its end. Some individual mills gave in and offered their spinners new prices. But authority took alarm: the spinners' committee was seized and imprisoned; and the operatives who were still on strike were driven back when the unions' funds were exhausted (considerable sums had been raised for them in the Midlands, but arrived too late). But many of the strikers were 'blacklisted' by the mill-masters.

The weavers' movement began with the Oldham fustian workers issuing public manifestos for wage-increases, which their employers conceded, apparently after an accompanying condition that other masters in their trade be induced to fall in line had been fulfilled. This success combined with the general industrial ferment of the region to stimulate wider pressure. A general delegate meeting of 'The Associated Weavers' was called in Bury, after which the muslin-weavers' societies began to deputize employers for a 7s in the £ advance. Some masters gave in, others made partial or conditional offers, others refused. At this, the Associated Weavers' delegates called a strike of all workers not receiving the increase.

[1] Aspinall's No. 234.

Several thousand workers were stopped in concert, and '. . . a simultaneous movement throughout the manufacturing district'[1] was set off as the strike spread to the plain cotton weavers of the north Lancashire towns. The Bolton and Manchester employers, at least, conceded about half the workers' demand, and most of the weavers concerned seem to have gained something. But the strike appears to have ended in division: a general delegate meeting of the Associated Weavers decided to call it off at this stage, against a Radical demand that it be converted to a general stoppage of all weavers in Lancashire and the neighbouring counties. Nevertheless the weavers of Bury and the northern towns continued the strike, in Preston to the point of complete defeat, in other places with a varying success: in Burnley the affair ended in conflict with the military.

The 1818 strike-wave had an aftermath of repression. The Manchester spinners, with their strike-leaders in prison and many others of their more active members arrested or 'blacklisted', were temporarily crushed. (Those imprisoned for their part in the 1818 strike-wave included John Doherty, then a young spinner recently immigrated from Ireland, but later famous as the founder of the National Association for the Protection of Labour and one of the great figures of the early working-class movement.) Some of the weavers' county and local leaders had also been arrested, and when the bleachers followed them in striking their committee, too, was promptly seized. Public meetings were forbidden, large bodies of troops had been moved into Lancashire. The following year's recession, when weavers' wages were cut again, brought no marked industrial action. The Bolton and Stockport weavers presented new petitions for minimum wage-fixing—this time, and apparently in despair of Parliamentary relief, direct to the magistrates. But working-class discontent in general found an outlet rather in the Reform agitation that culminated in Peterloo—in which tragic affair handloom weavers were especially prominent, of course. And though over 1819–20 there were strikes of cotton weavers in Yorkshire, in Carlisle, and most forcibly in Glasgow, the Lancashire weavers' loss of what they had previously gained from the 1818 strike-movement stirred them to no more than a gesture. The Bolton muslin-weavers apparently considered striking in concert with the Scots[2]; but the threat came to nothing. In Lancashire, at

[1] Aspinall's No. 280. See also Hammonds *Skilled Labourer*, pp. 96–119 for accounts of both spinners' and weavers' strikes. There are detailed differences in the various accounts.

[2] Aspinall's No. 362 suggests this, too.

least, their 1818 strike was the handloom weavers' last concerted industrial movement.

VI

Superficially at any rate, this middle phase of the early unions' history is thus dominated by an almost continuous resistance of the handloom workers to the decline of their status. Wood traces the average wages of Bolton fine- and quilt-weavers yearly over most of the period[1]: almost every step in their long descent can be linked with a movement amongst the weavers. Beginning at 29s to 30s a week in 1797–8, for instance, wages fall to 25s in 1799—the year of the first general weavers' union. After a recovery, they fall again, first slowly, then fast, to 18s and 15s in 1807 and 1808—the years of the Monster Petition and the Great Weavers' Strike. The fall is interrupted by a brief recovery in 1809–10, and especially in 1814, when wages reached 24s. But by 1817—the eve of the muslin weavers' turnout—they are down to 9s; the 1818 strike is the only significant case of weavers' militancy in a trade boom—but in this case, it was a boom from which they had benefited little. Their wages are a few pence up the year after the strike, but then fall again. (The last figure quoted by Wood, for 1834, is 5s 6d a week—less than a fifth of the wage of thirty-six years before. By contrast, the average wage of head carders in Manchester mills is given as between 20s and 28s in 1796, and between 23s and 26s in 1833[2]; and while *real* wages of most hand-weavers were 'near famine' level from the late 1820s on, those of factory operatives[3] apparently rose pretty steadily throughout the nineteenth century's first half—apart from a brief lag in the 1830s—more than doubling by 1850). But the breaks of relative prosperity that interrupt both the handloom weavers' decline *and* their sequences of collective activity are marked by the militancy of the spinners' combinations, which display a capacity for organization that grows as that of the weavers deteriorates.

The handloom weavers' temporary victory of 1818, in fact, signalled only their permanent defeat. When the Combination Acts were repealed, a huge general union of weavers was publicly re-formed, this time in conjunction with a similar 'Association of

[1] 'History of Wages in the Cotton Trade, etc.' (op. cit.) Table 32.

[2] Wood, Table 2. Head carders were skilled workmen at about the same pay level as the mule-spinners and usually paid on the spinners' earnings. They are the only male factory operatives for whom data originating at such an early date has been tabulated. Even so, their wage shows a greater subsequent fluctuation than that of the spinners.

[3] According to Cole's estimates (in *A Short History of the British Working Class Movement*, 1797–1937) from Wood's tables.

Weavers' in Scotland. But the divisions which were becoming apparent in 1818 cut off its development: almost immediately the new federation split up when the muslin-weavers, whose condition was still apparently less wretched than that of others, refused to accept the Association's financial obligations and broke away. The Scottish weavers seem to have retained some capacity for collective action—certain of their leaders were arrested in 1824 for the organized boycott of an employer. But the Lancashire mass now had no coherent force.

As the early unions moved into their third and last phase, two technical developments occurred that were finally to terminate their history. A power-loom had been available since 1785, and a completely automatic spinning-mule had been patented a few years after (the early powered mules still required 'working home' by hand, and so continue to be called 'hand-mules' like the preceding domestic machines). But it was only in 1822 that a quite satisfactory metal 'steam-loom' was put on the market by Roberts and Sharp: and over 1825 to 1830, the same firm put out successively improved versions of an efficient 'self-actor' mule.

The impact on the weavers was immediate: at the very time of their last general union's formation, a boom in 'steam-weaving' was well under way, as powered factories added the new looms—worked mainly by women—to their spinning plant. When a renewed and severe slump hit the industry (the Bolton weavers' wages fell to 7s over 1825–6) the handworkers could only produce a brief and spontaneous Jacquerie of machine-breaking. The outbreak began in Blackburn (when all the power-looms within six miles of the town were destroyed in a day), spread a trail of fighting down through the east Lancashire towns, and culminated in riots and fire-raising attacks on mills in Manchester. Over forty of the participants were transported or imprisoned. And after 1826 the hand-weavers, though in Scotland they preserved a seemingly effective organization for some time, were in Lancashire to all intents and purposes crushed. In that main region, their trade became increasingly casual. The 1829 recession provoked some attacks on weaving factories, and a quilting weavers' union was actually formed in Manchester. But a meeting to revive the hand-weavers' federation in 1831 drew only an insignificant response. And when a burst of power-loom installation in Lancashire over 1833–6 signalled their approaching disappearance as a class, the weavers could only respond with a gesture: their petitions of 1834 and '35 seem to represent a last initiative of the weavers themselves, although schemes for wage-boards and other measures to alleviate their condition continued to be aired in Parliament.

The spinners, by contrast, soon recovered from their defeats of 1818. Their revived activity, in fact, became a major stimulus to the new machinery: the invention of Roberts' self-actor mule could '. . . in a great measure, be attributed to the injurious effects resulting from turn-outs,' and to '. . . an anxious desire on the part of the proprietors of cotton-mills that some means should be devised to enable them to dispense with the labour of the spinners.'[1] It is perhaps significant that as they move through this third phase of early unionism the spinners' major activity begins to spill over into the intervals of trade recession—indeed, ends in a struggle against wage-reductions. Nevertheless, its main pattern of concentration in periods of trade prosperity remains; and in the early spinners' case development of the automatic machine was sufficiently tardy to permit them to produce meanwhile their most ambitious organized efforts. And since these contain several hints of more modern situations, they can perhaps be sketched less cryptically.

By 1822–3, with trade moving up to a boom, the Bolton spinners had already launched on a course of militancy (during which they claimed to have raised wages considerably above other towns[2]) which worked up to a strike for a seven and a half per cent advance in one firm's mills. The firm conceded half the demand, the strike began to spread, and the Bolton masters concerted to impose a new wage-list on the men under threat of locking-out the whole district. The operative spinners refused, and a stoppage of 5,000 operatives ensued. When their Bolton committee was arrested, it became apparent that the links between the spinners' Lancashire societies had already been re-established: some twenty such local organizations, as well as a number of mill clubs, had contributed to the Bolton men's support. In the same year the Glasgow employers complained bitterly of extreme exactions by the local union. And the spinners greeted the repeal of the Combination Acts in 1824 with an outburst of militancy. In Hyde they called a strike which lasted six months, and was 'reported to be fostered by some central organization',[3] to bring Hyde rates up to those generally paid. There were smaller strikes or lock-outs in Stockport, Chorley and other Lancashire towns. The Glasgow union initiated a train of mill disputes which culminated in a strike for the dismissal of a non-union chargehand.[4] Here again the masters combined to threaten a general lock-out unless the union withdrew: again, the union

[1] Andrew Ure, *The Cotton Manufacture of Great Britain* (Knight, London, 1836) Vol. II, pp. 194–5.

[2] Aspinall's Nos. 391 and 393.

[3] The Webb-Fielding MS. (loc. cit.).

[4] Aspinall's No. 392 gives detail.

refused, so that the resultant Glasgow stoppage was enforced for over four months.

In both their major affrays of 1824 the spinners were defeated: during the 1825–6 slump the Lancashire spinners at least, were quiet—apart from mill strikes against Oldham employers' attempts to impose a new wage-list. But during these and the ensuing years a rapid technical development of the hand-mule was pushing employers to attempt to reduce piece-rates in line with the improved machines' growing output.[1] As trade recovered, the spinners' resistance at individual mills—there were mill strikes in several towns—again drove the employers to concerted action. In 1829 the Stockport employers cut wage-rates and set off a six months' strike of the district, while the Manchester mill-owners took advantage of a temporary slump to confront their men with a district price-list of the masters' own dictation for fine-spinning. There, the union leaders were apparently anxious to temporize: but their members' anger pushed them to a final rejection of the new district list. When the fine-spinners struck, the employers ordered the coarse-spinners to cease supporting them under penalty of a wage-cut. The coarse-spinners too, refused; and a most bitter conflict ensued which was only ended after nearly six months, by the Manchester union committee's decision to over-ride the very substantial minority (at least) of the members that favoured its continuance.[2]

Out of this disaster arose the Grand General Union of Cotton Operatives of the United Kingdom. Their previous defeats had apparently already convinced the spinners' leaders—John Doherty was now secretary of the Manchester committee—of the need for a more extensive and more closely co-ordinated federation. In December, 1829, delegates from English, Scottish and Irish Spinners' Societies met in the Isle of Man to adopt a scheme for a national organization, under Doherty's secretaryship, with its own funds to be raised by a regular levy on its affiliates. And when, in 1830, the mill-owners of Ashton—a fast-developing spinning district—repeated the Manchester employers' attempt to impose a revised wage-list, the local spinners felt strong enough to resist: the threat of a district strike compelled the employers to raise the list-prices. Encouraged by reviving trade, strikes had already occurred there and in Bolton; while in Manchester, the spinners initiated a campaign to recover their losses of the previous year by systematically striking mills in turn—a method which was proving so successful that it was

[1] Note again that the term 'hand-mule' applies to the *semi*-automatic factory machine, not the original domestic one.

[2] An account of the Manchester strike, quoted from an uncited source, is included in the Webb-Fielding MS.

spreading to other districts. At this, fifty firms in the Ashton neighbourhood concerted to provoke a battle with the spinners' combination by imposing a wage-cut under threat of a lock-out. And the new Grand Union retaliated by calling out all spinners receiving less than the rates on which the Ashton men themselves were insisting.

The Ashton strike lasted ten weeks and stopped some 20,000 factory workers. In the upshot, the Grand Union's order for a widespread turn-out met with only partial response, and that limited to the districts near Ashton itself: and though the Union's leaders organized country-wide financial support, the affair ended in violence and a renewed defeat. When the mills were re-opened early in 1831 there was[1] 'a great influx of unemployed spinners' (many, no doubt, the stragglers of the spinners' 1829 Manchester debacle) and some hundreds of the 3,000 Ashton spinners involved were replaced. The Grand Union, in fact was broken by its own ambition, and although its second, 1830 Congress had revised its constitution, appointed Foster as full-time secretary,[2] and selected Liverpool as the centre for its next, intendedly six-monthly conference, there is no record of a subsequent meeting. While the Manchester union, till then the biggest in the country and the fulcrum of the spinners' movement, was so debilitated by these defeats and the diversion of its leaders' interest to the agitation for a ten-hour day that after its revival and re-organization in the mid-'30s, it could only count half its former strength of 2,000 qualified men.

Apparently the spinners' local activity continued nevertheless: new technical development was in any case undermining Manchester's natural leadership of the spinning trade. And after a brief recession, a general federation including at least the Lancashire societies[3] was again functioning in 1833. But the hand-mule spinners, too, were now moving into their decline. In the boom of 1833–6, they produced a new wave of militancy—beginning with a movement for an eight-hour day that culminated in an unsuccessful strike in Oldham. In 1836 the spinners at Bolton forced a sizeable wage-increase, and in the same year the Preston spinners were urged by delegates from the other Lancashire unions to demand Bolton prices, and in fact struck for a ten per cent advance. But this strike

[1] Account in the Webb Collection. W. A. Jevons also wrote an account of the Ashton strike—in the Social Science Association's *Report on Trades' Societies and Strikes* of 1860. See also *Skilled Labourer*, pp. 131–2. The accounts differ, as usual.

[2] Chapman (op. cit., p. 203) also quotes Doherty's reference to McGowan (appointed organizer with Foster at the 1829 Ramsay conference) as being an inspirer of the union.

[3] The Webb-Fielding MS. R. Smith (loc. cit.) reports a national organization of some kind in this year.

was particularly disastrous.[1] It not only exhausted the union after three months, but led to the introduction of the self-actor (which was already working in some sixty English mills[2]) to the rising north Lancashire spinning centre: while over a quarter of the Preston spinners were dismissed. In the following year's slump, the mill-owners counter-attacked. The Oldham union struck again against wage-reductions, failed, and temporarily distintegrated. And in 1837 the Scottish union was defeated in a similar struggle by the unusually well-combined employers of Glasgow, and its leaders were arrested and tried on various criminal charges.

The effect of new machinery on the spinners was much less drastic than on the handloom weavers—whose number fell from about a quarter-million in 1833 to some 60,000 ten years later.[3] The self-actor's introduction was relatively gradual, as it was adapted to finer and finer work. But a combination of this competitive threat, of exhaustion from their previous defeats, and finally of recurrent and deep depression from 1837 to 1843, left the hand-mule spinners much subdued. Although they continued to engage in mill disputes or small local strikes, for nearly a generation after the Glasgow Spinners' trial they put up no major trade action. A formal national federation was reconstituted in 1842, but this (as we shall see) was rather a different affair from its predecessor of 1829–30. And meanwhile, such militancy as the spinners preserved was largely diverted to other channels.

VII

We can, then, summarize the whole period here covered of the early cotton unions' history. Until the hand-weavers' final decline before the power-loom, nearly every recession in the cotton trade is marked by some outbreak of collective activity on their part. While from their first appearance, the mule-spinners greet nearly every boom with some act of organized militancy. This alternation symbolizes the contrasting motives of the two groups' trade unionism.

The handloom weavers' combinations are primarily defensive in character, concerned at first to preserve a status regarded as historically established, and later—as their trade becomes increasingly inflated with workers lacking personal memories of the conditions that status implied—to maintain a bare existence. The spinners' organization on the other hand, is aggressive; in so far as it is at all

[1] For a detailed account, H. Ashworth, *An Inquiry etc. . . . into the strike of the Operative Cotton Spinners of Preston*, British Association, 1837.

[2] According to Ure (op. cit.) p. 198.

[3] Wood (op. cit.) Table 39, quoting various sources.

concerned with the mere maintenance of a standard, this has no long historical justification. It represents only that established in the first rush of spinning's mechanical development—a standard which, as knowledge of the new skills spread, would become increasingly artificial.

Thus, the spinners' early strategy is essentially self-reliant and opportunistic. When trade is slack, resistance to erosion of their high wage-standards is confined to mill actions—stubborn though these might often be. The spinners' major strength is reserved for the times—1810, 1818, 1823–4, 1830 and again in 1834–6—when its exercise will be most embarrassing to their employers. And even then, an attempt is made to husband it. The spinners' 'rolling strike' technique, which first appeared in 1810, is consistently applied in their later big stoppages. And there is a similar opportunism in their choice of ground for striking. Their 1810 and 1824 strikes are called to level-up lower wage-rates: and this tactic was enshrined in the resolutions of their Grand General Union of 1829–30, which defined it as the responsibility of affiliated societies to raise individual mill rates to the better standards within their districts, but of the federation to support individual societies in attempts to raise lower district rates to the higher levels prevailing.[1] But on the other hand, the spinners' strikes of 1829 and '30—the so-called 'long-wheel' strikes—were effectively called to preserve the wage-gains of workers on superior machinery in the better-paid districts. And the Bolton strikes of 1821–3 were deliberately designed to edge an already well-paid district further up the scale.[2] So that the spinners' strategy was two-pronged.

Against this, the handloom weavers rely little on the strike weapon. Even in this history's first phase, when the weavers' general economic condition is improving, trade actions by them are confined to the intervals of depression; and when such actions do occur exhibit no considered strategy, but tend to involve the whole section or trade concerned. The weavers' strikes, in effect, are general movements of protest: this is especially true of their great Lancashire strike of 1808, but remains true even of the strike of 1818 and of those in Scotland. By contrast, the spinners' strikes, characteristically, are calculated attempts to exploit favourable turns of trade or local

[1] The Resolutions of the Grand General Union's 1830 Conference are included as an Appendix to *On Combinations of Trades* (Anon., London, 1831). See also Cole & Filson, *British Working Class Movements: Select Documents 1789–1875* (Macmillan, London, 1951) p. 247 et seq., for extracts of the 1829 Conference resolutions.

[2] For district differentials at these times, see Wood (op. cit.). Fine-spinning wages generally, and those of Manchester in particular, were consistently higher.

circumstance to enhance or consolidate their relatively privileged position.

Directly, the spinners' major strikes—though not their minor ones —were nearly all failures. Though it is hard to say whether this was because their objects were ill-conceived, because of their leaders' inability to control the spinners' militancy once let loose (and therefore to compromise at the propitious moment), because of the increasingly formidable employers' combinations with which they were confronted, or because of the persistent legal retaliation they encountered. But the indirect effect of the spinners' vigour must not be discounted: it is noteworthy that when the mill-masters associated to impose new wage-lists on them, these were usually designed to forestall wage-increases (in terms of rates or earnings) rather than reduce wages. And against the spectacular failures of the early spinners' unions, there remains the offsetting contrast of the persisting stability in the mule-spinner's wage in face both of 'automation' and of that mass of surplus labour which brought the hand-weavers down, by the 1830s, to a third or quarter of the spinners' earnings.

So much, however, by the way. The major point is that the flickering appearance of early trade unionism seems to arise, not from the absence of any continuing current of collective association among the cotton workers, but from the intermittence of their actual need for collective action. A boom presents the spinners, this new and aggressive class of factory hands, with an opportunity. But in a slump the employer's power is reinforced, not only by a greater readiness of other factory-masters to support him, but by the desperate mass of unemployed outside the factory gates. So it behoves the factory-workers' unions to avoid any challenge which will offer the always-immanent employers' alliance a chance to crush them (even if there were much point in their striking when under-employment and short-time were already widespread). The active motivation of the hand-weavers' associations, however, is defence. During intervals of prosperity, they may perhaps console themselves with its hopeful reflection of their traditional status. But in depression, the weavers are compelled to action by the danger, less of unemployment than of a cut-throat and catastrophic competition in output and piece-prices between outworkers desperately striving to earn the essentials of life. Thus, the situation that calls for organized militancy by the early spinners is quite opposite to that which calls for collective action by the hand-weavers. And for each group, in the intervals between its particular 'trigger' situation's recurrence, no general activity is indicated by its organizing motives. But for each group again, the promptness of the workers' organized response to every repetition of that 'trigger' situation suggests (and other evidence apart) that at least the elements of a continuing association have been preserved meanwhile.

Of course, one good reason why that association might, in the interludes between actions, have in any case avoided too obvious a show was its illegality. But a more important reason for the seeming impermanence of early unionism may be found in its particular organizational qualities—and this may also reconcile the conflicting expert views we noted in this chapter's opening. The labour historians who saw no early depth in textile unionism's roots seem to have been looking for formally-stable institutions, comparable—if only in a primitive way—with more recent union forms. The students of the cotton trade who assumed unionism's historical continuity there, on the other hand, have rather observed the persistence of certain reiterated collective pressures, of consistent tendencies to collective action. It is perhaps in these, rather than in particular institutional forms, that the essence of trade unionism consists. But that is for the next chapter.

II

TRADE UNION ORIGINS

2

The Character of Early Unionism

I

One explanation of the recurrent vitality of the early cotton workers' unions is what can be described as the essentially natural character of their organization—meaning by 'natural', perhaps what contemporary sociologists mean by their use of the word 'informal', but at any rate that the early cotton operatives' methods of association followed, without artificial contrivance, from the conditions of their work and life. Thus, the hand-weavers' unions probably had their roots, quite simply, in the regular social meeting of men working at the same trade in the same place. The frequency with which Lancashire magistrates found it necessary to warn inn-keepers against accommodating weavers' meetings is an index to the importance of the convivial social forum as a vehicle for collective action. The small-ware weavers' society of 1756 claimed to have been long preceded by an informal club. In 1809 a Scottish weaver's pamphlet spoke of the Paisley textile workers as having for a long time been accustomed to meet weekly 'in every decent public house' to discuss the state of trade and their disputes with masters.[1] The earliest mule-spinners had a common habit—one reviled by their employers—of taking Monday off after a good week's earnings, and spending the day (and the cash) together in pubs which had from regular use almost come to be recognized as their own.

The next stage—again, a natural growth from the practice of collections for unfortunate workmates or their families—was the friendly society. The 'box club' was the normal basis of the eighteenth-century weavers' organization (as, before them, of the Continental

[1] *An Answer to Mr Carlile's Sketches of Paisley*, by Wm. Taylor. (In the Webb Collection).

journeymen's associations). The recognition of their 'box' by the masters was one of the claims for which the check-weavers struck in 1758, and when about the same time the Manchester merchants warned the Oldham weavers to cease contributing to a 'box', the latter replied that to do so would mean withholding their charity from their fellows. The silk-weavers' union of 1768 was formed as a 'box-society'[1]. And several of the first spinners' unions were formally constituted as friendly societies—the 1795 rules of the 'Friendly Associated Cotton Spinners of Manchester', indeed, declared that '. . . persons (who) combine together to raise the price of their wages, contrary to law, shall be immediately expelled.'[2]

The Acts of 1793–5 that gave a legal protection to approved friendly societies incidentally gave also a means of trade association shielded from the Combination Laws: by 1801 there were over 800 such friendly clubs in Lancashire—more than in any other county. And while the later tendency was for the trade organization proper to separate itself from the friendly society—as was, indeed, advisable when the former's funds were liable to seizure—the friendly association frequently continued an auxiliary service to the union. Thus the weavers' general unions, in both Lancashire and Scotland, could plead their legality as being concerned to secure the application or reform of existing law. However, they not only drew on the friendly societies to help finance their petitioning deputations, but in their great 1808 and 1812 strikes appealed to the latter with some success for help[3]—as did the spinners (who by this time were operating in open defiance of the Combination Acts) in 1818. The friendly societies certainly provide a major continuity between those surges of active trade combination by the early cotton operatives that were traced in the preceding chapter. The insistence of the modern cotton workers on funeral benefit as (whatever else is provided) an essential 'friendly' function of their unions is perhaps a surviving preference of the earlier period.

The weavers' village trade club, with the 'box steward' as its principal official, at any rate emerged imperceptibly from these informal or 'friendly' beginnings. And one or two of the spinners' societies that were first formed in 'country' weaving centres—Oldham, for instance—adopted a similar form.[4] But in the cotton trade's capital city itself, an alternative but similarly-natural form developed. The Manchester smallware weavers' organization was based on the 'shops', which each sent one representative to the

[1] Wadsworth (op. cit.) p. 367.
[2] *Rules* in the Manchester Reference Library.
[3] See Aspinall's Nos. 97 and 100, also Nos. 262 and 302.
Copy of the *Rules* in the Webb Collection.

society's monthly meeting. It has been suggested that the 'shop' was actually the 'putting-out' merchant's warehouse, and the term may well have applied to that[1]. However, 'shop' (i.e. 'workshop') weavers already existed. And certainly in later unions the workshop or factory basis was common: the calico printers' society in Lancashire, for instance, operated through an assembly of shop representatives.[2] Particularly, the Manchester spinners' affairs were managed by a committee of 'head shopmen' who were also individually responsible for bargaining at their own mills.[3]

Between these simple basic units—the village trade club in the country centres of domestic industry, the committee of shop representatives in the city concentration of workshops, warehouses and factories—contact could be maintained by sending delegates as the need arose. Among the weavers, the 'bearing home day' provided, again, a natural system of communication; country hand-weavers would tramp very long distances into Manchester and other towns to exchange their work for materials. The first centres of factory mule-spinning—Manchester, Oldham, Stockport, Ashton, etc.—were well within a day's walking radius; and inter-town transport by coach, wagon and carrier—as well as by canal boat—was probably extensive enough in the developing cotton area for quite big distances to be readily covered. The practice of sending 'walking delegates' off to visit meetings of neighbouring societies in fact survived quite late among the Lancashire unions.[4]

The difficulties of communication, which several writers have considered to be a major obstacle to stable 'industry-wide' unions before the railway network was established, or efficient post and telegraph services available,[5] were minimized within the relatively concentrated industrial regions of the cotton trade's growth. So much so, in fact, that in case of a strike in one district, it was normal for the town's weavers to march in procession to 'turn out' the neighbouring centres—as in 1808 and 1818. In the general strike of 1842, the whole area of Lancashire, Cheshire and Derbyshire, extending some hundred miles from north to south, was stopped by this method alone, within three days of the original Ashton strikers' decision to seek support outside Manchester. The spinners' 'rolling strike' system did not require such methods, but they developed the 'delegate' system of inter-communication quite extensively.

[1] Daniels (op. cit.), p. 44.
[2] *Rules*, loc. cit.
[3] See *Rules*, and R. Smith (loc. cit.).
[4] See Chapter III, 1, section VI.
[5] See Cole, *Introduction to Trade Unionism* (op. cit.) p. 23, and even Chapman, though qualified (op. cit., p. 184).

Individual spinners' societies, of course, used it to canvass support from other local unions in strikes. But the spinners' federations themselves sent deputations to stimulate local societies into an observance of federal policy, and employed full-time delegates to scour the country for outside aid in their great disputes. Similar delegates were occasionally employed to concert the activities of the general weavers' unions in different regions. The whole 'delegate system', in fact, was viewed with especial alarm by the authorities—partly, no doubt, because the Radical societies' itinerant agitators were similarly called.[1]

The defect of this method was probably not so much its slowness. This was considerably offset, when compared with the formal and ponderous procedures of modern trade unions, by the speed with which a meeting could be convened and a decision taken once the delegate arrived. In the weaving centres, indeed, municipal officials often facilitated the assembly of the workers and helped publicize their meetings' decisions. The fighting with which the 1818 strike terminated in Burnley was set off by the town bellman's imprisonment as 'the active agent of the combination'; he was released by the weavers, whose ringleaders were in turn seized. The real problem of the delegate system of intercommunication—particularly for the spinners' strike tactics—was almost certainly the unreliability of its financial result, which in turn was traceable to the absolute autonomy of the local societies. Delegates from a striking society might arrive in another town to find another strike already in progress there. Individual unions might fling themselves into a dispute despite inadequate resources, only then to find the funds of other districts exhausted by unemployment or previous stoppages. Hence the spinners' repeated essays in federation. Their Assembly of 1810, their Grand Union and so on, were essentially systems of pooling and allocating strike support—the Grand Union not only planned a standard rate of strike pay but even projected a ballot to select the societies which had the prior right to strike. Given that essential function of a common strike fund, the definition of strike aims—standard wages or piece-prices, entry controls, etc.—was an unavoidable corollary. By contrast, the first handloom weavers' federations were primarily concerned with the enforcement of an imagined legal preference, and in any case included at most a few thousand weavers within a smallish radius. And their later general combinations, by intent existing primarily to compile and forward pleas for legislative regulation, could also manage with a flimsier superstructure than the spinners.

Even so, all the cotton workers' federal organizations remained

[1] See Aspinall's Nos. 308 and 315.

simple. The combination that conducted the 1758 check-weavers' stoppage consisted merely of an assembly of the 'box-stewards' from the districts surrounding Manchester—these were the eighteen men subsequently arrested. The local boxes contributed to a central box in Manchester, the trade regulations of which were accepted by the local societies, and which also issued 'franks' to duly qualified journeymen. The 1799 general Association of Weavers was a committee of local delegates, apparently appointed in proportion to their societies' respective strengths, which having agreed its aims left their implementation to the three officers they had appointed from Bolton, the strongest district. But even the earliest spinners' federations were similarly rudimentary. Their first great strike of 1810 was directed by an assembly of local representatives meeting in Manchester, apparently with no formal constitution, but under the 'chief leadership' of one Joseph Shipley, a 'respectable mechanic'.[1] The federation, in fact, was merely a logical extension of the delegate system.

It was only when the Lancashire spinners attempted formally to federate the cotton regions outside England itself—having previously sent delegates to organize the backward Irish centres—that they elaborated their structure, and in so doing turned the greater difficulty of communication the attempt involved into a major defect. The Grand Union began in 1829 with three separate national executives—for England, Scotland and Ireland respectively. The system was cumbrous (though perhaps mainly from the Lancastrians' viewpoint). At any rate the Union's 1830 Congress was persuaded to replace it with a single executive of five—three appointed by Manchester alone, and two from the neighbouring English districts in turn. The outlying districts' failure to respond to the subsequent call for a United Kingdom strike may well reflect a constitutional conflict between them and the Union's dominating (and impatient) Mancunian initiators. If so, the spinners would probably have been better-off without this piece of constitution-mongering. Their previous informal federations had rarely failed to produce generous support for the 'fighting branch' of the moment.

In such affairs, of course, it is not clear how far a redundant constitutionalism was induced by the middle-class sympathizers, whose participation the early unions occasionally enlisted but whose respect for, and knowledge of, respectably-institutional procedures was greater than their rank-and-file's. Foster, the 1830 secretary of the Spinners' Grand Union was, according to the Webbs,[2] 'a man

[1] The Webb-Fielding MS., citing an unquoted source—possibly a record then in the Bolton Spinners' possession.

[2] *History*, p. 118. Other evidence, however, is that he at least began as a working spinner, and may have been 'blacklisted' for his union activity.

of independent means' (by 1830 Doherty himself was on the way to becoming a full-time publicist). Of the spinners in 1818 it was at least said (though bitterly, since by an opponent) that their committee had 'strong common sense, though not cultivated education.'[1] The balance between these two qualities *may* have been altered by later influences. The occasional high-flown tone of early weavers' pronouncements, as well as some organizational ornatenesses in their societies, have also been attributed to outside advice.[2] Into very recent times, some of the still-surviving independent Scottish textile unions were actually dependent for their management on outside people—often local ministers.[3]

However, such a dependence on outside guidance could rarely have been significant in the early unions. And some of them certainly adopted pretentious terminologies or procedures autonomously. The old smallware weavers adopted a rule that the members should sit in a strict seniority at their society's meetings so as to '. . . cause a Reverence in the Beholder'.[4] And when the Manchester spinners called their panel of head shopmen 'the Arbitrators' they were probably trying to attach to their representatives a little of the legal prestige conferred on people nominated to settle weavers' price-disputes under the Cotton Arbitration Act.

However, such trimmings usually remained superficial. And despite the basic simplicity of the early unions' structure, they produced many examples of effectively-concerted action, undertook considerable organizational tasks (the weavers' Monster Petitions, for instance), and even collected surprisingly-large financial resources on occasion. The spinners' federation paid out £1,500 a week for several weeks[5] in 1810, and the much poorer Glasgow weavers raised £3,000 to plead their case for a legal wage-list[6] in 1812. The Webbs' reference to the spinners' 'contributions of 1d or 2d per week only' is in fact rather a misleading report of the early unions' financial capacity.[7] The subscription of both the spinners' Grand

[1] From Aspinall's No. 286.

[2] See, for instance, Wadsworth (op. cit.) p. 345.

[3] According to the Secretary of the Scottish Council of Textile Trade Unions, the Forfar operatives' association had a local hotel-keeper for secretary so late as 1951.

[4] This is, of course, the present practice of the TUC's General Council though, one supposes, for a different motive. But the smallware weavers also required all members to sit with their hats on.

[5] According to Mantoux (op. cit.) p. 462. The number of actual spinners involved was probably about 3,000.

[6] Chapman, p. 187, See also Chapter II, 1, section iv.

[7] *History*, p. 195—contrasting the spinners, as prior experimenters in national unionism, with the supposedly more 'liquid' New Model ASE. On this contrast, however, see Ch. III, 2, section I.

Union and the NAPL was certainly 1d per week, as was that of the weavers' general union of 1824: but these were federal bodies, the subscriptions to which were levies on individual unions, with their own financial rules.[1] The spinners' federations in any case, commonly exacted a sizeable entrance fee to prevent clubs or societies joining with intent merely to finance their own strikes cheaply. Their Manchester Society's acceptance fee for *individual* members, however, was 10s; and its standard contribution was 7d a week, to which were added weekly 'levies' of 3d to 6d according to need[2]—a total weekly contribution of 3 or 4 per cent of the spinners' average earnings at the time. Other spinners' societies had still higher rates. It was the *hand-weavers* whose fund-raising capacity was, naturally, more limited: the standard strike pay of the spinners' Grand Union was actually higher than the then-normal weaver's wage.

II

But perhaps the most important implication of the early unions' essential structural simplicity is the continuity of association which it reflected and facilitated. The formal disbanding of a society, even the seizure of its committee, funds and records, could of itself make only a temporary impact on its members' organizational capacity. The essential workplace units survived informally (as did the background resource of 'friendly' association), and could maintain their links with each other; the re-erection of an open organization was an easy matter. In many ways, in fact, the early cotton unions resembled the 'unofficial movements' which have so frequently embarrassed official British union leaderships in modern times. There is the same basis in the workplace group, which may have informal 'friendly' functions as well as trade ones. There is the same federal super-structure—the shop-stewards ('head shopmen' or 'box-stewards') forming the local committee, the representatives of local committees forming the 'movement'. And there is the same use of 'delegates' to communicate with other groups, and particularly to canvass support for local strikes.

The modern 'unofficial movements', like the early unions, show an apparently flickering activity. They come alive—often formidably so—in times that the workers they influence consider critical, and subside when these crises have passed. While even their intervals of passivity may provide an analogy with the antique operatives' organizations. In such interludes, the nominal apparatus of an

[1] Even so, this federal subscription was, in real terms, higher per member than that at present collected by the TUC.

[2] *CFT* (loc. cit.).

'unofficial movement' may today be maintained by a handful of politically-convinced 'militants'. But these may also be overwhelmed or replaced by other leaders when some twist of circumstance revives genuine rank-and-file concern—as for instance, the Communist leadership in the unofficial Portworkers' Committees was superseded during the Northern Dock strikes of 1955–6. Just so, it is possible that the persistent reports of radical influence in the early cotton unions are often to be attributed to the predominance of radicals among such union activists as remained when the generality of operatives was in a passive mood[1]—as well as to (another analogy to modern phenomena) the radicals' attempts to extend, stimulate and influence strikes despite their exclusion from the latters' direction. Thus the Reform agitators, having been active on the fringe of the great 1818 strike-movement,[2] afterwards attempted first to revive its inter-union by-product, the Philanthropic Society (although they were apparently restrained from exploiting it during its brief phase of genuine life), and then to transfer its focus—as the new General Union of Trades—to the thereafter more promising Midlands and London.

To the extent, then, that the early cotton unions were in fact (and as the Webbs suggested) 'ephemeral', this can now be reconciled with their persistent reappearance. What have later been thought of as the 'unions' proper were commonly either simple formalizations of certain natural links between the workers, or merely-superficial structures. But these were erected on a much more durable foundation—the habit of association between workers of a settled occupational group. This habit was probably of itself sufficient to convey and preserve such things as the spinners' entry controls and job demarcations, or the weavers' methods of adjusting piece-prices as between employed journeymen and 'independent' domestic operatives. Such things simply became what would now be called 'customs of the trade'.[3]

The habit of association was, moreover, probably of itself sufficient in such cases to produce, at need, an organization to deal with small disputes by 'deputation' or strike action—even were that habit not reinforced by such continuing and more formal links as friendly

[1] See Aspinall's Nos. 303, 309, 315 and 316.

[2] Aspinall's No. 234.

[3] The earliest weavers' societies were, of course, almost literally *trade* unions, often combining not only 'shop' workers, out-workers and journeymen, but also some small masters. The arrangements proposed by the striking check-weavers of 1758 were, in fact, very similar to those which actually obtained for trade regulation between the Yeomanry Organizations and the Livery Companies in London two hundred years earlier—cf. Daniels (op. cit.) p. 49, and Unwin's *Industrial Organization in the Sixteenth and Seventeenth Centuries* (MUP, 1904).

clubs. Small strikes of workers quite without formal union membership have occurred in modern times (for instance, the several weeks' strike of charwomen at the Burtonwood air-base in 1955); and several isolated 'mill clubs' only moved into a formal existence so as to join the spinners' 1810 federation. The habit of association may even have secured a disciplined behaviour in wider disputes. The mule-spinners' district societies probably had close to 100 per cent. organization in their factory towns. But it seems unlikely that the handloom weavers' general unions connected even a majority in formal membership: the 1799 Association of Weavers, for instance, may have had about 10,000 at first formation.[1] Nevertheless these unions drew very large numbers into their activities. As was said of the miners in a later period: 'They would constitute an inchoate or potential Union even if no formal union existed. (So that) . . . a common policy is sometimes pursued, and the hardships of a strike willingly endured, by a considerable fringe who are unconnected with the Union.'[2]

The habit of association broke only when the class concerned dissolved, or became too unstable or diluted to preserve it—as finally happened to the hand-weavers. Though even when these had generally reached a stage of social disintegration, it was notable that such sections of them as were protected from machinery or the flood of new entrants by a special skill quickly regrouped apart from the disorganized mass. A Quilting Weavers' Union, for instance, was formed as late as 1829—although their branch of the textile trade was old, and prices for it had been included in very early wage-lists.

On the other hand, such more elaborate and extensive superstructures as the early unions produced were mainly required to deal with specific general crises. The appearance of continuous activity which distinguishes modern trade unions from their predecessors (at least, in cotton) largely arises from the professional leadership of the contemporary organization. This leadership, with its accompanying administrative structure, gives the union as such an existence independent of its members' activity. Among the early cotton operatives, the needs that later induced professionalism in trade unions—the increasingly technical character of wage-fixing, the administration of large centralized 'friendly' funds, and so on—had not yet arisen. Nor did the absence of professional leaders inhibit

[1] Wigan was reported (Aspinall's No. 24) as having 700 members, and had two delegates on the General Committee, which was apparently proportionately-representative of the district societies.

[2] W. J. Ashley, *The Adjustment of Wages* (Longmans, London, 1903) pp. 12 and 13.

the development of what was often, in relation to the operatives' more elemental purposes, a quite skilled tactical direction. This is evidenced by such things as the Association of Weavers' apparently astute management from 1799 to 1807: their first manifesto, for instance, was nicely calculated, not merely at the same time to allay the ruling classes' fear of proletarian Jacobinism and to enlist employers' concern at cut-throat competition from small masters, but also to appeal to the pockets of the farmers and landed gentry (these, together with better-paid country weavers, were being taxed to subsidize low wages from the Poor Rates)[1]. While apart from the spinners' broad technique of wage-pressure, there are the minutiae of their strike arrangements—the allocation of picketing duties to ensure that all selected factories were covered, but no one by its own workers; the system of messengers to keep the strike-committee in hour-by-hour liaison with the mills; the organization of twice-daily processions to keep the striking spinners mobilized and orderly; and so on.[2]

It seems arguable in fact, that the modern elaboration of formal trade union structures was induced, not so much to *permit* central leadership as to control the professionalism which that leadership developed. The early cotton operatives' associations were apparently reluctant to see responsibility stay overlong in particular individuals' hands and—like other unions of the day—often spread it, in their formal organizations, by combining elective with more random methods of choosing their officers. The actual committee of the Manchester spinners, for instance, was selected from their panel of 'arbitrators' by simple seniority (the 'head shopmen' from whom the arbitrators were elected may have been appointed on the same principle). The Glasgow spinners' committee was chosen by lot from mill nominations. The check-weaver had no right of refusal if nominated for office in his 'box'. Very short periods of office were also common: the check-weavers' stewards, again, were elected only for three months, and the Philanthropic Society's rules changed one-third of its committee monthly, and the whole every quarter. Such systems, of course, sometimes had the advantage of sharing out the risks of victimization or arrest. But that would not apply to all of them; and suspicion of any tendency to an enduring concentration of power must also have been a factor. The possibility of a separation between the rank-and-file and even such a merely semi-

[1] The manifesto is reproduced at length in W. Radcliffe's *Origin of the New System of Manufacture* (Manchester, 1828) pp. 73 ff.

[2] See the numerous references to the 1818 strike in Aspinall's collection. This may be the first occasion on which the term 'picket' itself came into general use.

professional leadership as the Manchester spinners had in the late 1820s was, indeed, illustrated in their committee's alleged termination of the 1829 strike, against the members' wishes as expressed in a secret ballot, by falsifying the voting results.[1]

Of the connection between the constitutional elaboration of modern trade unions and the full-time officials' appearance, there will be more to say in later chapters. Its effect, however, is to make the modern union's internal structure, in a sense, artificial by contrast with that of earlier and less formal workers' associations—to convert the unions into 'institutions' with an identity to a significant degree independent of their membership. So that one might say, of many internal conflicts in modern trade unions, that when their members find the 'institutional' structure inadequate or obstructive to their desires, then the 'natural' structure tends to re-create itself as a rival (if now 'unofficial') vehicle of collective action. Such a juxtaposition rarely arose in the early unions.

III

In the early cotton unions, one region seems to have been notable for a special solidarity. And this is perhaps worth a brief glance, because it not only provides a further contrast in union method—and one that reinforces the previous section's argument—but incidentally raises an economic problem. The explanation of the Scottish unions' unusual strength is not clear. The law against combination was less rigid in Scotland: and that country's tradition of popular education was, in a contemporary view, also a major factor.[2] The Scottish weavers had—unlike the English—an informal general association before the handworkers' decline set in; one established, moreover, to secure a uniform wage-list by direct action, not merely to petition for a legal wage. It may well be that this early development established a special cohesion that survived the handloom weavers' later troubles. At any rate their subsequent actions were apparently more effective, and their strikes more disciplined and purposeful, than those of their English fellows. In their great 1812 stoppage, it was remarked that 'the (Scottish) weavers . . . act in concert with wonderful unanimity . . . and the leading men of their body are persons of wonderful coolness and ability'.[3] They procured

[1] According to the Webb-Fielding notes.

[2] 'The people of Scotland are superior to the English in discernment and reflection. They have the superior advantages of education . . .' J. J. Dillon's report to Viscount Sidmouth, December 18, 1812. (Aspinall's No. 133). The Factory Commissioners' reports show a considerably smaller proportion of children in Scottish mills.

[3] J. J. Dillon, again.

counsel's advice to keep within the law, and were careful to avoid any disturbance that might give the authorities an occasion to act forcibly against them (several thousand troops had been sent to Glasgow). They actually organized an internal police of their own to ensure their members' good behaviour—even succeeding, apparently, in keep the many Irish in Glasgow orderly.

In more normal times, the Scottish weavers' arrangements were similarly systematic. Their local societies exchanged delegates, and their general policy was managed by a federal committee of five, seemingly representative of district delegate meetings. After the 1812 strike's failure the committee set about a most ingenious attempt to enforce the wage-rates previously approved by the magistrates. It divided the country into areas to each of which it appointed a 'beamer' and assistants: the task of these agents was to put the work received by the weavers into the looms, but they would only do so after the weavers had both proved their membership of the association *and* shown satisfactory price-tickets for the work to be done. Local Scottish weavers' societies about this time even regulated working hours by having the town drummer beat at 8 p.m. And in 1834, when the remnant of the Lancashire weavers' general union was presenting its last hopeless minimum-wage petitions, the Glasgow and Paisley unions secured a full collective agreement, by which price-lists would be fixed and revised at an annual conference with employers' representatives.[1]

The first report of a spinners' union in Glasgow comes only in 1810—when several Lancashire societies were already well established. But in that year their organization's attempt to get standard wages and conditions provoked—like that of the federated Lancashire spinners—a widespread lock-out which in this case stimulated some violence. And by the 1820s the Glasgow spinners, 'exhaustively combined and daringly led',[2] had become the most formidable group of all. Indeed, it seems that they may by then already have attempted to sponsor a national spinners' federation, which would have anticipated the Lancashire-initiated body of 1829–30. In organization, the Scottish spinners had clearly learnt much from their weaver compatriots. Their committee, too, divided its area into districts, in each of which it appointed an agent who communicated the committee's policy to, and received the contributions collected by, the mill delegates. The union's subscription was extraordinary —2s 6d a week, to which special levies might be added, and which was in any case raised to 5s a week for those who were permitted to

[1] Sharp (op. cit.) p. 2.
[2] Chapman (op. cit.) p. 201.

enter the trade from outside the society's area.[1] The 'outsider' might also be required to pay an entrance fee of up to £5. And spinners from some 'outside' districts (seemingly unorganized ones), even in Scotland itself, were absolutely barred.

It is curious that the Glasgow spinners' union, unlike its Lancashire equivalents, appears to have organized no major strike of its district until its fatal conflict of 1837. It may well be that its drive to secure control of spinning labour at the level of individual mills achieved such success that it never had to resort to more general conflicts—until it was finally challenged by employers provoked to act in concert. At any rate, it seems to have been remarkably powerful: although having only half the adult-spinner membership of the Manchester union at peak, it appears to have achieved something like a 'closed shop'; its regulation extended not merely to wage-rates and entry, but to questions of mill arrangements, the appointment of overlookers and so on—a degree of interference to which the Lancashire unions forswore even the ambition.[2] One prominent employer, indeed, protested in 1823 that 'several of the masters in Glasgow and the neighbourhood have been obliged to give up part of the management of their own business and leave it in the hands of these united rulers'.[3] The protest seems to have had some substance: and the great 1824 lock-out was a concerted effort by the Glasgow cotton manufacturers to defeat '. . . this audacious attempt to turn all the mills into a petty democracy'.[4] But although the union suffered a setback on that occasion, it continued to support (at rates virtually equal to half-pay) the considerable number of its members who were blacklisted, and for the next year or two engaged in some prolonged mill disputes to support standard wage-rates. By 1826 it was at least enforcing its own wage-list on some factories: when the firm of Graham's put up their works at that time, for instance, it reported that '. . . the combination gave us a list of prices we were to pay'.[5] And within a year or so this standard seems to have been generally accepted by the employers.

The explanation of the Glasgow spinners' special power may well be that by the 1820s, whatever their society's formal constitution,[6] they had acquired a full-time leadership *de facto*—and one, at that, not of middle-class sympathizers or of intellectualized artisans but of 'persons whose turbulent spirits have excluded them from regular

[1] *CFT* (loc. cit.).
[2] Cf. *Resolution* 13 of the Grand Union's 1830 Congress (loc. cit.).
[3] Houldsworth (also a local magistrate) in Aspinall's No. 392.
[4] A contemporary Press description, quoted by Chapman (op. cit.) p. 213.
[5] *CFT* (loc. cit.) quoting the Report of the Committee on Manufactures of 1833.
[6] See section ii above.

employment.'[1] Probably, the committee-men were 'blacklisted' and thus became professionals: in any event, there is little doubt that the Glasgow leadership set about achieving its aims not merely by a prompt use and support of mill strikes, but by systematic intimidation and hired violence. The Lancashire spinners' strikes were often a cause of bitterness between them and other operatives; but the Glasgow spinners systematically subsidized at least those of the latter who might be tempted to take the spinners' place, and exploited the riotous tendencies of the factory boys to threaten employers and 'knobsticks'. Against the latter, moreover, Glasgow seems to have been the only place in which the 'vitrioling' of persons (as distinct from their materials) was deliberately employed by the union.

It is no doubt a commentary on the period that what was possibly its most effective trade union should have been almost a terrorist organization. As it was revealed in 1838, the conduct of the Glasgow spinners' society supports no charge of mere gangsterism, comparable with that which has afflicted some unions in the U.S.A.'s recent history. Their trial raised little doubt of the leaders' personal integrity. The oppressions and inhumanities of the raw industrial order were converted by the State's enforcement of it into a systematic social tyranny, and would have explained a Jacquerie. But whereas the Lancashire spinners attempted to challenge that condition in ordered and open battles, the Glasgow union chose rather the method of the guerrilla and Maquis. At any rate, when its leaders were brought to trial in 1838 their violent record did not deter a working-class sympathy almost as widespread as that which the Tolpuddle labourers aroused four years previously.[2] But it may also be symptomatic both of the special character of the Glasgow spinners' leadership and (more important for the general understanding of union development) of the extent to which the workers themselves had become dependent on—or involved in—their directorate's unusual mode of operation, that in cutting off the head of Glasgow spinners' unionism the 1838 trial there seems also to have destroyed the body. The general revival of spinners' trade unionism in the 1840s did not, apparently, extend to Scotland.[3]

[1] Houldsworth (loc. cit.).

[2] The indictment, with certain other extracts and notes on the trial is reproduced by Cole & Filson (op. cit., p. 291).

[3] The Spinners were not the only West Scottish trade union that, though very strong in the 1830s, collapsed utterly thereafter (see Chapter IV, 1, section i, for instance). An alternative explanation suggests itself to the writer, though he cannot explore it. Freemasonry, which remains in Scotland both more popular and more radical than elsewhere, was strong there in the eighteenth century and may have provided a background force to trade unionism—but was over whelmingly diluted, in the newer industries, by the accelerated Irish immigration of the 1840s.

The economic problem, however, is the special effect of the Scottish unions' early superiority on the regional industry's development. The weavers, by a special shrewdness and a soberly-ordered solidarity may have prevented their wages falling as fast as did wages in England: by an opposite ferocity, the Glasgow spinners apparently kept a wage-level close to that of Manchester itself.[1] These things, although the *general* level of Scottish wages (for unorganized factory hands, for instance[2]) was substantially lower than the English. But in 1787, with the factory revolution just beginning, west Scotland was a close rival to Lancashire in the exploitation of the new techniques—having twenty-four powered mills (nearly a quarter of the total in Great Britain) to the latter's forty-one. By 1835, however, Scotland had only an eighth of all the cotton factories, the majority of which were then in Lancashire.[3] This may suggest the Scottish factories' competitive power to have been hampered by the peculiar strength of their unions. But against this, the relative decline of the Scottish spinning industry seems actually to have accelerated after the Glasgow spinners' final defeat. While the handloom weavers' disappearance was apparently delayed in Scotland—about 1840, there were still over 50,000 of them there[4]. And whereas many of the English hand-weavers had become, in their attempt to compete with the power-loom the producers of an inferior commodity, the Scots were concentrating on higher-quality products which the new machine was slow to bring within its capacity. Did strong unions and artificially high wages cut off the Scottish textile industry's growth—or delay a decline that other factors made inevitable?

IV

It seems clear, at any rate, that the methods and character of the Glasgow spinners' leadership put their union into rather a special category. In other cases, violence in industrial disputes not only was much much more incidental—indeed, frequently restrained by the unions themselves—but probably had an alternative explanation.

Despite that difference in motivation between the early spinners' and weavers' unions which was analysed in the preceding chapter, they resembled each other in one aspect beyond the 'natural' character of their organizations. This was an essential sectionalism—indeed,

[1] Compare Wood's Tables 32 and 33 for weavers, 5 and 30 for spinners.

[2] See Wood, again.

[3] According to Burn (*Statistics of the Cotton Trade*, op. cit.).

[4] Chapman (op. cit.) p. 22, n. 3. The total number of handloom weavers about this time is unrecorded, but was probably between 100,000 and 150,000.

an attempted exclusiveness. That common quality is clearly shown by their policies towards entry into their respective occupations. The handloom weavers' unions almost certainly derived the idea of statutory wage-enforcement from the Tudor system of legal wage-controls. But the earliest weavers' societies are well-known to have been, if anything, more concerned to maintain the traditional apprenticeship than with wage-regulation.[1] The check-weavers, for instance, declared their intention of 1758 to be '. . . to support and maintain the trade with experienced and honest workmen and to bring it under the statute of 5 Elizabeth' (i.e. the Statute of Apprentices).[2] While the smallware-weavers attempted an elaborate entry regulation—including a restricted register of apprentices, a 'blank' system to certify the journeyman's qualification, and a blacklist of unqualified workers. The first formal spinners' societies—at Manchester and Oldham in 1795–6, as well as at Glasgow in 1810—similarly included apprenticeship regulations in their rules. Some years later, local spinners' unions were still from time-to-time demanding a limit on the number of 'apprentices', and in the 1820s were in effect attempting an even more direct restriction of entry when they demanded that vacancies in the mills be filled only from names submitted by them.

Apart from one or two specialized branches of the manufacturing trade, like smallwares and quilting, it seems likely that weaving apprenticeship had already become nominal in the heyday of the weavers' prosperity. As that prosperity receded, the weavers returned to a political demand for the entry limitation which they were by then incapable of enforcing for themselves. Apprenticeship regulation was a frequent object of the weavers' petitions—but was as frequently rejected. While in the last stages of handloom weavers' organization—and though the re-formed general weavers' federations, in both England and Scotland, included apprenticeship regulation in their objects of 1824—the demand for apprenticeship had become pathetically secondary to that for a minimum wage. The spinners' Grand Union of 1829–30, on the other hand, despite the development of the factory process since the mule-frame's first appearance, attempted to impose an even tighter form of trade exclusion—one restricting the right to learn to the relatives of established spinners.[3] Even the Woolcombers, perhaps the strongest of preceding textile unions, had merely given a *preference*

[1] See both Daniels, and Wadsworth, op. cit.

[2] From a manifesto cited by Daniels, p. 48.

[3] *Resolutions* 8 and 9 of the 1830 Congress (loc. cit.), substantially re-affirming a proposal of the 1829 Congress.

to the relatives of qualified men, and that confined to eldest sons.[1]

In at first attempting to impose an apprenticeship system, the spinners were merely imitating the weavers and other unions of handworkers. But that system impiled the mobility of qualified 'journeymen'. And this proved in practice inacceptable to the stronger spinners' societies: spinners from other districts of the Grand Union, for instance, were refused admittance by Glasgow. On the other hand the fact that, with the mule-frame's elaboration, every spinner came to require two or three young assistants made it impracticable to restrict the acquisition of skill, and defeated the spinners' attempts to limit the number of 'learners' or to compel employers to engage only men nominated by the unions. But the various formal 'rules of entry' the spinners proposed represented only experiments. The spinners, like the weavers before them, were subject to both the diffusion of their specialist skill and its reduction by mechanical progress and division of labour. In the weavers' case, the outworking system and the relative ease of setting up as a small master combined with these things to make it impossible for the weavers themselves to control the many entries to their occupation. But the spinners were advantaged, not merely by an initial solidarity but also by their early concentration in a few mills and localities. And their experiments quite soon produced a method of entry control empirically adapted to the new factory industry's condition. Some details of this method are perhaps better considered in other connections.[2] But its essence (though less formal than apprenticeship) was to put every spinner at the top of a vocational ladder erected in his own workplace—a position which could only be gained by climbing that ladder's successive steps as they were vacated by others. At any rate, by the 1820s the spinners' entry controls seem to have been sufficiently effective to materially re-inforce their strategic position.

A second aspect of the early unions' exclusiveness was their attitude to other groups of workers. The weavers, for instance, apparently made no systematic attempt to associate with their organizations the many ancillary workers to handloom weaving (it was estimated that of winders alone, one was required to every six weavers)[3] though local societies may have included some of them. Nor did they organize the many domestic jenny-spinners who, before the factory finally extinguished them, must have practised

[1] 1821 *Rules* of the United Societies of Woolcombers, reproduced as Aspinall's No. 126.

[2] See particularly Chapter III, 1, section v, and Chapter IV, 2, section II.

[3] Wood, (op. cit.) p. 126.

in weaving villages and included members of the weavers' families. The spinners excluded from union membership most, if not in fact all, of their own assistants: and their Grand Union deliberately excluded the female mule-spinners who at that time existed (though it recommended them to form their own associations). Nor did the spinners attempt to organize either the preparatory workers—cardroom hands, etc.—in spinning factories, or those engaged on such rival factory spinning processes as the water-frame and its successor, the throstle. The operatives of these latter machines were women; but even the male jenny-spinners in Stockport factories were obliged, apparently, to attempt their own society.[1]

In this respect, one major factor in the similar attitudes of the spinners' and weavers' unions is almost certainly that both the mule-spinners and the earlier hand-weavers were themselves employers of labour. As the handloom improvements raised the early weavers' output (it took several hand-carders and spinners to keep a 'fly-shuttle' weaver fully employed) they were obliged to look beyond their families for help. And sub-contracting of domestic spinning, as well as certain other ancillary work, continued even after the jenny's introduction—if only because, until factory production secured a consistent yarn for both weft and warp, the 'putting-out masters' themselves were not always able to discover bad work or fraud in yarn already wound by domestic spinners, and preferred to make the weavers responsible for their own thread. The factory mule-spinners, however, also paid their own assistants, and as the mules developed the number of these assistants that was required grew so that over half the young people in cotton factories were employed by adult operatives.[2]

V

Thus, the exclusive character of the early unions—and especially the spinners—may well be a partial explanation of the violence with which the industrial disputes of their period are so often associated. Attacks on people or machinery seem in any case to have emanated from several distinct sources and been of very different degrees. Bands of weavers collected the shuttles from their neighbours' looms to ensure the completeness of their 1808 strike, and a similar method animated the 'Plug Plot' of 1842 (mills were stopped by drawing the

[1] *Rules* of Stockport Society (the only known one of jenny-spinners), promulgated 1824, listed in Chapman's references as in the Manchester Library, but not found by the present writer.

[2] Hutchins & Harrison, *History of Factory Legislation* (LSE, London, 1911), p. 37.

boiler plugs or cutting their dams). As the more disastrous struggles approached their climax, it was easy for such things, and the already more-than-moral pressure on 'knobsticks' (strikebreakers, who were often imported in gangs by the mill-owners), to pass over into more extreme forms—into the breaking or vitrioling of the warp-threads of recalcitrant weavers, into personal violence, and into attacks on the mills of the most obstinate employers. The weavers' strikes were rare, and in the later days of the handloom industry already symptomatic of a desperation intensified, once a strike was launched, by the weavers' meagre capacity to raise strike funds. But even for them, the ordered public procession seems to have been the most usual strike demonstration. While the spinners certainly *attempted* to manage their strikes in sober fashion. In the great strike-wave of 1818, for instance, the Manchester strikers' conduct was disciplined until near its end, though riots and attacks on mills occured in out-districts.

The spinners' strikes, however, immediately put out of work masses of unorganized labour, which had no support from strike pay and was refused it from the public funds. Accounts of both the Manchester and Glasgow spinners' strikes make it clear that it was these unorganized workers—and especially the many boys and women amongst them—who were often responsible for disturbance and destructive incidents. They were under urgent threat of starvation, and thus mainly interested that the strike should end soon—while the spinners' strikes were often, by recent standards at least, extraordinarily protracted. Such strikes, moreover, often provided an opportunity for the mass of oppressed or unemployed from other trades to vent their desperation: by no means all the loom-smashing in 1826 was done by weavers. But only in the case of the Glasgow spinners is there much evidence that the unions deliberately exploited this tendency to violence on the part of the unorganized.

Attacks on machinery as such are, in any case, pretty clearly separated from the incidents to trade disputes—and are also rare. The selective character of the 1779 raids, for instance, makes it clear that these were aimed less at the newer spinning-machines than at their monopolization by wealthy masters: the riots' immediate cause was apparently an offer by one machine-owner to '. . . spin at lower prices than those generally given'.[1] Luddism in Yorkshire had an authentic basis in the obliteration of a strong old textile craft, the woolcombers, by machinery: but in Lancashire it secured only limited support—indeed, was to a large degree created by agent-

[1] According to Wadsworth & Mann (op. cit.) p. 499.

provocateurs.[1] The 1826 outbreak of steam-loom smashing was motivated by the failure, first of the weavers to remedy their grievances by political appeals, and then of their last resort to industrial combination. There is no record of spinners attacking the 'self-actor' mule (they did not even attempt to compete with it—as the hand-weavers did with the power-loom—by lowering the quality of their work to reduce its price). And in later affairs, the separation between different classes of operative was again as much a factor as a hostility to machinery itself. Thus Cooke-Taylor reports of his visit to the Chartist handworkers of Burnley: 'I heard more than twenty openly advocate the expediency of burning down the mills in order to compel the factory hands to join in an insurrectionary movement.'[2]

Of the early unions' relation with employers, hostility and potential violence were not invariably typical. Some union policies—like the specification of product standards and labour costs—appealed to the interest at least of groups among employers. In weaving, especially, groups of more substantial masters were sufficiently disturbed by the later fluctuation of wages and labour costs (by their own petition of 1808, 100 per cent. within three years) and by the effects of price-cutting by the 'little masters' in trade slumps, not merely to add their voice to the weavers' minimum-wage petitions, but to attempt joint compacts for the regulation of weaving prices—in 1808, in 1819, and again early in 1826. Some of the weavers prosecuted after the 1818 strikes, in fact, pleaded (unsuccessfully) that they had struck in understanding with certain employers: in one district the latter had even contributed to the weavers' funds. And magistrates frequently complained of employers' reluctance to proceed against their workers for combination. In such cases, sympathy with the weavers' poverty was certainly a factor in the attitude of the masters concerned. In spinning, the factory system set a sharper division between employer and worker; and as the spinners' unionism mounted to its climax of strength and systematization, their relations with the masters took on all the quality of an endemic, general and prepared industrial warfare. In spinning (and apart from occasional reports of firms surreptitiously subscribing to strikes against rival concerns) the few early instances of employer-union co-operation appear to have been largely inspired by the smaller employers' fears of competition from firms with more modern machinery. Thus the Glasgow union's campaign in the mid-'20s for standard wage-rates

[1] Hammonds, *Skilled Labourer*, Chapter X. Apparently, some spinners were attracted to Luddism by their 1810 strike's failure, but the evidence does not indicate more than a handful. Both spinners and weavers, however, contributed to the funds of the Midlands Luddites.

[2] *Notes on a Tour in the Manufacturing Districts of Lancashire* (London, 1842).

was supported by some local masters, and in 1830–1 some combination of 'small-wheel' owners and operative spinners in south-east Lancashire attempted to 'regulate the trade'.[1] But even in spinning, the idea of joint regulation (together, no doubt, with many incompatible ideas) had by 1846 gained to the extent that the Oldham spinners were substantially able to apply the hand-weavers' earlier suggestion (of 1810[2]) for meeting a trade recession. They persuaded their employers, who had proposed to reduce wages, to reduce output by short-time instead.[3]

VI

The would-be exclusiveness of the early cotton unions had, however, some broader consequences. One recurring problem of union development is the relation between general labour movements and those sectional organizations of workers which are usually identified as trade unions—at least, in the Anglo-Saxon world. In other countries, there have been many instances in which unions have appeared primarily as one possible expression (among others) of some much broader movement—political, social, religious or national—of which they are almost the dependent industrial agencies. And there is no reason to think this evolution less typical than the alternative one, in which unions appear as independent embodiments of separate group interests, which *may* link in some broader association, but will even so retain a standing apart from it. In the period of the early cotton unions' rise and fall, British labour history of course provides examples of both forms. Narrowly sectional associations of workers in several old-established crafts continued, certainly, from well back in the eighteenth century. While the latter end of the period—and particularly the decades of the 1820s and '40s—is remarkable for general movements of the working-class.

It is just the purposively sectional character of the early cotton unions that no doubt explains why there should be so little evidence of co-operation between the spinners' and weavers' associations themselves. The two groups remained rather apart even in 1818, when they were—for once—both striking at the same place and time. But particularly, this common sectional quality of the spinners' and weavers' associations perhaps explains what is at first sight surprising—the difference in their respective attitudes to workers in non-textile trades. The early cotton unions themselves promoted several general labour federations: and of these attempts the weavers might well seem the more likely source. After the outbreak of the great French Wars, the weavers' weakened industrial bargaining

[1] According to Chapman (op. cit.) p. 80.

[2] See Chapter II, 1, section v.

[3] According to Gayer, Rostow and Schwartz (op. cit.).

position drove them to fall back upon mass pressure on the political authority. So that—like the 'general' unions of our own day—they should therefore have had a strong interest in re-inforcing that pressure by sheer weight of numbers. But the weavers' thinking was still apparently preoccupied with the myth of their historical entitlement to a special status. It was, curiously, from the spinners, whose early history is essentially that of a determined and consistent attempt to carve out for themselves an aristocratic position in the new industry's structure, that the initiative to associate other labour groups into a broader organization came. However, it is perhaps significant that, even there, the attempt was confined to sections—largely of artisans—already organized. And whether the spinners themselves ever envisaged a recruitment of the unorganized mass of labour is not clear. But when that mass was finally stirred by the appearance of general trade union federations, the spinners appear to have retreated from the movement they had themselves played so large a part in launching.

The spinners' first move towards a general labour federation was stimulated by the 1818 strike wave—when they called a meeting of 'all trades' in Manchester, and formed the Philanthropic Society, primarily to support '. . . any trade that may be engaged in resisting oppression'. Its resolutions recommended affiliated societies to raise separate funds for 'the general benefit', and envisaged the control of sectional strikes by a federal body in Manchester with a representative executive. It included miners, builders and mechanics, but textile workers' unions were apparently predominant among its constituents. However, it so soon subsided that within a few months of its formation, the Crown Law officers were advising that legal action against it would only revive it. A 'General Union of Trades' is recorded as meeting, with delegates from the Midlands, Liverpool and the Somerset wool-weavers, in October of 1818 at Todmorden[1]—a centre at the same time convenient to both Lancashire and Yorkshire and suitably remote from the Mancunian magistrates' view. It was presumably a continuation of the Philanthropic Society, but made no further appearance in the textile districts.

Another attempt was made after the 1824 strikes. A confederal 'Trades Union' existed in Manchester in 1826, but '. . . expired before it became widely known'[2]—and was castigated at the congress of the

[1] According to a record of Mr E. Hopwood, formerly of the present-day Weavers' Amalgamation (see also Aspinall's letter No. 308).

[2] According to Chapman (op. cit.) p. 204. See also the Webbs, *History*, p. 115. It seems possible that this was an attempt to put on a permanent basis the committee the Manchester cotton operatives set up to oppose any re-enactment of the Combination Laws in 1825.

Spinners' Grand Union in 1829 for allowing its affiliates to strike against wage-reductions without authority. However, by far the best known venture is of course the National Association for the Protection of Labour, which the spinners initiated after the failure of their 1829 strike.[1] The NAPL intervened in their Ashton strike of 1830, and at that time had some 150 affiliates, including a score of spinners' unions. In several respects, the NAPL resembled the Spinners' Grand Union itself—it had, for instance, the same subscription—and though it spread to the Midlands and Yorkshire, and to several non-textile industries, it remained largely under their dominance.

It is noteworthy that, although a few local weavers' societies joined the NAPL, the main body of the surviving handloom weavers' associations kept aloof from it—as they had also, it seems, from the preceding Philanthropic Society.[2] The NAPL seems to have disintegrated by 1832, after the Lancashire unions refused to support strikes in the Midlands. And while both its leading spirit John Doherty himself and the Manchester spinners' committee made separate attempts at new federations—a body called the Manchester Trades Union was apparently functioning a year or so later—it is also noteworthy that the spinners remained detached from the later creations of the movement for 'National' unionism they had themselves helped to set off. They were, for instance, unrepresented in Owen's Grand National of 1834, although they took part in the great London demonstration for the remission of the Tolpuddle Martyrs' sentences. And though they sent delegates to the first meeting of the National Association of United Trades for the Protection of Labour in 1845, they never actually joined that organization, cautious as it was.[3]

So it does not appear that their leader Doherty's belief in the virtue of concerted industrial action to uplift the condition of labour at large was ever quite the motive that inspired his spinner followers. They, in effect, rather saw these general federations principally as a means to widen support for their own position—as a device which might supply the deficiency their protracted strikes revealed in their own resources. When it seemed that such general unions might impose a merely supporting role on the spinners themselves, the latters' enthusiasm evaporated.

A final effect of the early unions' essential sectionalism may perhaps be seen in—what is in any case difficult to separate from

[1] Accounts of the NAPL'S activities in G. D. H. Cole's *Attempts at General Union* (Macmillan, London, 1953) as well as the Hammonds' *Bleak Age* (Swan, London, 1934).

[2] Hammonds, *Skilled Labourer*, (op. cit.) p. 114.

[3] Webbs, *History*, p. 191.

their relations with broader labour movements in general—their political attitudes. For the weavers' organizations from 1799 onwards, political action was primary (it was, indeed, their combinations' ostensible purpose to plead for Parliamentary help or to apply existing law that accounted for the official toleration they received being, usually greater than that extended, to the spinners). But this action remained narrowly limited—to their minimum-wage petitions, and to a secondary extent to their demands for the enforcement of apprenticeship. Even at a late stage, it extended only to proposals for a tax on steam-looms and the prohibition of yarn exports—demands which strongly conflicted with the interests of other labour groups. For the spinners at this time, however, political action was very subsidiary. And when it did emerge, it was—apart from their participation in the Committee against the re-imposition of the Combination Laws—mainly confined to a single demand for the legal limitation of working hours. While the extent of even this demand's support by the unions' rank and file was doubtful. The Manchester spinners included a reduced working day in their 1818 strike claims; and the employers actually cut working hours after the strike, though saying they did this to forestall the Parliamentary agitation then developing rather than in satisfaction of the strikers' demand. Doherty recorded that the Manchester spinners continued to raise contributions for the 'Short-time Bill' even after their union's committee had been broken up. But at first, what most obviously pressed the operatives to demand shorter hours was trade depression; and that pressure was only intermittent.

There are other suggestions that—despite a working-day that ran up to fourteen and a half hours and work that was 'the most laborious known'—many of the mule-spinners were lukewarm in their enthusiasm for the Short-time Bill because they feared it would involve a reduction in their earnings. Certainly, their support of such campaigns wavered when they discovered that the 1819 Act restricted the hours of the children they employed themselves.[1] It appears probable, in fact, that it was only with the appearance of the self-actor's threat to the spinners' employment that their campaign to limit factory working hours became really determined. It seems mainly through this avenue, too, that an Owenite influence then entered their unions. Doherty and Owen were associated in the Society for National Regeneration, and the Oldham spinners' strike for the eight-hour day in 1834 was connected with that Society's central campaign for factory legislation. But after their subsequent defeats, the 'short-time' agitation for some years embodied the main

[1] See Aspinall's No. 393.

common activity of the spinners' clubs—just as these for that time provided most of the campaign's finances.

Many union members and leaders were no doubt reformist or revolutionary in their personal outlook. The fall of the Bastille was acclaimed by popular demonstration in Manchester, and there is evidence that thereafter 'Democrats infiltrated the Lancashire textile unions'.[1] In 1801 several such radicals were arrested, and about this time employers were dismissing 'Jacobins' from among their workpeople. But the policy of the unions was not obviously affected by these political militants. The weavers' general union of 1799 rejected the accusation of Jacobinism as a 'calumny'. And even though the delegates who returned in 1811 from the rejection of the weavers' pleas in London then resolved to press for the franchise, while the Lancashire Hampden Clubs of 1816 onwards drew their main strength from the handloom weavers, the 'Loyal Weavers' were still sufficiently strong in these workers' leadership two years later to over-rule the Reformer militants among them. The spinners were by then reputedly more radical in sentiment. They are supposed to have contributed funds for the Blanketeers' March of 1817. And their Stalybridge union invited others to join the Philanthropic Society in 1818 'in one body for Trade and Reform'. But the Philanthropic Society itself prohibited political argument at its meetings under penalty of a fine (Rule 8). While the spinners' Manchester committee repudiated a supposed Radical intervention in their 1818 strike.

It was only after the weavers' last hope of securing improvement through industrial combinations had evaporated in 1825—when their major unions were in fact disintegrating—that they appear to have become predominantly radical in outlook. The spinners were drawn towards the movements that culminated in Chartism rather through a series of setbacks—the failure of their Grand Union and NAPL, the disappointment first of their demand for a general 'short-time' Bill by the 1833 Act and then of their projected industrial campaign for hours limitation (their leaders had apparently considered a general strike[2]), their defeats of 1834–7. And the reactions of the two groups were then characteristically different. Said Cooke-Taylor again[3], of the north-east Lancashire textile workers, that '. . . they were all Chartists, but with this difference, that the block printers and handloom weavers united to their Chartism a hatred of machinery which was far from being shared by the factory operatives. The latter also deprecated anything like

[1] Aspinall's *Introduction.*
[2] According to Chapman (op. cit.) p. 100.
[3] *Notes on a Tour, etc.* (op. cit.) p. 43.

an appeal to physical force, while the former strenuously urged an immediate appeal to arms.'

VII

Among the cotton operatives, in effect, three streams united to produce the political ferment of 1837 onwards that closes the early phase of their trade union history. First, there was a desperate radicalism of the old handworkers, for whom almost any change could now be only for the better, and the more drastic the more so. Second, there was the factory aristocracy of mule-spinners: these had looked askance from the former summit of their strength on proposals—like Doherty's for producer co-operation in the 1820s—to do anything not obviously relevant to that strength's exploitation. But with their footing shaken by industrial defeats and partially undermined by technical change, they were now moving to a generalized desire to see something done about almost everything. And third, there was the growing mass of factory operatives excluded by the spinners' organizations. These new workers had nevertheless begun to be drawn towards trade unionism, however partial and temporary—to some extent by the 1818 strike-wave, still more by the Combination Acts' repeal, and particularly by the furore raised by the NAPL and Owenite unions. Among them, however, distinctly-formed sectional identities were as yet lacking; and to them the political movement must have appeared equally, if not more, meaningful than the industrial one. They were in any case drawn by any mode of action that others offered. Thus, political and industrial excitements alternate—until after the disappointment of the 1832 Reform Act, and the suppression of Owen's Grand National in 1834, they finally merge.

It is a comment on such general movements that the circumstance now common to all three groups of cotton workers was an instability of occupational status. At any rate, the twist that at last flung them together was very likely the appalling slump of 1837, and the impact of the popular revolt against authority's attempt to apply the new Poor Law to the North. By 1840 (when trade, after a brief revival, began to fall off again) Chartism's central ferment was shifting to Lancashire. And it was the Lancashire union lodges that M'Douall had recruited to Chartism that brought its formerly-ineffective 'sacred month' tactic—that of the political strike—near to realization. But it was an Ashton spinners' turn-out for 'the wages of 1840' that set off the great general strike of 1842: and when the new power-loom weavers of Stalybridge carried it into Manchester they then, apparently, voted against the Chartist assembly's decision to turn the strike into a primarily political one.[1] While it was probably the old handworkers who were mainly instrumental in spreading the strike's accompaniment of riot, street-fighting and attacks on factories out over the whole cotton region. It is curious, for instance, that a personal memoir of the time, by a Preston spinner who later became the local society's secretary, speaks of 'turn-outs' of the factory workers in desperation after three successive wage-cuts in 1841 and 1842, but does not mention Chartism as a cause of the strike—moreover referring to the attackers of local mills, and particularly to the bands who attempted to march on the town from the south-east, as 'the mob'[2].

However, the handloom weavers were now a fast-expiring class. The 'Plug Plot' was the greatest strike of the nineteenth century, and the world's first attempted General Strike.[3] But when it subsided in failure, Chartism was shown to have left little trace in the surviving unions' official policies. A union officer of more recent times may have been right in describing the old spinners' societies as 'all Chartist'.[4] If so, it was only the later, O'Connorist variety of Chartism that lingered—the Oldham spinners are reported to have rented land to employ members displaced by self-actor[5]—and this continued the Owenite Co-operative thought that had already influenced them in the 1830s. For them, as in a different sense for the other factory operatives, the 1840s represent a period of uncertainty and transition, of experiment in alternative forms of labour activity. In the upshot, the hand mule-spinners were to accommodate themselves with little discomfort to a gradual retirement before technical change; while the mass of newer factory hands were approaching their own mode of trade unionism. In the last wave of militant Chartism, the northern focus of disturbance shifted to the Yorkshire woollen centres.

*

However, the prime purpose of this account of the early cotton unions is just to set the background to their modern successors—

[1] R. Groves: *But We Shall Rise Again: A Narrative History of Chartism*, (Secker, London, 1938) p. 132.

[2] Thos. Banks, *A Short Sketch of the Cotton Trade of Preston for the last* 67 *Years* (Spinners' Institute, Preston, 1894). Banks himself began work as a seven-year-old factory lad in 1821; this address to his members recalls his memory of the times that followed.

[3] For some account of the strike's events, see *The Plug Riots of 1842 in Lancashire and Cheshire*, by A. G. Rose (Lancs. & Ches. Antiquarian Society, 1958).

[4] Fielding, in the Webb-Fielding MS. (loc. cit.).

[5] Chapman (op. cit.) p. 226.

the organizations of those newer industrial workers who have now been brought upon the scene. So the account can conclude with a general statement: the habit of association—'the natural gregariousness of similars' to which Ashley attributed the later strength of miners' trade unionism[1]—provided the early cotton union's stable base. But it does not fully explain their origin, because the formation of such a habit requires a certain occupational stability, the establishment of which was to some extent itself a result (clearly so in the spinners' case) of formal or informal regulation by the workers themselves. The early unions' history suggests a further condition of their appearance to have been the availability of a tradition of regulating working conditions derived from a previous age—or at least, of a nearby, suitable and functioning example of collective organization to follow. The handloom weavers inherited the Tudor tradition of the small master's trade monopoly: the factory mule-spinners took up the technique of the town journeyman's guild where the calico-printers left it off. But the spinners' brief initial phase as *domestic* operatives, drawn from or working beside domestic weavers and at first emulating the latters' organization, seems an essential link in their development.

Without this transitional connection, it is, in fact, difficult to explain the vigour of the early factory-spinners' unions. Their relative power has been attributed to their ability '. . . to turn out nine times their own number'.[2] In the factories, they were a group of men, identified by the practice of a common skill, amidst a labour force predominantly of women and young people. They controlled an early stage in the consecutive series of productive operations that made up the textile industry, so that a stoppage on their part immediately involved their own assistants, and must sooner or later involve the interdependent preparatory and manufacturing sequences. This disproportionate disarrangement of their business from spinners' strikes was certainly a cause of the special hostility with which, as the factory system developed, their activity came to be received by employers.[3]

But these same considerations would apply, with even greater force, to the male cardroom hands, who represented, at the factory's introduction at least, a group both similarly skilled and similarly situated in relation to the mass of operatives, but even less numerous proportionately and still more strategically positioned—at the preparatory stage of production itself. Moreover, as an occupation

[1] Ashley (op. cit.) p. 12.
[2] A report in the Webb Collection.
[3] See for instance Ure (*The Cotton Manufacture of Great Britain*, op. cit. p., 194 et seq.) on '. . . these tyrannical proceedings on the part of the "spinners" . . .'

the cardroom men's history antedates the spinners' by some years. The introduction of carding-engines (which required power of some kind) from the 1760s on was an important contribution to the concentration of economic power in the Lancashire cotton trade. And the mechanized preparation of fibre was (with the 'water frame' for spinning proper) an integral part of the Arkwright system, on which the first complete factories of the 1770s were constructed. Yet the cardroom hands produced no trade unionism until the closing years of the period here examined—in the early 1830s. And even then it was limited in coverage, of brief life only, and apparently touched off by the general labour movements of those years: it possessed no roots of its own.

Thus, these first cardroom workers' unions seem to have disappeared when the stimulus of general labour agitation was withdrawn. And this brings us back to the distinction made earlier in this chapter between a dependent trade unionism of their kind, and the independent sectional unionism that the early spinners' and weavers' associations must by now demonstrate to be deeply rooted in British labour history. The preceding discussion contains some hints of the character and sources of general labour movements. They seem to have had a frequent connection with occupational instability—as when the specialist hand-weavers' clubs merged into general weavers' associations, or all the cotton operatives' societies were drawn into industrial Chartism. It is equally obvious that the aims of such movements have a highly, if not primarily, political content. But of a stable sectional unionism, there appear two inter-related conditions. The traditions of the early weavers preserved active collective associations amongst them well into the period when their initial occupational identity was disintegrating. The early spinners were able to adapt preceding traditions to create an occupational stability. These two conditions—occupational stability, and an inherited or adaptable organizing tradition—provide the clues to the modern unions' development.

III

GROWTH OF THE MODERN UNIONS

1

The Theory of Labour Aristrocracy

I

Crudely sketched, the generally-accepted picture of British trade unionism's development would probably go rather as follows:—The unions' history really begins with the local 'trade clubs' of the eighteenth-century artisan. Occupational federations of such clubs occasionally rose to some brief power. But their effectiveness was generally limited by their essentially local basis, by the isolation and autonomy of their constituent units. This primitive organization in any case never touched more than a small proportion of wage-earners. Then came the Factory Revolution. The repeal of the Combination Acts set loose a much wider labour movement, in which political and economic objects were both nebulous and entangled. Thus, some of the surviving artisan trade clubs, together with many local associations of new workers, were swept into the 'Nationals' of the 1830s—loose mass organizations, militant in spirit, but weak in their basis and structure, and lacking in strategic and tactical realism. Upon the collapse of these general union organizations, the main force of working-class protest was for a while diverted to political channels. But meanwhile the skilled workers—several of whose groupings had in any case remained aloof from the ephemeral 'revolutionary' labour movement—once again drew together into reformed associations. And it was from these that an effective and durable form of trade union organization at last emerged. The 'New Models', the great craft unions of the 1850s on, owed their stability in part to their exclusive character.[1]

[1] Strictly, of course, the term 'New Model' applies only to the Amalgamated Society of Engineers itself. But it is conveniently used to describe the several re-groupings inspired and guided by that example.

But that stability also derived from their novel structure—the centralized amalgamation of former local or sectional unions. The craft unions provided 'The skilled labour base of English unionism . . .'[1] And it was their organizing experience—particularly, their elaboration of a sound trade union administration—upon which the permanent mass unions of the present century were at last founded.

There is rather more in such a sketch than a statement of the main order of historical events. There is also an implied theoretical proposition—that the organization of skilled workers is a necessary preliminary to the development of trade unionism in general. One might, indeed, describe it as proposing the labour movement's historical need of an aristocracy. And there is perhaps a secondary implication. The later 'industrial' and 'general' unions resembled the mid-nineteenth-century craft amalgamations in their monolothic organizational form—a form in which the degree of centralization certainly varied from union to union, but was always markedly greater than in the early 'Nationals' and the still earlier trade federations. And the sketch suggests that this form was, if not indispensable to mass unionism, at least a major factor in its growth and stability.

It is here, perhaps, that the textile unions' lack of a historian has most influenced the interpretation of union development. Because in them, the 'trade club' survived. By comparison with the centralized craft unions, the new cotton workers' 'Amalgamations' of the latter-nineteenth century were federal associations only. Their basic unit remained the autonomous local society—to this day colloquially known, in many places, as 'the club'. Upwards of two hundred such societies, rarely with more than a single full-time official, and the majority of them wholly administered by lay officers, have at one time or another composed the modern cotton workers' system of organization. And these societies have federated in several ways, of which the sectional or occupational Amalgamation is only the most prominent.

It is not clear, in fact, just how the sectional federations of the cotton operatives' local societies came to be called 'amalgamations' at all. The first such body to use the term appears to have been the East Lancashire Amalgamated Power-Loom Weavers' Friendly Association of 1858; and it seems very possible that the previous success of the Amalgamated Society of Engineers had identified the word, rather with the general idea of more united association, than

[1] Asa Briggs, in *The System of Industrial Relations in Great Britain* (Clegg and Flanders, ed., Blackwell, Oxford, 1954) p. 21.

with a particular organizational method[1]. The movement which produced the ASE was heavily concentrated in Lancashire; and the great lock-out of 1852 that tested and proved the mechanics' new organization itself stemmed from a dispute in an Oldham textile machinery works the previous year.[2]

At any rate, the cotton operatives made the old local trade club, and the federal association of trade clubs, work in a modern industrial context. One problem this raises is, of course, how they did it, and why they preserved that form. But this, we will put aside for a later chapter. A bigger question is raised by certain contrasts between the histories of the separate 'amalgamated' groups of cotton unions themselves.

It is not easy to present systematically the history of the numerous local unions and their inter-relationships: in the present scope, one can only isolate certain features. And what appears most significant here is the date from which a continuous formal existence can be recorded for the various local unions which now compose—or have composed (since not a few have in this century merged with neighbours, or dissolved on the disappearance of textile occupations from their locality)—the modern cotton Amalgamations. The date of each modern society's inception in this sense is plotted in the Chart 'Formation of Modern Cotton Unions', together with the formation dates of the main inter-union federations, and of some isolated but non-continuing unions which are of some interest.[3] The results fall into certain patterns: and these may at least open the theory of trade union development implied in this chapter's opening sketch to some doubt. The history of the cotton unions not only suggests that effective and stable unions of unskilled workers may appear *without* a prior organization of the skilled. There is some evidence in that history that where less-skilled workers do organize first, skilled unionism will be stimulated—and that where, on the contrary, the skilled workers are first to organize, the spread of trade unionism to others may be actually inhibited.

A question that must first be clarified, however, is the meaning of 'skilled' in this context. Few occupations 'in the cotton' are intrinsically skilled in the sense that their adequate performance necessarily requires any long preliminary training. Most of the work is simple

[1] It is notable, however, that though all the main sectional groupings of cotton workers are commonly described as 'amalgamations', to distinguish them from the local unions on the one hand and alternative types of federation on the other, three of those groupings avoid the word 'amalgamated' in their formal titles (see Chapter I, 2, section iv), describing themselves instead as the 'General Union' or 'National Association'.

[2] See James B. Jefferys, *The Story of the Engineers* (Lawrence & Wishart, London, 1945) Chapter I and II.

[3] This 'Main Chart' follows on pp. 112/3.

machine-tending—feeding the machine with its material, removing its product, keeping it clean and free from obstruction. Beyond that, by far the most common manual task is that known as 'piecing' (twisting together the ends of fibre), which involves only an acquired trick of manipulative dexterity. This is not to say that there is no great difference between old hands at such jobs and new workers. Many operatives acquire an intuitive perception of the performance of their machine and material, an ability to anticipate and forestall defects. But these capacities are not a product of training but of experience. And the difference they make are not so great that employers generally have refused inexperienced workers, or themselves installed any lengthy system of training. While several textile occupations that are usually regarded as more skilled, are so because other duties—like the supervision of other operatives, or the maintenance and setting of machinery—have been added to the fundamental task of machine-tending.

There are, in fact, few marked natural divisions of skill between the various jobs in the cotton trades. It is all a question of degree, and otherwise of the experience of individual operatives. But this situation is normal in industry rather than unique. The sharp demarcation between skilled and unskilled workers in, say, the building and engineering industries is largely a product of the traditional apprenticeship system, by reference to which those who may perform 'skilled' tasks are distinguished from those who may not. In that instance, the allocation of jobs has, in effect, been adapted to a classification of workers, rather than the classification of workers being based on the nature of the jobs they do. Of course, such demarcations may originally have derived from the possession of uncommon knowledge by a minority: but unless the latter's advantage is preserved by some artificial restriction, industrial skills usually spread all too easily from the point of view of their possessors —or are segmented into elements that can be readily communicated, or even reproduced mechanically.

Granted such a restriction of entry as apprenticeship, however, workers who have passed through that gate will naturally try to keep it narrow by increasing the tasks that new entrants must master, and by specifying those tasks as monopolies of the properly-admitted. While employers who are confronted with such a restriction will as naturally insist, since they cannot engage labour for 'skilled' jobs as they please, that the workers they *may* employ shall be as competent as possible. Several of the 'crafts' on which the nineteenth-century New Models founded themselves, in fact, only survived as such because of an earlier struggle to maintain the apprenticeship system in changed industrial and technical

FORMATION OF MODERN COTTON UNIONS

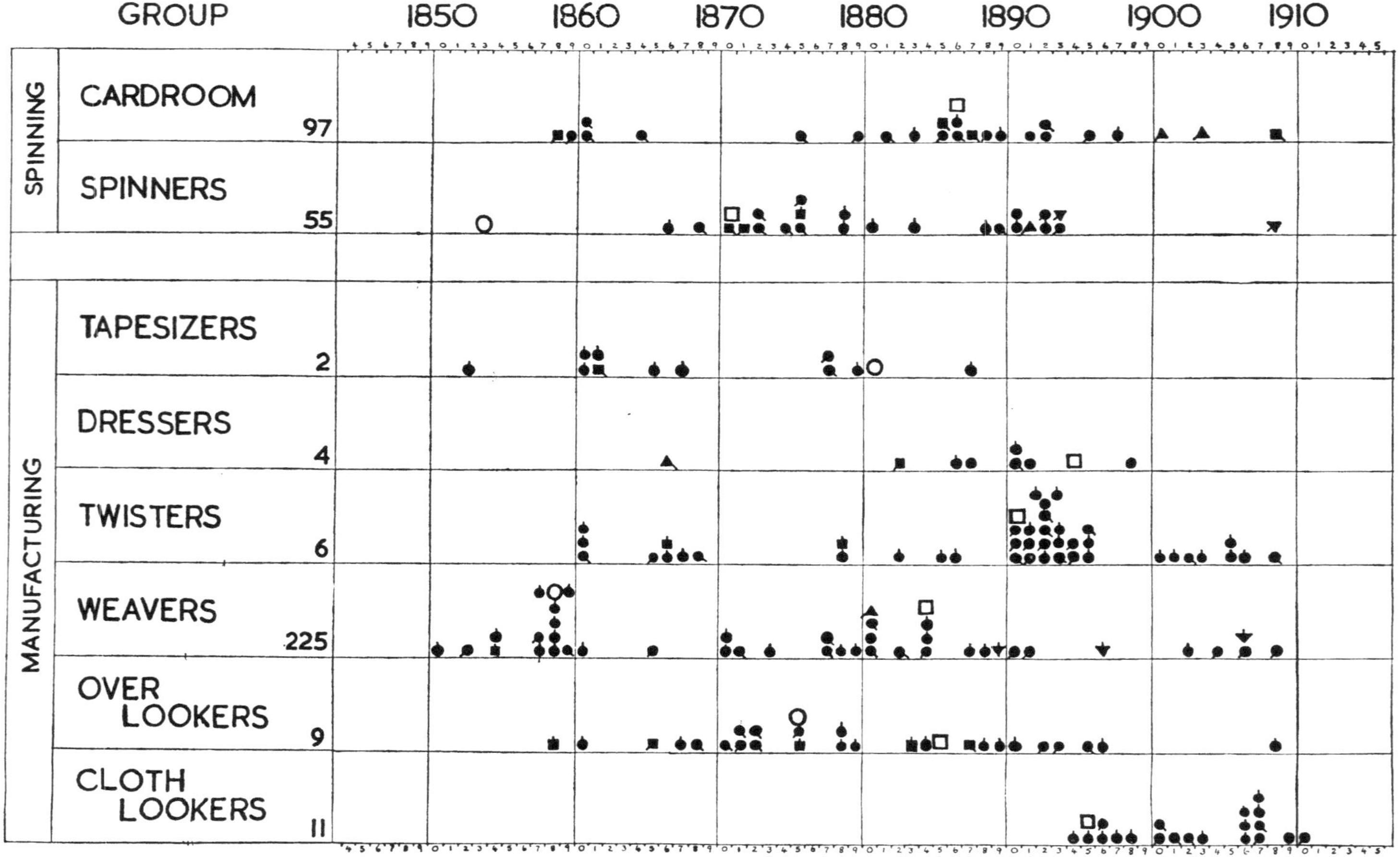

KEY:

LOCAL ASSOC^NS
- ● NORMAL.
- ■ MULTI-BRANCH.
- ▲ NON-CONTINUING.
- ▼ OPPOSITIONIST.

MARK TO LOCAL ASSOC^N SHOWS DISTRICT. eg:
- ● N. & N.E. LANCS
- ● BOLTON-M/C ('EGYPTIAN' AREA)
- ● S.E. LANCS ('AMERICAN' AREA)
- ● YORKSHIRE

AMALGAMATIONS
- ○ LIMITED
- □ GENERAL

MEMBERSHIP: TO NEAREST THOUSAND, FOLLOWS TITLE (EXCLUDING ▲ AND ▼), & IS AT PEAK (USUALLY 1920/21).

MAIN CHART

E

Information from various sources, particularly (for all groups except the Spinners and Warehousemen) the *Annual Reports* of the Labour Correspondent of the Board of Trade. In the case of the Weavers, these have been supplemented by notes on the history of local unions made by Mr E. Hopwood, their Amalgamation's former Assistant General Secretary, and in several other cases by the records of individual Amalgamations or unions. Such unions as are registered have been checked with the Registrar of Friendly Societies. The dates of the Warehousemen's local societies (which are, incidentally, described in the Chart by their original title of the 'Clothlookers') are from the records of the present Amalgamation only, and those of the Spinners' unions from an unpublished thesis by R. Smith, *The Lancashire Cotton Trade, 1873–96* (for the degree of Ph.D. at the University of Birmingham, 1954) with some additions from the Spinners' records, the Webb-Fielding MS., and other sources.

The list is not complete, although it includes over 200 unions and associations: about a score of smaller local unions which have been known to exist cannot be traced in this way. These include especially a group of minor spinners' societies. The spinners' unions in the 1880s were unusually diverse in size—about half of them having less than 100 members. Several of these were in such outlying places as Bristol and Derby and have been long extinct. The spinners were unusual in having locals so distant from the now-traditional cotton area in the mid-nineteenth century; but since these small outlying clubs appear to have been of hand-mule spinners, and thus survivals of (or descendants from) the earlier period when spinning was more widely dispersed, their non-inclusion does not materially affect the development the Chart portrays.

Three important general federations are not included. The UTFWA took its present form in the late '80s. And the International Textile Workers' Association was initiated by the British unions, responding to the time's intenser foreign competition, in 1894. The Northern Counties Textile Trades Federation linked the manufacturing Amalgamations in 1906.

circumstances. The Lancashire textile-machinery makers, for instance, reported of the introduction of the basic modern machine-tools between 1800 and 1840 that '. . . machinery (can be) made almost by labourers whereas before it required, without these tools, first-rate workmen'; but they also complained that they had been unable to take full advantage of this because the engineering operatives '. . . have combinations among themselves, and they are very tenacious of their rights'.[1] And there are cases on the other hand—a major instance will be developed later—in which a 'skill' has been quite artificially created, by the workers' gradual imposition of labour supply controls on a formerly 'unskilled' occupation.

From the viewpoint of trade union development, at least, workers are thus 'skilled' or 'unskilled' according to whether or not entry to their occupation is deliberately restricted, and not in the first place according to the nature of the occupation itself. From this angle, the cotton unions can be readily classified. All but two of the cotton amalgamations are composed of unions which are commonly called 'closed'. The Spinners, the Overlookers and the Twisters, the Tapesizers, the Warpdressers and to some extent the Warehousemen, all have systems of regulating the intake of new labour. These systems differ from union to union, and are in no case the traditional apprenticeship as it is known in the craft unions of other industries, but they are nevertheless effective—in some amalgamations for the whole membership, in others for the latter's major section. The Weavers' and Cardroom Amalgamations, on the other hand, consist of so-called 'open' unions, with no control over entry except in the case of one or two numerically unimportant departments.

II

One thing that clearly appears from the plotting of the unions' initiation dates is that no new organizations were formed after 1910. The structure of the cotton operatives' organizations was crystallized before the great 'general' and 'industrial' unions of the present day had emerged, and underwent no notable modification later. Considering the changes that have occurred in the labour movement at large since that year, and the violent transition in the cotton industry's own condition, this is itself a fact of some significance. But this again will be a matter for later discussion. For present purposes, the more important thing the Chart reveals is that no modern cotton union can trace a continuous history before 1850—this, despite the existence

[1] To the Select Committee on the Export of Machinery, 1841, quoted by Jefferys (op. cit.) p. 22.

of labour combinations in the industry over a preceding century. This is not to say, of course, that there were no unions of the modern classes of operatives before that date. But the relation between old and new workers was still undefined: the two classes were, in fact, in competition with each other—a competition often involving conflicts which were reflected in their attempts at organization.

Thus the Lancashire spinners reformed their federation in 1842—the year of the Plug Riots, and probably to resist the wage-reductions which seem to have been the main occasion of their participation in those events. And the new federation's title—the Association of Operative Cotton Spinners, Twiners and *Self-Acting Minders* of the United Kingdom[1]—indicated an attempt to bring in the new workers. This federation seems to have been very active for three or four years, organizing support for local disputes by irregular levies, and sending deputations to employers in particular towns in an attempt to ensure the payment of customary rates. A former secretary of the Bolton hand-mule spinners, S. Holmes, alleged that the federation '. . . caused poverty and distress in the federated districts by promoting strikes'.[2] But another spinners' leader, Fielding, said that it seemed '. . . to have been fully recognised by employers as representative of workers in the various localities.'[3] The federation's most notable activity, however, was its support—if not promotion—of the 'Short-Time Committee', which was now organizing an agitation to limit factory hours that was apparently more strongly-based than preceding campaigns of this kind.

But the federation had a fluctuating affiliation, and was itself based on Bolton—rapidly becoming the great centre of fine-spinning, and the district in which the advance of the self-actor machine was slowest. The federation could not, it seems overcome the hostility between the old hand-mule spinners and the new 'minders'. The old spinners not only feared undercutting by the automatic process in general; there were many specific causes of grievance between the two groups. Employers, for instance, would bribe away the hand-spinners' assistants to operate the new machines by offering (and this was not difficult) higher wages than the spinners paid them, thus dealing a double blow at the spinners' aristocratic position. And when self-actors were installed to beat or forestall strikes the bitterness was particularly strong. To this day, old operatives still have many tales to illustrate the contempt of the hand-mule spinners for the (to their thinking) unskilled 'minders'. Several societies

[1] Authors' italics. 'Twining', incidentally, is a process of doubling yarn on adapted mule-frames, now almost extinct.

[2] In a Note in the Webb Collection.

[3] Note in the Webb-Fielding MS.

excluded the self-actor men from their membership; in other towns rival unions were formed. In Bolton itself—which had at first apparently set out to recruit the new workers—a separate 'Self-Actor Society' was formed in 1861, and although this later became the most completely-organized of spinners' unions, it was not until 1880 that the hand-mule spinners there finally reconciled themselves to their diminished empire and merged the remnant of their union with the new body. Inside the 1842 federation, moreover, local unions linked up to form alternative groupings. The Oldham spinners' society, for instance, was re-formed in 1843 to resist an employers' demand that spinners supervise four or six mules instead of the customary two (which suggests that many of its members were already working self-actors). And this society developed into a federation of local unions in the coarse-spinning district about its headquarters town that rivalled the Bolton-dominated grouping. And after the 1847 slump, both Oldham and Bolton withdrew (together with Manchester) from the spinners' general association, which then remained only as an expiring federation of small societies.

The distinction between old and new workers was, of course, much more marked in the weaving than the spinning trade. The difference between the hand-mule and the self-actor when the latter came in was small; they were both powered machines, but the former was only semi-automatic. Later, it was found possible to convert powered hand-mules to self-acting; and the operators of both machines were to be found together in the same factory and even in the same workroom. The gap between the power-loom and the hand-loom weaver, on the other hand, was that between the factory and domestic worker—and one widened by sex difference. Though women were allowed to take over the hand-looms of husbands who enlisted for the great French wars, and afterwards the number of female workers probably increased as hand-loom weaving degenerated, most of the hand-weavers were still men. But the early 'steam-weavers' were women or boys. Nevertheless, combinations of factory weavers appeared very early. Indeed, their first strike occurred when a competitive powerloom was still under development in the Stockport mills.[1] There, the operatives were drawn into the great Lancashire strike wave of 1818—only, it seems, to be defeated in this initial battle. The weavers demanded a fifty per cent. wage-advance, but their employer brought in strike-breakers from the Midlands, and the affair ended in a riot and the calling in of the

[1] The *total* number of workers in powered weaving-factories at this time was put by Ellison at about 10,000 (quoted by Wood, op. cit., Table 39)—for Britain as a whole.

cavalry.[1] The power-loom weavers' reaction to the repeal of the Combination Acts was notably stronger than that of the domestic workers: those round Manchester struck again for several months in 1825. Four unions of factory weavers affiliated to the NAPL in 1830. And from then on there is a growing—if cryptic—record of activity on their part.

In the boom of 1834–7, factory weavers' unions were formed and re-formed in several major centres—Glasgow and Preston, for instance, and twice in Oldham, where the first district wage-list for power-loom weaving also appeared in 1834. But these unions seem to have suffered the same eclipse as the spinners' societies in 1837. (In fact, the whole pattern of the factory weavers' early activity clearly resembles that of the contemporary mule-spinners' combinations rather than that of the handloom weavers, though there is no evidence of any direct industrial co-operation between the two classes of factory worker beyond their brief association in the NAPL.) The power-loom weavers' recovery, however, seems actually to have ante-dated that of the much older spinners' organization. In 1840, when a temporary revival of trade occurred, they attempted a general association of some kind: the 'Powerloom Weavers of Great Britain and Ireland' was formed in Manchester, apparently to support a Stockport weavers' strike. Though little is known of this federation, and its career seems to have been short, the factory weavers' part in the great 1842 strike (the Plug Plot, again) has already been noted; and a fluctuating organization of power-loom weavers was maintained in Manchester itself for twenty years thereafter—until the modern society was established.[2] Power-loom weavers, like the spinners, sent observers to the meeting of the National Association of United Trades for the Protection of Labour in 1845. And by the late 1840s their militancy seems to have exceeded that of the spinning operatives. There was a spate of local power-loom weavers' strikes against wage-reductions in 1846, a similar upsurge for wage-increases in 1848, and for several years on, mill stoppages of weavers were recurrent.

In the latter nineteenth century, the characteristic concentration of the early factory operatives' activity in boom periods disappeared —something probably not unconnected with their acquisition of professional leaderships. Major stoppages were now occasioned by both wage-reductions and wage-demands. Even so, the early hand-weavers' and -spinners' roles seem to have been somewhat reversed in their modern successors: a detailed study of industrial disputes

[1] See Aspinall's No. 223.

[2] The 'modern society' itself, the Manchester and Salford Weavers' Association, has recently merged in the Ashton weavers' union.

in the nineteenth-century's last quarter, for instance, shows that whereas most spinning stoppages arose from wage-cuts (or equivalent causes), most weaving strikes were in support of wage demands.[1]

But it was not until the mid-1830s that it became clear that the future lay with the power-loom. The development of stable power-loom weavers' unions was, of course, also inhibited by the recurrent depressions of the following decade; several other classes of factory workers first formed unions about 1830 which apparently disappeared in the following great slump. And in weaving the transition from hand- to machine-work was much quicker, as well as more radical, than in spinning. It is also possible that, in weaving, the mere width of the gap between old and new workers limited direct friction between them—just as such friction was engendered in spinning by their closely shouldering each other at the workplace itself. Nevertheless, for many years after the 1840s surviving traces of the competition between hand- and machine-worker are to be found in the quality-weaving branches where the hand-loom persisted. The Bolton 'Excelsior Friendly Society of Toilet and Marseilles Quilt Weavers by Power' of 1865, for instance, forbade its members to instruct hand-weavers in power-loom weaving, and the formation of a rival hand-loom union in that town in 1880 (it survived at least till 1893) was probably stimulated by this rule's re-affirmation by the re-organized Bolton power-loom weavers' union of that year.

III

However, by the nineteenth-century's mid-point, a clear change in the cotton operatives' situation had occurred. In its recovery from the great slumps of the 1840s, the cotton trade itself had crystallized into a recognizably modern form. The violence of its expansion was now much diminished[2]: no new textile districts were opened up after this time—the later trend was rather to a concentration in certain existing centres. In some sections of the trade, indeed, subsequent growth seems to have occurred almost entirely in already-established firms.[3] The newer workers were still very mobile. There is a fascinating picture of the factory weavers' life about this time in the diary of an active trade unionist, John Ward.[4] The fragment was written in the far north-east Lancashire district.

[1] R. Smith, unpublished thesis (op. cit.).
[2] Compare the tables of Chapter I, 2, section iv.
[3] See, for instance, Turnbull (op. cit., p. 111).
[4] *The Diary of John Ward of Clitheroe, Weaver, 1860–64*, (Ed. R. Sharpe France) *Transactions*, Historical Society of Lancashire and Cheshire, 1953.

Ward himself came from the south-east, but on returning to visit his relatives—also weavers—found them all moved to other towns: during the four years the diary covers, one of Ward's brothers moved once, the other three times, while his only daughter married a spinner and left with him for another district. But this mobility was geographical, not occupational. The Lancashire landscape was now dominated by towns where cotton provided the major livelihood, between which workers moved readily to better themselves *in their trade*. This combination of occupational stability with geographical movement must itself have furthered the new unionism's spread.

Besides this settlement in their economic position, there were social changes among the workers—a reconciliation with the new order expressed in attempts to adapt it to their needs rather than to overthrow it. Revolutionary political ideas were losing their influence among them—a delegate meeting of the Bolton Spinners' Federation in 1846, indeed, pronounced that '. . . in future the Central Committee shall not be allowed to expend any money on any political subject whatsoever'; and in the next year the same body denied public reports that the unions had taken part in election campaigns because such activities '. . . are opposed to the principles of this association.'[1] The reaction was perhaps extreme: more generally, the operatives had just received a lesson in the possibilities of political 'pressure-group' tactics—for specific improvements as opposed to sweeping reforms. In contrast to the failure of militant Chartism, the largely middle-class campaign for the repeal of the Corn Laws secured cheaper food to the workers in 1846—and the landed interests in Parliament by way of revenge backed the Factory Bill of 1847, and thus fulfilled the operatives' own demand for the ten-hour day. The years of working-class political agitation, however, were not without an indirect effect—especially, it seems likely, upon the new classes of factory worker without native traditions of collective organization. Place wrote of the earlier Reform Movement that '. . . in spite of the demoralizing influence of so many of our laws, and the operation of the poor laws, it has impressed the morals and manners, and elevated the character of the working man . . . Within a few years . . . "Lancashire brute" was the common and appropriate appellation. Until very lately it would have been dangerous to have assembled five hundred on any occasion. Bakers and butchers would at least have been plundered. Now a hundred thousand people may be collected together and no riot ensue, and why? Why, . . . that the people have an object.'[2]

[1] Quoted by the *CFT*, May 19, 1933.

[2] Quoted by Graham Wallas in *The Life of Francis Place* (4th edn., Allen & Unwin, London, 1951) pp. 145–6.

The 1840s, the experimental and transitional period of the cotton workers' history, were thus also a period of practical education to them. The Ten-Hour Act itself helped them to complete the process. It gave a direct stimulus to the trade union revival, particularly among the spinners; between 1847 and 1850 there were many mill strikes against evasions of the new law. But the reduction in hours also fertilized a crop of 'Mutual Improvement Societies' in the northern towns: Ward the weaver was a patron of a local Mechanics Institute. This cultural progress, if moderate, was by no means unimportant to the unions themselves. Ward's diary and the memoir of Banks the spinner[1] both give a picture of conscientious, literate if self-educated men, serious students of their trade's condition, who despite personal poverty (Ward notes an Easter Sunday ham-and-egg breakfast as an annual feast) handled large sums of money on behalf of their fellows.[2] And an unreliability of elected officers had frequently handicapped the early societies.

The revived unionism itself reinforced the spirit that fostered it: a decline in the incidental violence of industrial disputes is noted by several commentators in the 1850s. And a middle-class observer of a northern textile area reported '. . . a very decided improvement, both physical, moral, economic and social . . . where Union prevails'.[3] The cotton operatives, of course, were merely anticipating a quite general phenomenon: the Social Science Association's Committee of 1860 recorded '. . . their opinion distinctly that the improvement in the management of Trades Societies has been most marked and satisfactory'. But in the cotton districts this progress was particularly advanced by the rapid growth of consumers' co-operation after the Rochdale Society (itself formed by weavers) found a practical operating principle in 1844. The Co-operative Societies seem, in fact, not only to have strengthened the individual worker's position (they helped many through the Cotton Famine of the 1860s) but to have offered, in many Lancashire towns, a similar support to the nascent unions as did the Friendly Societies to their predecessors. This they did by such things as extending credit to strikers (even gifts of groceries) and giving direct help to union organization in the form of meeting-rooms, office-premises and suchlike facilities; on occasion, they actually assisted in the formation or management of local unions.

These changes were beginning to be reflected in the workers'

[1] See Chapter II, 2, section VII.

[2] Banks became secretary to the Preston spinners' club in 1854 and Ward was elected chairman of his local weavers' club in 1860.

[3] A letter quoted by Ludlow and Jones in *The Progress of the Working Class, 1832–67* (London, 1867).

relations with their employers. By 1860 '. . . the spirit of hostility by which workmen had been so long animated against the heads of manufacturing establishments vanished'.[1] The change was probably more marked in the newly-developed factory districts of north Lancashire: in and around Manchester itself, conditions were still bad and a great deal of revolutionary feeling survived.[2] And even in the northern districts great conflicts were yet to come. But for the time being, at least, the manufacturers there were anxious to press on with their revived trade undisturbed, and an attitude of mutual acceptance was developing. Already by 1852 in the north-eastern cotton districts '. . . both sides (had) got tired of the constant trouble. This was the first time when the masters agreed to meet the men on an equity'.[3] The workers of Lancashire at mid-century were on the eve of a development which was to carry them in a decade—according to an observer of their condition in 1860—to '. . . the head of the English working class. They had the highest wages, and were, of all workers, the most intelligent and best organised.[4]'

IV

Despite the atomistic structure of the modern cotton unions, it is easier to trace the nineteenth-century growth of their organization than of their memberships. This is a pity, because the two do not always coincide, except in their generally improving trend. The expansion of union membership and the evolution of union organization are in general obviously inter-related. But it is also necessary to draw a fairly clear distinction between the two things.

Organizational development—that is, the formation of new unions or the re-organization and closer association of existing ones—is, for instance, partly stimulated by defeats. These, as will be shown, were certainly not the only factor; and their influence became clear only when the unions had acquired professional leaders, who responded to them by drives to improve the operatives' preparedness

[1] M. I. Tougan-Baranowsky, *Les Crises Industrielles en Angleterre* (Paris, 1913) pp. 398/9.

[2] See, of course, Engels, *The Condition of the English Working Class in 1844.* For a brief general picture of operatives' conditions in 1860, W. O. Henderson, *The Lancashire Cotton Famine, 1861–5* (MUP, 1934) Chapter 1.

[3] Eccles Shorrock: *A Letter to the Workpeople of North and North-East Lancashire* (Manchester, 1880). See also Shorrock's *Particulars as to the Progress of the Cotton Trade in Blackburn and the Formation of the First Council of Conciliation in 1852.*

[4] Tougan-Baranowsky (op. cit.). So far as the cotton operatives were concerned the statement about relative wages could probably only be substantiated in reference to such groups as the spinners or to family earnings.

for future conflicts. But they were definitely important. Thus the present Spinners' Amalgamation was formed, and its two biggest constituents—the Oldham and Bolton unions—re-organized, after the 1869 strike of the Preston textile workers against wage-reductions, which was defeated after seven months. This strike also seems to have inspired the forming (or re-organization) of several weavers' unions.[1] A major wave of union formation amongst the weavers was similarly set off by the movements against wage-cuts in the mid-1870s, which culminated in the 'Great Strike' of north Lancashire mills in 1878, when over 100,000 workers either struck or were locked-out for nearly two months. And another organizational surge in spinners' unionism followed the four months' stoppage of the Oldham district in 1885—again induced by wage-reductions; while this lock-out was also the direct cause of the present Cardroom Amalgamation's creation.

*

Defeats, on the other hand, generally also caused a fall of union membership. Recorded strengths of both the spinners' and weavers' unions, for example, show a marked decline after the Great Strike of 1878. We have few early membership figures for the modern unions—much less, continuous series. And such statistics may be misleading if, for instance, taken to indicate the degree of collective organization at the time, because many modern unions had less formal predecessors, the membership of which is unrecorded.[2] Moreover, the modern unions retained for a while some other qualities of the earlier associations besides the latters' essentially local basis. In particular, it is likely that the demarcation between unionists and non-unionists was at first less sharp than it became after the industrial impact of the great 1870s' depression forced the unions to tighten up their organization. Thus, they continued for some time to collect funds from and pay strike-benefit to non-members: the weavers' unions did not cease the latter practice until near the century's end, and some of them probably consisted at first of no more than a core of activists, who were nevertheless capable of mobilizing many times their own number when the need arose. And Rules of Warehousemen's local branches drawn up in the present century indicate that in this, the last of the cotton operatives' amalgamations to develop, strike-pay to non-members still continued: their Bolton Committee, for instance, is authorized '. . . in all cases of dispute . . . to grant pecuniary support

[1] These movements can be traced in the Main Chart.

[2] Statistics for the smaller Amalgamations need particularly careful handling up to quite recent times, because they are also much affected by secessions and re-affiliations.

to any person who might stand as an obstacle in the way of obtaining our rights.'[1] Certainly, the nominal membership of such unions is a much less conclusive indication of their strength than is that of the more-emphatically 'closed' spinners, or of the craft unions outside.

However, actual union membership would at least indicate changes in the solidity of the operatives' collective affiliation. But of it, we have before the 1870s only scattered notations: we are told, for instance, that three groups of cotton unions were represented at those precursors of the present TUC, the conferences of Organized Trades in 1866 and 1867—the 'Northern Association of Cotton Spinners' with 6,000 members, the 'Power Loom Weavers (Blackburn)' with 5,000 members, and the 'East Lancs. Power Loom Weavers' with 6,000 members.[2] But for the last body—which, of course represents the weavers' 'Amalgamated' association of 1858 already referred to,[3] and is usually and conveniently called by them 'The First Amalgamation'—it is possible to link up such items into something like a continuous series (this is charted in Graph II, which follows later in this chapter). And such information, when associated with later and more reliable records, does suggest one respect in which the unions' organizational and numerical growths may have coincided.

The epoch of the modern cotton unions' development (like that of their industry's expansion after 1850) is divided by the great depression of the 1870s. The flurry of industrial conflict at mid-century, culminating in the bitter Preston strike of 1853, introduced two decades that are certainly not to be interpreted as ones of industrial harmony, but in which conflict was at least relatively localized. If there were many mill strikes, and if one district strike in 1859 especially represented a protracted test of the new weavers' organization, there were no industry-wide struggles. And during this period, development was concentrated in the new factory towns of north and north-east Lancashire (as with the earliest textile workers, labour agitation always tended to focus on the most rapidly-advancing industrial centres).

The seven months' Preston strike of 1869 was perhaps an omen, but the scene certainly changes in the mid-'70s. The uncertain years from 1872 lead into a major slump (see Graph I, Ch. I, 2) and initiate

[1] *Rules* of the Amalgamated Textile Warehousemen, Bolton Branch, 1906.

[2] According to Ludlow and Jones (op. cit.).

[3] The unions have often been very loose in the use of their titles, which combines with the frequent similarity of the latter and the number of the former to create confusion. One agreement n this century, for instance, was signed by 'The Northern Counties' Amalgamation of Warpers and Winders', which on search proved actually to be the Amalgamated Weavers' Association!

a generation's extensive conflict. The Great Strike of 1878 was anticipated by major stoppages of the Oldham and Bolton districts in 1875 and 1877 respectively: and the period culminates in the 'Stalybridge' and 'Brooklands' lock-outs of 1891–2 and 1893—which each involved as many workers as the Great Strike itself, if not more. Over these two decades, the focus of industrial conflict shifted to the spinning centres of south-east Lancashire—so much so that one is tempted to call this whole period the Southern phase of cotton union growth, as against the Northern phase of 1848-70.

The shift, during the 1870s, in the geographical focus of both union development and industrial conflict was certainly remarked by contemporaries. 'We are glad,' said Banks the Preston spinner of of the 1885 dispute in Oldham, 'that the battlefield has been removed from this part of Lancashire to a younger battalion, whose souls are in arms for the fray.' The coarse-spinning trade was first to feel the sharpened foreign competition that followed the 1870s, and which by limiting the industry's further export growth intensified its internal competition. The trade responded with a heightened technical innovation, a general speeding-up of work, and an economic re-grouping. The joint stock company had been remarkably absent from the cotton industry before this time[1]: the typical employer was the owner/manager, who met his workers face-to-face. The new 'Oldham Limiteds', however, moved in a stormy labour climate of their own creation.

Some two-thirds of the local unions of which the initiation has been traced (see Main Chart) were formed after 1875. The majority of those originating before that date did so in the north Lancs. districts; while those formed afterwards were mostly in south Lancs. or in Yorkshire. Even if—as probably was the case for the spinners and weavers—the new local unions were only formalizations of already associated groupings, this itself signified an organizational development. While most of the unions of *other* operatives were certainly created after the mid-'70s: among these workers, the evidence is that organization was very weak before that time. And it is equally certain that in the next twenty years union membership generally was moving up to a new level.

Otherwise, however, membership is affected by several factors—by prosperity and depression, by the growing general acceptance of labour's right to organize (though the waves of unionization in cotton bear no very close correspondence to those outside), as well as by the mere passage of time, which increased not merely the degree of union affiliation among cotton operatives but also its

[1] According to Gayer, Rostow and Schwartz (op. cit., p. 416), of some 950 joint stock companies existing in 1844, only one was in cotton.

Graph II: UNION MEMBERSHIP

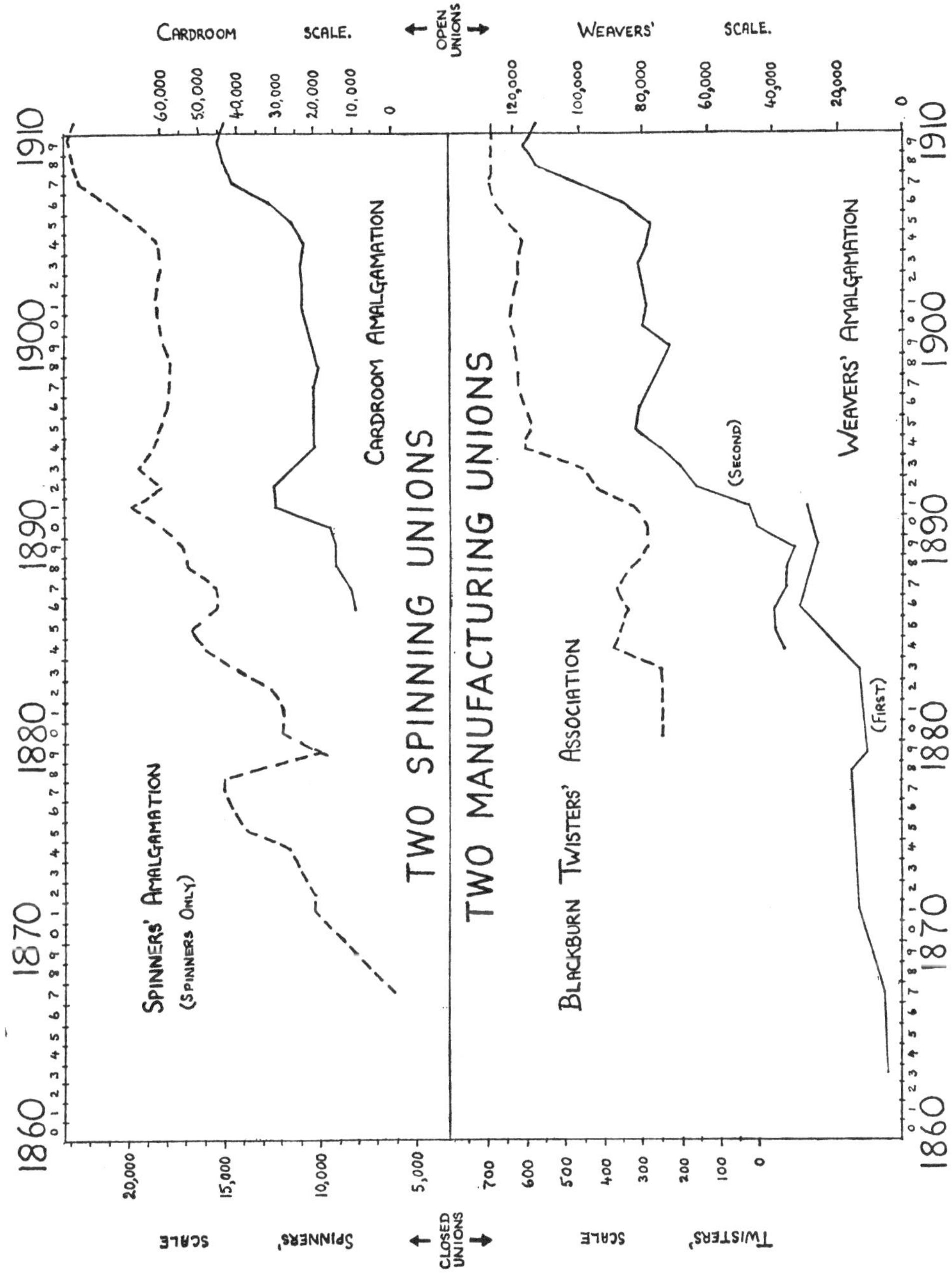

stability. For instance, the temporary falls in membership that followed unsuccessful strikes (as well as some successful but protracted ones) became notably shallower as the unions matured.

But there is one thing that the available membership records certainly illustrate. Graph II traces those of four labour organizations through the later period covered by the Main Chart. They include the two Amalgamations in the spinning trade—the 'closed' Spinners and 'open' Cardroom: and these are paralleled by two analagous organizations in the manufacturing industry, the 'open' Weavers' Amalgamation and a 'closed' twisters' union (the only such group in the weaving section for which a satisfactory membership record has come to the writer's hand). All four records are, of course, affected by the very broad trend sketched above. *Within* each of the cotton trade's two main sections, moreover, the detailed membership fluctuations of the open and closed organization respectively are very similar (though, as one would expect, the closed association's strength varies less widely). But *as between* the two sections of the industry, the changes in union membership differ considerably. For two or three years after 1886, for instance, the weaving unions' membership falls, probably as an aftermath to their exhausting twenty weeks' Ashton strike of 1886–7. But in the same years the spinning unions' membership is rising as the Spinners themselves recover ground lost in their hard-fought retreat at Oldham in 1885, and the new Cardroom Amalgamation scores its first successes. After their great lock-outs of 1891–3, however, the strength of the two spinning organizations falls significantly; but at this time the Weavers have secured their first 'industry-wide' wage agreement, and the manufacturing unions' membership continues to rise.

These differences were possible because the technical, economic and geographical divisions between the spinning and weaving sections were widening to such an extent, in the 1860s and '70s, as to make them virtually two separate industries.[1] And this fact makes it possible to compare union development in the two trades from the viewpoint of this chapter's opening discussion, of the role of a 'labour aristocracy' in union growth.

V

The Main Chart shows that in both the cotton industries, the first formally-continuing local unions to be established were 'open' organizations—of cardroom operatives in spinning, and weavers in manufacturing. However, the cardroom unions remained few and weak until quite late in the period covered by the Main Chart.

[1] See Chapter I, 2, section v, again.

Before the forming of their own Amalgamation in 1886, they had only a few thousand members. Apart from them, informal groups of cardroom hands from time-to-time conducted local negotiations, or even strikes; but as late as 1872 one such effort (in Rishton) was organized by the local co-operative society because of the cardroom workers' lack of association and experience.[1] Despite the spinners' comparatively late development of stable unions of a modern type, their associations dominated the cotton trade's spinning section. It was in fact, only on the eve of World War I that even their membership (including 'piecers') was overhauled by that of the cardroom unions, although the latter had a much wider field of recruitment. In the manufacturing industry, however, there is no doubt of the Weavers' pre-eminence, whether in terms of activity or membership; in the latter, they always exceeded all the other manufacturing unions together.

One element was common to the new unions' techniques. This was the political agitation for limited ends—a method inherited from the Short-Time Committees of the 1830s and '40s. The unions of the different groups of cotton workers co-operated, from 1871, in the Factory Acts Reform Committee, which seems to have been re-formed in 1883 and finally emerged as the United Textile Factory Workers' Association[2]—the body that now acts both as a federal link between all the various Amalgamations and as the vehicle of their affiliation to the Labour Party. Individual Amalgamations conducted campaigns of their own for legal improvements in their members' conditions. The Weavers, particularly, maintained a persistent agitation in the 1880s and '90s for the statutory control of 'steaming' in weaving sheds and on similar issues: such campaigns were clearly a major device by which their modern Amalgamation built up its strength. In their industrial techniques proper, however, there is a marked difference between them and the Spinners.

The emphasis of the Spinners' policy, over the interval between the decline of the old hand-mule societies and the stabilization of their modern unions, was on control of labour supply. When Roberts, Sharp & Co. marketed their perfected self-actor mule in 1830 they listed among its advantages: '*First* . . . the saving of a "spinner's" wages to each pair of mules, piecers only being required, one overlooker being sufficient to manage 6 or 8 pairs of mules or upwards.'[3] And it has been shown that saving wages was by no

[1] According to R. Smith, unpublished thesis (op. cit.).

[2] The UTFWA is usually given (by the Webbs, for instance) as having been formed in 1886, but Board of Trade reports give it as formed July '83, dissolved August '86 and re-formed October '89. The UTFWA itself does not have its own early records—or indeed, any systematic collection before 1932.

[3] From a leaflet reproduced by Ure (op. cit.), p. 199.

means the only motive employers had for escaping from their dependence on the spinners: the latters' collective militancy was also a major pressure. Nevertheless, the new self-actor minders reproduced exactly the old spinners' system of machine-manning and entry control. The minders themselves adopted the title and role of 'spinner': each continued to supervise just one pair of mules with its quota of two male piecers, from whom alone the minders were recruited and that in strict order of seniority at the individual mill. And that this system was far from being adopted at the employers' choice is shown by the many local battles that were fought over it. Its connection with an early revival of the Oldham union in 1843 has been remarked; as late as 1888 it was still an issue where hand-mules were undergoing a belated replacement.[1] It is notable that in outlying Lancashire districts where the spinners' unionism had been weak, women were employed on mules until well on into these times. And in Glasgow, where the spinners' association never recovered from its debacle of 1837–8, the working of mules by gangs of women under an overlooker became a regular—apparently by the 1880s, the dominant—system.[2]

The new power-loom weavers' trades unionism, however, developed in a context of free entry to their occupation. The old hand-loom apprenticeship had been virtually extinct (except in one or two small and isolated specialist branches) for at least a generation before power-loom weavers became at all numerous, and was in any case incapable of adaptation to their circumstances. In the few cases where they did attempt to regulate entry, it was by a system neither resembling that, nor identical with the Spinners'. And it was not until the new weavers' unionism was very well developed that it began to concern itself with its members' machine-complements. The power-loom weavers' pre-occupation was with the elaboration of standard wage-rates.

This is not to say, of course, that the spinners were uninterested in wages: the famous 'Blackburn List' of wage-rates, which in 1853 embodied the reconciliation of that district's employers to the fact of their workers' collective organization (and which some have called the Cotton Operatives' Charter), included a scale of spinning prices. And later major conflicts in spinning all concerned what were essentially wage-issues. But these were mostly *general* wage-reductions: the new spinners' success in establishing a regulation of labour supply by persistent local pressure itself guaranteed their *relative*

[1] The *Cotton Factory Times* for August 21 of that year carried an attack on the method of working 6 or 8 sets of mules by piecers (young assistants) with only one overlooker in charge.

[2] See Wood (op. cit.) p. 103.

wages. That success is shown in the rapidity with which self-actor spinners' wages overhauled those of the surviving hand-mule aristocrats: in Manchester about 1850, the formers' earnings were only some half the latters'; but by the 1880s the proportion had risen to over four-fifths.[1] However, the spinners' lesser concern with standard wage-rates is demonstrated by the fact that the various local spinning wage-lists were not finally merged until 1949, and this under governmental pressure. That the intensity of the weavers' drive for standard rates was much the greater is shown by their securing of a Uniform List of Wages over half a century before. When the weavers' so-called First Amalgamation revised its Rules in 1878, in fact, it declared its primary object to be: 'To maintain as far as possible a uniform rate of wages . . .'[2]

VI

It was, in fact, just their concentration upon standard wage-rates which induced the weavers' special contribution to trade union development, and one which seems the key to their own early consolidation. This was their adoption of full-time officials, and those of a type so distinctive that they might almost be described as trade union technicians. This invention was a direct consequence of the 1853 Blackburn List's agreement.

The payment of wages by piece-rates has been general in cotton factories since their earliest days, except for certain classes of operative who had no equivalent in the still earlier domestic industry. The factory industry, in fact, took over the piece-rate system from the domestic spinning and weaving trades (where it was inevitable), if for no other reason than that factory and domestic production were for a long transitional period complementary to each other —or in some cases, actually combined. At first, however, the system was relatively simple. The range of products was comparatively small, and for any one type of yarn or cloth, it was easy for a single price (and hence, piece-rate) to be determined, and held by custom, over a whole producing district—the more so because districts themselves specialized in particular types. But technical development permitted the diversity of products to be immensely widened, so that it became much more difficult to regulate any one piece-price

[1] Estimated again from Wood's tables (p. 27 et seq.). Over the same period power-loom weavers' earnings also rose somewhat in relation to hand-spinners, but only from rather under to just over a third. However, Manchester was never one of the modern weavers' best-organized districts.

[2] *Rule I* of the North East Lancashire Amalgamation of Power-Loom Weavers' Friendly Associations, formerly the East Lancashire Amalgamated Power Loom Weavers' Friendly Association.

by custom alone; written, formally-agreed 'lists' had already appeared in the domestic trades.[1] It was especially hard to maintain a systematic (or 'fair') relationship between the wage-rates for different varieties of yarn or cloth. And the difficulty was increased as employers on one side and workers on the other began to demand adjustments in piece-rates, not merely for multiplyingly-different varieties of product, but to compensate for changes in the process or conditions under which any one variety was produced.

The maintenance of a 'Standard Rate' in piece-work trades with a complexity of products and processes is notoriously a perennial problem of collective bargaining. One method of regulating piece-work wages, which was very common amongst organized trades in the nineteenth century, and which certain minority groups of cotton operatives to the present day retain, is to require each new piece-price to be fixed for the district or occupation as a whole. But this amounts to *ad hoc* bargaining, since each price is fixed separately, without systematic relation to other prices. Where products and processes are subject to continual modification it makes impossible demands on the district or national negotiators. And because each separate price is then mainly determined by the respective bargaining strengths of the employers and workers at the time it is fixed, the different prices in the 'List' may yield very different weekly wages. Another method is to fix only a basic time-wage by district or 'industry-wide' bargaining, leaving piece-rates to be fixed at the workplace itself but subject to the proviso that they shall yield earnings related in some way to the standard time-rate. The difficulty with this method is that the piece-rates for similar work may then differ widely between workplace and workplace—again because of variations in relative bargaining strengths. This may lead to a gradual nibbling away of wage-standards, the effect of weak bargaining by workplace groups being perhaps concealed by 'speed up' or intensified effort to maintain earnings. In any case, this method has usually developed where piece-work has come late to an originally time-working trade—as in engineering.

One or two groups of cotton workers have in recent years moved away from piece-work altogether, demanding a standard wage instead. But the Blackburn List of 1853 attempted to solve the problems of enforcing the 'Standard Rate' in piece-work occupations in a quite novel and ingenious fashion. The Blackburn List's descendants in cotton-weaving were subject to drastic criticism by official enquiries after the Second World War. But these problems have never quite been eliminated by even the most modern of 'work-load assessed', 'job-evalued,' and 'scientifically-incentive' wage-systems. And the

[1] See Chapter II, 1, section II.

Telegrams: "Deucalion, Westcent, London" *Telephones: Holborn* 8577 (3 *lines*)
and 8203

George Allen & Unwin Ltd

PUBLISHERS & EXPORTERS

All communications to be addressed to the Company
Please quote our reference

40, *Museum Street,*
*London, W.C.*1

MTDB/RB 23rd October, 1962.

The Industrial Correspondent,
Financial Times,
Bracken House,
10, Cannon Street,
London, E.C.4.

Dear Sir,

I am sending to you under separate cover an advance copy of TRADE UNION GROWTH, STRUCTURE AND POLICY, which we are publishing on November 8th. A review copy has already gone to your Review Editor, but we did feel that you would be particularly interested to see this.

Yours sincerely,

for GEORGE ALLEN & UNWIN LTD.

Martin Blackman

Blackburn List's principle certainly reduced them immensely. At any rate, that principle stood the test of a century's subsequent experience, and most cotton operatives apparently continued by preference to be paid according to it, at least until the scrapping of older plant in the cotton trade's 1960 re-organization sharply increased the proportion of workers on more recent systems.

The principle of the Blackburn List was to determine, first, a conceptual standard unit of each occupation's product, together with specified standard conditions of production. For this standard (or typical) unit of output, the standard piece-price was then fixed. Next, the possible variations from the standard product were graded systematically—as were also the foreseeable variations under each head of the specified conditions of production. Finally, for each point of variation, from either standard product or standard conditions, an addition to or subtraction from the standard piece-price was also fixed—so that these adjustments took the form of regular scales under each head of the 'Standard's' specification.

Thus, when Banks the Preston spinner in 1866 signed for his members a simple wage-list on the Blackburn principle, he took as the 'Standard' for weft yarn spinning an output of 100 lb. of '32's count' (i.e. of a fairly coarse grade) with 18·38 turns per inch, spun on a self-actor mule-frame with 640 spindles. The price of this unit was fixed at $42\frac{3}{4}$d (actually, the average of prices paid in neighbouring districts, which were mostly on the Blackburn List itself). To compensate for different outputs from bigger or smaller machines than the 'Standard', this 'Preston Self-Actor List' added $\frac{1}{2}$d. to the standard price for every 20 spindles below 600, and deducted $\frac{1}{4}$d. for every 20 spindles between 600 and 900. To fix the price of yarn of different qualities than the 'Standard,' the List provided a scale of deductions for each grade of coarseness, and of additions for each grade of fineness, these scales being determined by an agreed formula (for instance, yarn of 40's count—finer than standard—was paid at: the standard price $\times$ 40/32, plus 2%). While yarn with more turns per inch than Standard was paid an addition determined by a similar formula.[1] Another Standard was laid down for warp yarn spinning, with similar scales of variation. Then the Preston List detailed various

[1] Although the Preston Spinning List is simple enough to serve as a convenient example of the Blackburn principle, its paragraph on this point ran: 'In calculating the turns for counts of yarn, the turns to be calculated by multiplying the square roots of the counts by 3·25 for weft and 3·75 for twist. All extra turns to be paid for at the rate of two-thirds of the proportion' (from *The Standard List of Prices for Preston and Neighbourhood . . . For Spinning on Self-Actor Mules, adopted May* 11, 1866). The other mule-spinners' signatory was their chairman, William Whittle, probably a brother of the famous and mathematical Blackburn weavers' leader referred to later!

other scaled payments for such things as spinning weft yarn on warp mules (which were slower), spinning yarn on to non-standard reels or packages, and so on.

The effect of the 1853 Blackburn List was thus to transfer the normal fixing of piece-rates to the mill, but—provided they came within the range of products and technical conditions foreseen as possible by the Lists' negotiators—to make them largely an affair of applying the centrally-agreed formulae. District or (later) 'industry-wide' bargaining thus became mainly concerned with changes in the conceptual Standard Rate itself (implying a general increase or cut in wages), and otherwise with new products or processes not foreseen in the Standard List, or with disputes arising from abnormal conditions and from mill disagreements about the particular facts of production to which the standard scales were to be applied. But the List's principle involved a meticulous adjustment of piece-rates to meet changes in technical circumstances which, as the List came to be applied to the surrounding district, proved of almost infinite combination. When the Blackburn Weavers' Union was formally consituted after the List's agreement, it had as secretary a Ned Whittle, who had not only achieved European fame for his part in the great Preston strike of 1853–4 but was noted as a '. . . sound, profound and wonderfully proficient mathematician, who contributed frequently to periodicals and magazines and in their pages proposed the solution of many difficult and interesting problems.'[1] But despite this asset, the Blackburn union's branches in neighbouring towns apparently grew dissatisfied with the assistance it could provide them, and in 1858 broke away to form, as a federation of some half-dozen independent societies, the Weavers' First Amalgamation. And this body's practical purpose was '. . . the continued support of a skilled calculator of prices, able to defend the operatives' interest in the constant discussions which arise upon the complicated Lists of piece-work rates now in existence'[2]—an object which it decided, two or three years later, would be best fulfilled by selecting its secretary after examination.

It is clear that there was at this time a network of power-loom weavers' associations in Lancashire—apart from the Blackburn union, the new First Amalgamation's affiliates, and one or two unions in the southern cotton districts that appear to have existed continuously since the mid-1850s. Banks and Ward between them refer to organization in half a dozen towns not covered by any of these, and imply it in others. There seems even to have been already

[1] From an account recorded by Mr E. Hopwood, formerly of the present AWA.

[2] *Constitution* of the East Lancashire Amalgamated Power Loom Weavers' Friendly Association.

existing a loose federation of all these weavers' societies, with which both the new Blackburn and 'Amalgamated' groups were linked.[1] In the great Preston dispute of 1853 a manifesto of the Masters' Association complained '. . . that the operatives have put themselves under the guidance of a designing and irresponsible body who, having no connection with this town nor settled position anywhere . . . dictate to the operatives the means of enforcing the conditions upon which they shall be PERMITTED TO LABOUR'. But these associations were exactly of the 'natural' type already described as characteristic of the handworkers' unions[2] (which explains why direct record seems non-existent). Their organization, that is, was one of local societies maintaining contact by 'delegates', who might meet for a broader co-ordination; the whole producing only an intermittent formality of structure. It suffered from the same drawback as the earlier unions in handling industrial conflict. Ward, for instance, recounts how, while already contributing heavily to a strike in Colne, the Clitheroe society itself struck and sent out delegates (some literally 'walking') round other districts to appeal for funds. In Preston, the Clitheroe delegate found himself addressing the weavers' meeting in competition with others from Bolton and Darwen on an identical mission, and was reduced to reminding Preston how 'we had helped them on a former occasion' (probably the great 1853–4 lock-out). Particularly, however, these 'natural' organizations were unable to meet the new development of collective bargaining that their own success initiated. The Blackburn List of 1853 was arranged with a committee of operatives: but such bodies soon proved incapable of dealing with the List-system's application and implications.

District after district fought for an agreed wage-list, and succeeding, encountered similar difficulties. So that, as the value of the First Amalgamation's original appointment of a full-time official was demonstrated, the modern weavers' unions, each centred on

[1] The First Amalgamation's members in 1863 (the earliest Report surviving) were Darwen, Church, Accrington, Padiham, Chorley, Haslingden and Great Harwood. Oldham and Radcliffe associations can also claim continuance from the 1850s. Banks refers to Oldham, as well as to a Stockport union, as helping the Preston weavers in 1853. Ward mentions Bolton, Colne, Clitheroe, Preston, Rochdale and 'Enfield' (possibly Edenfield, near Bury) in 1860-2, and refers to Evans of Rochdale as 'the delegate of the Executive Committee' (although the present Rochdale union dates only from 1878), and to a meeting of this EC in Blackburn. There is even some confusion about Ward himself, since the present Clitheroe union is elsewhere recorded as formed in 1860 with a Chick Knowles as president, but Ward notes his own election as chairman at the 'annual meeting' of that year. It is possible that Ward's own group was at Low Moor (where he worked), or that 'the union' was some broader inter-local body.

[2] See Chapter II, 2, section v.

the employment of a professional negotiator, crystallized out of their 'natural' predecessors. And it was this corps of officials who both gave the new unions their subsequent stability, and were mainly responsible for the later development of the weavers' trade unionism in general.

The First Amalgamation immediately survived what its later secretary, Birtwistle, described as an attempt by the employers 'as one body to crush the Union in its infancy' at Padiham,[1] where it fought a twenty-nine weeks' stoppage which essentially concerned its main policy objective '. . . to keep up our present rate of wages to the (Blackburn) Standard List . . . and *more particularly* to bring up the prices of those who are at present paying the lowest rate of wages'[2] The First Amalgamation survived perhaps a still greater test in the Cotton Famine of 1862–4, when for three years the trade's activity was halved (see Graph I, Ch. I) and when many of the less formal local unions disappeared. More societies joined it (at peak it seems to have had some fourteen affiliates), while other local unions selected officials of their own. But this new group of professionals found their appointed task of establishing standard rates hampered by unorganized localities which were competing for trade with their own, and by variations between local piece-rates. So they concerted to organize backward districts, and formed a 'Wages Committee' amongst themselves to co-ordinate policy.[3] And it was they who, after the Great Strike of 1878 revealed the weakness of the new unions' resources for major conflicts, initiated a reorganization.

The First Amalgamation's affiliates had unequal funds, and its wealthier local committees were unwilling to throw theirs into a common pool. In 1880, Birtwistle and the officials of some independent local unions formed 'The Northern Counties Weavers' Association' (actually from the First Amalgamation's office in Accrington) as a vehicle of common negotiation by the various weavers' organizations. In 1884, after a disastrous strike in Blackburn for the restoration of pre-1878 List-rates, they promoted an all-Lancashire delegates' meeting from which the present Weavers' Amalgamation emerged.[4] And the first act of this 'Second Amalgamation' was to levy its twenty-nine affiliated societies to raise a central strike reserve of £5,000.

[1] From a speech some years later. There is an account of the 1859 Padiham strike by W. A. Jevons in the 1860 *Report* of the Social Science Association *On Trade Unions and Strikes*.

[2] Author's insert and italics.

[3] According to R. Smith (unpublished thesis, op. cit.) this functioned informally in the 1870s.

[4] The original title was the Northern Counties *Amalgamated* Weavers' Association, the first two words being dropped only in 1907. This last change seems to

The First and Second Weavers' Amalgamations for nearly twenty years maintained a curious co-existence, part competitive, part co-operative. For a while they had nearly equal memberships (see Graph II), and overlapping but by no means co-incident affiliations. But the Second Amalgamation proved itself in the twenty weeks' Ashton strike of 1886–7, when the local weavers actually cracked before the new federal body ran out of strike pay—thus reversing the pattern of former defeats to the operatives. And its bargaining efficiency was established in the protracted negotiations that produced the 1892 Uniform List. In the interval, the First Amalgamation's bigger affiliates withdrew their subscriptions, leaving it as a minor federation of unions that could not afford their own officials, while the Second Amalgamation's form became a model for other groups of cotton workers.

VII

Despite the increasing effectiveness of the Spinners' labour controls, it was only when they adopted the Weavers' new system of professional administration that the spinners' unionism was stabilized. Between the decay of the 1842 federation and the final establishment of the present Spinners' Amalgamation, there were two further attempts at a general association of spinners. In 1853, during the movement to recover the wage-reductions of 1846, an 'Equitable Friendly Association of Hand-Mule Spinners, Self-Acting Minders, Twiners and Rovers of Lancashire, Cheshire, Yorkshire and Derbyshire' was formed.[1] The great Preston lock-out of that year was set off by the local spinners' initial success in that movement for wage-increases. The employers closed the mills to defeat other operatives' demands for the same concession: but whereas the latters' resources dwindled despite a national (indeed European) contribution of funds, the Spinners' new Association organized support for its Preston affiliate which grew throughout the protracted stoppage. Banks says the local union was actually in a better financial position at the end than the beginning of the thirty weeks' dispute, and was able to support its 'blacklisted' and displaced members subsequently. But afterwards, the new spinners' federation again declined. A second attempt to revive it followed in 1860: the inspiration is not clear,

have had no particular significance: the same geographical denomination had been adopted by a broader inter-union federation in 1906 and probably caused confusion.

[1] 'Rovers' in this title referred to a small class of operatives on mule-frames adapted to produce 'rovings'—strands of fibre partially twisted in preparation for spinning.

but there was a wave of local strikes about this time (the peak of the boom that preceded the Cotton Famine), and the Preston Spinners—then the most militant group—had just secured their first district agreement for self-actors.The reformed federation's attempt at improved management suggests that it was influenced by the previous success of the weavers' First Amalgamation: its rules provided a standing executive of the three principal officers only, in place of the old (and typical) representative Board. But the members of this triumvirate were themselves primarily agents of local unions: the federation remained without its own officials, and had no regular funds. In disputes, individual spinners' unions sent delegates out to beg for support, just as in the earliest power-loom weavers' organization. The federation was weakened by the abstention or secession of important societies: in 1869 its secretary pronounced the spinners '. . . more divided in action, and as a class more split up into sections than were their predecessors of 25 years ago'.[1]

In all this, the technical division between hand-mule and self-actor spinners was a factor of decreasing importance. The conversion of the then great Preston centre to self-acting was largely completed in the 1853–4 conflict. By the 1860s, the automatic machine was everywhere an irreversible fact, and hand-mules were becoming the exception in the South-Eastern coarse-spinning districts of Lancashire. The central hindrance to continuous co-operation between the various spinners' societies now was less the competition between older and newer workers than the unwillingness of the better-placed local unions to contribute *regularly* to an organization necessarily dominated by others, and which societies with poor financial resources might exploit. The Cotton Famine, however, reduced the technical split still further: there was a considerable mortality of small firms with old equipment. And with the recovery, and the spread of the new Wage-Lists in spinning, the lessons of the weavers' experience began to sink in. The spinners' Oldham union appointed a full-time secretary in 1868 (they were already negotiating a standard wage-list). And after the defeat of another major Preston strike in 1869, the spinners' federation took a permanent form. The constitution adopted by a meeting of delegates in 1870 provided for a regular levy on affiliated societies, part of which was to be allocated to a reserve fund, and part for the management of the new organization itself.

The new spinners' unionism had now reached an organizational level comparable with their predecessors' Grand Union of 1829–30. But its consolidation was not yet complete. Like the power-loom

[1] *Circular* to affiliated societies, in the Webb collection.

weavers' First Amalgamation, the new '*Amalgamated*[1] Association of Operative Cotton Spinners, Self-Acting Minders, Twiners and Rovers of Lancashire and the Adjoining Counties' failed the test of the 1870s' depression. Its reserve fund helped the Oldham spinners' in their 1875 strike but was exhausted by the Bolton dispute of 1877: in between, the local unions' autonomous conduct of a strike in the North-East[2] proved it to have little influence on its affiliates. The number of these, having risen in 1875, fell again; and for some years the Amalgamation seemed once more in danger of disintegration. For a time, in fact, a rival centre of authority threatened. The Oldham union (now the biggest) had in 1880 linked up its neighbouring societies into a 'Province'. This device was encouraged by the Spinners' Amalgamation so as to concert the actions of unions under similar wage-lists, and to enable smaller societies to call on a full-time official. But in 1882, the Oldham union formed a 'United Movable Committee' which came to connect spinners of American cotton (Bolton mainly used Egyptian) as far afield as Yorkshire, thus associating 7,000 workers[3]—well over half the Amalgamation's membership. So that the Spinners' 1870 federation seemed threatened by similar rival leaderships and secessions to those which had destroyed its predecessor of 1842.

However, in 1878—the year of the Great Strike in North Lancashire—the Spinners' Amalgamation had appropriated another weavers' technique by appointing its new General Secretary after examination. And he initiated a series of detailed improvements—completed by a constitutional reform in 1884 (again, the year of the modern Weavers' organization's formal embodiment) that gave the Amalgamation practically its contemporary shape. Within a few years, the Amalgamation's influence recovered and the 'United Movable Committee' declined. Local unions adopted the same selective appointing method—which the Webbs, of course, regarded as mainly responsible for the modern cotton unions' success.[4] Only half a dozen spinners' unions were, in fact, both wealthy enough *and* sufficiently concerned for the problems of wage-fixing to have full-time officials (there must have been twenty or thirty in the Weavers' associations at this time): but this handful of professionals came to constitute what was virtually a permanent cabinet of the Spinners' Amalgamation. Within a year or two of its surmounting

[1] Author's italics: another hint of the external influence, but now more probably of the Weavers than of the ASE.

[2] See Smith (unpublished thesis, op. cit.) for details.

[3] According to a reference of Chapman (op. cit.) p. 235.

[4] *History*, pp. 307–9.

the great Oldham dispute of 1885, that Amalgamation had become one of the most powerful of all labour organizations.

*

Thus the modern spinners' and weavers' unions alike arose from the 'natural' associations the new factory operatives formed before the nineteenth-century's mid-point. But the Weavers first evolved the permanent and professional administration that distinguishes modern trade unionism in general. And this advanced development they owed just to their concentration upon the direct control and improvement of wage-rates as an organizing basis. Trade unions can attempt to control the supply of labour, so that its price will be raised automatically. Or they can try to fix its price, leaving supply and demand to adjust themselves. The two methods are, of course, not mutually exclusive. But an emphasis on the first technique marked the mid-nineteenth-century 'New Model' craft organizations, just as the non-craft workers' 'New Unionism' of the 1890s was mainly characterized by the second. And it is with the latter group that the major preoccupation of the weavers' unionism identifies them. While the Spinners' contrasting preoccupation with the regulation of entry makes them most akin to the great craft unions of non-textile industries. The cotton weavers' associations of the 1850s, however, anticipated the dockers' and gas-workers' unions by over forty years: their First Amalgamation, in particular—and though it also antedated not a few of those exclusive labour societies which have been thought the period's typical product—might well have claimed to be the first of the New Unions.

III

GROWTH OF THE MODERN UNIONS

2

'Closed' Versus 'Open' Unionism

I

Few things supply a better index to the differing character of the major cotton workers' organizations than their subscriptions. In the 1880s, average contributions to the Spinners' federated societies were equalled, among all unions covered by Board of Trade Reports, only by the Amalgamated Society of Engineers, at 1s 2d a week per member. And this excluded the regular levy made by the Spinners' 'shop-clubs' for the expenses of their organization in the mills; while their Oldham union's average subscription at the time was 2s, excluding both 'shop' *and* 'Amalgamation' levies. By contrast, the average weaver's contribution was under 1½d weekly (and that of the cardroom unions only fractionally greater). The Spinners, like the great craft amalgamations outside the textile trade (and although their dispute expenditure much exceeded those unions') provided a variety of 'friendly' benefits to their members—unemployment, 'breakdown and stoppages', accident, 'leaving trade', emigration, superannuation, funeral. The weavers' First Amalgamation had included limited friendly assistance in its objects ('the respectable interment' of members is particularly notable), and their local unions also provided occasional but always small benefits of that kind. The weavers' Second Amalgamation, however, like the later general labour unions in other industries, paid only for disputes. Since the Spinners and Weavers at first dominated labour history in their separate (if related) industries, we can proceed to compare the differing impacts of 'closed' and 'open' unionism—which the Spinners and Weavers respectively embodied—on workers' organization at large.

The possibility of such a comparison—though it involves disentangling a complicated history of inter-union relationship—is facilitated by another curiosity in the development of textile trade unionism. This is the seeming absence in that development of any strong direct connection between the Spinners and Weavers themselves. There is, of course, their early association in specific political campaigns like those for a shorter working day. And under the circumstances of their evolution, a certain cross-fertilization between the two industries was inevitable. It has been shown for instance, that the Spinners' organizational development turned very much on their adoption of the Weavers' professional leadership system. But these things were all, so to speak, 'at the top'. A permanent political alliance between the spinning and weaving groups, in the United Textile Factory Workers' Association, appeared only when their Amalgamations all had the same type of full-time officers. And it was then largely a creation of those officials: even before that, these had long tended to form a single block when it was a question—at the TUC, for instance—of pushing particular cotton trade interests against competing external claims. But it was only after the First World War that some co-operation between Spinners and Weavers in central negotiations with employers developed—and it then remained uncertain and intermittent. At a district level, such co-operation was much weaker: the inter-union 'Local Textile Trades Federations' for instance, were (and are still) mainly composed by manufacturing operatives' associations. And at a factory level, it seems to have been virtually non-existent, despite the obvious occasion for it in 'combined' mills.

Even when the Spinners and Weavers were involved in the same great disputes—as at Preston in 1853—they appear to have kept apart. About the time of the 1878 Great Strike, there is some record of a 'Special Emergency Wages Committee of the Cotton Operatives in Lancashire, Yorkshire, Cheshire and Derbyshire', which apparently included both spinners and weavers.[1] But it is not clear whether this was an 'official' or 'unofficial' body; it certainly made no mark on events, and was quite ephemeral. While the lack of direct interchange was evident even where spinning and weaving was conducted at the same factory—as in the old North Lancashire 'vertical' mills of the 1850s and '60s. Ward the weaver, for instance, was employed at just such a mill: but the spinners played no part in the disputes his diary describes, and he mentions a later spinners' strike there as a quite remote affair. To the present day, a firm in this district still keeps a spinning factory and a weaving shed in the same yard: according to a local union officer, the operatives enter by the same gate, but there has never been any co-operation between them—

[1] According to Smith (unpublished thesis, op. cit.).

indeed they barely know each others' names. In this relative detachment between the two leading union groups, it seems the Spinners were more responsible than the Weavers. But the immediate point is that here it reinforces the separation which had developed between the spinning and weaving industries themselves. The initial development of both self-actor spinners' and power-loom weavers' unionism involved, in each of the cotton trade's two sections, only a part of the operatives employed. In each section, we can thus analyse the evolution of collective organization among *other* workers—and especially the effect on that evolution of the particular form of unionism that the section's leading group had already adopted—in the assurance that the influence of developments in the sister industry was relatively secondary—or at least, indirect.

Of the effect of the Spinners' exclusive technique the outstanding illustration concerns, of course, their own assistants—the 'piecers' ('big' and 'little') who by the century's end outnumbered the spinners themselves by three to one. Piecers had been casually admitted to the early hand-mule unions, and generally continued to be accepted by the latters' successors, though always on inferior terms. But the spinners' attitude to the organization of piecers remained ambiguous. Spinners generally earned from about two to four times as much as even their senior piecers, so on the one hand they were interested in maintaining their very marked wage-differential—and very real control—over their assistants: but on the other, they wished to prevent them acting as strike-breakers (members or not, they often had to give them strike pay), and 'to early inculcate . . . trade union principles'[1] in the minds of those who would ultimately become spinners themselves. Local unions solved this dilemma in different ways. Some virtually ignored their piecers; those in the now technically-advanced Southern districts (where most assistants were required) encouraged them to join.

In the upshot, the degree of piecers' organization remained low, and no very systematic attempt to recruit them was made until they threatened to organize themselves independently. And this is one of the few points at which external labour movements seemed to have directly influenced the cotton unions' development. About 1890, some Bolton piecers, aided and encouraged by local socialists, started an agitation which led, in 1891–2, to the forming of a 'Lancashire Piecers' Association'.[2] This move apparently induced an

[1] Jewkes & Gray (*Wages and Labour in the Cotton Spinning Industry*, op. cit.) p. 195.

[2] This is one of the two 'breakaway' unions shown in the Spinners' group of the 'Main Chart' of Chapter III, 1, section i.

enthusiastic response[1]; and the spinners' reaction was immediate. Their Bolton union enforced a 'closed shop' against the rebels by making its spinner-members responsible for collecting subscriptions (to itself) from their assistants, meanwhile promising an improvement of the latters' treatment. Other local unions, with the Amalgamation's support, formed separate 'Piecers' Associations' of their own, nominally to encourage trade unionism amongst these workers; but these organizations always remained under the spinners' control and censorship—forming, in fact, a sort of trade-union 'company union.' So it is understandable that the piecers' dissatisfaction apparently continued. In 1894 there is even a report of a strike of 'little piecers' (aged 10 to 14!) who called a meeting at a public house and elected officers.[2] Several years later, in the general upsurge of trade unionism about 1908, a 'National Cotton Operatives' Association' of piecers was formed, but also came to nothing against the Spinners' resistance.[3] It was only in 1920, after a more serious breakaway movement in Oldham, that the Spinners' Amalgamation itself accepted piecers as eligible for (limited) membership and thus for Amalgamation benefit. It seems doubtful, however, that as many as half the piecers have at any time been trade unionists.[4]

The spinners' attitude to their piecers has attracted several commentators. The Webbs, for instance, refer to the piecers as 'brigaded' into a subordinate place in the spinners' unionism.[5] But this attitude also affected other and more numerous groups of operatives in their industry—for instance, the women in spinning processes proper. The spinners had, of course, early fought against the employment of women as mule-spinners: in the 1818 strike-wave, mills using that system were even fired. About 1870 (when the present Amalgamation was formed) and according to Chapman, women were 'expelled from the Unions'[6]—and this presumably refers to women mule-spinners, since their retention as such led to occasional strikes in the '80s, although the Spinners still had nearly 2,000 women in local membership thirty years later. Many of these, however, were probably employed as piecers under men—a system already declining. More important were the women and girls on alternative spinning processes, first the 'throstle' and later the 'ring-frame'—

[1] See Jewkes & Gray (op. cit.).

[2] *Bolton Chronicle*, July 5, 1894.

[3] Board of Trade Reports give it as having 200 members, and winding up in 1909. This is also shown as a 'breakaway' in the Main Chart.

[4] Estimated from Board of Trade Reports, which give memberships 1903–10, and from post-1920 Amalgamation returns. Jewkes & Gray give a figure for 1895, source unquoted.

[5] *History*, p. 7.

[6] Chapman, op. cit., p. 214, footnote.

on which foreign cotton-factory industries have been almost exclusively based. In the 1890s one or two local unions in the South-East accepted ring-spinners into their puppet Piecers' Associations (this probably accounts for the rest of the Spinners' reported female membership). But the Amalgamation gave their recruitment no encouraging, and later recommended their exclusion. They were taken up by the new Cardroom Amalgamation, but remain one of the worse-organized groups of cotton operatives, although in recent years the ring-frame has rapidly supplanted the mule as the principal spinning instrument. Here, the spinners' exclusiveness has encouraged competition from badly-paid female labour, and thus helped to cut off their own occupation.

The Spinners also had interests in stages of production both preparatory and subsequent to spinning spoper. The 'rovers and twiners' who appear in the Amalgamation's first title[1] were men who respectively worked yarn up for spinning, and 'doubled' it for special uses. These were working variants of the mule-frame, however; they operated similar labour controls to the spinners, who accepted them as equals (even providing special representation for them on the Amalgamation's Executive). But the great majority of doubling operatives were employed on other (some, on rival) processes. A successful six months' strike of these doubling workers occurred in 1881 at the Oldham mills because they had been refused a wage-increase secured by the spinners.[2] But the latter made no attempt to encourage the strikers' informal organization, which then subsided. Doubling workers' efforts to form permanent unions of their own are recorded only in this century—at Bolton in 1900 and in Manchester in 1903; the first survived only by merging with the local Cardroom union, the second became extinct.[3] Doubling workers are now organized (not highly) by several other bodies, including both cotton and general unions—the latter having come in during the 1890s at Stockport, when the local doublers failed to secure other support. One group of male doubling workers are known as 'gassers' (from the process of 'gassing' certain types of yarn). And there is a local story (no doubt apocryphal) that the old Gasworkers' Union—now, of course, the NUGMW—first undertook to negotiate for them under a misapprehension as to their trade's nature.

[1] Chapter III, 1, section VII.

[2] According to Smith (unpublished thesis, op. cit.).

[3] These unions are shown in the Main Chart as 'non-continuing' unions in the Cardroom group. A Doublers' Association apparently existed in Stockport in 1896 (letter in *CFT*, August 14, 1896 refers) but was already declining. The writer has been told that the Spinners' Amalgamation at some point definitely refused doublers, but cannot confirm this.

II

However, perhaps the most interesting part of the story of curious relations between the different groups of cotton-spinning operatives concerns the Spinners' early dealings with the preparatory workers whose unions now form by far the bigger organization, the Cardroom Amalgamation. The flimsy and limited character of trade-unionism, before the 1880s, in this oldest-established class of factory operatives has already been noted.[1] In the late 1850s there seems to have been some fairly widespread organizing movement among them: about 1857–8 an attempt at a general organization appears to have been made from Bolton, where the 'National United Association of Cardroom Operatives' was formed. It is possible that the small group of South Lancashire cardroom unions that date from this time (as the *Main Chart* shows) are the residue of this effort, which otherwise came to nothing—as did a similar attempt in 1860, this time from Hyde. After the Cotton Famine, there are references to cardroom unions in North Lancashire—especially in Blackburn, then the focus of the fast-developing weavers' organization. There, the cardroom overlookers in 1866 appealed to the employers to support their authority against combinations of their operatives.[2] While Eccles Shorrock, the North Lancashire employers' leader, said a union was formed there in 1872 but its 'representative became so insolent and abusive that the masters refused to see him'.[3] This movement among the cardroom workers seems to have been quite widespread. However, it produced no surviving organization. The change came with the depression of the 1870s, and particularly with the subsequent intensification of work and technical development (especially marked in preparatory processes) which was associated with the competitive rise of the new firms known as the 'Oldham Limiteds'.

It seems fairly clear that the handful of cardroom unions then surviving were mainly of men—the 1860 organization, for instance, called itself the 'United Central Association of Card and Blowing-Room Operatives' (card and blowing machines are alike operated by men and boys). They ignored the female workers in associated processes (frame-tenters and so on) who composed the majority of the spinning industry's operatives. They were, in fact, rather ineffective attempts to imitate the spinners' unionism, which was, of course, already very active, though it had not yet produced stable formal organizations: the 1860 effort at a county cardroom associa-

[1] See Chapter II, 2, section VII.
[2] According to Smith (unpublished thesis, op. cit.).
[3] 'A Letter to the Workpeople . . . etc.' (op. cit.).

tion may itself have been inspired by the re-forming of the spinners' federation in that year. And a similar attempt in 1880 by the then existing handful of cardroom societies (now slightly increased in number—see the *Main Chart* again) to construct an 'Amalgamated Association' also failed. About this time in the Ashton district there were even competing clubs—two breakaways from some original society having followed, first a disagreement over the exclusion of Irish workers,[1] and then a personal quarrel among its leaders (one product of this became known simply as 'White's Union'). But the Oldham union, in the centre of new economic development, was apparently changing its character. It had begun to organize women operatives successfully—by the 1890s, it had a 90 per cent. female membership. It formed a federal 'Wages Committee' of cardroom clubs in the surrounding district, using as an inducement to association with itself a central 'Accident Fund', which cardroom unions in other districts began to join. And it seems to have acquired a full-time secretary by the early 1880s.

The decisive event in the cardroom unions' history was the great Oldham lock-out of 1885. Preparatory workers' wages were customarily varied with the spinners'; and they were usually put out of work by the latters' strikes. But now the new Oldham federation assumed a more positive role, and undertook an independent resistance to the wage-cuts that caused this dispute. It persuaded other cardroom unions to levy their members in its support; and after the stoppage, it re-organized its own local federation on the lines of the Oldham Spinners' 'Province'. But the lock-out had convinced it of the need for a wider organization, and the success of the Weavers' Second Amalgamation had demonstrated the possibility of achieving that aim. In 1886 the Oldham association called a conference of cardroom societies by which the Cardroom Amalgamation itself was constituted.

The Oldham Province at first provided over half the new body's membership, although by now some twenty or so local societies (of a varying organizational formality) had declared themselves. But the Amalgamation's establishment tapped a spring of discontent among the hitherto unorganized preparatory operatives: in its second year it handled over 600 disputes (mostly on behalf of women operatives), confirmed 21 strike notices and supported 7 local strikes.[2] In 1888 the new Amalgamation acquired its own full-time General Secretary and headquarters, though the (now) two Oldham officials continued to hold other leading positions in it. It launched a successful independent wage-claim for preparatory workers in

[1] This arose from a local incident about 1868, known as the 'Murphy Riots'.
[2] *Annual Report* of the Cardroom Amalgamation for 1887–8.

'American' spinning districts (the Bolton union, still much smaller and largely male in membership, managed its affairs for some time apart from the Amalgamation, though affiliated with it). The Amalgamation's membership began to rise fast.[1] Solid unions were established in localities hitherto unorganized or in which only informal clubs had existed (a development which is again traced in Chapter III, 1's *Main Chart*). Each such union, like the weavers' societies, centred on the employment of a qualified professional agent. And though local Cardroom unions imitated the Spinners' 'Provincial' organization to facilitate this, their Amalgamation itself again resembled the Weavers' in having a strike fund as its main plank. Within five years of its formation it included over a third of all preparatory operatives.

In all this, it is not evident that the Spinners offered much assistance. Indeed, the Cardroom Amalgamation's first years were marked by one of the most extraordinary events in the history of inter-union relations in general. The new body began immediately to press for standard wage-rates, so underlining its kinship to the Weavers and to 'unskilled' unions in general. In particular, its militant Oldham Province conducted from 1887 on a campaign for a Cardroom Wage-List that two years later culminated in a series of official strikes. And the Oldham Masters' Association ordered all their mills on to short-time in retaliation. The employers, however, were at this time much divided amongst themselves: older firms thought the Masters' Association dominated by the new 'Limiteds' and refused to conform to its instruction. But it happened at this time that the employers were themselves in dispute with the cotton-merchants of Liverpool, who had formed a ring to keep up the price of American fibre. A newly-formed federation of South-East Lancashire master-spinners, to which the Oldham Masters' Association was itself affiliated, decided to break this 'Liverpool Cotton Corner' by working short-time in all its districts. The Operative Spinners, in support of the employer federation's action on this question, ordered their members out of all mills not obeying that federation's instructions—thus, incidentally perhaps but nevertheless effectively, completing the lock-out against the Oldham cardroom workers!

By 1891, however, the cardroom operatives' organization was an established fact: and it was clear to the Spinners' leaders that they were themselves heading for some general conflict with the employers. They then concluded a mutual aid pact ('The Cotton Workers' Association') with the Cardroom whereby each Amalgamation would support the other in mill strikes, and would contribute

[1] The growth of the Cardroom Amalgamation's membership is traced in Graph II of the previous Chapter.

to a common fund for this purpose. The pact was of considerable prestige value to the Cardroom Amalgamation and encouraged its recognition by employers: but it shortly found that spinners' claims on it much exceeded those of cardroom workers, and that the fund was draining the Amalgamation's limited resources. The agreement was revised to pay only workers who struck 'in sympathy' from the common pool, not the original strikers in any dispute. But this would have had the effect of giving the partner which *initiated* fewer strikes —the Cardroom in practice—the greater claim on the joint fund. And the agreement appears then to have become ineffective.[1] The great 'Brooklands' lock-out of 1892–3, in fact, exhausted the Cardroom Amalgamation's resources: its membership fell heavily thereafter, and did not much recover for a decade. It was only after this recovery that a satisfactory joint agreement with the Spinners was made,[2] and the latter for the first time accepted (in 1905) a Cardroom proposal to present a joint wage-claim. The Cardroom Amalgamation remained comparatively weak meanwhile. Its major agreements with employers were all made only in the few years before World War I.

III

It is pretty clear that the cardroom unions' development occurred, if anything, rather despite the Spinners than with their encouragement. And the Spinners' permanent recognition of the cardroom workers' organization effectively dates from the time that it became too powerful to be ignored. But one other illustration of the effects of the Spinners' 'closed' unionism on the organization of other operatives is to be seen in their relations with their own peers—the other, but less numerous, 'skilled' or supervisory workers in their industry.

Early hand-mule clubs admitted storemen, clerks and so on to membership, but excluded them from their committees;[3] these workers established no tradition of organization. The modern spinners' unions appear to have largely ignored such employees: but about the late 1880s, when the new Cardroom unionism was establishing itself in Oldham, the wave of organization appears to have affected several minor groups of specialist workers. Two such

[1] Sir Alfred Roberts, the Cardroom Amalgamation's present General Secretary, wrote a souvenir history of that organization from 1886 for its 1936 Golden Jubilee (*After 50 Years*) and says the agreement was abandoned because of 'difficulty over the pooling of funds'.

[2] *Agreement . . . for Securing Joint Action in Case of Individual Strikes* of May 2, 1904.

[3] According to Chapman, and the *Rules* of the early Manchester Society.

were the under-engineers and roller-coverers—the former concerned with the maintenance of mill power plants and drives, the latter with refitting the innumerable rollers in preparatory and spinning machinery. Each of these groups formed unions in the Oldham district about 1891–2. Apparently feeling too small to survive without some supporting alliance, but not caring to associate with the proletarian Cardroom, they were accepted as affiliates by the Oldham Spinners' Province. Both their memberships subsequently declined, the Under-Engineers' Association finally becoming extinct.[1] The roller-coverers learnt the lesson, and in 1912 transferred their allegiance to the Cardroom Amalgamation, within which their society still enjoys a modest prosperity.

Some spinners' unions in the 1880s also accepted warehousemen and overlookers. The warehousemen, however, only finally preserved their organization by emulating the roller-covers' example and transferring to an 'open' union; but the spinning overlookers were apparently unable to swallow the lowering of status this might have implied. In the result, overlookers in the spinning industry have never approached an effective trades unionism, and tend rather to regard themselves as managerial staff than as operatives. And by the time the Cardroom Amalgamation rivalled the Spinners' influence, this attitude had crystallized and become mutual, so that cardroom unions in turn excluded workers promoted to supervisory jobs, or restricted their membership rights.[2]

Such skilled and supervisory workers as these appear to have been initially accepted by spinners' unions that still felt insecure. In the early 1880s about a quarter of the self-actor men in Oldham Province, for instance, were not yet unionists; and the incompleteness of their own organization at that time may explain the local spinners' initial willingness to accept certain other workers. But their own aristocracy once established, the spinners in effect withdrew encouragement from the organization of others who might by occupational status claim to share their position. Fear of being compelled to share their privileged standing, however, would not explain the spinners' attitude to the general run of the industry's

[1] The Under-Engineers are shown as a non-continuing union in the Spinners' section of the *Main Chart*, the Roller-Coverers in the Cardroom group.

[2] The *Rules* of the Cardroom's North Lancashire Provincial Association, for instance, provide that a worker promoted to carder or under-carder may retain membership with benefit rights, provided that he conforms to *all* union regulations but attends no union meeting and takes no other part in union management. The Spinners' Amalgamation permits spinners promoted to overlooker to retain full membership: but membership, under its *Rules*, may only be held through an affiliated union—and some spinners' societies (including Oldham, the biggest) now require men promoted overlooker to resign it!

operatives, who were not claimants to a superior position. On the contrary, the co-operation of the preparatory workers, for instance, would have been helpful to the spinners because it would have cut off any possibility of their own assistants acting as strike-breakers against the spinners themselves. That the Spinners' attitude to the industry's other workers in general was influenced by an overriding motive was suggested by Chapman, who thought separate unions of the different occupations necessitated '. . . in the fact that an enlarged share in the joint product secured by the one might be at the expense of the other'.[1] At first sight, at any rate, this proposition is not easy to reconcile with the apparent willingness of the Cardroom Amalgamation, by contrast with the Spinners, to encourage the organization of other groups than its initial membership. But that the Spinners accepted this view is also clear—most, in the treatment of their own piecers. They may well have been influenced—like the craft unions of the time—by contemporary economic doctrines to the effect that the total share of wages was inexorably limited. They were certainly well-informed by their officials in trade matters, and accustomed to think of the 'margin' between raw material and product prices, which indicated current levels of profit, as also determining wage-possibilities. And as the group with an established and prior hold on the industry, it must at least have appeared to them that organization of other workers was as likely to be to the spinners' own cost as to that of their employers.

Whatever the motive, it seems pretty clear that the prior establishment of a powerful 'closed' union in the spinning trade at least gave no encouragement to the general spread of trade unionism there, and in some cases inhibited or actively frustrated it. In other industries there are one or two cases where the existence of an organized and dominating labour aristocracy at least drove other workers to associate in self-protection. In the metal industry, for instance, a relation very similar to that between spinners and piecers existed between the top iron-and-steel workers and the day-wage men who acted as their helpers. It was on the day-wage men's resentment of this relation that the Steel Smelters' Union was largely built up,[2] in the years before World War I—with such effect that it came to outnumber the old Associated Iron and Steel Workers of Great Britain, which was then induced to merge with it. The Spinners were more powerful than the Iron Workers, and effectively blocked every parallel threat from their own assistants.

[1] Chapman (op. cit.) p. 243.

[2] There is an account of the establishment of what was to become known as 'Hodge's Union' in John Hodge's autobiography, *From Working Man's Cottage to Windsor Castle* (London, 1931).

IV

With these effects of the 'closed' Spinners' early domination of labour organization in spinning, we can now compare the general development of trade unionism in the cotton manufacturing industry, where the 'open' weavers' unions were first to consolidate. An immediate respect in which the general structure of unionism in cotton-manufacturing evolved differently from that in the spinning industry appears from the previous Chapter's *Main Chart*. In spinning, at the peak union membership of just after World War I, the 'closed' Spinners' Amalgamation had some 24,000 spinner-members, plus a subordinate 30,000 of their assistants: while the 'open' Cardroom, with nearly 100,000 members, constituted the mass organization of other spinning and preparatory operatives. In manufacturing, the Weavers' Amalgamation provided a much more powerful 'open' association, with a handful of 'breakaway' or unaffiliated societies making up its record strength to perhaps a quarter-million members. But the workers who were able to construct a 'closed' unionism in the weaving trades were organized in eight separate groupings,[1] with a total membership of over 30,000—exceeding that of spinners proper in the parallel industry.

The weavers' societies show (*Main Chart* again) two major waves of formation. The first runs from 1850 to 1860, and includes both the Blackburn Union's establishment and that of the First Amalgamation. It is significant that this wave is followed by an upsurge of 'closed' union organization, briefly interrupted by the Cotton Famine in 1862–3, but thereafter resumed.[2] A crop of overlookers' and tape-sizers' unions, for instance, appears in the decade after the formation of the Weavers' First Amalgamation. The second major wave of union formation amongst the weavers runs from 1877 to 1891, and is again pursued by similar movements to unionize warpdressers and (with a lag) the clothlookers and warehouse workers. 'Closed' unions often appear in the same districts as their weaver predecessors. Indeed, the clearest example of the connection between the unionization of weavers and of other workers is that of the twisters, the formation of whose societies closely follows on the two major waves of weavers' unionism both in time and in area. While the construction

[1] The Main Chart shows only five brief headings for these. But the Tapesizers actually had two 'Amalgamated' associations. An Amalgamated Mill-Warpers' Society, now extinct, is shown as a non-continuing union with the Twisters, as the next-of-kin. While an association of Chain-Beamers (now merged with the Warpdressers) also existed independently till 1928, but the writer has been unable to trace its formation and it is therefore not included in the Chart.

[2] The two years 1862 and '63 appear to be the only ones from 1857 to 1910 in which no new cotton operatives' organizations were formed, except 1899.

of unions for the strongest of the 'closed' occupations numerically, the overlookers, is not only renewed after the forming of the weavers' Second Amalgamation but also stimulated by the minor surge of weavers' organization around 1870, so that the overlookers' first wave appeared more prolonged than that of the twisters'.

The workers organized by these new closed unions appear to have no significant previous history of collective association. Their occupations were almost entirely a creation of the factory industry (the invention of dressing and sizing machinery in the early nineteenth century, for instance, was an important step in the development of a practical power-loom industry). Some clubs of power-loom overlookers, tape-sizers and 'cotton-yarn dressers' affiliated to Doherty's National Association for the Protection of Labour in 1830, but seem to have been an ephemeral creation of the then general labour ferment. Between the 1830s and the appearance of the stable unions traced in the *Main Chart*, such workers produced only one or two pure friendly societies.[1] The timing of the various groups' later nineteenth-century organization was, of course, affected by their particular circumstances. The warpdressers, for instance, appear to have enjoyed a special status until very late in the period. They were a small class of individual specialists, who possessed equipment of their own and sometimes set up as independent artisans, taking in work on commission. They earned more than mule-spinners up to the 1890s, when they still had about twice the average weaver's wage.[2] Old members of their association say that, early in the present century, warpdressers still emphasized their independence and status by refusing to enter the mill of a morning until all the other operatives were at work, and insisting on leaving first. The clothlookers, on the other hand, though receiving little more than the average weaver, were regarded by the employer as in a sense his agent, and so were particularly liable to victimization if they adopted trade union sympathies.[3] Thus the comparatively late organization of warpdressers and clothlookers may be explained by the opposite extremity of their circumstances. But a general conclusion that the 'skilled' groups were stimulated to associate by the organization of the 'less-skilled' weavers seems inescapable.

The stimulus, of course, could well have been in part a protective

[1] A Warehousemen's Philanthropic Society seems to have been formed in 1850, for instance, but by 1890 had only a handful of members. An Overlookers' Provident Society is recorded in Yorkshire in 1844. (Both Board of Trade notes.) The latter, however, may have been an association of spinning workers.

[2] See Wood's tables (various, but particularly No. 42).

[3] The Warehousemen's former General Secretary, Mr Fred Lee, also produced a souvenir history for their Amalgamation's Jubilee: 1895–1945. *Fifty Years of Progress and Endeavour* (*ATW*).

reaction. Wood's infinitely meticulous work permits a comparison which seems good evidence that the surges of weavers' organization were associated with a reduction of the more-skilled workers' relative wage-advantage[1]:

	1833	1850	1860	1877	1880	1891	1900	1906
Dressers' and Sizers' Wages Index	100	90	90	144	126	130	133	144
Power-Loom Weavers' Wages Index	100	100	114	155	146	164	173	188
Ratio Dressers' and Sizers' Wages to Weavers' %	252	227	200	235	219	200	195	195

Thus (and comparing the table with the *Main Chart's* record of unionization's progress), dressers' and sizers' wages fall over the early decades of the factory industry, which is what one would expect to happen—in the absence of collective organization—as skills become less scarce. But they are stable when weavers' wages rise in the decade of the latters' first major organizing wave. Between 1860 and 1877, when the sizers are unionized, the 'skilled differential' is restored to a level at least equal to that ruling before stable unions gained a footing amongst the weavers. But this differential falls again after the Great Strike of 1878, apparently because the skilled groups are as yet less able to resist wage-reductions than the weavers. And the fall continues apace in the 1880s, when the weavers complete their union structure and gain much bigger wage-increases. The narrowing, however, is first slowed and then halted as trade unionism extends to the dressers. So here, in effect, the skill differential's movement over three-quarters of a century closely reflects the relative development of trade unionism among skilled and less-skilled workers respectively.

In the case of the overlookers, the defensive reaction to the weavers' unionization was direct. Overlookers (or 'tacklers')[2] in the mid-nineteenth century were responsible not only for setting-up and maintaining looms, but for the performance of (usually) eight

[1] Calculated from Wood's Table 42, average weekly earnings in each year. The critical movements seem relatively unaffected by 'compositional' changes, etc.
[2] They were also called 'tuners' in Yorkshire.

or ten weavers apiece. They hired and fired weavers, and were paid according to the latter's output. And in the early days of the power-loom industry, they rarely began their careers as weavers themselves. In the circumstances, conflict between the weavers and overlookers was inevitable. Complaints of 'driving' or victimization by the over-lookers were frequently taken up by the weavers' unions. Their Second Amalgamation conducted a campaign against the 'slate system', whereby the earnings of individual weavers were chalked up in the shed each week—often with accompanying comments and warnings—and which the weavers held to have caused several suicides.[1] Weavers not infrequently struck for the dismissal of a particularly obnoxious overlooker; but weavers might also strike because they considered their earnings reduced by an overlooker's technical incompetence. Thus the Objects of the Chorley and District Overlookers' Association of 1878 (for instance) specifically included the support of members whose work was stopped by such action on the weavers' part. An element of the same relation existed between the weavers and the clothlookers, who were responsible for passing the weavers' work as satisfactory for payment. But the friction here was much less: the clothlookers got little extra for their trouble, were not paid by results but risked dismissal if they were too tolerant, and were perhaps as much to be pitied as resented.

Nevertheless, the closed unions clearly based their organization on the Weavers' experience—in many ways, directly imitated the latter. The earlier groups to associate, for instance, almost exactly repeat the Weavers' structural development. Their first improvement on the primitive local club is, like the Blackburn Weavers' Society of 1854, the multi-branch association, expanded to cover the surrounding district. The overlookers formed just such a union in 1858, the tapesizers another in 1865, and the twisters yet another in 1866—all centred on Blackburn. While the now extinct mill-warpers formed a similar association in 1866 in Oldham, where the weavers had anticipated them with a wide-area union by seven years. Then came the partial federation of local societies—often themselves hived-off from the multi-branch district unions—on the lines of the Weavers' First Amalgamation. Thus, the 'National Confederate Associations of Power Loom Overlookers' is organized from Manchester in 1875, and the 'North, North-East and South-East Lancashire Amalgamated Tapesizers' Association' appears in 1880. And finally, after the success of the weavers' Second Amalgamation more or less complete federations of the closed unions also emerge—

[1] References to several cases appear particularly in the Weavers' General Council's minutes for 1901–3, when it instructed local societies to hold public meetings on the issue.

the overlookers' present 'General Union' in 1885, the Twisters' Amalgamation in 1889. The tapesizers, for reasons which are now quite obscure, never completed this progression, a separate multi-branch district union continuing to operate in the South-East (the 'Friendly Protective Society' of 1861). But the groups that organized latest were, of course, able to jump whole stages of the Weavers' more experimental evolution. The Warpdressers start by forming a multi-branch district union in Manchester in 1882 and move to a complete Amalgamation in 1894: the clothlookers leap straight from a district union (again at Blackburn) in 1894 to an Amalgamation the following year.

There are other respects in which the closed manufacturing unions resembled the Weavers. The Overlookers, for instance, apparently attempted to found their local organizations, despite the latters' relatively small numerical strength, on the employment of a full-time secretary, so that they had ultimately about as many permanent officials as did the Spinners, although the latters' peak membership was five times greater. And the closed unions seem all to have adopted low membership subscriptions. Although overlookers and tapesizers in the 1880s and '90s were, like the warpdressers, getting about twice the average weavers' wage, the union contributions of all three groups ran usually at 3d or 4d a week only; while those of the twisters, who were paid up to half as much again as weavers, ran at 1d or 2d. Such contributions were quite comparable with those of local weavers' societies. The closed unions paid more and better benefits than the latter: but they seem to have raised their funds partly from entrance and 'learning' fees (typically, about equal to a full week's wages). In fact, their system of controlling entry to their members' jobs may itself be yet another illustration of the Weavers' influence on them.

One or two of the modern power-loom weavers' unions appear to have begun by attempting to regulate the intake of new labour. These, particularly Bolton in 1865, were formed just after the first major group in North Lancashire. But their members were mainly engaged on high-quality or specialized work—quiltings in Bolton, velvets and fustians in Oldham. They seem to have been more prosperous—Oldham, for instance, whose trade fluctuated much less than that of more typical weaving districts, frequently helped the Northern group in strikes. And it is possible that they in turn were influenced by the spinners' unionism that dominated their centres. But their attempted control was quite different from the spinners' 'mill seniority' system, which was based on now old-established practice and involved a quite detailed regulation of the operatives' grading and machine-complements. Instead, the names of would-be 'learners' of power-loom weaving were to be submitted before admittance to the local union committee, which would then determine whether the trade could support them—in effect, a crude and direct restriction of the supply of labour.

Whether this attempt failed of its own accord, or whether the weavers' unions concerned lost interest in it as they were drawn into the general weavers' movement for standard wage-rates, is not clear. At any rate, although the system did not survive among the weavers' unions,[1] it was taken up by all the succeeding closed unions in manufacturing and developed by them into their present normal method of entry control, by which learners are accepted only against such actual vacancies for qualified men as occur at individual mills —and as the members there and their local union agree should be filled[2]—but for which no unemployed member is available. The only exception was that of the twisters, who were confronted with rather unusual technical circumstances. Their work was very similar to that of another occupation, the drawers, each of whom, however, required an assistant usually called a 'reacher-in'.[3] The twisters' unions dealt with this situation by accepting twisters and drawers as virtually interchangeable but providing that each mill should recruit to the combined occupation only to meet actual vacancies *and* from its own reachers-in, according to the latters' order of seniority at the mill itself. The Twisters' method of entry control thus rather resembles the Spinners'—except that the two upper grades have equality of wages and union status, and greatly outnumber the subordinate grade of assistants. So that if their system *was* a variant of the Spinners', it was at least a democratic one.

But it is also clear that the weavers gave more than an organizational example, and the stimulus of protective reaction from the

[1] The Oldham union still enforces a rule that no member shall train a new worker who does not also belong to the society, but this is now used to oblige new entrants to join the union, not to limit entry to the trade.

[2] Even when a management offers a vacancy, a local union of overlookers, tapesizers or warpdressers may refuse to fill it for any one of a variety of reasons —for instance, that the mill concerned is not thought likely to need the extra man permanently, that employment generally is insecure, or that the management has refused some union demand. The union's qualified members at the mill concerned will then refuse to teach any candidate for the vacancy which has been thus rejected by the union—and such instruction 'on the job' is the only form of training generally accepted.

[3] Roughly, the twister's job is to join the threads of a replacement warp beam into any loom which has used up its supply of warp material. The drawer, on the other hand, arranges the threads for any *new* pattern to be put into a loom, using a frame through which the 'reacher-in' passes him the 'ends' of thread. There are some mechanical 'knotting-frames' which require three operatives (one a juvenile), and on these the drawer becomes the 'man-in-charge'; but most work is still done, at time of writing, by hand.

weavers' own unionization, to the unionizing of what are now the manufacturing industry's closed occupations. In fact, local weavers' unions very generally accepted such more-skilled workers before their own unions appeared—just as they already organized such lower-paid ancillary operatives as winders. The twisters and cloth-lookers, particularly, with several related classes of more-skilled operatives, seem to have been widely recruited by earlier power-loom weavers' societies. While some of the weavers' original wage-lists (Blackburn, for instance) even included lists of prices for warpdressing. There appears, however, to have been no resentment on the Weavers' part at the formation of independent skilled unions. On the contrary, the Weavers attempted to secure the latters' co-operation. Thus, a 'Joint Committe of Weavers' and Overlookers' Associations of North and North-East Lancashire' was formed to present a united front 'against the encroachments of the employers' in the bargaining that preceded the Great Strike of 1878. And when, three years afterwards (and twelve years before the better-known 'Brooklands' procedure was adopted in spinning), the manufacturing employers' federation agreed to set up a joint committee 'for the settlement of Weavers' Complaints', the association of the new closed unions with the much more powerful Weavers was a material aid to the formers' securing a recognition from employers.

At a later stage, in 1896, the several manufacturing Amalgamations, including the Weavers, actually approved a scheme for a general federation with its own officers.[1] The scheme fell through because the Tapesizers and Warpdressers had already abstained, and the Overlookers' Amalgamation swung against it as (among probably more important reasons) implying a distrust of the overlookers' power . . . 'to manage our own affairs'.[2] The surviving federation of rather less aristocratic groups (twisters, clothlookers and mill-warpers) with the Weavers was never completed or effective.[3] But a renewed attempt ten years later produced a looser but comprehensive alliance between the Weavers and the smaller union Amalgamations; this was the Northern Counties Textile Trades Federation, which has since 1906 acted as the recognized common negotiator on behalf of all workers in the cotton manufacturing industry. And meanwhile a great deal of local co-operation developed. Local Textile Trades Federations were by then established in most of the manufacturing towns, to provide 'mutual assistance against disastrous strikes', to prevent strike-breaking by one society's

[1] *CFT*, September 25, 1896, for report of delegate meeting.
[2] *CFT*, October 23, 1896.
[3] The 'Federation of Amalgamated Associations of Weavers, etc.' is not reported after 1898.

members in another's disputes, and to 'help to induce' all workers to join the union appropriate to their occupation.[1] It is notable that no such local co-operation developed in the spinning industry: and in all these movements, the Weavers apparently played a leading part. Moreover, at a higher level the Weavers' officials not infrequently helped the weaker closed unions in negotiation. The Clothlookers' Amalgamation, for instance (by then known as the Warehousemen's), secured its first general agreement only in 1920, and that with the direct help of the Weavers' General Secretary.

V

Thus, and whereas the Spinners neglected or discouraged the collective association of other operatives, the Weavers actively encouraged it. But the most striking effect of the relationship between the mass Weavers' organization and the small closed unions in manufacturing is to be seen in the changing status of the overlookers. Early overlookers' societies often went out of their way to declare their lack of connection with trade unionism. The Overlookers' Provident Society No. 3 of 1868, for instance (what happened to Nos. 1 and 2 has not emerged), announced that 'We are not connected with strikes and lock-outs'.[2] Instead, it declared that its aims were solely to provide sickness and unemployment benefit, to secure and notify members of information about vacancies, and to give 'by mutual intercourse, younger members . . . such knowledge from the experience of older members as will benefit them in the duties of their occupation.'

This attitude was already changing in those districts where the Weavers were strong. The Oldham Overlookers' Association of 1870 included in its Objects not only 'to help the members to find work' but '. . . to regulate and equalise as far as possible the number of looms an overlooker shall be allowed to superintend, according to class and quality of work: and according . . . to establish one uniform and corresponding rate of wages'. The overlookers' partial Amalgamation of 1875 was 'to avoid unpleasantness between employers and employed'.[3] But its method of promoting peace seems to have been a warlike preparation: its main function was apparently to accumulate a strike fund. However, the Overlookers' association with the Weavers in the preliminaries to the great 1878

[1] Quotations from the *Rules* of the Nelson, Colne and Brierfield Textile Trades Federation, 1903.

[2] The *Rules and Objects*.

[3] *Objects* of The National Confederate Associations of Power Loom Overlookers.

strike of the North Lancashire weaving centres apparently provoked a dissenting movement in the area round Manchester. The Pendleton Overlookers' society, which had grown, from its first formation as a 'Mutual Assistance Association' a decade or so before, into a multi-branch organization of the district, and still declared that 'This Society is not a trade union and we do not acknowledge strikes,'[1] now organized a 'National Association' in rivalry with the near-trade-unionist federation of 1875.

By this time, however, it was becoming not uncommon for weavers promoted to overlooker to retain their membership of a weavers' union despite the existence of separate overlookers' societies which they also joined. In 1883–4, the Blackburn weavers struck for six weeks against a wage-reduction: and local overlookers refused to obey their employers' instruction to both weave themselves and bring their families (their wives and children were often weavers) to work the looms. Afterwards, an agreement between the overlookers' and weavers' associations for mutual support was discussed: it was suggested, for instance, that weavers might refuse to work under overlookers expelled by their own union. But many overlookers were still 'jumped-up lads', some without significant experience as weavers: and the agreement came to nothing. In the depression of 1893, particularly, complaints of overlookers 'driving' their weavers increased—probably because the former were trying to make up their 'poundage' on weavers' earnings reduced by wage cuts—to such an extent that the Weavers' Amalgamation advised its members that '. . . it has become absolutely necessary that some protection be made against your mental depression' and required all cases of alleged 'driving' to be reported for 'instant action'.[2]

The overlookers, however, had meanwhile formed their own new Amalgamation, and one that was definitely trade-unionist in its objects—which were announced as '. . . to provide against the encroachments of employers on our rights and privileges'. In 1887 a group of the conservative National Association's affiliates broke away (as the 'United Association of Power Loom Overlookers'), and both sections later joined the new Amalgamation. Individual unions of overlookers at this time were joining the Weavers in the Local Textile Trades Federations, which often included such objects in their rules as the abolition of the 'slate' system, and prescribed automatic sympathy strikes for any overlooker discharged for refusing to operate it. Some of these Federations also provided that overlookers should give preference to union members in engaging weavers, and that weavers in turn should give no help to non-

[1] The *Rules*.

[2] From a circular of the Weavers' General Council.

unionists attempting to learn the 'closed' trades. And similar objects were adopted when the various manufacturing Amalgamations themselves federated in 1906—with the significant additions that the overlookers themselves agreed to press for a standing weekly wage instead of the 'poundage' on weavers' earnings, and to refuse the promotion of non-union weavers to learn overlooking.[1] It now became usual for the closed societies generally to accept only members of the mass Weavers' organization as new entrants. But over the whole period the character of the overlookers themselves was altered. Not only did they—and by contrast with their counterparts in the spinning industry—become one of the most powerfully-organized occupations in the cotton industry (their Amalgamation is the strongest of the closed union groups in manufacturing) but they definitely shifted over from the role of employers' agents to the side of the operatives. There has, in fact, been a steady tendency for the overlooker to shed his supervisory functions and become more and more a mechanical specialist.

In general, therefore, the prior organization of the weaving industry's mass occupation both directly and indirectly encouraged the development of trades unionism among the more-skilled workers—and that to an extent found in few other industries. In engineering, for instance—the home of the 'New Model' craft amalgamation itself—the organization of supervisory workers remains at the present day so weak that the unions there are compelled to accept the separation of 'staff' from 'operatives', and the formers' associations are not allowed to join the latter in collective bargaining with employers—or to bargain so extensively. While the engineering foremen themselves are little-unionized, and their tendency in that direction continues to be inhibited by the employer-approved Foremen's Mutual Benefit Association. Even in mining, where the overlookers ('under-lookers' in Lancashire, perhaps to distinguish them from their cotton equivalents) are unusually well-organized, their association with the mass miners' unions has never come so close as in the cotton manufacturing industry.

VI

The direct encouragement the Weavers gave to the organization of the more-skilled does not, of course, imply a special altruism on their part. The Weavers' power rested entirely on the strike weapon: few weavers could undertake the more-skilled work, but most more-skilled operatives could weave if it came to the point. And in the cotton towns, whole families lived by textiles: a third of the operatives

[1] *Objects* of the Northern Counties Textile Trades Federation.

at the present time are married women, and the employment of children as 'half-timers' continued well into the present century. So the skilled men's own families were often engaged in weaving, and the formers' hostility or co-operation was thus important to the solidarity of the weavers themselves. Many operatives' associations made a great point of the family relationship: 'It should be the duty of all members of Amalgamations comprising this Federation to see that all members of their families, over whom they have control, are members of the Associations connected with the trades in which they are working,' say the Rules of the Northern Counties Textile Trades Federation, and the precept is repeated in many local federation and union rules.

But particularly, there was the key position the more-skilled groups occupied in the weaving industry's structure. When the overlookers still hired weavers themselves, for instance (and that in towns where little alternative employment to weaving offered itself), their opportunity to victimize trade unionist weavers would have been almost infinite had they exercised it systematically. On the other hand, more-skilled workers had opportunities to forward the weavers' interests as well as damage them. A mill could carry on if half its weavers walked out, but the withdrawal of a handful of tapesizers or warpdressers would—if their occupations were effectively organized—stop it dead. To the weavers' unions, several considerations thus argued the desirability of a sympathetic organization of the more-skilled workers; and since the latter patently preferred to form their own associations where they could, the Weavers could best serve their own ends by encouraging that development.

In some respects, of course, the organization of the more-skilled—indeed (since, again, the Weavers also recruited to their own ranks many of the less-skilled ancillary workers in their industry) of other operatives generally—might seem contrary to the weavers' own interest. Particularly, it could involve a smaller share than they would otherwise secure in their industry's total wage-bill. But it seems more than probable that the Weavers took a different view of that wage-bill's determination to the Spinners. They started, in the 1830s and '40s, at a wage-level little above that of the unorganized mass of women and girls in other factory processes—which, since many men were then taking up power-loom weaving, must have meant not much above subsistence level.[1] The doctrine that wages were held down by the pressure of over-plentiful but uncombined

[1] In 1840 weavers' average earnings were (Wood, Table 42) 10s 6d a week, with 5s for 'helpers' (juveniles). From the same source it can be estimated that other 'unskilled' wages in cotton were rather over 8s for females (including girls), and about 12s for men.

labour is implied in the assertion—repeated so often by weavers' leaders that it appears as a fundamental article of their economic faith—that low wages were caused by an over-production which they in turn encouraged. The Weavers were certainly not socialist in their unions' formative period—though they always took a more radical standpoint than the Spinners (their officers later stood for Parliament as Liberals when the Spinners' leader stood as a Conservative). But the view that wages could and should be raised at the employers' expense, not that of other workers, and would be more likely to be so raised if trades unionism became general, seems implicit in their organizing policy.

Similar considerations to these would, of course, have explained the new Cardroom Amalgamation's willingness to recruit other groups of operatives to its initial membership—though at a later stage the cardroom unions' policy took rather a different turn to the Weavers'. Nevertheless, if one wished for a further illustration of the *indirect*—as opposed to the direct—stimulus that the organization of less-skilled workers has given to that of the skilled, that too is possibly provided by the development of the two major organizations of spinning industry operatives.

The Spinners' attitude to the cardroom unions' growth has been previously recounted. Although some cardroom societies can claim a longer *continuous* existence than any spinners' association, there is no doubt as to the very much deeper historical roots of the spinners' unionism. It may be, in fact, that since the latter based itself on establishing conventional controls of labour supply that amounted to 'customs of the trade', it had less need of formal organization than associations—like the Weavers', or the first effective cardroom union in Oldham—that depended on collective bargaining. At any rate, the probability that the first stable cardroom unions of the 1850s turned initially to the Spinners' unionism as a nearer model than the Weavers', attempting—ineffectively—to consolidate themselves as exclusive and closed associations rather than as a mass organization, may well account for the lag in further cardroom union development. (And that the cardroom unions have continued to be influenced by the Spinners is shown by their adoption of the latters' 'Provincial' organization—a system which permitted the Bolton cardroom clubs, which were slower to break away from the exclusive form, to operate as a distinct grouping in the same Amalgamation as the more aggressive Oldham Cardroom union.)

Nevertheless, the cardroom unions' growth does seem to have had a certain 'feedback' effect on the Spinners' organization. The Spinners' modern unions show two waves of local development (see, again, the *Main Chart*). And despite the Spinners' undoubted supremacy in their industry, each of these waves follows a surge of cardroom organization. The Spinners' major wave, from 1866 through the 1870s, pursues the first tentative movement of Cardroom union formation in the late 1850s. While the Spinners' minor wave, from 1888 to 1893, follows the forming of the Cardroom Amalgamation itself. And wage-movements supply other evidence that moves by the mass of operatives to organize induced the same protective reaction in the skilled spinning workers' combinations as they did in manufacturing. Thus, in the 1860s, after the appearance of the first cardroom unions, cardroom wages jumped sharply, rising nearly twice as fast as those of spinners. After the final construction of a permanent spinners' federation in 1870, however, the spinners again held their own for a period. But in the five years after the Cardroom Amalgamation's establishment in 1886 the spinners were again being overhauled.

It is not easy to summarize this wage movement because of the variety of occupations involved in the cardroom case, but roughly:

Percentage Increase in Weekly Wages[1]

	1860–71	1871–86	1886–91
Spinners (self-actor)	24	4	16
Cardroom hands (male and female)	40–50	0–10	20–30

It is arguable that the tendency for technical innovation in the second half of the nineteenth-century to concentrate in the processes preparatory to spinning would in any case have raised cardroom wages, and reduced the spinners' differential over the latter. But that pressure was at work throughout the period—indeed, was probably most intense in the late '70s, when the relation between spinners' and cardroom hands' wages was, however, stable. And in any case, the preceding and subsequent jumps in cardroom wages specially advantaged male workers, who—as will be shown later—were also to gain most from the preparatory workers' unionization in general. That the improvement in the preparatory operatives' wages relative to the spinners' was at least partly associated with the cardroom hands' organizing campaigns seems incontrovertible. And it seems equally likely that—just as in the weaving industry—this movement of the lower-paid provoked a defensive reaction on the skilled workers' part, thus stimulating the Spinners' re-organizations.

[1] Estimated from Wood's Table 42, again. The overall cardroom increase may be affected by changes in the proportion of female operatives who were juveniles, but not in its detailed timing.

It is at this point, incidentally, that one cannot discount the further possibility, in spinning labour movements, of certain cross-influences from the manufacturing industry. If the Spinners' re-organizations were in part provoked by unionization of lower-paid operatives in their trade, the two waves of cardroom union formation themselves follow hard on those of the Weavers' (see the *Main Chart* again). While another curiosity is the very close parallel between the growth of spinners' local unionism and that of the major skilled occupation in manufacturing—the overlookers. From 1865 to 1893, the formation of new local unions by the Spinners and Overlookers respectively runs parallel, not merely in timing but in area. But it has been shown that, of all the 'closed' manufacturing groups, the Overlookers' development was most nearly determined by that of weavers' trade unionism. What all this may suggest is that the organization of the weavers gave an indirect but double stimulus to that of the spinners. First, in that it set off a general movement to organize the less-skilled operatives that overflowed into the spinning industry. But second, in so far as the organizing of more-skilled manufacturing workers that it directly provoked and aided, in turn encouraged the Spinners' counter-reaction to the new labour movement in their own trade.

At any rate, in the upshot, this counter-reaction certainly dominated the history of spinning's labour during that industry's continued rise. One effect of the Spinners' successful effort to re-assert their supremacy is that by the early twentieth century they had more than restored the advantage in relative wages that they had held over the general run of their industry's workers in the mid-1870s[1]—an advantage they then retained up to the Second World War.[2] Whereas in the weaving industry the egalitarian trend in wage-differentials continued late, and was recently renewed.[3] A condition of the spinner's relative re-instatement, however, was that the degree of organization among spinning workers *as a whole* remained lower than in manufacturing.

VII

Of the contrasting effects of 'open' and 'closed' unionism on workers' organization at large one can find, even in the cotton trades, still

[1] Estimated as for the preceding Table. In 1906 self-actor spinners' relative differentials over their own piecers and cardroom women were the same as in 1877, and over the less-organized spinning females actually increased.

[2] See the present writer's 'Trade Unions, Differentials, and the Levelling of Wages' (Manchester School, September 1952).

[3] Cf. the Table of section IV above, and otherwise as footnote 2.

other illustrations. In a final selection, perhaps the most remarkable case is that of a group which, though numerically small, now occupies a leading position in the Cardroom Amalgamation—the strippers-and-grinders. These workers (who service the carding-machines proper, as opposed to the cleaning and mixing machinery that precedes them in the spinning process, as well as to the various combing and roving frames that follow them and on which the bulk of female spinning operatives are employed) are the direct descendants of the oldest class of men factory workers—the operatives of the eighteenth-century carding-engines. From those earliest years on, however, their status declined—supervisory and mechanical functions being removed from them, and their machine-tending work sub-divided—until by the 1850s their position differed little from that of general labourers. It was they who formed the ephemeral cardroom unions that affiliated to Doherty's NAPL, and who probably gave the main drive to the mid-century attempts at cardroom organization. But after that limited upsurge of the 1860s, their status again declined: in the mid-'70s their wages were actually falling when those of every other class of cotton operative were still moving up.[1]

The strippers-and-grinders were again most prominent, however, in the Cardroom Amalgamation's own formation. At that time (and according to family memories of the trade) in some coarse-spinning districts they were little better than casual labour. Entry to their jobs was quite free (men were in fact taken on as 'jobbers'), and employers dismissed workers and engaged new labour as the fluctuations of trade dictated. But following the successful initiation of the Cardroom Amalgamation, the strippers-and-grinders set about a determined attempt to elevate themselves. One of the Amalgamation's first acts was to press for (and secure) a preferential wage-increase on their behalf: its Second Annual Report noted that '. . . their status and position as *skilled* artisans has during the year made gigantic strides towards the ideal that increasing numbers think it should be'.[2] And to that aim both the unions and the operatives concerned worked persistently. The two then separate occupations of stripper and grinder were gradually merged from the 1880s on. Their members exploited every minor technical change in carding to increase their responsibility: while according to the Amalgamation's present General Secretary, strippers-and-grinders in his own original district had taken, in the 1920s' to setting their own machines despite managerial prohibition. By 1903 they had already secured agreements effectively specifying the ratio of men to

[1] Wood's Table 42, again.
[2] Present writer's italics.

machines. And by World War I they were operating a unique form of 'apprenticeship' in several districts which was confirmed by general agreement in 1919, has since been progressively improved, and now operates as a most effective restriction of entry. The method varies a little between districts, but its essence is that a would-be recruit must be accepted into the union and work for some time before a specified age (in Bolton, twelve months before seventeen) as a 'can-tenter'—a boy assistant. If he completes that period, he will be put on a district rota for vacancies as 'junior' or 'apprentice grinder,' and can meanwhile work at any other job. When a vacancy turns up (which may, even now, take quite a few years) he does two years 'learning' at a little below the full rate. But he is then entitled to work anywhere in the district, not only as a grinder, but at any other male cardroom job.

At any rate, within five years of the Cardroom Amalgamation's establishment, strippers'-and-grinders' wages had been raised by nearly a third—much more than any other cotton occupation's. And they, unlike other operatives in the spinning trade, continued to overhaul the spinners subsequently. By 1920 their wages had risen to nearly three-quarters of the latters'—a ratio that held through the inter-war period, when differentials in most industries were widened.[1] And in more recent revisions of the spinning industry's wage-structure,[2] they have succeeded in putting themselves on a level very close to the still-aristocratic mule-spinners. The strippers-and-grinders comprise only a small proportion of the Cardroom Amalgamation's membership, despite the great role they have played in that body's development. But they have, in effect, been able to exploit the strength that mass unionism provided to make their own occupation 'skilled'—and certainly 'closed'. It is impossible now, of course, to say how far their persistent endeavour to raise their sectional status is attributable to a tradition of the cardroom men's high original position in the first factory industry. The history of the Cardroom Amalgamation might perhaps be interpreted as that of an old skill's struggle to re-assert its originally-distinctive standing. But the point here is that it was only able to do so after first organizing the mass of cardroom workers.

A further example of that central point is provided by the cloth-lookers in the weaving industry. Their Amalgamation of 1894 led a struggling existence for several years—a decade after its formation the total membership of its affiliated locals was only 1,000. But they

[1] See J. W. F. Rowe, *Wages in Theory and Practice* (LSE, London, 1928) Tables III and IV, pp. 48 and 49. Rowe then graded strippers-and-grinders as 'semi-skilled', against his 'unskilled' weavers.

[2] On this, see *Trade Unions, Differentials and the Levelling of Wages* (loc. cit.).

seem then to have decided that a closed union of their own occupation alone offered an insufficient basis of organization, and they began to accept warehousemen generally into membership (adding those workers to their title). There were, however, other pockets of relatively-unskilled workers, male and female, who had not been drawn into the weavers' unions; and by simply ruling that 'men' in their organization's amended title included women, the clothlookers also began to organize the latter. Their Amalgamation's membership rose fast, reaching (now as the Amalgamated Textile Warehousemen) 11,000 by 1921. And (though they never quite regained that peak) by becoming, in effect, a partly 'open' union the clothlookers held their strength much more than most of the cotton Amalgamations in the industry's subsequent retreat.

Another smallish group of skilled workers (this time in spinning —and it is another commentary on the broader impact of the Spinners' closed unionism that several such occupations were only drawn to organize in the time of the 'New Unions' outside) also began to form societies of their own in the early years of this century. These are the cop-packers, a class of specialists in the packing and storing of cotton yarn to preserve its condition. And they apparently came to the same conclusion as the clothlookers about their prospect of maintaining an independent and exclusive organization, but preferred linking themselves with a stronger body to opening the ranks of their own. In the coarse-spinning districts of Oldham and the South-East, where they were probably warned off associating with the Spinners by the previous experience of the under-engineers and roller-coverers, they anticipated the latters' affiliation to the Cardroom Amalgamation.[1] But their union in the fine-spinning Bolton district was unable to accept so proletarian an association, and instead merged with the clothlookers. In each case, however, the cop-packers then continued a flourishing existence. So that in their case, again, the stability of a skilled group's status and organization has also depended on its association with a broader alliance of workers.

By contrast to all these, the small Amalgamated Millwarpers' Society determined to preserve both its exclusiveness and its detachment. Though one of the longest-established of the cotton-trade's closed union organizations (it was formed in 1866), it declined fast in the inter-war period—according to a contemporary account because it was by then so restrictive (the occupation had become virtually hereditary) that employers determined to dispense with its

[1] See section III above. The Oldham cop-packers are shown with the *Main Chart*'s cardroom group at their date of formation, 1908, though they did not join the Amalgamation until 1913.

members' services.[1] It has since expired. It seems, in fact, to have become too inbred to survive hard times. And this is clearly a general risk of closed unionism—including its equivalent forms in non-textile industries. The occupational group that it circumscribes may not prove big enough to give it an enduring basis. But if it does, the very technique of this form of trade unionism involves a definite rigidity: unless the closed union's members are also numerous enough and sufficiently diverse in their experience for the entrance of modifying ideas to be permitted, the organization may lose all capacity to adapt itself to circumstance. At best, the union itself may then decline and disappear, as several such societies (like the Sawyers' Unions that were strong in the nineteenth-century building trade) have done—and a course on which the once-great Spinners' Amalgamation also seems now well set. At worst, it may destroy its own members' occupation by an excessive inflexibility of practice. A firmly-closed unionism is not necessarily in the interest of skilled workers themselves: several of the New Models' modern descendents—most notably the Amalgamated Engineering Union itself—owe their present power to mergers and to openings of their ranks. More to the historical point, the narrowly-closed form of association is not one which could be adopted and preserved by all skilled occupations. The effective organization of many such workers has had to wait on the appearance of broader types of unionism than that which the exclusive unions of the mid-nineteenth century provided.

*

In the previous chapter, we compared the development of the Spinners' and Weavers' Amalgamations themselves—and saw that it was by no means inevitable that stable trade unions should first be formed only by more-skilled workers. We have now compared the effects of the Spinners' and Weavers' differing techniques on the growth of trade unionism at large in their respective industries. And this permits us to extend the previous conclusion—by adding that where less-skilled workers organize first, this has apparently provided a better basis for trade unionism in general than has an initial organization of skilled workers alone. Indeed, it appears that what are nowadays regarded as 'skills' have themselves sometimes achieved that status (or retained it) because of just such a prior organization of unskilled labour. While on the other hand, where an already-skilled group has organized first, this has often frustrated or inhibited the spread of collective association to others.

[1] See *Are Trade Unions Obstructive?* (Hulton, ed., London 1935).

These conclusions are derived from the cotton trades; but their implications seem sufficiently interesting to test by reference to the evolution of the labour movement outside that area. Meanwhile, it in any case also seems that trade union development is as much to be understood in terms of the clash or coincidence of sectional interests among workers, as in terms of the evolution of any general struggle between wage-earners at large and employers.

IV

SOME COMPARISONS

1

The Gap in Trade Union Development

I

The preceding Chapter's broad argument was that the closed unionism which the modern Spinners adopted from their predecessors had a stifling effect on the growth of collective organization among other operatives in their industry. The Weavers' open unionism, on the contrary, actively encouraged the development of a broader labour organization—and this, nearly half a century before a widely-based trade unionism re-appeared in other industries than cotton manufacturing. Historically, the Weavers are usually grouped, because of their early consolidation, with the 'Old Unions', in opposition to which the 'New Unions' of the 1890s appeared. But we have already seen that they were, in a major sense, the first of the New Unions themselves.

But why was it, then, that so long an interval elapsed before a similar mass unionism emerged in other industries? Between the mass labour movements of the 1830s and '40s—the part-economic, part-political upsurges which comprise what is sometimes called the British labour movement's 'revolutionary' period—between that sequence and the wave of general labour organization set off by the seamen's, gasworkers' and dockers' strikes of 1888–91, only three groups of workers produced a substantial and solid trade unionism. These were the miners, the cotton operatives, and the artisans of the established crafts—printers, builders, and several minor groups of tradesmen, but particularly the workers of the great metal and wood-working crafts on which the engineering and constructional industries alike were founded, and which produced the 'New Model' unions of the 1850s and '60s. True, trade unionism not merely survived among certain boot-and-shoe making tradesmen over the whole intervening period, but in the 1860s and '70s extended to the new mass-production operatives of the footwear industry. The boot-and-shoe operatives' unionism, in fact, seems to provide an interesting analogy to that of the cotton workers'.[1] However, they were too few to represent any substantial re-inforcement of the mid-nineteenth-century labour movement: the Amalgamated Society of Boot & Shoe Makers, just after its formation in 1874, had only some 4,000 members—perhaps about 1 per cent. of total union strength at the time. Similarly, there were associations of railway footplatemen and guards that had a continuous history from the 1840s. But these were almost pure friendly societies, as such tolerated (even subsidized) by the railway companies, which suppressed attempts by several grades of railwaymen in the 1860s to adapt the 'friendly' organization to trade union purposes. Indeed, even in the case of the miners, trade unionism was little more than sporadic outside one district: only the colliers of the North-Eastern coalfield achieved any wide and stable organization before the formation (in 1889 again) of the Miners' Federation of Great Britain itself. Previous attempts at national unionism by the mine-workers—in 1841 and in 1869—each collapsed after a few years, bringing down in the process most of the county associations from which they were constructed.

But each of these three major groups—the 'craft' artisans, the cotton operatives, and the miners—had, of course, displayed a large degree of organized activity before the 'revolutionary' decades' mass labour agitation. The pre-history of the modern craft unions is well known: but among the miners also, brief associations (at least) of wage-earning colliers are reported as early as 1662, when 2,000 miners of North-East England petitioned against owners' and overmens' oppressions.[2] Even in the newer coalfields, strikes are reported before the close of the eighteenth century: and early in the nineteenth, regular combinations appeared. One of Scots miners, for example, was suppressed in 1818, reappeared when the Combination Acts were repealed in 1824–5, and seems to have been especially systematic —at least in the Lanarkshire mines near Glasgow, where it operated a quite elaborate control over working conditions until (like the Glasgow Spinners' Union) it was destroyed in 1837.

The great movements of the 'revolutionary' period reached very widely. And if one element in them was certainly a last protest of the old-style hand-worker against inevitable extinction, their influence among the newer classes of industrial workers greatly outweighed

[1] This is referred to again in Chapter IV, 2.

[2] J. U. Nef, in *The Rise of the British Coal Industry* (Routledge, London 1932), vol. ii, p. 177.

that phenomenon in significance. Even the farmworkers, among wage-earners in all experience the group least accessible to labour organization, were stirred into the 'Labourers' Revolt' of 1830; while the Tolpuddle Martyrs' case of 1834 itself shows that attempts at trade unionism continued for a while amongst them despite the violent suppression of that protest. And yet the agitation of the 1830s and '40s left behind it few permanent additions to the ranks of those workers who had previously developed some form of collective association. Why?

The 1889 outbreak was of course preceded by other major attempts to unionize non-craft workers. The uprush of union membership from 1869 to '74 carried several new groups into organization—there was the first significant movement of general labourers in the Beckton gasworkers' strike of 1872, the revival of agricultural workers' trade unionism by Arch's organization, the formation of what was later to become a stable railwaymen's union, as well—quite important to the later development of 'general' unionism—as of an initial tinplate-workers' association in South Wales; and so on. But the recruits of the early 1870s proved mostly ephemeral: the new organizations were largely dissolved by the 'Great Depression' of 1875 on. It can perhaps be argued that had not that economic collapse intervened, collective organization would have stabilized itself among the 'unskilled' much earlier than the 1890s. But the weakness of mass unionism's resistance to such an economic setback, and the long years of delay before it effected a substantial reappearance, must themselves demonstrate how insecure was its previous tenure. Even the already-well-established ironworkers' association, whose strength apparently rose sharply to over 30,000 in the early 1870s, relapsed after the depression to an exclusive society of a couple of thousand members, largely confined to the North of England.[1] Contrast with these events the Lancashire weaving unions' survival, in the previous decade, of the Cotton Famine—a recession which, if less enduring than that of the 1870s, was certainly, in terms of the industry it most affected, very much more severe.

In any case, against the evidence of earlier movements towards a universal form of trade unionism than that of 1889, there is the fact that even the latter, despite its symbolic impact, achieved only a narrow footing. It was not for another twenty years that the 'New

[1] The South Wales tinplate workers were apparently not associated with either the old Iron & Steel Workers' or the later Steel Smelters' union, but after re-forming their organization in 1887, allied themselves with the dockers and became a main support of that branch of 'general' unionism which culminated in the modern T & GWU.

Unions launched, in the industrial struggles that immediately preceded the First World War, upon an extension that carried them by 1920 to a rivalry in strength with the long-established craft organizations and cotton operatives' unions, and with the more recently-consolidated miners' associations. And even then, their stabilization was to a large extent attributable to the almost accidental support they received from war-time legislation which, designed to minimize industrial disputes by compulsory arbitration, virtually compelled their recognition by employers in the process.

In fact, one could probably present a picture of trade union development throughout the nineteenth century up to World War I in terms of a series of waves, occurring roughly one in each generation—around the early 1830s, 1850s, 1870s, 1890s and 1910—in only the last of which (and that doubtfully) did unionism extend so widely, relative to the wage-earning population, as in the waves of the 1830s.[1] And of that, the explanation cannot be that the workers who were untouched by labour organization for so long after the 1840s had in no case yet acquired that stability of occupation which trade unionism, to be both stable and spontaneous, usually requires. Though new manual occupations were still appearing with the elaboration of industrial processes, the main structure of many industries had settled by the 1850s, and the great labour migrations were over. On the other hand, it is notable that some old-established occupations which were preserved by the Industrial Revolution had previously produced early forms of unionism that in this period relapsed. There were, for instance, outbreaks of combination among the watermen and sailors of the North-East coast ports, from the seventeenth century on, that continued under the Combination Acts; and there was a strike as late as 1851.[2] And at that time a national federation of seamen's unions actually existed. But it was only in 1879 that (what was later Havelock Wilson's) Maritime Union formed in the North-Eastern ports—despite the strength of the neighbouring miners' and shipbuilders' unions—and not (again) till 1889 that it achieved more than a local scope. And it is perhaps worth remembering that even such groups as the London dockers were not entirely without historical traditions of organization. Effective guilds of coal-porters and others flourished in the port and

[1] In the textile trades, at least, one could certainly argue for the existence of an earlier 'wave' about 1810—in the decade following the Great Weavers' strike of 1808 (see Appendix B).

[2] Nef (op. cit.) gives an account of the earlier affairs; Aspinall has several later references. The 1851 strike is referred to by Welbourne in *The Miners' Unions of Northumberland and Durham* (Cambridge University Press, 1923) p. 108.

markets of London well into the eighteenth century, though by the late nineteenth that tradition appears to have withdrawn into the small and then-exclusive association of stevedores.

Indeed, outside the groups which had already produced, by the 1850s, a stable 'institutional' trade unionism of the form we have mainly identified with the acquisition of professional officials, there seems thereafter little development even of less formal associations, analagous to what this study has described as 'natural' trade unions in the case of the early cotton operatives' combinations. Even the briefer type of 'unofficial' uprising, such as that set off among non-union engineering operatives by the Nine Hours Movement after 1869, appears to have been a rather rare event.[1] The 'New Unions' of the nineteenth century's end had no such background of primitive or informal association among their members as had their predecessors. What has to be explained, then, is not merely a near half-century's delay in the appearance of solid mass unionism in other industries than cotton manufacture, but an apparent *decline* in the general degree of collective association among workers.

II

One of the most illuminating clues to this feature of British labour's development is provided by the contrast between the strength of trade unionism in cotton over the past century, and its weakness in other major textile trades—particularly in woollens, worsteds and textile-finishing. The workers of these latter industries may well claim to have the oldest of union histories: the wool workers and tailors were the first to form what the Webbs and later authorities recognized as trade unions.[2] While 'Discontent was the prevalent attitude of the operatives engaged in the wool industries for centuries'.[3] And the modern woollen industries share many qualities with the cotton trade. They are geographically concentrated, the wool and the worsted districts separated from cotton by the Pennines,

[1] The railwaymen are perhaps an exception, since about the same time there were several 'unofficial' strikes on the railways—a movement that culminated in the formation of the 'all-grades' Amalgamated Society of Railway Servants of 1872. As in the case of the early cotton operatives, the railway friendly societies may have encouraged collective association: the 1872 Society retained an emphasis on 'friendly benefits', but was so cautious that first the ASLEF and next the General Railway Workers' Union were later formed as 'breakaways'.

[2] See, for instance, Milne-Bailey's 'Introduction' to his *Trade Union Documents* (Bell, London, 1929).

[3] Burnley, *A History of Wool and Woolcombing* (London, 1889) p. 160. The Hammonds' *Skilled Labourer*, of course, gives a very detailed account of the handworkers' agitation in the wool trades from the 1790s to the 1820s (Chapter VI).

and the finishing industry overlapping the areas of all three of those trades. The three spinning and manufacturing industries (cotton, woollen, and worsted) have several fundamental machines and techniques in common, and therefore many similar occupations: their economic conditions are much alike, each being largely dependent on imported materials and foreign markets. The worsted industry, in particular, even has much the same 'horizontal' economic organization as cotton. And yet in modern times the woollen textile trades have presented, among industrial workers, one of trade unionism's weakest sectors. As late as 1936, in fact—after all agreements in the wool and worsted industries had been for nine years suspended by the employers—it was actually proposed to a Board of Inquiry into industrial relations in these industries that worsted spinning be put under a legal Trade Board. How is the nineteenth-century decline in textile trade unionism outside cotton—contrasting so sharply with labour organization's precocious advance in cotton itself—t › be explained?

The very early development of workers' combinations in the wool, worsted and finishing trades arose, of course, from the growth in them (before a significant cotton industry existed) of a capitalist domestic and workshop economy. There were active and powerful operatives' combination very early in the eighteenth century—of woollen weavers in the West Country, worsted weavers in East Anglia, calico-printers in London. The calico-printers' subsequent rise has already been sketched.[1] While the woolcombers' national federation was one of the most formidable of the latter eighteenth-century labour organizations—in 1801 it was alleged to have 60,000 members.[2] As Yorkshire and Lancashire became the great textile regions, these unions moved into them. The early decades of the nineteenth-century were a period of great union activity in the woollen and textile-finishing industries. Both woolcombers and calico-printers virtually ignored the anti-Combination Acts (though the printers' committee was arrested at Bolton in 1815). And several other groups were organized and militant. In Yorkshire, these included wool and worsted spinners and weavers, as well as cloth-workers (the 'shearmen' or croppers); while dyers' and bleachers' activities are frequently reported in Lancashire.

But several of the old unions became involved in a hopeless opposition to machinery. The shearmen were the core of the Yorkshire Luddites, and went down early. The worsted weavers rioted against power-looms in 1822 and again in 1826; and just before the

[1] See Chapter II, 1, section iii—and Turnbull's *History of the Calico-Printing Industry* (op. cit.) for a more detailed account.

[2] Hammonds, *Skilled Labourer* (p. 200).

latter outbreak, they joined with the woolcombers to make a united resistance, in a combination which was crushed after a protracted strike. The calico-printers became similarly committed to a struggle against the march of mechanisms: their 1813 Rules declared that 'No printer, being a fair workman, shall assist or have anything to do with . . . the surface machine,' and laid down detailed instructions for its members' action if machinery were introduced to their workshops.[1] By the 1840s, however, all three occupations were advanced in decline—over 90 per cent. of all calico-printing, for instance, was then done solely by machinery.

In the woollen trades proper, the situation seems to have been rather different. The early improvements in spinning and weaving equipment actually strengthened the independent master-workman's position, and the adoption of the power-loom was much slower than in cotton—handloom weavers were still common in Yorkshire in the 1860s. Here, the workers' pre-occupation was rather with the competition of the big manufacturers. Woollen weavers and clothiers early combined with the shearmen to demand limits, not only on the use of new machines but also on the number of apprentices, spindles and looms individual manufacturers could employ or operate.

These, of course, were mostly domestic workers. But factory operatives' combinations certainly also existed in the non-cotton textile trades about this time. One of wool or worsted operatives is reported as early as 1818 at Colne Bridge[2]—perhaps an outer ripple of the great North-Western strike wave of that year (which also stirred bleachers and dyers around Manchester into collective action[3]). And the Yorkshire 'General Union of Weavers and Spinners' formed at Dewsbury in 1822 presumably included the newer factory operatives, since it gave evidence to the Short-Time Commissions of 1824. While factory workers were no doubt involved in the 'Leeds Trades Union' of 1830—apparently a Yorkshire equivalent to Doherty's National Association for the Protection of Labour, but based mainly on the woollen and worsted trades—which was crushed with the Owenite unions in 1834. But the old handworkers' organizations, concerned mainly to resist machines or preserve an unusual economic independence, neither organized the factory hands nor offered a model which they could imitate.

[1] *Rules for the Conducting of the Union Society of Printers, Cutters and Drawers in Lancashire, Cheshire, Derbyshire, etc., 1813* (in the Manchester Reference Library).

[2] According to Ben Turner's autobiography *About Myself* (Toulmin, London 1930) p. 88.

[3] See Chapter II, 1, section v.

Except in one case: the machine calico-printers' union adopted just its handworking predecessor's technique of organization and entry control, secured an apprenticeship system, and made itself into a craft union. But this shut out the mass of operatives in its industry, as did one or two other small and closed organizations that survived, in the new factories, the old handworkers' decay. So that the collapse of the 1830s' wider labour movement left—despite occasional strikes of woollen factory weavers and other operatives in the late 1840s—no general tradition of association in the woollen and finishing industries.

Into this vacuum came, from the 1860s on, the new cotton unions' influence. The Lancashire weavers were interested primarily in the control of wage-rates, which were determined largely by the condition of cotton manufacturing itself: and to that industry's two or three centres on the Pennine fringe they restricted such deliberate organising efforts as they undertook in Yorkshire.[1] But the more-skilled workers in cotton manufacturing were at this time forming closed unions to regulate the intake of new labour, and to this aim the possible entry of unorganized operatives from similar jobs in the wool trades must have presented a real threat. Moreover, these unions' particular system of entry control, since it usually aimed at directly limiting the total number of qualified workers to the actual number of available jobs, in any case implied mobility of labour. At any rate, in the 1860s local overlookers' societies appeared in all the main wool and worsted towns—their major units, as at Bradford and Leeds, by appearance similarly-organized to the original Blackburn Overlookers' multi-branch union of 1858. And the Yorkshire overlookers' societies later formed a federation of their own. A number of twisters' unions also appeared at this time, in Yorkshire as in Lancashire. And when the warpdressers began to organize in the 1880s they very speedily set up Yorkshire societies.[2] The Lancashire Spinners' control of entry via promotion virtually barred the movement of qualified workers between districts (though two or three wool spinners' unions were formed in Yorkshire in imita-

[1] Indeed, in one sense, Yorkshire may be said to have had more influence on the Lancashire weavers than these did on Yorkshire. The special militancy of the Colne Valley cotton-weavers' associations may be partly attibutable to the immigration of some of the most vigorous Yorkshire weavers, either drawn by higher wages in cotton, or expelled from wool for trade union activities.

[2] In the *Main Chart* of Chapter III, 1, only those Yorkshire organizations which actually federated with the cotton Amalgamations are shown. Since the Overlookers' and Twisters' Amalgamations were initially 'strike fund' associations, designed to deal with the cotton masters, their woollen equivalents had no interest in joining. But the Warpdressers' Amalgamation acted as an employment exchange from the first, and federated Yorkshire and Lancashire.

tion of them); and they, like the Weavers, remained uninterested in their woollen equivalents. But the Spinners' re-organizations appear to have set off a different movement: about the time of the Spinners' revival in the 1860s,[1] a group of skilled workers in the finishing trades around Bolton (where they were largely engaged on the processing of fine yarns) also formed local closed unions which then federated, very much on the local Spinners' lines, as the 'Bolton Amalgamated Dyers, Bleachers and Finishers'.[2] So that by the decade's end a substantial cluster of closed unions was established in the wool, worsted and finishing industries.

But this fostered no development of mass unionism. Indeed, the early memoirs of Ben Turner, who became the most notable of the Yorkshire textile operatives' leaders, give a picture[3] of a relation between the organized aristocrats and the general mass of workers in the 1880s strikingly similar to that so commonly reported of the cotton trades a century before: 'The weaver was looked down upon by the overlookers, and . . . a woollen spinner and a woolsorter despised the company of men in ordinary grades of labour . . . the woolsorter had his special chair in his special snug at his customary public house and a woolcomber or a labouring factory worker had to be above the ordinary if he was allowed in that place.' There were occasional weavers' strikes in the 1860s and '70s, but these produced no surviving organization. While the Huddersfield Weavers' Union, formed in 1881, was just such an informal organization as the early cotton-weavers' unions—but without their degree of customary solidarity. This union was composed of delegates from mills where operatives had paid 6d for a membership card, and collected no regular subscriptions. Turner thought the union 'almost valueless' and, after a catastrophic defeat from want of funds or support in its 1883 strike against an employer-imposed wage-list, he led a move to re-organize it on Lancashire lines. But the Yorkshire weavers were too demoralized (or poor) to pay a regular contribution, and the union languished still.

The Yorkshire dyers were rather better placed than the weavers, partly because they included many more-skilled if still unorganized workers (and the rest mainly men), partly because they were mostly employed by a small group of big firms with strong cartellist tendencies—and these, once the finishing workers had produced a trade unionism sufficiently militant to constitute a potential threat to

[1] See Chapter III, 1, section VII.

[2] The writer has heard this referred to by old workers simply as 'The Bolton Amalgamation'. At one stage, it actually seems to have been linked with the cotton unions' Factory Acts Reform movement.

[3] *About Myself*, p. 130.

the continuity of production, proved willing to come to quick terms with it. Even so, an attempt to form an Operative Dyers' Society ('Amalgamated' like the Bolton group) failed at Bradford in 1871: and though the re-formed Bradford union of 1878 succeeded ten years later in securing recognition and a nine-hour day by strike action, it remained narrowly-based and limited to its particular local centre—as did a similar (but 'National') association later formed at Leeds.

What loosed a wider movement in the wool and finishing industries was the general wave of 'New Unionism' in the 1890s. Turner of the Huddersfield Weavers and Hayhurst of the Bradford Dyers were aggressive exponents of the new doctrines. And the Yorkshire factory towns were a fertile field: Leeds, particularly, was a centre of the garment workers' and gas workers' activity, and the miners' unionism revived in the surrounding districts. The new or re-suscitated popular unions helped each other, often through (again, new or revived) Trades and Labour Councils. And they were stimulated, encouraged and aided by Socialist agitators—to whom several of the union leaders were fervent recruits (Turner actually joined the Knights of Labour's European branch): one may, indeed, speculate how far the late persistence of militant Chartism in the Yorkshire towns—itself perhaps a symptom of trade unionism's earlier disappointment and defeat there—made them especially receptive to the new mode of labour organization. At any rate, the Huddersfield Weavers' Union became involved in a Bradford strike in 1890 and re-formed as the West Riding Power-Loom Weavers' Association. The title suggests an emulation of the Lancashire cotton weavers; and about this time the *Cotton Factory Times*—the Lancashire unions' semi-official journal—started a Yorkshire satellite. But only one wool-weavers' union in fact established itself on the Lancashire model, and that at Saddleworth, on the fringe of the cotton area. The new West Riding Association was already taking a different form; a few years later (largely under the influence of Turner) it renamed itself 'The General Union of Weavers and Textile Workers', and began to organize other operatives. And in 1900 it formed a Textile Workers' Federation with the Leeds Dyers' Union. Meanwhile the Bradford Operative Dyers' Amalgamation organized strikes over a wider area, and in 1894 secured an extraordinarily favourable 'union security' agreement from its own monopolistic employers. It sent out organizers to other regions, and by sheer friction stimulated the old Bolton Amalgamation, first into a broader activity, and then into another (though uneasy) federation with itself—as the National Federation of Dyers, Bleachers and Kindred Trades. Meanwhile, the 'New' Gasworkers' and General

Labourers' Union began to organize in both the worsted and finishing trades.

In these movements, the now quite long-established skilled workers' organizations played no part—they held aloof from the Textile Workers' Federation campaign for an eight-hour day for, instance. And, in fact, the proportionate effect of all this activity was small. Turner's General Union of Textile Workers had a membership of some 2,000 only at the close of the century, and that declining. The second national wave of general labour organization, that immediately preceded World War I, carried union membership in the dyeing and finishing trades to some three-quarters of their total employment. But in 1913 the woollen and worsted unions, in all, still had only about 15 per cent. organization. In particular, their membership of women—the majority of their trades' operatives—was confined to four or five thousand, against the cotton unions' 150,000 of 1910 (and this, the year before the Lancashire Weavers fought a county lock-out on their policy of refusing to work with non-unionists). And although the Yorkshire unions' membership grew with the First World War's national extension of mass unionism, their inter-war weakness has already been noted. It was, no doubt, this continued weakness which largely persuaded the modern woollen and worsted operatives—like their predecessors, the hand-workers of a century before—to merge their own organization with a stronger. By successive amalgamations in 1922 and 1936, they combined with the dyers' and finishers' unions to form the present National Union of Dyers, Bleachers and Textile Workers. While even the Woolcombers' Union, heir to the strongest of the old-style exclusive societies, was driven in 1936 to merge into the NUGMW. So that trades unionism in the non-cotton textile industries now has a very different shape to that which it assumed in cotton itself.

Despite the very early appearance of trade unions in the pre-factory industries, modern union structure in the woollen and textile-finishing trades thus represents a not untypical product of the partly socialist-inspired movements to mass labour organization associated with the Match Girls and the London Dockers. So that its main feature is a single large and primarily 'open' union, which has developed a solid core in the finishing trades, but becomes progressively weaker as it spreads out through the woollen and worsted industries into several minor textile sectors. But the great *general* unions also organize sections, not merely of these minor textile trades, but of the woollen and allied industries themselves. Whilst alongside these alternate products of the same New Unionist movement to mass association, there is a handful of minor closed unions which, though long-established, have played little part in the broad development of textile labour organization.[1]

One reason for the present form of trade unionism in the woollen and finishing trades is that the tactics and techniques of its early predecessors, the old handworkers' associations, were not such as could be adapted to the factory operatives needs'—indeed, were rather alien to the latter, since the handworkers were so much preoccupied with resistance to machinery or the preservation of the independent craftsman. But the major point here is that neither the survival in the factory industry of fragmentary closed unions from the earlier epoch, nor, particularly, the importation by certain skilled groups of new forms of closed unionism from the Lancashire cotton trades in the 1860s, stimulated (*or* encouraged) any general movement. Unionization on an extensive scale had to wait on the later intervention, if not quite of an outside force, at least of an influence that was national, and partly political, in character—and which has largely moulded the present form of trade unionism in the non-cotton textile industries. There is thus a clear contrast with the cotton manufacturing trades, where the open weavers' unions were first to appear—not merely in the structure and solidity of trade unionism there, but especially in the promptness and pace with which a broad organization of labour developed, in its native vigour, and its independence of external stimulus.

III

When one looks at the growth of trade unionism in individual industries one usually finds that it has depended on the establishment—in a particular district or occupation within the industry, or in a closely allied trade—of a core of organization: a group of workers whom special circumstances have permitted to develop a technique of collective association and action in advance of their fellows. Sometimes other workers imitate the original group's methods; sometimes the group itself is actively interested in extending organization to others. In either case, from this group organization spreads. The cases of the Blackburn district weavers in cotton manufacturing, the Oldham strippers-and-grinders in the cotton spinning trades, the Yorkshire dyers and finishers in the other textile industries, are repeated in the history of a number of unions—by Co-operative Society employees in the Union of Shop, Distributive and Allied

[1] Several of them are, of course, now associated with the Textile Workers' Union in the National Association of Trade Unions in the Textile Trade (NATTU). But this federation was a product of the movement to consolidate 'industry-wide' bargaining after World War I.

Workers, to take a more recent instance. But what seems to have happened to mid-nineteenth century trade unionism is that its potential cores of development—the groups that had already succeeded in establishing some kind of continuing collective association—nearly all turned to a form that not merely gave no encouragement to the growth of trade unionism in *general*, but actively discouraged it.

There are no doubt, cases—in some Continental countries, for instance—where broad political-social movements have by themselves inspired the development of stable trade unions. But for that to happen, such movements must at least continue long enough for participation in general agitations to pass over into a habit of mutual support in more humdrum sectional issues. And the defection of the already-organized groups of workers from the early British 'revolutionary' labour movements largely robbed the latter of momentum. The mid-nineteenth century Spinners were, of course, by no means alone in their reaction from the preceding period's political exuberance: the branches of the ASE 'do not allow any political matter to be discussed at all nor entertained among us,' said Newton of the Engineers in 1856. It was only by a skilful campaign of persuasion that the 'Junta' leaders edged the 'trade societies' back to a cautious support of such political demands as those for manhood franchise; and the established unions were drawn into a substantial political role anew as much by the series of legal threats to their existence and practice that followed the public reaction to the Sheffield outrages of 1866. While their political aims then remained cautiously limited—to questions affecting their own status in a social, political and economic order they broadly accepted: the major political objectives of the craft amalgamations had probably been realized by 1875. After the decay of Chartism, it was principally the non-craft associations of the cotton operatives and miners that again took up the method of political pressure. And they did so in relation to narrowly-specific issues—the regulation of female and child labour in textile factories, such aspects of working conditions there as 'steaming' and so on, in the case of the cotton workers; questions of safety, the prevention of cheating by employers in payment for work done and the like, in the case of colliers. But by themselves political campaigns for such issues supposed the existence of collective organization in the trade concerned: they could not create it. In the pressing case of safety regulations for shipping, for instance, the national seamen's federation of the early 1850s had agitated to improve the Merchant Shipping Acts; but no such organization existed to support Plimsoll's Bill twenty years later.

In the industrial sphere proper, there was of course a fairly general withdrawal by established unions from interest in promoting organization outside their own occupations. Some of the craft societies—like the printers and engineering mechanics—had in any case remained aloof from the early general union movements. But even the Operative Builders, whose great 'General Union' of 1831–4 apparently organized labourers as well as tradesmen,[1] withdrew from that enterprise when the Union broke up into the craft societies among which were later to be numbered one or two of the New Model's most powerful representatives. One group of internal dissentients to the General Union's expansive ambitions called themselves, significantly, 'The Exclusives'.

The builders' case is of some special interest, because there—unlike most other craft trades—the threat of strike-breaking by unorganized labourers showed itself substantial. Yet the next attempt to organize building labourers came from an outside body, the 1845–6 National Association of United Trades for the Protection of Labour, with the brief career of which the building crafts themselves had small association. The Building Labourers' Union that was formed in London during the great 1859 lock-out broke away and disintegrated before the stoppage was over, possibly because of discrimination in strike pay.[2] When the 1872 London building lock-out stimulated the labourers there to a new effort at unionization, the assistance of both Applegarth of the Carpenters and Coulson of the Bricklayers was largely directed to guiding the infant association towards 'sound amalgamated principles': the Amalgamated Builders' Labourers' Union in fact disintegrated the next year just because of that attempt to impose centralized financial control on its local lodges. And although one union of building labourers that was formed in 1889 survived until it was quite recently absorbed by the bricklayers' amalgamation, it never had more than a few thousand members. In the upshot, unionization of building labourers (like that of less-skilled engineers) was only finally achieved by general labour unions with a base in other industries. Had the

[1] There is some dispute about this. The Webbs (*History*, p. 125) listed labourers as one of the seven sections of the Builders' General Union—as does a recent reporter, Francis Williams (*Magnificent Journey: The Rise of the Trade Unions*, Odhams, London, 1954, p. 57), but presumably after them. Postgate's *Builders' History* (NFBTO, London, 1923, p. 67) says the Webbs were mistaken, and that the slaters comprised the Union's seventh section, though labourers may have been organized with the main crafts which the sections otherwise represented. However, Postgate later refers (p. 89) to an independent action by Manchester labourers *within* the Union, and quotes the intention of leaders of the Union to include them, together with certain other badly-organized groups, in its intended 'productive' offshoot, the Grand National Guild of Builders, 'as soon as they can be prepared with better habits and more knowledge to enable them to act for themselves'.

[2] See Postgate (op. cit.) p. 175.

craftsmen genuinely wanted their labourers organized, the daily working relationship between the two grades is such that these things could hardly have happened.

It is understandable that the organized craftsmen should have had little enthusiasm for the extension of trade unionism downwards —or even, sometimes, outwards to other groups who might reasonably claim skills allied and comparable to their own. For the crafts themselves to organize the lower-paid workers involved the possibility of claims on those funds to the accumulation of which the craft amalgamations had become devoted. Particularly, their attitude cannot but have been influenced by the chance that any gains secured by an unskilled workers' organization might well be at the expense of the tradesmen's wage differentials or of their claims to monopolize the allocation of better-class work. What is more curious is that the separation of a privileged section of wage-earners from the mass, the exclusion of the generality of factory operatives and workers from better-paid jobs, did not provoke those excluded to combine in retaliation. Especially, because the relationship between the aristocracy of wage-earners and the rest often went beyond such things as the enjoyment by the former of disproportionate wage-differentials or an exceptional security, and included an element of obvious exploitation—as where (a not uncommon system) the skilled man was responsible for his helpers' payment, and openly appropriated the lion's share of their joint product—or even authorized the labourers' actual maltreatment.[1]

True, at this stage the closed unions themselves offered no model which could be imitated by occupations without customary entry requirements that could be converted to deliberate entry restrictions, and too badly-paid to raise the subscriptions entailed in attempts to eliminate surplus labour. Yet cases like the Spinners, in which the aristocrats' societies actively *prevented* their assistants forming independent unions, are perhaps few. Nevertheless, it seems significant that where trade unionism of the lower-paid was achieved independently of the outside 'New Union' agitation, this was often attributable to the initiative of some group with existing organization which had, however, failed to gain its members a secure aristocratic status. This was so not merely of the cotton cardroom workers, but in the case of the successful protest movement in the iron and steel industry already referred to.[2]

[1] See Alexander Somerville's account (*Autobiography of a Working Man*, 1818 —pp. 86 et seq. of 1951 edition) of the masons' attitude to their labourers.

[2] See Chapter III, 2, section III: 'Hodge's Union' was originally a small Scottish society that actually excluded helpers for demanding promotion rights, but then saw in the latters' dissatisfaction an opportunity of extending into England.

What seems likely is that the exclusive unions' methods, in the general absence of effective examples of an alternative form of trade unionism, now created among the unorganized a hostility to unionism as such. On the one hand, the continued development of industrial technique itself imposed on closed unionism a certain obviously anti-social quality. The exclusive unions relied upon a monopoly of certain jobs: but jobs were changing, so they were compelled to attempt to extend their monopoly to match. Thus much of the new, better-class work that technical innovation created was withheld from the lower-paid workers: even the disputes which led to the ASE's formation were partly caused by the craftsmen's demand that labourers be excluded from new machines. So that on the other hand, the conflicts in which the closed unions themselves became involved were also rarely such as to stimulate wide sympathetic movements. To the contrary, in fact: many of them were so strictly struggles between rival monopolists that they not merely hindered the latters' own development (in both building and engineering, demarcation and similar disputes were a continuing drain on the great new craft amalgamations' energies) but could have induced nothing but resentment in the labourers and others whom they put out of work. Add to these things a natural reaction from the open contempt with which craftsmen commonly regarded such attempts at self-protection as their labourers made.[1] And John Burns' comment of 1885 falls into place: 'The great bulk of our labourers are ignored by the skilled workers . . . (so that) ostracized by their fellows, a spirit of revenge alone often prompts men to oppose or remain indifferent to Unionism . . .'[2]

In the end, of course, the craft unions' traditional attitude to the labourer provoked an opposition within their own ranks which helped to modify their exclusiveness. Less notice has been attracted by the attitude of most 'Old Unionists' to women workers. The general hostility of trade unions in the 1860s and '70s to the women's cause in fact led to several attempts to form independent female unions, and to the establishment of the Women's Trade Union League. 'Eminent historians of the Labour and Trade Union movements have preferred to scuttle hurriedly across this dangerous ground,' writes a recent commentator on the women's social movement of the time; 'the women's battle in the unions was with the men rather than the employers—with the domestic, not the economic

[1] The 'labourers,' said Coulson the Bricklayers' secretary (despite the Builders' dubious record in their respect) 'cannot be organized.'

[2] *Justice*, January 24, 1885. (Extract in the Webb Collection).

boss.'[1] And indeed, the Secretary of the TUC himself declared the function of unions to be '. . . to bring about a condition . . . where their wives would be in their proper sphere at home, instead of being dragged into competition for livelihood against the great and strong men of the world'.[2] Up to the 1890s, in fact, the cotton unions constituted an honourable exception to the major unions' attitude on the social claims of women: and the further growth of their organization, in the established Weavers as well as the new Cardroom Amalgamation, has been described as 'of first importance' to the women's suffrage movement,[3] into the leadership of which the Oldham mill-hand Anne Kennedy then brought a working-class element. There followed, over several years, a campaign which included pressure on the cotton unions' M.P.'s by their women members, and the presenting in 1901–2 of nearly 70,000 women textile operatives' petition for the vote. In Lancashire, there was a major effort to bring the women's economic and political struggles together. But at this stage other union leaderships were still largely indifferent—if not hostile: even the Miners, who in other respects at this time were by no means to be identified with an 'Old Union' viewpoint, opposed the joint Labour/Women's candidature at the mixed cotton-mining constituency of Wigan in the 1906 election.

IV

That the frustrating effects of exclusive tendencies were by no means confined to the 'craft' industries seems, in fact, sufficiently shown by the Miners' own history. And their example is particularly interesting because, otherwise, the miners show many close analogies with the cotton workers—with whom they made up half of known union membership in the early 1870s. The mining industry, like the textile industry, produced a numerous wage-earning class long before the Factory Revolution. In the seventeenth century, many mining enterprises already employed upwards of a hundred workers. And by the eighteenth century the industry was largely dependent on capitalist finance, and had developed a separate managerial class. Indeed, as typical industrial wage-workers the miners can probably claim not merely a longer history than the cotton operatives, but a more continuous one. The transition from the early mining system, by which groups of free workers jointly contracted with coal-owners to work pits or seams, to the large-scale hiring of individual wage-labourers that became almost invariably usual in the nineteenth

[1] Fulford, in *Votes for Women* (Faber, London, 1957) pp. 107/8.
[2] Henry Broadhurst, to the 1875 TUC.
[3] By Fulford (loc. cit.).

century, provides a certain analogy with the transition in cotton from independent domestic weaver to factory operative. But in the coalfields that developed first and fastest, at least, this democratic group-contract system was never generally predominant.

Otherwise, however, the analogy between miners and cotton operatives is continued to recent times in their unions' structure and policies, which contrast sharply with those of the craft amalgamations. There is the same foundation on the local society (the pit or district 'lodge' in the miners' case), itself sometimes employing a full-time officer concerned primarily with the details of wage-fixing. There is the same essentially federal superstructure—except that the county or regional miners' federation largely replaces the sectional 'amalgamation' of the cotton unions. There is the same tendency—as in the case of the Northumberland and Durham cokemen, enginemen, mechanics and deputies from 1864 on—for occupational groups to split off while retaining a federal link with the broader association (a tendency recognized in the modern NUM by the establishment of separate 'Areas' for craftsmen, etc.). And there is the same trend for such general federations—up to the Miners' Federation of Great Britain itself—to form for general wage-movements, the accumulation of strike reserves, and political pressure. But the analogy continues in another respect: the historical role of the closed spinners' unions in relation to other cotton operatives seems substantially reproduced, in coal, by the relation of the North-Eastern Miners' Associations to the miners of other coalfields. The North-East district largely dominated the history of miners' unionism for half a century from 1840. And that history conveys a large suggestion that the more general instability of mining trade unionism during this period is connected with the North-Eastern colliers' aristocratic tendencies.

Long before the Factory Revolution proper, the miners' condition had taken on a quality which went beyond that of a distinct occupation and made them virtually a separate social caste. In early times, the very handling of coal entailed a social ostracism. The miners themselves were already largely isolated in colliery communities, dependent on mine-owners for housing and necessities, and subject to elaborate employers' disciplinary codes. The conditions and danger of mining were such that labour for the immense seventeenth-century expansion could only be provided by forced impressment and kept by severe legal restraints. In the most rapidly expanding areas—those with access to North Sea transport—mine ownership was, moreover, identified with political and social power. In Scotland, the great landowners' influence in the state produced the peculiar legal slavery of the miners there. But in the North-East—

which by 1700 produced nearly 40 per cent. of British coal—local life was dominated by the great Newcastle merchants, the 'Hostmen' who legally monopolized the region's sea outlet, and from that base straddled local enterprise and government.

Thus for any defensive movement of miners in the North-East, the situation in which the Spinners' Grand Union of 1829–30 found itself, of confrontation by a formidable combination of large-scale capitalist employers, was reproduced a century before that time—only intensified by the even greater political power of the North-Eastern mine-owners and by the still sharper social rift of employer from worker. There was, however, this difference in the North-Eastern pitmen's situation: that the Newcastle merchants' monopoly—which continued until well into the nineteenth century—also acted in some measure to protect the miners' conditions, since the mine-owners could pass customary labour costs on to consumers. So that there was already an element of the paternalism that now often accompanies monopolistic conditions.[1]

In the early eighteenth century, the mining industry's expansion slowed. And it was then that two features of the North-Eastern miners' conditions crystallized that were later to become of major importance. First, technical improvements reduced mining's previous dependence on the underground porter: coal haulage became a boy's job, and the hewers—the coalface workers proper—began to emerge as an aristocracy among colliers. The 'butty' system (essentially a form of gang-labour) which became so common in the newer mining areas of nineteenth-century development was never adopted in the North-East coalfield. Under its older technique, the hewers worked individually or in pairs, with only occasional supervision: they were paid on output, the available working places in each mine being customarily shared by lot to prevent favouritism by employers' agents. They developed a skill, independence and solidarity that made them stand out as 'a sturdy band, apart from the motley mixture of common humanity'.[2]

But secondly, and immediately more important—the 'Yearly Bond' became the normal North-Eastern method of engagement. Much later, the Bond was to be an object of miners' resentment. But at this time, it provided relatively high standards of wages and security—not only specifying piece-rates in some detail, for instance, but including a form (perhaps the first instance) of 'guaranteed

[1] According to Welbourne (op. cit., Chapter. 1) the 'Hostmen' appear in the seventeenth century to have stopped their agents from paying pitmen in truck, and to have levied coal in stock to support the miners during their own disputes with the London consumers.

[2] Boyd, *Coal Pits and Pitmen* (Whittaker, London, 1895).

wage'. From then on, attempts by the owners to modify the Bond's terms were a cause of major disputes in the North-East. Thus, the great strike of 1765, which lasted with widespread violence from August to October, arose from a reported owners' combination to restrict the pitman's freedom to change employers at binding-time. And in 1810 the defeat of a strike which was similarly widespread (and not dissimilarly causated) entailed such an aftermath of unrest that the next year the owners agreed to meet together a deputation of miners representing each colliery. That meeting drew up an agreed Bond, to be observed by all the district's pits and colliers.

The North-Eastern miners had thus established a considerable collective regulation of their working conditions—had even come close to large-scale collective bargaining—before any systematic trade unions are recorded amongst them. But in the early nineteenth century their situation began to change. An influx of new capital opened up new collieries; and the new employers did not share the old monopolists' respect for customary labour costs. Terms of the Bond that were favourable to the miners were withdrawn—or increasingly evaded—and its restraints more onerously enforced. The repeal of the Combination Acts freed the miners to retaliate openly: in 1825, they formed 'The Colliers of the United Association of Durham and Northumberland'. When the new owners refused to deal with this union, the miners' attempt to counteract speed-up by imposing their own output limitations led to local strikes that culminated over 1831–2 in general conflict.[1] The great 1832 strike's defeat confirmed the owners' refusal to revive the old central agreement; and the miners' discontent was afterwards partially diverted to Chartism. That movement's suppression in 1839–40 was facilitated by a period of prosperity: but when another slump revived the North-Eastern miners' unionism, it is significant that the movement now took the form of a national combination.

'The Union of Miners of Great Britain and Northern Ireland' of 1841 affiliated county miners' associations from the now rapidly-growing coalfields of the Midlands, Lancashire and Yorkshire as well as from Scotland. Nevertheless, the Northumberland and Durham men played the forward role in it: and it was their aggressive defence (including their hiring of the swashbuckling Chartist solicitor, Roberts) of colliers in 'breach of bond' cases that drove the owners concertedly to abandon the annual Bond altogether. The North-Eastern miners' consequent demand that the owners accept a six-monthly Bond of the miners' own formulation provoked a

[1] Page Arnot, in *The Miners* (Vol. I, Allen & Unwin, London, 1949, pp. 35–6), says the 1831 union was actually a new one, the 1825 combination having meanwhile broken up.

conflict that temporarily broke the North-Eastern association. But the new national union's decision to support their great 1844 strike also involved the more immature miners' organizations of other districts in the subsequent collapse. The national union was effectively extinct by 1852.[1]

The North-Eastern miners maintained sufficient natural solidarity to organize local strikes, present a common front on re-binding terms where the annual Bond was preserved, and to conduct occasional wider campaigns—for mine-safety inspection for instance. But they had apparently lost interest in the national miners' movement: other developments were already swinging them back to a conservative policy. Technical progress had elaborated and consolidated the originally-primitive hierarchy among the North-Eastern miners. The perfection of blasting had long made it unnecessary for a pair of hewers to work its place together; the two partners now divided the working day up, working two separate shifts of six hours each. The 'putters', haulage and ancilliary workers, however, continued to work the full day. At the same time developments in underground transport and the increasing size of pits multiplied the number of haulage workers. And that also increased the steps in the ladder of advancement from boy entrant to high-earning hewer. A rigid seniority became by custom the rule in all questions of promotion and job-security at each pit. While the number of ancilliary operatives who were not on the promotion ladder also increased with technical development—some of them craftsmen and specialists, but many in lower-grade jobs. The hewers, in fact, were assuming a position in the North-Eastern mines remarkably similar to that of the mule-spinners in the cotton industry. To them, at least, such further security as the Annual Bond once offered was now small compensation for its restraints and penalties.

Thus, when in 1862–3 an owners' attempt to revive the Annual Bond provoked the North-Eastern miners to re-form their regional union, it displayed an attitude much closer to the craft societies outside the mines than to that of their own association of twenty years earlier—an attitude which was confirmed and embodied in the new permanent officials they appointed.[2] And the Northumbrian miners almost immediately demonstrated their new exclusiveness by breaking away from those of Durham who, more diluted by expansion of the Durham field, had proved too weak to resist the

[1] According to Fynes' *The Miners of Northumberland and Durham* (Sunderland, 1873) p. 139.

[2] 'Even now,' said Welbourne (op. cit., p. 11) in 1923 of the North-Eastern collier, 'he is apt to look upon the miners of other districts as navvies rather than miners proper.'

annual Bond's re-imposition. 'The Northumberland men felt that to them it was like being connected with a body of death.'[1] But when the Durham Miners' Union recovered, it adopted a policy very similar to that of Northumberland. And the attitude of *both* the North-Eastern Miners' associations to those then reviving in other districts was reserved. They were prepared, like the spinners in cotton, to join in a federation for legislative pressure—the Miners' National Union of 1863, which they effectively dominated.[2] But their unwillingness to co-operate with other, and less-organized, miners' districts in industrial action compelled several of these to form the rival Amalgamated Association of Miners of 1869, for mutual support.

The later history of the miners' unions is well known. The re-formed North-Eastern unions, after surmounting some initial conflicts, soon came to terms with their own employers. Between the 1830s and 1850s, the North-Eastern miners had demanded a general minimum wage and successive reductions in working hours; such demands they now abandoned. They accepted instead the principle that 'prices should rule wages', and turned to the elaboration of detailed wage-fixing and arbitration procedures. And this implicit settlement was for nearly forty years to divide the North-Eastern aristocrats from other miners. The sliding-scales (varying wages with coal prices) which they accepted as the logical expression of their new position were imposed on the lower-wage miners of other districts by employers. The rival Amalgamated Miners' Association was too weak to support alone the South Wales miners in their 1875 dispute and collapsed. Trade unionism in most other districts than the North-East withered to nominal proportions, while from the Welsh coalfield it virtually disappeared for twenty years. The ultimate revival of general miners' unionism under the MFGB of 1889 occurred in face of North-Eastern opposition to moves for a full national federation; and the MFGB's demands for a minimum wage and an eight-hour day were now just the grounds of the North-Eastern unions' abstention from it. And that abstention continued, despite dissent from lower-wage, long-shift miners in the North-East itself, for nearly twenty years—until trade unionism was solidly established in all other coalfields, and the North-East's power eclipsed.

[1] J. Wilson, *A History of the Durham Miners' Association* (Veitch, Durham, 1907), p. 6.

[2] This federation was, of course, first titled 'The National Association of Coal, Ore and Ironstone Miners', and was originally regarded as a continuation of the 1841 association: it seems to have become known as the Miners' National Union only after the rival 'Amalgamated Association' appeared.

All this is clearly reminiscent of the Spinners' role in cotton.[1] Indeed, the analogy with union development in the cotton spinning industry is extended by the Yorkshire miners, who seem to have played a part in the final establishment of mass miners' unionism (though that event was much more closely identified with the outside New Unionist movement) remarkably like that of the Cardroom Amalgamation's strippers-and-grinders in cotton spinning. Just as some cardroom clubs apparently antedated stable spinners' societies, the South Yorkshire Miners' Association could trace a continuous history back to 1858, several years before the North-Eastern miners' unions were re-formed.[2] But, as in the cardroom, early miners' unionism in Yorkshire remained comparatively weak, and very much under its more solid neighbours' influence; to Durham and Northumberland it virtually acted as auxiliary in the Miners' National Union. However, the Yorkshire organization shared the consequences of the rival Amalgamated Miners' Association's defeat in the 1870s, though it survived the depression. And afterwards, the Yorkshire miners broke away from the conservative North-Eastern grouping, and played the leading role in the establishment and consolidation of the MFGB—which they then for manv years dominated.

The history of miners' unionism seems, therefore, not untypical of the general pattern in industries where exclusive unions came to the fore in the mid-nineteenth century. After the first appearance of a wage-earning class, some groups achieve a real degree of collective regulation by informal, 'natural' workers' associations. A new industrial expansion—induced here by the Factory Revolution itself—plunges them into a period of uncertainty. Partly in an attempt to maintain their own customary or traditional standards, they promote or support wider demands and mass organizations of workers not previously organized. But among the original groups, the consolidation of an internal aristocracy in regular 'institutional' unions leads to their withdrawal from the general movement, the

[1] That the relationship between the North-Eastern miners and others was partly between workers in different areas, while the relationship of spinners' to cardroom unions in cotton was between those in different occupations, does not materially affect the analogy, since in both coal and cotton-spinning the groups concerned occupied complementary roles in their respective industries' productive structure. Thus, a difference in the markets of the North-Eastern coalfield (which developed as an exporting district, while most of the other fields—particularly those of Yorkshire and the Midlands that were most forward in the MFGB's formative years, expanded as home-market suppliers) perhaps facilitated the North-Eastern unions' pursuance of a separate course of evolution.

[2] See F. Machin's *The Yorkshire Miners* (Centenary Publication of NUM Yorks. Area, 1958).

collapse of which then breeds disillusionment and a retreat from organization among others. While, when the mass movement finally reappears, it may even encounter—as in the notorious case of the miners' Eight-Hour Day, of which the MFGB's final achievement by political pressure was protested by a strike in the North-East—the established aristocracy's active hostility. That, in mining, the North-Eastern hewer's achievement of an aristocratic position was critical to this pattern of events is perhaps confirmed by the contrasting history of the West Scottish colliers. Their early union of the 1820s had striven, even more deliberately, for an exclusive control of entry and promotion. But that attempt collapsed, and—after an interval as one of the Miners' most backward and worst-organized districts—the Lanarkshire miners became ultimately identified with the MFGB's most radical wing.

V

All this, of course, supports the preceding chapter's proposition that a very large part (at least) in trade unionism's evolution has been played by the struggle of conflicting labour interests. But the comparison of trade union development in cotton with that in other major industrial sectors between the 1840s and 1890s now suggests a further general conclusion. The mid-century's undoubted but narrow consolidation of trade unionism largely represented, less an advance than a retreat—and a retreat, in most instances, to bases already prepared by a much earlier development. The new craft amalgamations, and their associated exclusive groups in non-craft trades, achieved a major step in the legitimation of trade unionism: but that was indispensable to their own security. And the price of their consolidation was to cut off the infant general labour movement of the 1830s and '40s, and postpone its substantial reappearance for half a century.

It could, of course, be argued that the mid-nineteenth century's withdrawal from universal labour movements was inevitable. Both they, and the political radicalism with which such movements have usually been associated, were as much the products of a common despair as of a common inexperience—as the closing stages in the cotton handloom weavers' history demonstrate. At the nineteenth-century's mid-point, the pressures that earlier forced both the traditional artisans and newer industrial aristocrats towards an alliance with the mass of formerly-unorganized workers were lifting. The old manufacturing handworkers, of course, were no longer a significant factor. The stabilization of the industrial structure, together with a gradual absorption of the mass labour surplus, had reduced the insecurity in which the Factory and Agricultural Revolutions together had plunged every occupational status. The living standard of the surviving artisan trades, apparently sharply depressed during those Revolutions (though as much by the effects of prolonged wars on prices as by the Revolutions themselves) had probably recovered to something like its level of a century before.[1] And all this was naturally reflected in a reversion to sectional associations as the major instrument of labour activity.

But if the establishing of solid sectional unions, each primarily concerned with its own members' immediate economic interest, was an essential step in the development of the labour movement at large, that by no means automatically implied the inhibition of its further growth. The consolidation of the power-loom weavers' unions in cotton at this time actually stimulated, first the formation of similar sectional societies by previously-unorganized workers, and second the association of the various cotton operatives' unions in a new broad alliance. The Weavers, however, were the outstanding exception to the common pattern of mid-nineteenth century unionism. And it was to the predominance of this pattern—of 'closed', exclusive unions—that the subsequent gap in union development seems attributable. That there was nothing logically inevitable about this pattern's adoption seems demonstrated not merely by the Weavers but by the later case of the gasworkers, who, despite a natural job-hierarchy apparently ready-made for an entry control of the Spinners' type, provided a main core of the ultimate general labourers' organization. Just why did the unions that dominated the latter-nineteenth century's labour scene take an exclusive form? And just why were the cotton weavers the exception to that rule?

Here the theory of historical priorities in union development from which we began an earlier chapter's discussion of the modern cotton unions' emergence—that skilled workers are always first to organize—has something to say. It can be argued that, just as skill gives its possessors a measure of indispensability to their employer that supports them in collective bargaining, it also makes the defence of their position dependent on excluding other workers from competition for their job. However, it has since been shown, not only that 'skilled' workers have not in fact always been the first to form trade unions of a modern type, but that 'skill' itself is not a factor wholly independent of collective organization. Not merely do individual skills tend to dissolve in the absence of trade unionism

[1] See, for instance, E. H. Phelps Brown and Sheila V. Hopkins, 'Seven Centuries of the Prices of Consumables compared with Builders' Wage-rates' (*Economica* November, 1956). The reference is to Southern conditions, of course: it is not clear that real wages in the North followed quite the same course.

(or some similar collective regulation) but—as in the cases of the self-actor spinners or of the strippers-and-grinders—many 'skills' are actually the product of trade unionism itself, instead of *vice versa*. In the light of the British textile workers' history, indeed (as well as of the more recent history of labour movements in several newly-developing countries), one could as fairly argue an opposite proposition about the priority of different unions' historical emergence to that usually accepted. Namely, that the divorce between labour and the ownership of its tools first causes workers generally to associate, but that this general movement has levelling implications that in turn provoke better-paid workers to separatist organizations.[1]

But similarly, 'skill' is not a sufficient explanation of certain unions' exclusiveness, because in some cases 'skilled' groups have also formed the core of solid 'open' unions. And subsequent experience suggests this alternative pattern to have offered considerable advantages to the 'skilled' themselves. That was so in the Cardroom Amalgamation: and the merger of the old ironworkers' union with Hodge's oppositionist smelters' organization also led to the senior workers assuming a leading role in the new amalgamation, and this in turn confirmed their aristocratic economic status.[2] Only one thing can explain both the order in which trade unionism established itself among different groups of workers *and* the particular forms their various organizations took. And this takes us back to the conclusion previously drawn from the history of the old cotton handworkers' union. The vital factor seems always to be the presence of a tradition of collective organization or regulation—a tradition either preserved in the group concerned itself, or conveyed to it by another group with which it has had a close historical association.

The capitalist entrepreneurs of the Industrial Revolution used three methods of recruiting their labour. First, the immediate shortage of skills obliged them to employ many established crafts. It has been usual for modern reporters of labour history to follow the Webbs in rejecting any connection between the mediaeval guilds and trade unions. But this ignores a fundamental survival of the mediaeval corporate controls—the apprenticeship system itself. As the guilds weakened, apprenticeship was embodied in the state economic regulation that took their place. The decay of the guilds, however—or the spread of industry outside the corporate towns—deprived the apprenticed journeyman of a traditional *social* support,

[1] The history of a major North American 'industrial' union, the United Automobile Workers, would seemingly fit this proposition admirably. It is referred to later, in Chapter V, 1, section vii.

[2] See Chapter III, 2, section iii, and 'Trade Unions, Differentials, etc.' (loc. cit.).

and induced him to form his own associations for mutual help. And these—as the eighteenth-century 'trade clubs'—sometimes acted to preserve the customs of their craft. But on the whole, the small-scale employers of handicraft production's later epoch could probably be relied on to maintain the apprenticeship system as much as lay in their power, because it restricted entry to their own ranks. So there was little need for the journeymen's clubs to go much beyond their original 'friendly' functions. The large-scale employers of the Industrial Revolution, however, found the apprenticeship system an obstacle to the spread (and hence cheapening) of skills, and neither they, nor the State in which they had become so influential, were at all concerned to maintain it. So the journeymen were driven to assume the burden of its enforcement alone: and in the process their societies emerged as the modern craft unions, to which the preservation of apprenticeship was, and continued, the essential aim.

In the process too, of course, apprenticeship itself rather changed its character. The mediaeval apprenticeship was not merely a learning period (one in any case longer than now, and to which the worker's time as a journeyman was originally seen as an extension while he widened his experience). It was also envisaged as a period of service given in exchange for the right finally to enter the trade as a master. So that apprentices were themselves a major source of labour, both artisan and auxiliary. And when the journeymen's prospect of independence was cut off, they were obliged to attempt to limit further the number of apprentices to prevent them competing for the jobs on which the journeymen now depended—thus incidentally creating a new need for unapprenticed, 'unskilled' assistants. While in general it was the restrictive aspect of the apprenticeship system that now came uppermost. But its adaptation to industrialism was facilitated because the Factory Revolution left certain trades aside; and in these apprenticeship, though diluted and weakened by the general industrial expansion, suffered no direct attack by employers, and survived naturally. Printing, for instance, remained comparatively unaffected by technical innovation until after the mid-nineteenth century.[1]

But of central importance were the traditional woodworking crafts: these retained a base in the building and furniture industries that was relatively little touched by changes in technique. And the woodworkers provided much of the skill on which the new metal-working industries were founded. The tools of their trade—the lathe, plane and drill, the vice and file—were all adapted by the producers of the new factory machines; it was only the material that differed.

[1] See A. E. Musson's history *The Typographical Association* (Oxford University Press, 1954).

In the earlier stages of the Factory Revolution, in fact, the machines themselves were still largely constructed of timber, and it was only gradually that metal replaced it. While to the present day one key engineering craft—that of the patternmakers—remained essentially a woodworking skill. In the construction and equipment of factories, the millwrights, members of a mediaeval craft the core of which was a mastery of woodworking techniques, were increased by the entry of woodworkers from other branches. The journeymen-millwrights' societies were the first of the 'New Model' ASE's progenitors; and, when machine-tools appeared, their craft practice was emulated by the new 'engineers'. But many woodworkers also remained mobile over a range of industries—building, furniture, vehicle-making, ship-construction and engineering—and carried their independent craft tradition with them. It was perhaps no accident that Applegarth's Amalgamated Society of Carpenters and Joiners should have been the most perfect expression of the 'New Model's' spirit.

However, the industrial transformation also required skills that the traditional crafts could not supply—and in the knowledge of which the merchant-capitalists who first promoted that transformation were themselves lacking. In these cases, the latter simply farmed-out the work to adventurers into the new occupations, furnishing equipment, stock, or workplace to those who would undertake to supply them with products at specified prices. These sub-contractors themselves then employed such additional labour as was necessary. This form had many variants, but was nevertheless common to several rising industries—iron, coal, and cotton-spinning. In cotton-spinning, indeed, some early mule-factories virtually reproduced the capitalist domestic system under a single roof: the factory-owner merely supplied room, 'steam', and rovings (fibre carded and prepared for spinning) to the spinners at set prices, buying their output on the same basis.[1] In such circumstances it was perhaps natural for the sub-contractors to combine to deal with their employer on prices. And once combined, it was equally natural for them to attempt to prevent their assistants becoming competitors for their own places. Even so, they seem to have produced effective organizations only when (as in the mule-spinners' case) they were influenced by some preceding tradition of association. There are certainly other instances in which the sub-contractors declined to an inferior position—most notably, perhaps, in the Midlands

[1] Robert Owen, for instance, worked on this system in his early venture into the cotton industry. (See 'Robert Owen, Peter Drinkwater, and the early Factory System in Manchester, 1788–1800'. by W. H. Chaloner, *Bulletin* of John Rylands Library, Vol. 37. No. 1.)

chain-making trade which was one of the first 'sweated' occupations selected for legal protection under the 1909 Trade Boards Act.

In some such cases, of course, the vital tradition was still that of the apprenticed journeyman. The major building and engineering crafts resisted the use of sub-contracting—or piece-work—by their employers as tempting members to break craft customs (not least by excessive effort). But the Boilermakers in iron shipbuilding adopted the apprenticeship system despite the prevalence of sub-contracting in that trade. In other cases (as in bespoke tailoring) another branch of the apprenticeship tradition—that of the apprenticed small master rather than the employed craftsman—was preserved by the sub-contracting workmen. In both these instances, the old method of entry regulation was directly taken over, the associations based on it otherwise concerning themselves mainly with the fixing of piece-prices.

But the cases where the sub-contracting system was combined with an apprenticeship method of regulating entry are not the major ones, and generally this new class of sub-contracting workmen evolved alternative restrictions. In the cotton industry, the old hand-mule spinners had the tradition of combination for piece-price bargaining from the domestic handloom weavers, and the additional stimulus of the calico-printers' example in factory workers' organization. But the increase in the number of their assistants prevented their use of apprenticeship and (like the iron and steel smelters) they converted the sub-contracting system itself into a method of entry control—by enforcing the selection of spinners exclusively from the ranks of their own employees, and that in due order of seniority at the workplace. And the mid-nineteenth century self-actor spinners simply adopted their predecessors' customs and organization. In the mines, of course, no form of apprenticeship had ever been present. But instead, there were the North-Eastern traditions of the Annual Bond (itself a contract), of association to deal with monopolistically-combined employers, and particularly of the hewers' special status—already protected by a customary regulation which arrived at much the same procedure as the spinners by an only slightly different evolutionary route.[1] So that out of the

[1] The origin of the Annual Bond itself is obscure. There are suggestions (in both Nef and Welbourne—op. cit.) that the early Northumbrian miners were mainly recuited from small farmers. In which case the Bond may well have been adapted from the Annual Hiring contracts for 'free' agricultural labour which are still preserved in parts of Northumberland. As regards the further development of sub-contracting in the North East, the employment of 'putters' by hewers seems to have become normal as the coalface itself became the point at which managerially-owned techniques were least applicable (the major technical

sub-contracting system emerged an alternative form of exclusive unionism to that of the crafts.

There was, however, a third means of recruiting the labour the new employers required for their industrial processes. Where they themselves possessed the technical knowledge on which these processes depended—or where they were able to hire it in men capable of organizing the work of others—they simply took the cheapest labour available and put it into gangs, each member of which performed a relatively simple task under the direct supervision of an overseer.[1] This, in essence, was the 'butty' system that was operated in newly-expanding mining districts in the nineteenth century. It was the system of the great constructional engineers—the builders of roads, railways and canals—of the great port employers, and many others. It was (as the later history of mule-spinning in Scotland has illustrated[2]) the system to which originally skilled occupations themselves usually degenerated in the absence of effective resistance by their members. But it was also the system with which many new trades were initiated. Arkwright's frame-spinning mills in Lancashire—the first effective powered factories and the heralds of the Industrial Revolution proper—operated on just such a system. Indeed, in cotton the system continues as the general mode of organizing employment in other preparatory and spinning processes than mule-spinning itself—as in many other forms of mass-production. And since it required in its workers no special qualities beyond a minimal physical fitness to the labour involved, it was into just those trades which used this system that the mass of uprooted, immigrant, and enforced-unemployed were inevitably directed.

Such gang workers, it would appear, could have no common tradition. And yet the early power-loom weavers were workers of exactly this kind. The first economic steam-looms were built by established spinning and machine-making concerns, operated as

---

developments in mining, until the present century, concerned such things as shaft-sinking, underground tunnelling, transport and ventilation, etc). For some other varieties of sub-contracting, see Fay's *Life and Labour in the Nineteenth Century* (CUP, 1920).

[1] Clark Kerr (in *Productivity and Labour Relations;* Institute of Industrial Relations, California, Reprint 96) has described the modern systems of labour relations which have descended on the one hand from the journeyman-apprentice system, and on the other from the sub-contracting form, as the 'Guild' and the 'Manor' respectively, because they are characterized by contrasting restrictions on labour mobility and similarly-contrasting concepts of workers' rights. If one wished for a similar historical analogue with the system here described, one might call it the 'Plantation'.

[2] See Chapter III, 1, section III.

adjuncts to their existing factories, and served by teams of women and boys in charge of overlookers. How then, to explain the survival of the power-loom weavers' unionism from the 1830s? The weavers, of course, had not merely the stimulus of that period's general labour agitation: they had a near example of militant organization in the hand-mule spinners, who were already employed at the same mills. But so did the cardroom and preparatory operatives, who with a longer history as an occupational group than the factory spinners, produced no durable combinations at this stage. Yet the power-loom weavers' unionism proved even more resilient than the spinners'.

The explanation must lie in one source from which the immense expansion of power-loom weaving in the 1830s recruited its labour. Between 1830 and 1845 the number of factory weaving operatives trebled, rising by some 100,000: in the same time, the number of handloom weavers fell from perhaps a quarter-million to about 60,000.[1] In the earliest days of power-weaving, it may be (as some historians have said) that the handworker scorned to sacrifice his independence for the factory. But by the 1830s—if not before—that independence was already unreal: many handloom weavers were by then directly dependent for work on the factories' intermittent inability to meet a press of trade. And the catastrophic fall in handloom wages must in any case have made such independence as they still had seem insubstantial compared with the double (and more regular) earnings of factory hands. Certainly, the employment of men at power-looms was common by the 1840s. While it seems in any case impossible that an industrial transformation of this order could have occurred without many handworkers entering the mills. And with them they would have brought their experience of the handloom weavers' combinations.

But that experience was of the handloom-workers' last phase—the epoch in which their once-closed sectional societies had merged in general weavers' movements, when their attempt to preserve apprenticeship had long been defeated, and the weavers' agitation was concentrated in direct pressure to maintain (and at last, in the great 1818 strike, to increase) wage-rates, and in political pressure for the minimum wage. And even had these new power-loom weavers brought with them any experience of apprenticeship as a working form, one factor alone would have made it impracticable of adaptation to their circumstances. This was the presence amongst the power-loom operatives of an established and already great majority of women. Since women were so liable to interrupt their working life and return, meanwhile to be replaced by other women,

[1] Various sources, quoted by Wood (op. cit.) Table 39.

it was impossible for the power-loom unions to apply any effective form of exclusion from their occupation. That those unions were influenced by the declining handworkers' societies is perhaps sufficiently indicated by the fact that they adopted very much the same form of internal organization. But of the external policies that the handloom weavers had attempted, their factory successors inherited only those which in fact constituted the characteristic techniques of 'open' unionism.

In each, then, of the three major sectors of its mid-nineteenth century consolidation—the crafts, coal and cotton—trade unionism took a form to which it was impelled by just the traditional background that there ensured its survival. The 'revolutionary' and universal labour movements of the preceding decades stimulated these early sectional unionisms directly or indirectly. But in most cases that strengthening also incidentally reinforced elements in the latters' traditional make-up that were ultimately to separate them from the general movement, and encourage the latters' disintegration. The case is fairly clear in the pre-history of the craft unions, whose predecessors were in any case often held back from direct association with the universal movements by an almost purely exclusive tradition. In the early spinners' and miners' combinations, there were mixed elements—on the one hand, a tradition of collective bargaining and political pressure, on the other a customary labour hierarchy: and it was the latter that came to dominate their successors. But the power-loom weavers inherited no tradition of restrictive labour controls. It was notable, for instance, that when it was found possible for weavers to increase the number of looms they could operate—and hence their earnings—by employing a juvenile 'tenter' (an arrangement already common by the 1850s) no attempt was made to convert this form of sub-contracting into an entry restriction; while at a later stage, the 'tenter' system was sacrificed almost unnoticed to other union objectives.[1] The Weavers were almost entirely reliant on wage-bargaining and political action: and to this they were directed by the very tradition that also ensured their organization's survival.

[1] See Chapter V, 1, section v.

IV

SOME COMPARISONS

2

The Evolution of Trade Union Forms

I

The 'ambiguous effect' of the New Model craft amalgamations on the labour movement's general development was, of course, noted by the Webbs, and that comment has been repeated by most later historians. What we have now shown is that the restrictive—in fact, depressive—impact of the mid-nineteenth century consolidation of exclusive unionism was by no means limited to the trades dominated by craft associations. In this respect, indeed, the craft amalgamations were only one embodiment—and not necessarily the most important—of a general phenomenon, that took different forms according to the particular traditions with which, in individual industries, it was identified.

However, these effects of the exclusive unions' crystallization on the general growth of trade unionism might be accepted. But it could still be held that such effects resulted only from the exclusive policy of those unions, and that they made other innovations in union government, administration and practice that provided a guide by which more widely-based unions were later able to erect (what the early general labour movements had failed to achieve) a sound and durable organization. And to be sure, the New Model craft amalgamation has usually been thought the most significant development of mid-nineteenth century trade unionism. But *was* the 'New Model' a model? What is at issue here is not the undoubted stimulus the Amalgamated Society of Engineers' survival of its 1852 lock-out gave to the idea of closer grouping in other trades where the seeds of organization had already taken firm root—a stimulus that probably extended (witness the 1858 Weavers' federation's quite inexact description of itself as 'amalgamated') beyond the crafts proper—but rather the extent of the New Model's contribution to the later development of mass unionism.

Consider first what we have called the external practice of trade unions. The mass 'New Unions' of course, when they came, were —like the established weavers' associations—open organizations, making no direct attempt to control labour's entry into the occupations they organized. Nor did they attempt to strengthen the individual worker's bargaining position by benefit payments. When they did begin to add mutual insurance to their functions, it was as a 'friendly' assistance and an encouragement to union membership rather than an economic weapon. The first such benefit to be paid by Tillett's Dock, Wharf & Riverside Labourers' Union was funeral —just as in the Weavers, again—and the Webbs noted that funeral grants were usually the first the New Unions added to strike pay.[1] Effectively, collective bargaining enforced by strike action and political pressure provided the New Unions' only modes of action.

The great building and engineering crafts, on the other hand, were in the main concerned with collective bargaining, at any level above the workplace group (where it was often inevitable), only to the extent that it was forced upon them by organized employer resistance to their own attempt to regulate their trades autonomously. To the craft union, the 'Standard Rate' was not primarily an objective to be secured by employer agreement. It was rather an intended minimal condition on which the union's members should offer their labour—a determination of how far the union, by its unemployment benefit, would back them in refusing to accept work on terms they thought unfavourable. Particularly, the union rate was often a test of eligibility for membership itself. Despite their foundation on apprenticeship, the nineteenth-century craft unions were usually compelled to recognize many workers who had entered 'skilled' occupations irregularly. To bar all such workers from membership would have been to make them active opponents and competitors; to include them was to enlist their support for the apprenticeship system's future enforcement. But equally, to admit *any* operative who was performing work within the craftsman's claimed competence would be—in face, for instance, of the multiple gradation and specialization of work in engineering—to virtually abandon all restriction on entry. The solution was simple: it was to accept the market's assessment. Where a man could produce no other evidence of qualification than his present work, the question then became: is he, or is he not, receiving a rate equal to the least an apprenticed craftsman would command in the circumstances? (At the extreme, indeed, the London plumbers operated no formal

[1] *History*, p. 420, footnote.

apprenticeship at all before the First World War, accepting as a competent member any 'plumbers' mate' to whom employers would pay the high minimum rate specified by the union as appropriate to a qualified plumber.) And since the market rate for a particular craft would naturally vary—in the absence of any deliberate attempt by the union concerned to level it up—from area to area, it was probably this technique (rather than local variations in living costs, as has been held[1]) that explained the variety and range of district rates the major craft unions ordained, until quite recent times, as 'standard'.[2] In the hands of the craft amalgamations, the 'Standard Rate' represented less a principle of social equity or of economic strategy than a method of exclusion.

Since the great craft unions were mainly concerned to raise the *individual* worker's 'supply price' by creating a relative scarcity of labour and providing him with an alternative maintenance to wages, they also made little systematic use of the strike weapon. It is significant that the only two substantial and 'official' stoppages of craft industries between 1850 and the New Unions' appearance—the engineers' affair of 1852 and the London builders' dispute of 1859—were lock-outs. The background issues here—the limitation of piece-work and, particularly, of hours—involved a logical extension of the craft unions' general policy of restricting labour supply from the dimension of numbers to the dimensions of time and effort. But it was easier for employers to combine against the threatened changes in general practice which that union policy here entailed, than against the end-pressure to raise individual wage-rates to which it was directed. The unions themselves would have preferred to apply their policy workplace-by-workplace. To *defend* the nine-hour day the ASE spent nearly as much on local strikes in 1879 as in the twenty previous years of its history; but against the resistance of a powerful district employers' federation the engineers' nine-hour day itself was first won, several years before, by the 'unofficial'—indeed, largely non-unionist—movement that fought the North-East Coast strike of 1871.

Moreover, with their fundamental policy of autonomous regulation, the attitude of the crafts to political pressure was also of a piece—an attitude that came to a head, again, over the New Unionist demand for the legal eight-hour day. Fraternal feeling and the need to preserve an alliance which protected them from legal or political attack might persuade them to support, in the Trades

[1] See the Webbs, *Industrial Democracy*, pp. 320/1.

[2] The Amalgamated Society of Carpenters and Joiners had, about 1900, twenty district rates, the lowest district's being only half the highest. Until 1950 the AEU recognized no less than forty-seven district rates.

Union Congress for instance, the sectional demands of miners, cotton operatives and others for legislative regulation. But suggestions that political action be applied to their own trades in a fundamental way were suspect: to invoke the Law's aid was also to invite its interference. Between the three classic methods of trade union action, any union would—assuming that they could be equally effective—naturally prefer that which minimized the necessity of compromising with external interests. It would thus prefer 'autonomous regulation' (which includes the Webbs' 'Method of Mutual Insurance'[1]) to collective bargaining; and it would prefer collective bargaining to legislative enactment. But even though the nineteenth-century craft unions achieved only a partial success in their attempt at independent control of their trades, their whole tradition so predisposed them to the method of autonomous regulation that they made little positive attempt to explore the alternative techniques.

Thus, it was the great piece-working trades that were responsible for the nineteenth-century development of collective bargaining. And it was in these industries—and overwhelmingly in coal and cotton—that the major strike experience of the period from the 1840s to the 1890s accumulated. The 1844 and 1863 strike of North Eastern colliers, the great strikes of 1853 and 1878 of North Lancashire cotton operatives, the miners' stoppages in 1875 in South Wales and 1888 in Yorkshire, all dwarfed the two most famous craftsmen's stoppages. And these are only the most notable examples: the 1880s in cotton witnessed a whole crop of major strikes or lock-outs.

In such industries, even the exclusive unions were compelled to pay much attention to the elaboration of bargaining techniques. They inherited from their membership's sub-contracting origins a wage-system already set in piece-work form—and on their shrewd exploitation of which depended the reward of their aristocratic position. Under piece-work, the technicality of processes, the variety and flux of products or working conditions, in any case involved the danger of their wage-standards' imperceptible undermining by employers. And this made it impossible for them to deal with wages as did the time-worker craft union—by setting a minimum and leaving its members, in groups or individually, to strike the best possible bargain above it. Moreover, the activity of early unions in these industries had already driven their employers to combine, in a fashion strengthened by the local concentrations also characteristic of these trades, and this compelled their modern unions to negotiate at least in relation to substantial districts. And it was probably this,

[1] *Industrial Democracy*, of course. I believe the broader, and more adequately descriptive, term 'autonomous regulation' is attributable to Mr Dennis Bell.

as much as tradition itself, that in turn explained the Spinners' and North-Eastern Miners' preservation of political action as an industrial instrument: where the employers were organized and immovable, the disadvantages of legislative intervention were outweighed by its utility as a lever.

It was, in fact, the unions that combined systematic collective bargaining with an exclusive restriction of entry that achieved by far the greatest solidity and effectiveness. Thus, the United Society of Boilermakers and Iron Shipbuilders was obliged, despite its membership's craft organization, to undertake large-scale collective negotiation by the already-established system of piece-work subcontracting in the shipyards, and to develop the office of full-time 'District Delegate' to deal with the powerful local employers' groups. In consequence, however, and next to the Spinners' Amalgamation, perhaps only the Northumberland Miners' Association and the London Society of Compositors could approach the Boilermakers' claim to be the strongest major union of the period.[1] Each of these unions, by the century's end, had virtually 100 per cent. membership of the workers with which they primarily concerned themselves. By contrast the Carpenters certainly, and the Engineers probably, had failed to secure even majority unionization. The Spinners and Boilermakers, indeed, could reasonably be argued the most powerful unions British labour history records.

Nevertheless such unions did not preside over collective bargaining's fullest elaboration: the concept of the single Standard Rate applicable to a whole occupation, of the Minimum Wage to which even its unorganized sectors should be entitled—and at that, irrespective of the varying prosperity of employers—had small place in their policy. The indifference of the Northumbrian miners to the conditions of those in the competing steam-coal districts of South Wales was as marked as the Spinners' indifference to the wage-levels of women on alternative spinning processes. What wage-policy the Spinners would have pursued in the absence of formidable employers' combination it is impossible to say. But if the latter's growth prevented them from emulating the 'rolling strike' tactic of the old hand-mule operatives' federations, they equally showed little interest in extending the scope of wage-agreements beyond the areas of particular masters' associations, but (like the Boilermakers)

[1] For a contemporary account of the Boilermakers' position, see G. von Schulze-Gaevernitz's *Social Peace* (Swan Sonnenschein, London, 1900, pp. 239–43). It is perhaps significant that a relation in some ways similar to that between the spinners and their piecers then existed (and to some degree still exists) between the sub-contracting platers of the Boilermakers' union and their helpers in shipbuilding.

tolerated a significant diversity between districts in both rates and earnings for similar work.

In one respect, indeed, the Spinners were unfortunate. Their status as a class of 'key' workmen was superimposed by their own efforts on their natural position as members of one of the cotton-spinning industry's most substantial class of production operatives. So that any systematic attempt to raise their wages inevitably provoked similarly-systematic resistance from employers. By contrast, such closed unions as the Overlookers and the Tapesizers in cotton-manufacturing each represented a much smaller fraction of that industry's labour force and costs. They have thus been able, not merely to maintain an even greater diversity of district rates than the Spinners, but to treat even district negotiations as largely secondary to direct bargaining with individual mill managements. So that one might say that—just as in the case of exclusive unions in other industries, but much before their time—the Spinners adopted large-scale collective bargaining mainly because it was forced on them by employers.

It was the Weavers, rather, who saw in the growth of employers' organization itself (and though that growth was primarily a reaction to trade unionism) a possibility that permitted them to abandon as an inferior instrument their predecessors' demand for a legal minimum wage. The whole question of the interdependence of collective organization's development among operatives and employers is really a subject in itself (on which, see this study's Appendix). Suffice it here to say that the Weavers' lack of any control over entry made it inevitable that the degree of unionization among the operatives in which they were interested should be uneven—especially in an industry still fast expanding. But it also made their maintenance of wage-agreements with particular mills or groups of employers largely dependent on their ability to bring other firms into line. The answer was to press for *centralized* negotiation, the result of which would not only bind all the associated employers, but to which the latter would then themselves have an interest in inducing others to conform—and which would, moreover, entail a recognition of the unions that would help them to strengthen their weaker sectors, and would give them an entree to unorganized mills.

Hence the Weavers' pressure for *general* minimum rates and for 'industry-wide' conciliation procedures. They still remained to a greater degree than their contemporaries dependent on legislative support. For instance, the 'piecework particulars' clause of the 1891 Factory Act (which enlisted the aid of government inspectors in compelling textile manufacturers to provide details of the price and specification of each operative's task) was important to their enforcement of the Standard Rate itself; so that it was a triumph for the Weavers' Amalgamation that one of its leading officials, Thomas Birtwistle, should have been appointed to the Home Office staff to enforce that provision. While the weaving trades were to fall back in the 1930s on the actual legal enforcement of collective agreements.[1] Nevertheless, the Weavers' development of collective bargaining also drove them to the concept of a general association of local and sectional unions as essentially a central strike fund. And this concept was basic both to the ultimate national miners' federation of 1889 and to the great amalgamations of transport workers' and labourers' unions in the 1920s.

II

So far as their *external* character goes, then—their admittance to membership, their technique of action, the purpose of their Amalgamation—we see again that the Weavers represent the first substantial and stable trade unionism of the modern type. There *was* one external respect in which they differed from later mass unions: by comparison with the diversity of jobs and trades that certain of these (and particularly, the 'general' unions proper) came to organize, the Weavers' occupational coverage was restricted. And the reasons for such differences in the occupational shape of 'open' unions are themselves of some interest, since they have been critical to the general structure of British trade unionism. But here, the exclusive unions' occupational horizons—even those of the New Model craft Amalgamations—were still more restricted than the Weavers'.

So that if the mid-nineteenth-century development of exclusive unions provided any example for modern mass labour organization, this must rather be sought in their internal administration. And it was in its internal structure that the Weavers' organization mainly differed from most of the later mass unions—and in which these, on the other hand, could also be held rather to follow the craft amalgamations. The local association survived—indeed, survives—as the final centre of sovereignty in the coal and cotton unions.

[1] It is notable that even the Act of 1934, which made the Weavers' Uniform Wage-List legally enforceable and thereby introduced a quite exceptional practice into peace-time wage-fixing in Britain, in fact revived a very old principle in cotton. The Cotton Arbitration Act of 1800, which the handloom weavers attempted to use as an instrument of collective bargaining, in the first instance legalized agreements reached between representatives of the parties to disputes; and it was this, rather than an externally-fixed minimum, that several of the early weavers' wage-petitions demanded. While the Factory Act's 'piecework particulars' clause virtually reproduced a similar clause of the 1800 Cotton Act.

But in the 'New Models' it became—just as in the great modern general and industrial unions—a mere branch of the national body. The actual degree and pace of centralization in the craft unions during their formative period may have been exaggerated: but there is no doubt as to their administration's centralizing trend. As Rowe noted: 'The third quarter of the last century really saw the evolution of two 'New Models', that of the engineers, with the dominant characteristic of a centralized constitution but local bargaining, and that of the cotton operatives, with the dominant characteristic of a local constitution but centralized bargaining.' However (said Rowe) the Webbs '. . . *rightly realized that the former was the more generally important, and gave it the exclusive use of the title.*'[1]

But in the craft union the pressure to centralized administration was quite different in kind to that which moulded the later mass union's structure—and their resultant organizational systems thus in fact differed radically in function and form. In the craft amalgamation's case, the most generally-advanced explanation of central authority's growth has been the need to control local strikes. But this need arose from no general bargaining strategy, because such unions as the Engineers and the Carpenters, at least, did not possess one. 'A co-ordinated trade policy' the Engineers' official historian noted of the old ASE, 'was conspicuous by its absence.'[2] To the craft amalgamations the strike was not a tactic of advance but a last defence against some fundamental attack on their right to exist (as in the case of the 1859 Builders' lock-out) or on their mode of operation—their control over jobs or labour supply—as in the Engineers' disputes of 1852 and 1897. The strike, in fact, was a nuisance. More, it endangered their attempt to strengthen the individual worker's hand by benefit payments. The control of strikes was thus necessary, not to direct their aim, but to restrain expensive local militancies and free union funds for quite other purposes (a factor in the new craft leaders' attitude that possibly contributed to the cotton unions' reluctance to associate with the formers' 'Junta'). The accumulation of benefit reserves, however, has been a quite general pressure to centralization. It helps, for instance, to explain the greater concentration among the cotton-spinning unions than the Weavers. How the Oldham cardroom union's Accident Fund helped induce neighbouring cardroom clubs to merge in a relatively centralized 'Province' like that of the area's Spinners' association has already been shown.[3] And the gathering

[1] 'Wages in Theory and Practice', p. 123, footnote. Present writer'si talics.
[2] Jefferys (op. cit.) p. 159.
[3] Chapter III, 2, section II.

of a majority of mule-spinners themselves into the two Provinces of Oldham and Bolton is not explicable by the need to deal with strong district employers' associations, or to create a professional staff to apply the resultant wide-area agreements. Confronted by very similar needs the original Blackburn Weavers' Association and later the weavers' 'First Amalgamation' in turn split off independent local units, relatively equal in size.

However, the Spinners' need to conserve benefit funds did not quite suffice to overcome their tradition of local autonomy. Indeed, in one respect it strengthened the latter: the great Provinces were much more formidable in relation to the central Amalgamation than was the independent local weavers' association. True, the provision of substantial benefits by the spinners' unions was designed, less as an instrument of their policy than to mitigate certain consequences of it. The customary principle of promotion to mule-spinner only to vacancies in, and by seniority at, the individual mill involved effects which only became apparent as the cotton industry's rate of growth progressively slowed. First, a spinner who fell unemployed could not take another place at an *existing* mill because the latter's own senior piecers regarded the vacancy as their right. For this reason, the Spinners' officials themselves attempted, from the 1880s on, to modify the workplace seniority system, and to substitute the principle that promotion from grade to grade should go by vacancies in the upper grade *as a whole*, mobility within that grade being permitted. But the case for that emerged only as the piecers themselves began to show a spirit of independence; and the principle would have lessened their chances of promotion, the piecers' sole compensation for subjection to the spinners. In fact, the mill seniority rule for promotion to spinner seems to have strengthened rather than relaxed: even such compromise arrangements as the Bolton rule, that one half of spinners' vacancies might be filled by already-qualified men from outside the mills where they occurred, seem to have become increasingly inoperative.[1] Secondly, moreover, the Spinners' entry system also gave employers who had piecers grown adult and experienced in their mills a strong motive for ridding themselves of senior spinners whose pace of work was past its peak. And whereas the Spinners' resistance to other 'infringements of their rights' was virtually cast-iron, to this discrimination it

[1] As recently as January 1959, the *Quarterly Report* of the Spinners' Amalgamation commented on opinions that the cotton industry ought to be more compact, that these 'ignored the human consequences . . . (because) the members of this Amalgamation cannot have, and never have had, the opportunity of transferring their labour from one mill to another, except in a few isolated instances, and where new plant has been erected.'

was again weakened by their piecers' ambition for promotion. So older spinners were much more liable to unemployment than their counterparts in craft trades.

Thus, the Spinners' benefit rules seem frequently designed to get displaced members right off the occupational labour market. Such pure 'friendly' payments as disablement or widows', for instance, are usually restricted to a single and modest lump sum. Under Oldham rules, unemployed benefit was automatically withdrawn from a member made incapable of work by illness. The difference to craft union attitudes (that qualification carried a 'right to the trade') is illustrated by such provisions as the rule that a spinner who did not work as one for a year lost his membership—and with it, his right to work. If, however, having exhausted his 'out-of-work' benefit entitlement he started as a piecer, he was transferred to the Piecers' Association, with its inferior rights. At one time some local unions even made grants to members to set up on their own account—a practice contrasting strongly with the then contemporary hostility of the building and printing unions to a multiplication of small masters.[1] And one or two spinners' associations still provide 'leaving trade' grants, made only on condition that the recipient undertakes not to re-enter the occupation. The Spinners' Amalgamation, itself originally conceived as a central strike fund, added to its provisions emigration grants and a superannuation benefit supplementary to that provided by local unions—and payable under its 1902 rules, at so early an age as fifty-two.[2]

'Mutual insurance' was only necessary to the Spinners' unions, therefore, insofar as it became desirable to mitigate certain ultimate

[1] See, for instance, Musson (op. cit.) p. 94. In general, of course, such grants were made to set unemployed spinners up outside the trade (for instance, as window cleaners). But there seem also to have been cases of assistance to members setting up as independent twiners or in other cotton specialities permitting small enterprises.

[2] The age was raised to sixty in 1944—the 'old spinner problem' having been much eased by a shortage of young men. Such benefits were probably first undertaken by the Amalgamation additionally to the district unions because prematurely-displaced spinners might move to an 'illegal' job in a more backward and weakly-organized area. And superannuation now consists only in small grants to the union's twenty oldest members paid from a capital fund originally founded in memory of James Mawdsley, a famous Secretary of the Amalgamation, which otherwise now limits its 'friendly' provision to lump sum accident grants.

Apart from dispute pay, incidentally, the most common cotton union benefit now consists in 'out-of-work' pay—but of rather a special kind. It is often designed to deal with short interruptions of employment; this arises, not merely from the liability of the cotton trade itself to frequent fluctuation, but from the use once made by employers of short-time working as a device to exhaust the operatives' resistance—e.g. in advance of an anticipated conflict. So that 'out-of-work' pay was in a sense an extension of dispute pay. Dispute pay, however,

consequences of their customary labour controls. To the craft unions, however, it was an essential economic technique. Nevertheless, in the crafts there was a still more powerful drive to centralization, from which their concern for benefit funds itself originally stemmed. The craft organizations did not attempt, as did the closed cotton unions, to regulate the entry of new workers strictly in accordance with the vacancies that actually occurred. Their apprenticeship itself, with its five- to seven-year period of preliminary qualification that also carried the 'right to the trade' when completed, would have prevented that. Their method, therefore, was rather to restrict the total flow of new labour—usually, of course, by limiting the ratio of apprentices to craftsmen that individual employers could engage. But this method necessarily implied—if it were not in any case by origin inseparable from the 'journeyman' system—mobility of labour. The apprentice/journeyman ratio could be adapted to the *average* circumstances of a trade; it could not be adjusted to particular local circumstances because that would open the occupation's doors in weakly organized districts.[1] But unless craftsmen were mobile, the ratio would in one place produce a surplus, in another such a shortage as might drive employers to extremes of resistance.

This dependence on mobility inevitably implied central control. The apprentice-ratio could only be fixed by a body that could view the whole field over which the union's members might move. The regulations for apprenticeship and admittance must, like the ratio itself, be standard for all the crafts' local units. It was desirable that the number of members actually on the move in search of work be minimized because they represented a potential labour surplus as well as a drain on funds: so the random element in 'tramping' must be reduced by the regular collection and circulation of advice on local employment situations. All these things could perhaps have been undertaken by a merely federal body. But mobility also

usually includes a special category, 'Victim Pay', at much higher rates, and this is used by the closed unions to support members dismissed, not merely for union activity as such, but for standing by union labour regulations—e.g. in the Tapesizers, for refusing to teach a learner not properly authorized by the local union.

[1] The ratio actually adopted by individual crafts seems to have varied quite widely—from as high as one to three, to as low as one to ten. This was no doubt partly a reflection of different union strengths. But no union could impose too rigorous a restriction without trying employers too far. Since many employers would not bother themselves with apprentices once they could no longer be used as cheap labour, and since on almost any ratio smaller establishments would be prohibited from accepting them, one supposes the ratio to have been empirically adapted to the condition and structure of each trade.

involved an attack on the fundamentals of local sovereignty—the control over union finance and the right to strike. If decisions about dues and expenditure remained in local hands, subscriptions, benefits and funds would vary from place to place: unemployed workers would leave districts where subscriptions were inadequate or funds exhausted by over-liberality, and move into those where benefits were high. If the locals could strike without external restraint, their neighbours would find themselves burdened with the victims of ill-considered conflicts. Mobility without central control, in fact, compelled cautious and well-conducted locals to pay for the improvidence or rashness of others; and that would ultimately break up any broad association. The standardizing of dues and benefits, the centralization of funds and strike decisions, thus all followed from the mobility entailed by the craft system itself. Just as a main 'friendly' function of the old local journeymen's club was the reception and support of 'tramps',[1] so the preference of benefit-funds to strike-reserves that distinguished the 'New Model' craft amalgamations was an extension of mobility's implications.

It is easy, at a century's distance, to overlook the central and formative influence of mobility upon the modern craft unions' development. 'Tramping' was the backbone of their historical predecessors,[2] and literally kept such unions as the Stonemasons—the strongest of the original building unions and the first to possess a continuous national association—alive in difficult times.[3] If tramping declined after the 1850s, this was perhaps as much due to the craft unions' efforts to reduce its costs and to make movement more efficient, as to a change in economic conditions or a decline in mobility itself. The reform of tramping (by a system of labour direction and the standardization of unemployment relief) was a prime motive in the forming of the 1845 National Typographical Association.[4] And that the printers should ultimately have been the only major craft that failed to achieve a single unified association is obviously connected with the London Compositors' insistence that mobility cease at their own union's boundaries. The ASE itself set

[1] Even such near-universal friendly benefits as 'funeral' were influenced, in the crafts, by mobility. Thus the Unicorn Lodge (Hull) of the Stonemasons provided in 1848 '. . . for the Burial of *all* Brothers who coming into this Town in search of employment may happen to die, or . . . of any Brother working in this Town . . . whose Friends are not in a condition to bury them respectably which is to be decided by . . . a meeting convened for the purpose.'

[2] See, for instance, E. Hobsbawm: 'The Tramping Artisan' (*Economic History Review*, Vol. III, No. 3, 1951).

[3] See the account of Henry Broadhurst (the 'Stonemason's M.P.') quoted by Postgate (*Builders' History*, pp. 157/8).

[4] See Musson (op. cit.) p. 65 and pp. 265/6.

up an internal system of 'Mutual Aid Clubs' to promote the movement of members, and its 'Monthly Report' published the state of trade in every branch's area. In that union's early decades, provision for the travelling member certainly remained an important part of its daily business: between 1865 and 1874, for instance, it issued over 13,000 travel cards—equivalent to more than a third of its average membership over the period.[1] While at this time such sectional engineering societies as the Patternmakers were still more active in fostering labour mobility; and even at the nineteenth-century's end, a period of 'travelling' was still a quite normal stage in the craftsman's early career.[2]

Professor Ulman's recent study of national unionism's development during the latter nineteenth century in five American occupations—each of which seems to have imported the European apprenticeship system—has shown how the growth of a national labour market promoted centralization in certain United States unions.[3] But the impact of mobility, as an instrument of union economic practice, on the *structure* of the unions concerned can be illustrated from the cotton trades themselves. In cotton manufacturing, all the closed unions imitated more or less closely the Weavers' federal association of local societies. And all of them permitted some movement from mill to mill within each district. But they generally made transfer to another district conditional on the permission of the local union concerned. And only the Warpdressers developed mobility as a central characteristic of their system. The 'tramp dresser', with his lease and rods, was still a familiar figure in North Lancashire districts in the present century's early years; and the Warpdressers alone systematically organized in the Yorkshire woollen trades.[4] The Twisters, on the other hand, worked out an entry system which (like that of the Spinners) much restricted mobility—vacancies being generally filled by promotion from the subordinate grade of 'reacher-in' at the individual mill where each occurs: and among the twisters mobility is generally only now permitted to the extent that a man may work *temporarily* at a

[1] Estimated from Jefferys' data (*Story of the Engineers*, particularly p. 61).

[2] To judge by the account of the Webbs' ex-craft unionist assistant, F. W. Galton, reproduced by the former (*History*, pp. 431–451) as typifying the trade unionist's life at the time.

[3] Lloyd Ulman, *The Rise of the National Trade Union* (Harvard University Press, 1955) particularly Chapter II.

[4] An interesting sidelight on the effects of the Warpdressers' basing their labour controls on mobility is that—whereas the Spinners gave grants to their members to set up in business—the Warpdressers pursued the opposite policy of buying-up one-man concerns (which at one time did work for mills 'on commission') to prevent them competing for jobs with the union's members.

neighbouring mill, if he is not fully employed at his own. The Twisters' and Warpdressers' separate Amalgamations were, at peak, much of a size. The Warpdressers' Lancashire membership, however, was concentrated in only four local associations which later fused into two, covering between them the whole cotton region. But the original local Twisters' Societies multiplied themselves by fission until their Amalgamation had over forty independent unions in the Lancashire cotton districts alone—more than the then giant Weavers' Amalgamation itself, for over thirty times the Twisters' membership.[1]

The craft amalgamations' tendency to centralization was thus intimately related to their characteristic restrictive technique. And in them, in any case, the local autonomy of the former 'Trade Club' was confronted by an alternative and still older tradition. The old local journeymen's clubs were by origin only auxiliary to a more universal system—the code maintained by guild regulations, public law or masters' convention. And the craftsman's mobility must itself have blurred local loyalties. Many of the inter-local conflicts that still occurred after the craft amalgamation's appearance—such as that in the carpenters between Applegarth's Amalgamated Society and the Manchester-based General Union—were less concerned with any local demand for self-determination as such than with the resistance of surviving groups of militants to the new leaders' cautious policy.

It is perhaps significant of more than a geographical or political convenience that, as their professional leadership crystallized, the power-centre of important craft unions shifted from the Northern industrial areas (where the impact of an involvement in earlier general labour agitations still lingered in local attitudes) to London, in which old artisans' societies had continued a relatively peaceable and unchallenged existence through the nineteenth-century's critical early decades—and in which even the guild form survived late. The City Companies controlled most London trades over the greater part of the eighteenth century, and were still quite important up to the 1830s, when employed people actually had a majority in them.[2] It is possible that in their development of centralized government, as in their economic practice, the craft unions were in a real sense expanding on an ancient model—that of the great urban guild. At any rate, their occupations' traditional background was not altogether hostile to the concentration of authority that their distinctive economic practice required.

[1] See *Main Chart* of Chapter III, 1. Note particularly the proliferation of Twisters' societies in the 1890s.

[2] Postgate, *History of the British Working Class* (op. cit.) p. 8.

III

The centralized organization of the modern mass unions thus cannot be explained by the factors that pushed the craftsmen's amalgamations towards that pattern. And the later mass labour unions were certainly not predisposed to centralization by any such background of traditional corporate rule as that of the crafts. But nor, it now appears, was centralization a functional requirement of their characteristic techniques. It was unnecessary to collective bargaining: the decentralized cotton unions produced the nineteenth century's most extensive and elaborate bargaining system, and its most efficient strike organization. Nor was it essential to political action —rather the reverse, since a merely federal relationship permits groups which are unwilling to merge for other purposes to associate for particular legislative demands: the Miners' Federation of Great Britain was probably the most effective agency of political pressure that any section of British workers has so far developed. In the New Unions of the 1890s and their present-day successors, centralized rule seems in fact to have been largely an incidental product of the circumstances of their formation.

Between the New Unions, the Weavers, and the craft amalgamations, the vital difference is displayed by the character of their officials. The professional union officer was, in fact—and here both craft and cotton unions were alike—by far the major innovation of mid-nineteenth-century trade unionism. Not that earlier unions were quite without full-time officials. But such as they had were of mixed types—the activist workman briefly financed by his fellows as a 'delegate': the victimized strike-leader or committee-member who continued to be supported by his society: the militant agitator who had succeeded in converting his devotion into a vocation with union funds: the sympathizer of 'independent means'; occasionally, the lay secretary or chairman whose time came to be so much demanded that the union was obliged to subsidize him. In most cases, the career of such men was brief and uncertain: and their trade and administrative expertize was generally little above that of their members. It was only about the 1850s that it became a regular thing for unions to employ full-time agents. The practice, of course, reflected the stabilizing of the unions themselves. But with it, union office became an alternative career, if only for a handful of men, that attracted some of the ablest and most devoted of their members.

It is the appearance of this professional trade union leadership (the term 'civil service,' though suggestive, is hardly adequate) that really marks off the modern institutionalized union from its 'natural' predecessors. But even in the great craft unions, the formal change in union constitutions was—at this stage at any rate—limited: and where such changes occurred, they were usually gradual. The Carpenters' Amalgamation was a new creation, modelled on the ASE. But the Boilermakers, for instance, retained their original constitution of 1833, with its rotating lay exective selected by a 'governing district' only, substantially unmodified until 1897. In their case, the old constitution gave the union's nominal governing body an inexpert and unrepresentative character that actually facilitated the assumption of directive control by its secretary, acting in personal liaison with the union's group of full-time 'District Delegates'.[1] The 'New Model' ASE itself, in fact, largely took over the organization of its main predecessor, the 'Old Mechanics'—an association in which the nominally-independent branches were in practice already limited to the administration of an elaborate national code of benefit rules.[2] The ASE merely raised the already high subscription to cover 'trade' benefits and set up district committees to advise on the latter's use. For William Allan, who continued as full-time General Secretary, the reorganization in effect only extended the scope of his office. Even without such inherited aids, Harnott was able to achieve an almost despotic control of the old Stonemasons by sheer force of personality, and held it for many years without modifying the union's federal constitution. In the craft union, centralization was thus rather expressed in an increasing direction of policy by its officials—and particularly by its national secretary, who was usually the first to be elevated to a full-time status—than in formal reorganizations.

By contrast, the modern cotton unions' first professional officers had (like those of the Miners) to deal with an undivided tradition of local self-government. The natural basic unit of the first handloom weavers' associations was the village society: and this fundamentally local form was repeated in successive movements of cotton operatives, old and new. The village club usually grew, with the multiplication of factories, into the town association. But in the Weavers, at least, the full-time officials appear to have made no attempt to extend their particular society's area. Quite the contrary, in fact: Birtwistle and his associated professionals in North-East Lancashire

[1] See the Webbs' account (*Industrial Democracy*, pp. 28–32) of the state of the Boilermakers' administration before the reforms of 1895–7.

[2] According to Jefferys (p. 22) central control of benefits had been first required to permit the Journeymen Steam Engine and Machine Makers' ('Old Mechanics') Friendly Society to secure legal protection as such. The Society had already, moreover, opened its ranks to other engineers, promoted the wider "Mechanics' Protective Society", and itself provided for separate 'trade' action.

actively promoted the forming of permanent unions in other districts, which then acquired officials equal in status to themselves. The area of the individual official's influence was, indeed, occasionally reduced by secession, as the weavers at this place or that felt strong enough to support a secretary of their own: and the process seems to have been painless.

If, however, the officials accepted the customary pattern of cotton workers' organization, it was they who saw the need for greater co-ordination between the local unions' activities than was provided by either the irregular delegate assembly or such contact between the officials themselves as occurred both informally and in the way of business. But that did not require centralized government. In the major Amalgamations, the General Secretary had no great status in relation to the local officials. His power in relation to the local association, for instance, is still limited to that of 'visiting, advising and reporting.'[1] In their prime, the Spinners', Weavers' and Card-room Amalgamations put no more than an assistant and a clerk at their respective Secretaries' disposal—a smaller staff than that of each Amalgamation's larger affiliates. And even the role of spokesman or public representative of the Amalgamation would not infrequently fall to its part-time President—himself otherwise a local officer. For the cotton operatives' purposes, co-ordination enough for essentials—those of collective bargaining—was secured by the regular and frequent delegate meeting (almost invariably, the Cotton Amalgamations meet at least quarterly) at which officials and lay-members represent their societies together, and by the still more frequent meeting of the Executive or General Council, where the most influential local officers are invariably found. Beyond that, the conversion of the *ad hoc* strike fund (the characteristic financial link between the earlier unions) into a permanent reserve that could usually be drawn upon only under conditions specified by the Amalgamation and subject to its delegate meeting's advance approval, gave the federal body a powerful influence on local policy.

Indeed, the development of centralized collective bargaining itself, so far from demanding (as it has often been suggested to do) a parallel centralization in union government, appears from the cotton unions' case to have actually reduced the need for further moves in that direction. The consequent growth of employers' organization, and the elaborating of conciliation procedures, in fact ensured that any mill or local dispute which raised an issue of broader interest was almost automatically referred to a level of negotiation that brought Amalgamation policy to bear. *Before* the forming of

[1] *Rules* of the Amalgamated Weavers' Association.

the Second Weavers' Amalgamation, however, the need to restrain individual societies from 'jumping the gun' in local disputes was an important factor in their own officials' pressure for a formal sequence of conciliation with the employers—a procedure actually achieved after 30,000 operatives of the Blackburn district in 1880 struck for the return of wage-cuts imposed two years previously, and the major cotton employers' federation of the time, wearied by repeated disputes, agreed to the appointment of a standing 'Joint Committee for the Settlement of Weavers' Complaints'. And this arrangement was later elaborated into 'Joint Rules' providing successive stages of dispute-reference, from the mill to local and central meetings.

If, then, in both the cotton trade and others the new officials modified the practice of their unions, if their very appearance required a formalization of the latter, and if the officials in turn occasionally promoted structural amendments, these changes were not discordant with traditional patterns. But as between unions the officials themselves were the product of different functional needs, and hence were of very different types. In such unions as the Engineers and Carpenters, they were fundamentally financial managers, concerned largely with the husbanding of benefit funds. And it has been usual—following the Webbs—also to separate pretty sharply two other types of official: on the one hand the specialist negotiators of the established cotton and miners' unions (as well as of bodies like the Boilermakers that also developed collective bargaining), and on the other hand the 'labour organizers' of the later general workers' unions.[1] In fact, however, in neither the nineteenth-century weavers' associations nor the 'New Unions' was the distinction between these two latter types of officer quite so definite. The Blackburn weavers' association of 1854 certainly chose its first official to be a calculator of piece-work prices; but those appointed in imitation by other weavers' organizations early realized that effective bargaining involved more than trade and mathematical

[1] The Webbs, of course, also distinguished a fourth, the trade union 'Political Officer'—the specialist in the political representation of union interests. There are possibly one or two outstanding examples of this type—the late George Tomlinson, the weaver who became Minister of Education, perhaps, and the current Presidents of the Agricultural and Distributive Workers. But otherwise, the group of trade union M.P.s have not, as such and in recent times, made such a distinctive impact that it can be considered important. Effective political functions seem now usually grafted on to the prime ones of negotiating and administering, and embodied in the major union leaders themselves. If one were looking for a significant fourth type these days, it would—to judge by the T & GWU's recent nomination of its former Research Officer to the TUC General Council and the appointment by the TUC itself of its one-time Research Officer to its General Secretaryship—rather be found in the back room of the union office.

expertise, and required the backing of a forceful and extensive organization. They therefore set themselves to combine the role of 'trade officials' with that of recruiting agents and propagandists, touring other districts to stir them to action or build up union membership there, and frequently adopting a militant attitude to rally the operatives.[1] So that Eccles Shorrock, the North-East Lancashire employers' leader, contrasted Birtwistle and other leaders of the Weavers' Amalgamations unfavourably with the original Blackburn Weavers' Secretary, apparently regarding them as agitators.[2] On the other hand, the leaders of the later New Unions (to whom the description 'agitator' might be thought more apt) were quite soon forced to occupy themselves with the technicalities of collective bargaining and industrial policy. So that if the organizing and agitational functions of the Weavers' officials declined as their unions were consolidated, that only forecast the ultimate evolution of other mass unions' bureaucracy. And when external pressures finally compelled the great craft amalgamations to involve themselves in large-scale collective bargaining and to organize the non-craft worker, these, too, were obliged to press their own officials into a similar mould. In such respects, therefore, the Weavers' secretaries were the prototype of present-day union officialdom.

There were, however, two important differences between the Weavers' first officials and those of the New Unions. One, that the Weavers' full-time secretaries were grafted-on to an already existing (if sometimes informal) organization, through which they had themselves acquired the experience that led them to office, and the broad outlines of which they were in any case obliged to accept. The later mass unions' members had—except in the Miners—no such surviving organizational tradition to guide their leaders. The latter were often thrust into prominence by spontaneous strike-waves, and only thereafter entrusted with the establishment of permanent organizations—a task for which the very absence of traditional sectional loyalties among their initial membership often necessitated recruitment on a wider basis. Secondly, these leaders

[1] In fact, of course, the 'examination' which candidates for full-time office in the cotton unions have usually been required to undergo was not confined to technical matters, often including a paper and questions on general policy. While the 'examiners' might recommend a particular candidate on other qualifications than technical ones, or merely submit a panel from which the final choice was made by popular vote. And in the present century a large proportion of the Weavers' officials have been drawn from the militant Nelson district, which participated independently in the first moves to form a Labour Party, and was known as 'Little Russia' for its radicalism in the inter-war period.

[2] See *A Letter to the Workpeople*, etc. (op. cit.).

were themselves sometimes drawn (like several leaders of the earlier 'revolutionary' movements) from outside the ranks of their followers. So that such leaders had a different, and political, inspiration. They saw trade unionism as an instrument of class rather than of sectional advancement. And where the Weavers' officials stood primarily as the agents of particular occupational discontents, they stood rather as the apostles of a new general movement, of which they regarded their own unions as recruiting centres. In these circumstances, the organizations that emerged from their efforts focused, inevitably, on themselves. And in that arrangement's consolidation, one cannot exclude the effect of many such leaders' own position as a politically-convinced minority among their own followers: this particular pressure to central control must have strengthened as the officials' leadership was later challenged, from World War I on, by still more radical fractions. The New Unions tended to a centralized form because they were constructed around their professional leaders.

IV

It was just the relative absence of established sectional solidarities from their background that conditioned the shape of the New Unions, in terms of their occupational coverage—as well as making it inevitable that they should also become big unions. In the Weavers, the only previous open unions of substance, expansion was limited, of course, by the geographical isolation that followed from the weaving trade's growing segregation in specialized factory towns. But it was limited above all by a habit of occupational association and its consequences in union form and practice. The local weavers' associations occasionally organized textile workers from non-cotton trades with which they were in close contact and who had no unions of their own. And the Weavers' Amalgamation itself accepted, in quite recent years, the affiliation of a whole union of silk operatives. But such things the Weavers did almost accidentally: their own success gave them little practical interest in such recruits, and no arguments of principle urged them to assume the expense and responsibility of organizing campaigns outside those occupations which were contiguous to their original membership.

Even where cotton operatives in other regions than the 'cotton area' proper were concerned, the Weavers took little initiative. Thanks to the efficiency of the Lancashire industry, such workers represented no competitive threat: and the local unions' horizons were too limited for them to see such workers as a case for assistance. Their Amalgamation, as a central body, could have been well placed to undertake external recruiting; but its affiliates were reluctant to entrust it with more power than was recognizably necessary for their own purposes. When, in the present century, the open cotton union again acquired members in outlying regions (usually as a result of an initiative from the workers concerned or the extension of Lancashire-based firms) the Cardroom societies, which were much closer to the New Unions in the time of their consolidation and therefore in original tone, permitted their Amalgamation itself to administer outlying branches. But the Weavers insisted they be allocated to the nearest local society.

By the time that unorganized workers outside the cotton industry were again stirring independently, the Weavers had in any case adapted both their methods of collective bargaining and their legislative programme so closely to the circumstances of their own trade that they no longer offered a model to non-textile occupations without previous organizational experience. In particular, their enforcement of the standard rate through an inherited system of piece-work payment, the natural intricacy of which was only systematized by the Weavers' own effort to mould it to a comprehensive schedule, then concentrated their officials' bargaining experience in a meticulous and mathematical expertise which was largely irrelevant to conditions outside the cotton trade. The Weavers' minimum wage was thus no longer recognizable as the simple demand for a basic standard of life that gave the New Unions their appeal.

The New Unions' leaders needed the strength of numbers to consolidate their position. But that lack of established solidarities in the occupations where each first began to organize, which drove them to seek reinforcement among other groups, at the same time set few traditional frontiers to bar them from recruiting a diversity of workers. By their leaders' original intent they were, in any case, often less sectional associations than anti-sectional. And if the existence of the established 'Old Unions' prevented them in fact becoming truly general organizations, both circumstance and their initial political drive combined to give them at least a multi-sectional form. Thus, among the New Unions, the occupational shape of particular organizations often had an almost accidental character, being largely determined by the recruiting opportunities that presented themselves to their separate leaderships. The Textile Workers' Union in the wool and finishing trades, for instance, has assumed an apparently 'industrial' shape, less from deliberate design than from two other circumstances. First, that its foundation groups were of workers in occupations fairly specific to the textile industries, rather than of the more mobile types of lower-skilled labour from which the alternative 'general' unionism sprang. But second, that other New Unions, and particularly the general unions themselves, established a prior footing in the chemical and other industries contiguous to textiles, and thus prevented it assuming a broader form: it would otherwise probably have been a short step from Turner's General Union of Textile Workers to a 'Textile and General Workers' Union'.[1] However, had the general unions widened their hold on certain sections of the woollen and allied trades themselves before the native textile unions did so, the latter would probably have rather stabilized as an 'occupational' association of more-skilled finishing workers only.

The New Unions, however, grew from scattered individuals or groups, and first established themselves as a considerable number of distinct organizations. This was of no great consequence during their first decade or so, when they were mainly holding on to a membership secured by virtue of such agreements as a few employers had conceded during their initial outburst. Then, they were still largely isolated from frictional contact with each other by their own smallness. But the sharp increase in their membership from 1911 onwards, together with the competitive response which that growth and the consequent development of collective bargaining induced in several longer-established and once-exclusive unions, involved the New Unions, in many places and industries, in a competition too complex to be resolved by merely jurisdictional agreements, and in which no one of them could hope to emerge supreme—nor few to achieve even a reasonable stability. Moreover the division, between several organizations, of occupational groups who had by then begun to acquire a distinct solidarity as such, encouraged the possibility that sections of the unions' members would break away—a danger that heterogeneous and centralized unions have never wholly defeated (as the dockers' recent history outstandingly suggests). And finally, competition and division exposed the New Unions to criticism from the socialist theory that had often provided their own inspiration.

One answer, of course, would have been the re-allocation of memberships acquired by more or less indiscriminate recruiting, between a limited number of unions related to each other by some rational pattern of specialization. But that would have involved the wholesale break-up and reconstruction of several now-established organizations. And the New Unions, by the present century's second decade, were too far on the way to becoming quite as 'institution-

[1] Even the 1889 General Railway Workers' Union, which had similarly a nominally 'industrial' scope, according to the Webbs (*History*, p. 405) also organized general labourers.

alized' as the Old for that possibility to be seriously considered. The only solution that was consistent with the maintenance substantially intact of their separate officialdoms was the merger of existing unions into larger ones. It is possible that in some instances the 1920s' decline of union membership—which most severely affected the newer, open organizations—gave a final push in that direction. The only notable change in the cotton unions' structure since World War I, for instance, has been a reduction in the number of local unions by merger. And there, the trend has been supported—indeed promoted—by the officials because it helped to ensure units reasonably capable of maintaining professional agents. Similarly, the amalgamation of some more recent unions may have promised their new-expanded full-time staffs at least a lesser insecurity than did their continued separation. But the biggest amalgamations were mooted by the previous decade of expansion, which really made mass unionism an irreversible fact. And with their conclusion, the main outlines of British trade unionism's present structure were also settled.

A critical factor in determining the shape of particular mergers was thus the prospective position of existing leaders in the various possible re-groupings that were open to them. But fortunately theory permitted alternate forms of amalgamation. Where—as in the classic 1913 merger of railway unions, or in the later wool and textile-finishing workers' amalgamation—a New Union had expanded little beyond certain recognizable frontiers, within which older associations existed that were prepared to merge, the new grouping could now be blessed by the doctrine of 'industrial unionism'. And where, as especially in the Gasworkers' case, early expansion had been too vigorously unselective for that, amalgamation into a still more general organization could be justified by reference to 'class unionism'. But that the blessing of such a doctrine implied no particular restriction to its implications has been shown by the subsequent immense and universal growth of the T & GWU—the clue to which was that, though originally a near-industrial merger of dock and road-transport unions, its structure was, of all the new amalgamations, best designed for the subsequent accommodation of small societies in any trade that doubted their continued power to maintain a viable independent existence.

During this period of their renewed development and merger, the New Unions' governmental structures also crystallized. The relative absence of traditional solidarities from their background accounted for their final size—indeed, the tendency of groups that (like the dockers) evolved a conscious occupational identity of their own to split off was a continual embarrassment to their leaderships.

But it equally gave them no traditional pattern of self-government. The New Unions' original constitutions were makeshift affairs, often imitations of existing structures: and in their amalgamated forms there were, of course, differences that reflected their particular histories, a tailoring to fit particular personalities and groupings in mergers, and so on. But an underlying similarity emerged, which was elaborated by the professional negotiators and administrators who gradually replaced their founder propagandist-organizers.

In their original and amalgamated forms, the New Unions remained in a real sense their leaders' product. Since they were expressions of social democracy, they could hardly avoid a formally-democratic constitution. But the type they assumed effectively consolidated their leaders' authority. The procedure of electing for life their principal official—one adopted by most of the major unions that appeared after the MFGB—virtually confirmed the leader's position by popular demonstration.[1] His authority could rarely be effectively challenged by the members of predominantly-lay executive councils, elected for a year or two only, meeting infrequently, and drawn from a diversity of places and occupations. The large-scale annual or biennial conference gave such leaders a platform from which to sway their membership through the most active branch workers, who usually composed the exclusively lay delegates. And as they began to reconstitute their full-time staffs, the appointment of subordinate officials by lay committees, subject to the leaders' own advice and influence, gave the latter a control of the union's professional hierarchy which included in practice a certain power to appoint their own successors.

All this was quite foreign to the craftsmen's governmental pattern. In the crafts, just as in cotton and in most of the miners' unions, the officials had been initially grafted-on to an existing association, established or immanent. The New Unions of less-skilled workers, significant as they were, first appeared only during a broader awakening of labour consciousness that was in fact reflected more in an increase of the membership and militancy of established unions than in the formation of new ones. The intimacy of the rank-and-file cotton operatives' relationship with their local official—a man appointed and both closely and continuously scrutinized by an active local committee—largely prevented tension between professional agent and members from appearing in the cotton unions. But the major craft unions experienced a realization of, and a

[1] Of 127 unions of which the method of appointing their general secretary is tabulated by Allen, 53 elect him for life by some form of popular vote (estimated from Table I, *Power in Trade Unions*, op. cit., pp. 74 to 99).

reaction against, the *de facto* concentration in their national Secretaries' hands of an authority the remoteness of which was aggravated by their renewed growth of membership. The ASE in 1892 replaced its old lay executive council by a small full-time body of elected regional representatives, and adopted also the Boilermakers' system of full-time District Delegates. And these measures together not merely permitted a more active 'trade' policy, but—especially since all these officers were elected only for limited terms—in effect reduced the Secretary's power and returned some of it to the localities.[1] The Boilermakers in turn adopted, in 1897, the ASE's full-time regionally-elected Executive Committee; and the same device, usually together with that of the periodically-elected, full-time local official, was later imitated by other important craft unions—the Woodworkers and the Foundrymen, the Plumbers and the Painters. Thus, in the crafts the stimulation of rank-and-file interest by new movements in fact induced a reversal of the previous centralizing trend.

This internal change in the craft unions was under way at the very time when the New Unions were establishing themselves, and occurred before these settled into a final form. It also coincided with a period when the craft unions themselves were, from force of such circumstances as the renewed development of national employers' organizations as well as from the new influences in trade unionism, being drawn both into large-scale collective bargaining and into modifications of their exclusive attitude that were to end, at least for the New Model ASE, in its own conversion to a mass organization. While in that union the system of checks on central authority was later elaborated by such things as the reconstitution of rank-and-file Appeals Committees, the reduction of central staffs in favour of more local officers, and finally, of course, by the erection of the shop-steward to a status in actual union government that probably more than compensated for the previous decline in branch autonomy. In the modern AEU's case, indeed, central authority has been dispersed to a point at which it sometimes seems to disappear. It is a comment on the fundamental difference between the New Model's and the New Union's evolution, that whereas in the former's great descendant the AEU, coherent policy and consistent activity seems now only to be secured by the influence of a determined and co-ordinated political fraction, in the New Union's greatest contemporary representative, the T & GWU, only such a minority has

[1] Under the AEU's present constitution, of course, the role of principal agent is in any case divided between the President and General Secretary, the former being in several respects—particularly as the union's public mouthpiece and representative—the more prominent.

presented a substantial challenge to the authority of an established leader.

V

It has already been demonstrated that the centralized government now characteristic of many major unions is not connected with the growth of large-scale collective bargaining. Quite the reverse, in fact: the great craft unions' retreat from centralization was actually facilitated by collective bargaining's development, since it reduced their reliance on benefit funds and the apparatus of 'autonomous regulation' they evolved from the apprenticeship system. Nor is centralization, as some commentators have suggested, an inevitable result of the modern increase in union size.[1] A federal organization was found quite suitable by the cotton and miners' unions at their peak, when they had respectively nearly half-a-million and a million members. We have just shown that the New Unions did not become centralized because they were big, but that both their centralization and their size sprang from their original character as organizing centres. While it was, moreover, just when the great craft amalgamations were becoming mass unions that they reversed their former tendency to centralized control.

Nor, finally, is the predominant centralization of modern union government explained by more recent imitation of a once-successful earlier form—that of the New Model. The latter's major significance was that it embodied the professional union official's emergence as a dominant figure in the labour movement and, with him, the transition from 'natural' to 'institutional' unionism. But here, the New Model was far from providing that phenomenon's sole expression—or, ultimately, its typical one. While it is a further illustration of the importance of inter-sectional conflicts and competition to trade union development that it was the New Unions' arrival that drove several of the Old ones to modify their own character substantially. So that it might well be said the New Unions' present form owes less to their predecessors' than does their predecessors' modern form to them.

Summarily, it is with the more recent mass unions that centralized government is now particularly identified. And here their organization contrasts strongly with that of the one major grouping among older-established unions that otherwise anticipated their techniques.

[1] See, for instance, Allen (op. cit., p. 23): 'Once unions reach a certain size they inevitably centralize their administrations. This is a lesson learnt from the "New Model" Unions of the last century . . .'

The Weavers retained their federal form because it was founded, together with their methods of external action, in the very traditions of occupational association that accounted for their unions' early appearance. The New Unions, however, owed hardly anything to tradition and little more to example—beyond the generally encouraging effect of preceding instances of regular collective bargaining, successful strike action, and effective political pressure.

Thus the New Unions' form (one only elaborated in the mergers their haphazard expansion obliged them to enter) differed from the Weavers' because of their early dependence on their leaders, and because of the latters' frequent political inspiration. The New Unions, in the absence of tradition and by contrast to the Old, became in shape multi-sectional where the latter were (at least originally) sectional, and in internal structure centralized where the latter were (or were again becoming) decentralized. Both these qualities of the New Unions arose from their initial function as recruiting centres. But they were preserved (even to some discomfort, as the New Unions' established and amalgamated descendants came to deal with the growth of separate occupational loyalties among their members) when that recruiting function dwindled, as the leaders themselves became professional negotiators and administrators and their propagandist and organizing qualities withered.

Most students of trade union government since the Webbs have noted its great diversity of method. And confronted with a baffling variety of constitutional devices, all ostensibly intended to combine democratic rule with an effective administration, it is understandable that some should have attempted to simplify the whole problem of explaining this profusion systematically by supposing a general tendency to centralization. But if that supposition has here been shown incorrect, the opposite interpretation, which attributes trade unionism's constitutional diversity to an almost random empiricism, has been equally rejected.

Some part of this diversity is attributable to the occasional survival (or even revival) of what might be called 'pre-institutional' forms long after the emergence of the full-time official had generally made them inappropriate. Such devices of early trade unionism as government by the general meeting, the referendum, or the rotating executive, are still sometimes found. It has been noted, for instance, that the printers' unions did not go through the mid-nineteenth-century amalgamation movement and its aftermath in the same way as other craftsmen's associations, because it was obstructed by their local restrictions on labour mobility. Thus the London Society of Compositors' supreme body remained the general meeting even when its membership approached 14,000.[1] And it is curious that even such a comparatively recent union as the Ministry of Labour Staff Association itself should have a 'General Purposes Committee' consisting of the officials plus three area delegates nominated by the association's districts in alphabetical rotation.[2] Moreover, the MLSA's rules also provide for both the referendum and the 'initiative' in policy decisions—constitutional devices which are generally identified with the antiquity of trade unionism. So that it is not merely in very old unions that such primitive forms may still be found.

Nevertheless, it has also been suggested that three major themes can be distinguished in the evolution of British union government from 'pre-institutional' types. There is the development of the craft amalgamation—first towards centralization, then away from it. Here, the typical structure consists of a small Executive Committee, in the larger unions wholly or partly full-time, which is subject, together with all other full-time officials, to regular election—each officer usually being voted directly by the constituency of the union to which his office relates. The E.C. and officials will commonly be subject to a smallish supervisory or scrutinizing council of elected lay members. Thus the AEU's National Committee, though it normally meets only annually, does so for at least two weeks, and arranges its debates on the prime assumption that it is *instructing* the E.C.—not merely hearing and commenting on the latter's report. Or there may also be a separate 'appeals committee' of elected lay members which may meet at need to hear complaints against the full-time leadership, and is empowered to overrule its decisions, as in the case of the Patternmakers. Alternately, again, the lay supervisors may be a 'General Council' which meets more or less frequently—as in the Woodworkers' and Woodcutting Machinists' Unions—or a body (like that of the Plasterers and Blacksmiths) which meets infrequently but lengthily to regulate the union's rules. Sometimes the E.C. will even be subject to more than one such controller: the AEU, for instance, has an appeals committee as well as its annual lay council.

The second major type is that evolved by the mass successors to the 'New Unions'. Here, the supreme formal authority of the union is almost always a very large annual or biennial assembly of local delegates, which between-times entrusts its authority to a largish

[1] Just prior, that is, to its recent transformation—by amalgamation with a smaller body—into the London Typographical Association.

[2] This is distinct from the E.C. of the MLSA which is a broader—and apparently less functional—body corresponding to what in other unions might be a 'General Council'.

executive committee predominantly or wholly of lay members. The executive will usually be responsible for the appointment of full-time officials. But to this rule there will be an important exception: the General Secretary himself will be elected independently, by a direct ballot of the membership or some similar procedure (like a national vote of branches) and will then hold office for life. This appears, indeed, the most common method by which unions nominate their major official: and most of those that do so have the other features identified here with the more recent 'open' unions' development.[1] And among them, the role of the leading official (or in one or two special cases such as the Distributive and the General Workers' unions, officials) in relation both to the union's general administration and to the formally-supreme annual or biennial conference is usually much more positive than in the case of the form evolved from the old craft union: conference debate, for instance, is usually conducted in relation to an Executive Report the critical points of which will be presented by the General Secretary himself.

The cotton unions are now the outstanding contemporary representative of the third major type. This is the federal form, in which authority lies primarily in the hands of the union's local or sectional units. Of course, many unions allow a certain discretion to their local or sectional divisions—in such matters, for instance, as the calling of small strikes, or in affiliation to outside bodies. But this discretion is granted and withdrawable by some central or general body. In the federal type, the position is reversed: the powers of the central organ consists only in what its affiliates have conceded. And the concession is not necessarily permanent.

The federal form of the miners' unions—which provide its other great historical example—is now somewhat concealed by the modern NUM's apparently monolithic façade. Apart from cotton and coal, only one or two small craftsmen's associations, like the coopers', and some professional or non-manual workers' organizations such

[1] The minority includes a number of very small unions, whose supreme authority is still the archaic general meeting of members, and which appoints the General Secretary. That several of the closed printing unions (like the Typographical Association) ballot their General Secretary for life is probably explained by their growth from such small local societies. Thus, they have generally adopted a special variant of the craft constitutional form: their government is usually in the hands of a smallish lay E.C. of district or sectional representatives, subject to a review (except in what was the LSC) by a Triennial Delegate Meeting. But in the two or three cases where the period of the General Secretary's election is indefinite, a procedure for his dismissal is specifically included. Otherwise, the group of unions which elect their General Secretary for life also includes several—like the Potters and the Bakers—which have roots in the period before the 'New Union' movement, and which prescribe a preliminary (and probably decisive) stage of examination or selection by the E.C.

as that of insurance agents, have retained it in an obvious or substantially-unmodified way.[1] Nevertheless, other major unions with substantial roots in the period before the 'New Unionist' movement, but without a background of craft tradition, have at least evolved from a federal form. For instance, the boot and shoe operatives, who outside the crafts, coal and cotton, comprised the biggest organized group before the nineteenth century's close, re-formed their National Union in 1890 from large town branches, each appointing its own full-time official, conducting district negotiations and controlling its own funds. The Webbs detected in the NUBSO a tendency to sectional federalism, as well as local, since the different classes of operatives in each town formed separate sub-branches, and the Union was obliged to meet certain demands for sectional representation in its central government.[2] (The NUBSO actually emerged, rather like the cotton unions though later than them, by separation of the new machine-operatives from a much older organization of handworkers.) The present steel-workers' union (BISAKTA) was formed by gradually taking over the membership of a previous federation of sectional and local unions. A federal structure appears, in fact, to have been quite typical of such 'Old Unions' as were not also craft organizations. And even where originally-federal forms have been extensively modified in these unions' descendants, the latter often retain some distinctive constitutional feature of the type. Thus their leading official may be appointed or subject to preliminary selection by the governing body. And the latter will itself commonly be no larger than is required to secure a fair balance of the affiliated interests.[3]

[1] We exclude here, of course, such bodies as the National Federation of Building Trade Operatives, the Printing and Kindred Trades Federation, and the Confederation of Shipbuilding and Engineering Unions. These are federations mainly of *national* unions, existing for limited purposes—usually of joint negotiation with particular employers' alliances—so that a union may belong to two or three such bodies. The critical point is that they usually have no reserve fund of their own. They thus resemble the UTFWA, rather than the 'Amalgamations' in cotton.

[2] *Industrial Democracy*, p. 127. It is in any case often difficult to distinguish local from sectional interest-demarcations, since in many industries districts may also specialize in different products or processes.

[3] It is thus interesting that the BISAKTA, one of our nearest equivalents to an 'industrial' union, has resisted the seeming attraction of the annual conference, besides continuing to have its E.C. appoint the General Secretary. The NUR—though much more obviously a product of modern mass unionism—has modified the latter's typical form in a rather similar direction—by providing for examination of officers before election and much restricting the size of its annual conference. These things may suggest that the 'New Union' form is ultimately unacceptable to a union that combines 'open' and 'closed' occupations in the same industry.

All this, of course, does not suggest that the structure of individual unions has not been influenced by that of others. Where their external shape is concerned, the opposite is clearly the case. Among the New Unions, as we have shown in the non-cotton textile trades, the direction of particular organizations' growth was largely conditioned by the presence or otherwise of competing bodies in the fields of recruitment which were accessible to their original leaderships. While the later expansion of certain major craft organizations was not merely stimulated by the need to compete in bargaining strength with the newer mass unions that infiltrated their own industries, but often justified by the same ideological concepts—of 'industrial unionism' and so on—as in those unions' case. So that, among the three constitutional patterns here sketched (or four, if one includes the 'pre-institutional') it is perhaps also significant that the least change on earlier forms appears among unions which have been least susceptible to external rivalries that have led them into a wider occupational coverage, like those in coal, cotton—or print.

Similarly, the internal, constitutional evolution of trade unions has been affected by cross-fertilizations which have somewhat blurred the distinction between its main strands. Thus, several craft organizations—like the Electricians and the Woodworkers—have recently adopted the large annual conference on the argument that this is more 'democratic'. Usually, they have had reservations about its powers in relation to other channels of union authority: the introduction of this device was especially advocated by their Communist members. In other cases, a constitutional type has been modified to reconcile the parties—whether interests or personalities—to inter-union mergers. So that both the USDAW and the NUGMW, for example, had to give other officials a status close to that of their General Secretaries, to accommodate the leaders of the separate unions now amalgamated in these bodies.[1] And in still other cases, a pattern has been modified by sectional idiosyncracies. Thus several modern unions of non-manual workers have adopted very much the general form of the newer 'open' manual unions by which their own growth was much inspired—the mass annual conference, the large lay E.C. and so on—but have departed from that form by having their E.C. appoint the General Secretary. In this, they followed such older non-craft unions as those of cotton and steel workers. But in their case, it seems likely that the departure was attributable to a vocational familiarity with procedures of appointing officials by examination, interview, or selection board: several of the unions concerned—the civil service clerks', the

[1] On the NUGMW, see H. A. Clegg's *General Union* (op. cit.).

post office workers', the post office engineers'—are of public servants![1]

Despite such variants and modifications, the distinct main patterns seem adequately recognizable in modern union constitutions; and their differing historical derivation from earlier forms of association has been traced. It has also been shown how such internal differences between unions are linked with differences in their occupational coverage, which are similarly derived from the historical situation of their particular predecessors. So that the factors which, as the previous Chapter suggested, have determined both whether different groups of workers have been early or late to organize *and* their respective unions' original operative techniques, have also conditioned those unions' internal organization and external shape. Trade union forms are a product of trade union origins.

[1] The POEU has actually gone so far as to advertise its General Secretaryship, and appoint a non-member from the applicants.

V

UNION STRUCTURE AND UNION GOVERNMENT

1

The Morphology of Trade Unionism

I

In the development of trade unionism, we have looked at union structure in general from two viewpoints: from the outside, at the shape of individual unions—in terms of their occupational coverage or recruiting ambitions—and their relations to each other; and from the inside, at the internal government of particular organizations. To the internal structure of trade unions, and their relations with their members, this study will return later. But from the first of these viewpoints, that of external structure, it can now consider the morphology of trade unions.[1]

Any student of trade unionism will be familiar with the inadequacy of the classifications commonly used to describe the diverse external forms it may assume. Such categories as 'craft' or 'occupational', 'industrial' and 'general', may sometimes indicate a union's original shape or the recruiting doctrine by which it has at some time been influenced, but as a guide to its present character they are rarely very illuminating. Thus, the cotton unions are often described, by their own members and officers[2] as well as by outsiders, as 'craft' organizations. The term has a certain prestige value, but in its strict sense, it is obviously inapplicable to them. The classic craft union is distinguished by the apprenticeship system, the restricted entry of boys solely as learners into an occupation to which the union confines itself. Though recruits to one or two skilled cotton occupations

[1] So far as unions in general are concerned, a more preliminary, but in one or two respects more detailed, application of the analysis that follows is contained in the present writer's 'Trade Union Organization' (*Political Quarterly*, Jan.–Mar., 1956).

[2] See, for instance, 'Trade Unionism and the Cotton Industry', by Ernest Thornton, M.P., a paper to the annual Cotton Board Conference, 1953.

are now sometimes called 'apprentices', only one trade—the strippers-and-grinders—has adopted an entry system which *might* be considered approximate to the historic apprenticeship. And this trade is not organized in a separate union of its own.

The description, 'craft union', however, is often used in a looser way, to describe an association of workers marked off by some superior skill. And this use is superficially suited to those cotton unions which have here been called 'closed'—the Spinners, Overlookers, Tapesizers, Twisters, and so on. The difficulty that the Spinners also organize the piecers and mule-assistants, while the Twisters recruit reachers-in, can be overcome by regarding these less-skilled workers as also 'learners', or at least, as on the ladder of promotion to the union's principal occupation—in the same way as the Associated Society of Locomotive Engineers and Firemen (which sometimes also describes itself as a 'craft' union) organizes the engine-cleaners from whom footplatemen are recruited. The term is perhaps already stretched a little in the case of the Spinners, whose assistants outnumber themselves, and had (until the quite recent past at any rate) only a minority chance of promotion. But what is one to do when one finds that in Yorkshire the Spinners also organize many sorts of cotton operative other than those on the mule-spinning process—or that in several districts the Twisters organize beamers, who are not on their promotion ladder and are also less-skilled?

In fact, only two of the cotton amalgamations are 'closed' in a virtually pure sense. Both the Overlookers' and Tapesizers' membership is for practical purposes confined to those more-skilled workers described by their unions' titles (though the writer understands that even in the Tapesizers—whose tendency to shroud their occupation in a certain 'mystery' makes them perhaps closer in spirit to the old crafts than any other cotton union—one or two local clubs have accepted labourers into membership). Of the other closed unions, the Warpdressers not only organize the twisters, drawers and reachers-in of Yorkshire mills, but in Lancashire itself have absorbed a small independent association of specialized operatives called chain-beamers, and also now organize so many other workers concerned in the mechanical preparation of cotton yarn for weaving that these probably outnumber their nominal membership group. While the way in which the Warehousemen abandoned their original limitation of membership to clothlookers has already been described.

Finally, the term 'craft' is sometimes used, still more loosely, as an alternative to 'occupational'—to describe a union that, while not necessarily having any control over the entry of new labour, nevertheless restricts itself to a single occupation, or at least to so narrow a range of related jobs that it cannot reasonably be classified as some other kind of animal altogether (such as an 'industrial' or 'general' union). And in the sense that the nucleus of each cotton operatives' association was usually a membership in one particular occupation, the adjective 'occupational' is certainly more appropriate than 'craft'. But in the Cardroom Amalgamation's membership, the original core of male cardroom workers proper has been numerically quite overwhelmed by other operatives from the spinning trades. And the Amalgamation now covers so many other occupations that it could better be described as an 'industrial' union for the cotton-spinning industry—a role which will become still more apparent as the Spinners' Amalgamation continues its decline before technical change.

The Weavers' Amalgamation, had not several predominantly male groups in cotton manufacturing split off from the modern weaving operatives' associations at an early stage in their history, might well have assumed a similar place in that industry. The difficulty in fitting the Weavers strictly into the 'occupational' classification, however, arises not only because there remain a substantial number of other jobs than weaving proper, the occupants of which may be recruited by the Weavers, but because that Amalgamation has spread somewhat beyond the cotton manufacturing industry itself. The Weavers' entry into cotton spinning, for instance, is explained by their early inclusion of winders, reelers and warpers (a very numerous group of operatives on machine-processes intermediate between spinning and weaving) who were also employed in some spinning mills with weaving departments. From this the Weavers acquired a general interest in these operatives, although in the Bolton district the same workers have been organized by the Cardroom Association. But the Weavers have also organized independent mills in the doubling trade, where not only the Cardroom Amalgamation but the General and Municipal Workers' Union have memberships. So that in one or two places the Weavers' local association now has a minority, not merely of weavers, but of workers in cotton manufacturing proper. Other local weaving unions have organized workers in hosiery, asbestos, and rubber firms. And their Amalgamation's acceptance in 1951 of affiliation by the Amalgamated Society of Textile Workers and Kindred Trades, a silk-workers' union from outside the cotton districts, for a while encouraged a suspicion among other unions that the Weavers had ambitions towards becoming a general union of textile and 'allied' operatives.

Inside the cotton manufacturing industry itself, on the other hand, the coverage of the Weavers' Amalgamation would have been wider had it not encountered competition from other unions which were also expanding their occupational scope—the Warpdressers to include chain-beamers and dry-tapers, the Warehousemen rather more widely. These overlaps have usually been resolved by roughly classifying and allocating the disputed operatives on a 'departmental' basis within the mills. But they have sometimes involved the temporary partition of an occupation (as in the case of the chain-beamers and related operatives under a 1943 agreement between the Weavers and Warpdressers), or the nominal separation of two almost similar occupations—as among certain operatives previously described by collective agreements simply as 'odd hands about the mill' under a 1937 agreement between the Weavers and Warehousemen. And the elasticity of any formal principle of jurisdictional partition between unions is perhaps demonstrated by the Warehousemen's portion under this last arrangement, which was itself the product of several years' disagreement between the two Amalgamations about their jurisdiction among 'ancillary workers'. At any rate, the Warehousemen's finally-agreed share included not merely the various workers in the warehouse and packing departments of mills, but also the tapesizers' labourers and those in winding rooms, as well as the winding overlookers—although the agreement recognized the Weavers' exclusive claim to the winders themselves.

One difficulty with an 'occupational' principle of demarcation between unions (and therefore, in classifying them) is that occupations change: in the dispute just referred to, for instance, an earlier agreement (of 1923) between the Weavers and Warehousemen had broken down owing to technical developments which disturbed the classifications involved. But another difficulty with the 'occupational' principle is that unless it is reinforced by some second principle, like a restrictive and specific qualification for entry to the founder occupation, there will always be *other* occupations so close to the latter in content, employment conditions or some other quality that an organization based on it tends to spread, so losing its original form. Thus, when put to the test of a disputed claim to organize particular groups of workers, cotton unions have accepted 'occupational', 'industrial', 'departmental' (or sub-industrial), 'geographical' and other demarcations as expediency suggested. And where no such test has arisen, their boundaries are often vague.

However, a factual reluctance to fit into accepted categories—categories which unions themselves use to indicate their organizing intentions—is not restricted to the cotton unions alone. Indeed, it is perhaps rather less marked in their case than in others. There are, in fact, quite close parallels between the external union structure of the cotton trades and that of other industries. The respective situations of the Spinners' and Cardroom Amalgamations in spinning, for instance, are not dissimilar from those of the ASLEF and NUR among the 'conciliation grades' of railwaymen. Moreover, the relation between the Weavers and the other cotton manufacturing unions is rather like that ruling, in the non-cotton textile trades, between the big Dyers, Bleachers and Textile Workers' Union and the several smaller unions which also belong to the federal 'Association of Unions in the Textile Trade'.

II

The apparently haphazard quality of British trade union structure has been a matter not merely of common comment but of occasional major controversy for at least half a century. It is significant, for instance, that from 1874 on, the TUC itself has adopted successive resolutions in favour of 'closer unity' in union organization, and that its General Council has on two occasions (in the early 1920s and again between 1943 and 1946) undertaken very substantial enquiries into inter-union relations—each time making large proposals for reforming them—and has recently revived its interest in the question.[1] It is still true that no industry of any size, and few substantial occupations, are organized by a single union alone; while few sizeable unions, on the other hand, restrict themselves to a single occupation or industry. The practical disadvantages of this situation are certainly much less than they used to be. The Webbs' remark, that '. . . to competition between overlapping unions is to be attributed nine-tenths of the ineffectiveness of the trade union world',[2] has lost much of its force with the reduction in the number of unions by amalgamation, and with the TUC's development both of a procedure for conciliating jurisdictional disputes and of a code of good behaviour between unions (the 'Bridlington Rules'). While a mutual recognition of established 'organizing rights' has grown with the acceptance and consolidation of the newer unions.

These things have, of course, to some extent only transferred the structural problems of trade unions—from their external relations to their internal administration. But despite them, situations still persist in which the form of union organization seems, to either trade unionists or managements, not just incompatible with any rational principle, but inconvenient and wasteful for practical business. For instance, a large general engineering firm may have to deal with thirty or more separate unions, while in many sectors of industry different unions maintain duplicate negotiating staffs and administrations for the same class of workers—a situation, of course, that particularly affects the two 'general' unions which, under some

[1] TUC *Annual Reports*, 1924 and 1946, as well as 1959/60.
[2] *Industrial Democracy*, Introduction to 1902 Edition.

sixty or seventy national agreements alone, are both concerned with the representation of less-skilled workers. And crises in inter-union relations have been sufficiently frequent in recent years to lead the TUC in 1955 to seek and secure some extension of its powers to intervene in its affiliates' conduct of disputes.[1]

At one time, it was possible to regard such crises as the product of a fundamental disagreement among trade unionists as to the principle upon which their organizations should be based—a disagreement reflecting a still deeper division of view as to the purpose of trade unionism itself. The 'sound amalgamated principles', that the leaders of the mid-nineteenth century New Models erected into a philosophy to attack the various militant opponents of their cautious and consolidating policy, merged into a conscious and defensive 'craft unionism' in those leaders' successors when in turn attacked by the socialist labour organizers with the (alternate) doctrines of 'industrial' or 'class unionism'. This controversy, of course, was loudest in the years of mass union recruitment immediately before and after World War I. But the TUC's *Report on Trade Union Structure and Closer Unity* of 1946 still devoted an introductory discussion to the issues of principle involved in it. It retains at least a formal life in certain inter-union relationships—for instance, as between the Chemical and Rubber Workers' Unions on the one hand and the two great general unions on the other. One *might* attribute the failure of so many unions to embrace the complete membership indicated by their announced organizational ideal—as of the 'industrial' NUR to become a comprehensive union for railwaymen—to the inspiration of competitors by a rival theory of organization. And inter-union disputes can often be interpreted in the light of a controversy between organizational principles. So that when the London Typographical Society contests the NUR's claim to the printers of railway timetables,[2] or the bricklayers' and masons' union (the AUBTW) disputes the National Union of Funeral and Cemetery Workers' right to organize monumental masons, they can be regarded as illustrating the clash of 'craft' with 'industrial' doctrines.

However, similar situations have occurred when no such clash of principle was involved. So far as the writer is aware, jurisdictional disagreements between the cotton unions have never been expressed in the language of doctrinal debate. And it would be difficult to

[1] The 1955 amendment to the TUC's Rule 11, effectively permitting the TUC General Council to intervene in a dispute if negotiations *seemed likely* to break down (instead of, as previously, after that event) was largely suggested by the fact that the three major stoppages in the preceding year—in the docks, newspapers and railways—each involved an inter-union conflict.

[2] TUC *Annual Reports*, Disputes Committee.

rationalize at least the more recent disputes of the National Union of Public Employees with such bodies as the General and Municipal Workers' Union or the Confederation of Health Service Employees in the terms of rival organizing theories. Many unions which once announced adherence to a particular structural principle have in any case accepted limits which compromised it—as the general unions have long abandoned 'class unionism' by their agreements with other organizations *and* by their notable failure to merge with each other. Still more to the point, many unions once inspired by such a principle have entered fields apparently incompatible with it. Thus major 'craft' unions like the Woodworkers and Electricians—and most notably, of course, the AEU—have accepted workers of successively less obvious degrees of skill. The AUBTW, having appeared above in a 'craft' role in the case of the Monumental Masons, was very shortly afterwards judged guilty by the TUC Disputes Committee of 'poaching' labourers from the General and Municipal Workers.[1] The 'industrial' NUR has organized busmen, and the steel workers' union (BISAKTA) has recruited certain operatives in engineering establishments even though these were already employed under wage-rates fixed by other unions. While the 'general' unions have extended what was once their *de facto* role as organizers of less-skilled labour at large, by recruiting more-skilled workers in several industries—the T & GWU even having a special section for clerical, supervisory, and administrative staffs.

Even in the printing trades, where craft unionism would probably find its nearest contemporary ideal, and where the technical lines of distinction between jobs are probably much clearer than (say) in the metal and wood-working industries, there have been significant lapses from strict organizational purity. Thus the Operative Printers' Society (NATSOPA)—a major union of those printing and paper workers originally excluded from the old craftsmen's unions—argued in the Printing and Kindred Trades Federation's 1956 discussion of wage-policy that there was now '. . . so much overlapping by the printing unions that they could no longer be put into categories of craft and non-craft'. It had certainly itself recruited among several classes of skilled printing workers: while among the printing 'crafts' even the supremely-aristocratic London Society of Compositors has recently accepted a body of workers (the printing machine-managers) not recruited by its own strait path of apprenticeship, and who may also be organized by the 'non-craft' print unions. The LSC, indeed, changed its name to the London Typographical Association mainly to cover that extension. And so on.

Of course, the general unions are still 'general' in the sense that

[1] TUC Disputes Committee, *Annual Reports*.

they will in principle recruit any workers except such as they have agreed not to. And other customary classifications of trade unions also have a rather more than historic value in so far as many unions still fit one or other of them closely enough for it to describe their predominant membership's common quality. But other unions—including certain of the biggest—are now virtually unclassifiable. It has been shown that the AEU, for instance, retains important internal features of traditional craft unionism: but in other aspects it is a would-be industrial (or multi-industrial) union for the engineering and allied trades: and in still others it appears as an occupational union of mechanics and metal-workers at large. And how does one classify the Union of Shop, Distributive and Allied Workers? It is not an occupational union of shop and warehouse workers because it recruits laboratory and office staffs, as well as transport workers. It is not an industrial union for the distributive trades because it organizes factory operatives. It is not (as its major predecessor, the old NUDAW, predominantly was) an 'employment' union of co-operative societies' employees, because it now has a substantial membership in private trade and manufacture. Yet its interests are not yet quite so varied as to make it a third general union.

The difficulty in confining such unions to a category is partly that the categories themselves often fail to yield a sharp jurisdictional definition in practice. Demarcations by industry prove as vague as those by occupation: the superficially-clear boundaries between the Cardroom and Weavers' Amalgamations dissolved before the facts of jobs common to both spinning and weaving industries, and of the existence of 'combined mills' and independent intermediate processes. Even demarcations by craft often break down because these can be based alternately on the qualifications of the worker or on the job that he is doing: and the same job may be done by workers of different qualifications, while workers of a particular qualification may do different jobs. Apart from the 'general' union—which is hardly a category at all—only two such union types provide definite boundaries: 'craft' in its narrowest sense, of the common possession of a distinct and formal vocational qualification (such as many 'professional associations' make a condition of membership): and 'employment' in the sense that the union concerned restricts its membership—like several organizations of banking and insurance staffs—to those on the payroll of a particular concern.[1] And rather few trade unions fit either of these two categories.

[1] Theoretically, one supposes, an 'employment' union might also be one which accepted only the employees of firms that belonged to a specified employers' association. However, the writer has never heard of a union that based itself on such a demarcation.

However, the inherent vagueness of other jurisdictional definitions would be of only secondary consequence by itself, since, if that were the only problem in determining a union's membership frontiers, it could always be resolved in a quite arbitrary way—as by the United States National Labour Relations Board ruling of 1948 that dual or multiple union representation could only be granted in concerns that were not 'integrated' technically.[1] Much the bigger problem is the apparent reluctance of many unions, when it comes to the point, to sacrifice a potential membership for the sake of a pre-announced structural principle. Organizational theories have, in practice, often served for little more than to justify the immediate recruiting ambitions of particular unions. So such theories have proven proportionately adjustable to subsequent expediency—and opportunity.

III

Classification is not a mere scholastic exercise. Its point is partly to separate the elements in a situation that would otherwise appear confused and chaotic. But as such, it is also an essential preliminary to the understanding of any order of events, and to useful generalizations. Since certain important classifications of union types have their origin in the slogans of dead ideological debate, rather than in objective description, they neither explain the present morphology of trade unionism nor illuminate its likely behaviour. For such purposes, it is perhaps worth considering whether the simple division into 'closed' and 'open' unions, used by cotton operatives to distinguish between their own organizations—and in the preceding chapters to interpret those organizations' development, as well as that of others—is not more realistic.

One clue to the structure of British trade unionism is the concentration of membership in a few very large trade unions. Over half of the TUC's total affiliation currently belongs to six unions only, out of some 180 affiliates in all. Another clue, however, is the apparently comfortable survival, despite this century's general trend to merger and amalgamation among unions, of a number of relatively small organizations, like the Tapesizers in cotton and the Patternmakers outside.

The larger unions are 'open', at least in the sense that they are able to impose no restrictions on entry into many of the occupations that they organize, but are content to recruit all workers in those occupations whom the employers themselves engage. Such unions are almost

[1] This is the so-called 'National Tube Doctrine', from the case in which it was first concluded. The ruling, however, has since been extended to several other American industries.

inevitably expansionist in tendency. Since an open union is usually unable to bring pressure to bear on employers through controlling the supply of labour to a key stage in the production process, it is bound to rely on strength of numbers for its bargaining power instead. An open union, like the Cardroom Amalgamation (at least in its early days), may be unstable because the workers it recruits are not strongly attached to a particular occupation: the union is therefore obliged to attempt to compensate for the resultant low occupational solidarity of its membership by attempting to build up an insitutiona stability in the union itself. This in fact, and as the Cardroom Amalgamation discovered, means a staff of permanent officials, which its original membership group may be inadequate to support: so the latter must be expanded. Open unions, moreover—like the weavers' Second Amalgamation—rely partially on their capacity for political pressure, and this involves not merely an ability to mobilize votes, but also to finance political campaigns, candidatures and representatives. The open cotton unions' concern for '100 per cent, trade unionism' became notably more marked after their decision, very early in the present century, to support independent labour representation in Parliament. All these things require funds, and in the context of a membership largely recruited from lower-paid workers, the accumulation of funds again involves a large numerical recruitment.

The smaller stable unions, however, will generally be found to be predominantly closed. They are also restrictionist, not merely in the sense that they base themselves on a capacity to control the supply of labour to particular occupations and maintain an exclusive claim to employment within those occupations, but also in the sense that they have little intrinsic interest in increasing their merely numerical strength. Indeed, their interest lies rather in the opposite direction—of limiting the intake of labour to the jobs that they control, and thereby restricting also the membership of the union itself. Thus the shape of British trade unionism in general might be described as one in which open, expansionist unions have spread around islands of stable closed unionism—as the open Cardroom Amalgamation spread round the closed Spinners' Amalgamation in the cotton spinning industry. The principle animating the apparently haphazard growth of British unions has therefore been the elementary one that nature abhors a vacuum. Organizational vacuums have generally been filled by the nearest union to hand that was under a pressure to expand.

So far, then, the cotton unions' broad dual classification seems quite generally applicable. However, it is obviously possible—and may be useful—to refine it. The Yorkshire Spinners' recruitment of other operatives than mule-minders is not substantial enough to change materially the 'closed' character of the Spinners' Amalgamation. Nor are the strippers-and-grinders sufficiently numerous within the Cardroom Amalgamation for their success in 'closing' their occupation to make one hesitate about that union's classification as 'open'. Nevertheless, one must clearly reckon with the likelihood that closed and open sections of the membership will be so evenly balanced in some non-textile unions that these can only be described as 'mixed'. But the point particularly raised here is that whether a union is to be regarded as closed or open really depends on whether or not it controls entry to its predominant occupation. And in rather few unions is the membership restricted to one occupation alone. An open union, certainly, to increase its size would sooner or later be obliged to multiply the number of occupations amongst which it recruited its membership. So that another aspect of external union structure consists in the *diversity* of occupations each union organizes, and the relation of those occupations to each other.

Thus, one natural line for a union's expansion would be to recruit workers who were employed together with the members of its founder occupational groups—as labourers and similar operatives are employed with weavers, for instance, or (outside cotton) storemen and clerks with shop assistants. But another natural line of growth will be for the union to follow the movement of its existing members into new occupations. In some industries—like railways and coal (at least in their palmier days) or steel now—there is relatively little movement of labour in and out of the industry apart from the recruitment of juveniles and retirement of old employees, but workers will normally move from lower-grade jobs in the industry to higher-grade ones. In this case, the union itself may move up with its members, as both the early power-loom weavers' federations and some cardroom associations recruited cotton overlookers. So that, to take another instance, despite the existence of a separate union for locomotive engineers and firemen, about 10 per cent. of the workers of these grades on British Railways belong to the NUR, having been promoted from other grades and having retained their original union membership. However, in many other trades promotion to more-skilled and better-paid jobs is barred by the apprenticeship system, and lower-paid workers will rather move horizontally from one industry to another. The labourers whom the ancestral organizations of the present general unions recruited were particularly mobile between industries, so that unions founded on these workers naturally tended to spread from trade to trade.

But a final pressure influencing the direction of a union's expansion is the extent to which—and the direction from which—such standards as it is able to establish for its membership may be threatened by competition from other groups of workers. Thus, the leaders of the Weavers' First Amalgamation were driven to encourage organization outside the specialized districts of the manufacturing trade on which that body was founded, as well as to recruit ancillary operatives whose acceptance of low wage-standards might otherwise have threatened the weavers. In just the same way, the unskilled labourers' unions outside cotton found it impossible to confine their attempts at organization and bargaining to one or two industries alone, because it was difficult to maintain high wage-rates for one organized group of labourers while those in other trades and industries in the same locality were unorganized and badly-paid. On the other hand, an important motive in the expansion of the Amalgamated Engineering Union downwards from skilled engineering mechanics, to recruit lower-skilled engineering operatives, was that the standards of the former were threatened by the lower wages of the latter, and by the increasing technical possibility of replacing skilled by less-skilled labour.

The shape of an individual open union will therefore largely depend on the employment structure within which it commenced to operate. And it may be convenient to distinguish between 'horizontal' and 'vertical' lines of growth according to the opportunities and pressures indicated by that environment. Which is not to say that these directions are mutually exclusive. Most larger unions will be found to have grown, to some extent at least, in both directions—that is, horizontally to include occupations of about the same status as its original membership in other trades and industries, or vertically to include workers of higher or lower status within the same industry. And in some major cases, the difficulty of fitting the unions concerned into an orthodox classification seems to arise very largely from the fact that their growth—like that of the Warehousemen in cotton—has been about equal in each direction, and thus diffuse. The USDAW has expanded from its original membership of shop assistants on the one hand outwards to include warehousemen, transport workers, factory operatives and so on, who happen to be employed by the same concerns, and on the other hand upwards to include supervisors, managers, officials and technicians. Similarly, the AEU has spread partly by recruiting new groups of skilled metal-workers or mechanics in a variety of trades, which somewhat balances its membership among the growing class of less-skilled operatives in the engineering industry proper. But other large unions *do* exhibit a predominant direction of growth. The so-called 'industrial' unions—like the railwaymen's, the miners' and the steel workers'—generally operate in industries where, to each occupation, labour is recruited vertically from a lower grade in the same industry. The general unions on the other hand, because they began with workers whose chances of promotion within a particular industry were limited or barred, have in the main expanded horizontally—to include, particularly, the newer industries like chemicals and several forms of mass-production, into which their original membership was naturally transferable.

However, it is not merely amongst open unions that one may distinguish alternative vertical or horizontal lines of occupational diversification. Of the cotton operatives' various organizations, for instance, we have noted that only the Overlookers and the Tapesizers are *simple* closed unions in the sense that they are restricted to members of a single occupation. In the closed union's case, one factor in its extension may be just the method by which the union restricts entry to its principal occupation. Unions that control entry through an apprentice system, like the traditional craft unions outside cotton, or through regulating the acceptance of 'learners' like the Overlookers and Tapesizers themselves, will usually insist on the prior acceptance of these trainees into membership. And since these then constitute for their training's duration an inferior grade within the union, this itself adds a minor vertical element to the latter's form. But this factor is much more important where the union controls entry by regulating promotion from grades of worker subordinate to its principal membership, like the Spinners in cotton, or the Twisters & Drawers. Such a union often comes to include these workers (unless another union gets there first—indeed, sometimes it will do so to forestall that hazard) if only as a means to strengthen and regularize the 'promotion ladder' on which it depends. Thus, the open NUR, in extending upwards to the footplate grades of railwaymen, met the engine-drivers' own union, the closed ASLE & F, coming down; so that the latter has assumed a similarly vertical shape.

A closed union may also extend horizontally. This partly arises because even closed occupations are rarely demarcated by absolute boundaries. The problem of the potential substitutability of different kinds of labour has concerned closed unions as well as open ones: it has particularly affected the metal-working crafts, and partly accounts for the formation of the original ASE. The Spinners, for instance, were obliged to accommodate both the old hand-mule operatives and the new self-actor minders before they could stabilize their organization, and still accept twiners as of equivalent status to mule-spinners proper. While the ASLE & F, again, now joins the motormen of diesel and electric trains to its primary footplate membership. But a closed union may diversify its membership for other reasons than the imprecision of occupational frontiers. Thus the Warp-dressers in Yorkshire have recently merged their surviving local associations there into a 'Yorkshire Society of Textile Craftsmen', with the intention of organizing not only other skilled cotton-manufacturing operatives (the union already recruited twisters and drawers in the Yorkshire region) but analagous workers in the wool and worsted trades. In this case, the union's motive is apparently to preserve its subscriptions and administrative strength in face of the decline of its original membership. But the development of 'industry-wide' collective bargaining, which confronted exclusive unions in other industries both with powerful employers' associations organized on a national basis and with a greater need to finance professional negotiators, has similarly been a certain pressure on closed unions to extend their occupational coverage outwards.

It is important, however, that such extensions of unions' particular memberships have often occurred by way of mergers between separate organizations, rather than through further recruitment by individual unions. Indeed, since the 1920s amalgamation has in general been more important than new recruitment in determining the shape of individual unions. It is clearly for the major open unions, to which occupational diversification—as in the cardroom associations' case—has been a natural route to power, that the opportunity of acceptable amalgamation has been most significant as a determinant of their present external forms. For an established closed organization, any step which is likely to blur its membership's occupational identity and selectness will usually be taken only with reluctance, and as a response to powerful external pressures. Nevertheless, such pressures *have* operated. The development of the old ASE, for instance, took place just by way of amalgamation between separate exclusive unions.

This, at least—and though it may well come in the future—is a form of horizontal development the closed cotton unions have not so far much displayed—unless one includes those abortive nineteenth-century affiliations to the Spinners which have been traced, or the old-established mill-engineers' association's recent merger with a 'breakaway' from the AEU, as examples of that form. One reason for its relative absence in cotton is that in the manufacturing industry, the members of the closed occupations are usually employed in twos and threes at individual mills. Their numbers are too small in relation to the total payrolls of the firms in local masters' associations for the latter to have considered the *actual* wages paid to skilled groups to be a vital element in the wage-bill, or likely to set patterns which would spread to the other operatives at large. Unions like the Overlookers and Tapesizers have therefore been able to join in negotiations for *general* wage increases in the weaving trades, which have relatively benefited the members of lower-paid open occupations, whilst retaining the power to bargain for supplements locally or with individual mills which have substantially preserved their members' status.

But as we have already noted of the Spinners, the bigger closed unions in other industries have represented too large a proportion of the operative strength for the national employers' federations—themselves a response to the growth of mass open unions—to extend them such licence. Thus, 'craft' unions which had formerly been able to deal with employers on a workplace or, at worst, a district basis, now found themselves faced with a concerted refusal by employers to deal separately with the old craft and the new mass unions, or even to distinguish between their separate memberships in, for instance, general wage increases. In several industries (and particularly in engineering) older craft associations thus found that their apparent strength in relation to the employers was less important than their power at a previous stage of wage negotiation—that of the preparation of joint union claims.

To present a united defence of the better-paid's relative status is a motive for the horizontal merger of closed unions which, though quite old, has of course been revived by the succession of general wage increases over the past twenty years—with their accompanying pressure on previously-established wage differentials. So that it is interesting to see mergers of this type now again advocated, in certain industries, by some still predominantly-closed unions which have felt themselves outvoted in the policy decisions of the inter-union confederations which there deal with employers, and outweighed in bargaining by the bigger memberships of open unions. Thus, the Boilermakers' Society deliberately excluded the AEU from the conference of engineering craftsmen's unions that it called, in 1957, to advance proposals for mutual amalgamation; and for a while in 1958–9 it seemed possible that the century-old division between the regional and sectional unions of printing tradesmen might be overcome precisely by their common fear of the greatly increased strength of the open printing and paper unions. Decisions then taken by the craft printers' unions to attempt amalgamation were a direct consequence, on the one hand of their sense of failure in maintaining their members' relative status in face of the employers' insistence that skilled and unskilled be treated alike, and on the other hand of a proposed merger between the two open printing unions themselves. So that, just as in the nineteenth-century cotton unions, conflicts of group interests between workers still play their part in trade unionism's structural development.

At any rate, the importance of mergers between unions as a vehicle of their occupational diversification introduces a final moulding influence on the shape of the individual union: namely, the limits and obstructions to its growth that have been presented by rival unions' previous seizure of particular occupational territories. Even the simpler closed unions have in some cases been prevented from completing their restricted recruiting ambitions because some group within their occupation has succeeded in organizing a stable, and perhaps more privileged, position. It is probably for this reason that the Lancashire Tapesizers have never succeeded in establishing a united federation. While on a larger scale, we have already noted that a major obstacle, for almost a century, to a united organization of compositors has been the ability of the London Society to exclude from employment in the London area not merely workers who were not properly apprenticed to the trade, but even printers who have served a due apprenticeship in the provinces. Similarly, the Amalgamated Society of Woodcutting Machinists has found it impossible to establish itself in one small area of the North where a local union of packing-box makers has long held a traditional wage differential over the rates normally claimed for this class of work.

Again, however, inter-union competition for memberships is a problem which naturally much more affects the open, intrinsically expansionist unions. The present shape of many open unions—like the Weavers in cotton or the Textile Workers' Union in other textile trades—has clearly been set, not only by the determination of more-skilled operatives to construct or preserve their separate exclusive associations, but by the extension of other open unions into their own vocational neighbourhood. Sooner or later, any open union extending into a new field of recruitment has encountered another busily ploughing from a different point on the field's periphery.

The critical thing here is the extent to which a union in this position can still achieve a viable base—in terms of finance, bargaining power, capacity for political pressure, etc.—despite the existence of rivals. It has been previously suggested that the great movement of union amalgamation in this century's second decade arose largely from a realization by many of the then-new organizations that it was impossible for them to secure such a stability in competition. But a second phase in the amalgamation movement has set in since the 1920s, and is probably much more responsible for the persistent decline in the number of separate trade unions over the past twenty years. This sprang from the inability of a number of small unions either to grow further when confronted with the giant amalgamations, with their interests (and claims to 'organizing rights') in so many different fields of potential recruitment—*or* to establish and maintain a secure basis for occupational exclusiveness. In one textile trade, the old Woolcombers' merger with the 'general' NUGMW was probably motivated by just such a sense of insecurity. In the case of the cotton unions, the growth of both the Cardroom and Warehousemen's Amalgamations was partly due to their willingness to accept the affiliation of such minor bodies. And we have also noted how far the growth of the Transport and General Workers' Union has been attributable to an internal structure ingeniously contrived to encourage such small organizations to merge in it—as well as its inspirer Bevin's assiduous pursuit of such mergers.

Thus, the morphology of trade unionism has been conditioned by the latter's alternative operational techniques. The individual union's occupational coverage mainly has depended on whether it could function effectively by controlling the supply of labour to its founder occupation, or was driven back on collective bargaining and political pressure. In the first case, the union's shape has been heavily influenced by the particular method of regulating entry it adopted, and the hazards for its initial membership group of substitution or competition by other occupations. In the second case, however, the union has been under much greater pressure to expand and thus to diversify its membership. The direction of these occupational diversifications has been largely indicated by the pressures—including various forms of inter-union competition—and opportunities presented by the employment structure within which each union started, by the existence or otherwise of other unions along the indicated routes of expansion, and by the incentives to merger between unions thus confronted with each other.

IV

The distinction between closed and open unionism, therefore, pretty adequately explains not merely the cotton unions' external structure, but the general pattern of British trade union organization. It also, however—and this is something that the customary typologies of trade union external structure certainly fail to do—explains some important differences in the normal behaviour and preoccupations of various unions.

One would naturally expect, for instance, that open unions should be rather more preoccupied with wage questions, while closed unions will be concerned with issues affecting their control of labour supply and employment. But the difference is also exhibited in more detailed aspects of wage policy itself. Thus, on the whole it has tended to be the open unions in major industries which have taken the lead in the general wage-movements of the past generation: the general pattern of wage demands and increases throughout the cotton trades from 1939 on was largely influenced by the determination of the Weavers' Amalgamation to compensate its membership's inter-war experience of low and unstable earnings. The closed unions have been much more concerned with the relative status of their members in the wage-structure, rather than with the level of wages in general. Indeed, the most notable interventions of closed unions in post-war wage movements have taken the form of protests against the relative narrowing of wage-differentials occasioned by general wage increases themselves. In the cotton trades the increasing resistance, particularly of the spinning industry's male aristocracy, to that narrowing (from which they were unable to escape, as did the closed groups in cotton manufacturing, by mill and local bargaining) led the unions to revert to demands for common percentage wage-increases, which disturbed wage-relativities no further. But in other important cases—as in the printing stoppages of 1950 and 1955, and of course the engine drivers' strike of 1955—this resistance in effect involved an inter-union dispute between the open and closed organizations in the industries concerned. And this is certainly true of the events which led to the withdrawal of the 'open' NATSOPA from the Printing and Kindred Trades Federation in early 1958: the immediate cause of that secession was the closed print unions' support of a proposed new system of wage-negotiation which would have involved the separate consideration of wage claims from the craftsmen and from other unions.

The distinction between closed and open unions also means a good deal in terms of detailed inter-union relationships. Thus, the typical inter-union problem of open trade unionism is the 'jurisdiction' dispute—about which union should have what members. Disputes of this kind were settled by those Weavers' agreements with other manufacturing unions described earlier in this chapter; and they consitute the TUC Disputes Committee's main pre-occupation. The typical inter-union conflict of closed trade unionism, however, is the 'demarcation' dispute—about which union's members should have what jobs. Partly for technical reasons, such disputes are rare among the closed cotton unions, if not altogether unknown; but they are endemic in several traditional crafts outside.

Similarly there is a difference in attitude to union membership. The closed union is identified with the 'closed shop'—that is, the insistence on acceptance into the union as a prior condition of employment. The open union is characteristically associated with the form of compulsory union membership best described as the 'union shop'(but sometimes improperly called '100 per cent. trade unionism'), involving a requirement that entry into a job which the union organizes shall be followed by joining the union. And it is probably true that there is a considerable difference between the attitudes of closed and open unions to employers. Since the essential technique of closed trade unionism is a system of 'autonomous regulation', it is with unions of this type that trade rules and customs of a kind which are often described by managements as 'restrictive practices' are largely associated. The open union's dependence on collective bargaining, however, involves at least the employers' acquiescence in that, and preferably their co-operation. To this end, the militancy which was at one time identified with the New Unions is only one tactic, and one which in their case was as much required by the need for a propagandist recruiting appeal as by the contemporary obduracy of employers.

With the growth of a general willingness on the part of managements to recognize trade unionism as such, and particularly in the presence of a prolonged prosperity which made firms reluctant to see output interrupted by industrial disputes, not a few of the big open unions have found it easier to establish themselves in a new concern by approaching the latter's management than by directly canvassing its workers. In such cases they have often been willing to trade what amounted to trade union co-operation in meeting managerial needs, for recruiting facilities, managerial recognition and bargaining concessions. This tactic has certainly been used by certain cotton unions in the post-war period: but it has even become an instrument of inter-union competition. For instance, one or two mills now established outside the traditional cotton area have been organized by the general unions rather than the cotton unions proper; and here, this appears to have arisen less from any tardiness of approach by the latter than from the management's preference for unions which would be more tolerant (or less expert) in their attitude to the details of payment and employment conditions. Thus, the militant unionism of this century's opening decades merges into the 'business unionism' of the present day.

But of course, the frontier between open and closed unionism is not rigid and permanent. So that a closed union may become open—or develop open sections within its membership. Since the general conditions of effective closed unionism are an occupational stability on the part of the workers it organizes, and a system of restricting entry to their jobs, the most obvious cause of such a transformation in a closed union's character is a technical change which undermines the permanence or blurs the identity of its members' occupation. Whether the union will in fact then modify itself depends largely on the pace of the technical revolution with which it is confronted. Thus, in cotton (and until recent years at any rate) the Lancashire mule-spinners have appeared quite content—like the millwarpers before them—to have both their occupation and their organization gradually die. Their unions seemed able to adapt the supply of labour to a steadily diminishing demand by simply restricting new entrants to the trade, and rival processes were not so intensely competitive as to create significant unemployment among existing members or to undermine their wage standards. So far as they were concerned, 'the job would last their time'. In a rather similar way, the old sawyers' unions in the building trade were apparently content to disappear gradually before the new powered sawmills, and made no attempt either to organize the latter's operatives or to demand their jobs for themselves.

The Lancashire Warpdressers' recent extensions of membership to allied manufacturing operatives is only partly attributable to the fact that some of these represent new processes which rival its traditional occupations. The situation, however, is rather different for a union which is confronted by a technical revolution as violent as that which affected the old-established National Union of Vehicle Builders in the 1920s. The immense rise of mass-production in the motor-car trades made it impossible for the union to maintain a monopoly of vehicle construction in general which was adequate to guarantee its existing memberships' employment—or even to maintain, on an exclusive craft basis, sufficient strength in the motor-car trades themselves to bargain. The union therefore opened its ranks to mass-production operatives, in an attempt partly to secure thereby some control over the new jobs' multiplication, partly to reserve some of those jobs for its older membership, and partly to establish a significant bargaining force in relation to the very large firms which rapidly became the industry's type—as well as in relation to the other, and largely open, unions which now threatened to dominate its field of interest. On the railways, again, it now seems at least possible that technical change may thrust the ASLE & F into much more general competition with the NUR than hitherto: having accepted electric and diesel motormen as of equal status to its steam footplatemen, it recently amended its rules to permit the admittance of '. . . *porters or any grade* where such grades are by agreement in the line of promotion to motormen'![1]

Beyond such things, those pressures that have sometimes led to mergers between closed unions may alternatively impel an exclusive union to open its ranks. Its *members* may be indifferent to a prospect of decline which is sufficiently long-term: but if the union has full-time officials it will possess a separate drive to institutional self-preservation. Thus, in the Spinners' Amalgamation, the Yorkshire

[1] Author's italics. This arrangement is, the writer understands, already operative on the London Transport Executive's electric railways.

district's recent abandonment of its exclusiveness (by changing its name to the Yorkshire Cotton Operatives' Association, and commencing to recruit workers from any section of the cotton trade in that area) had as its explicit motive the Yorkshire spinners' inability to support their full-time negotiating staff in face of the attrition of their own numbers. In Lancashire, it has been said that a major reason for the Warpdressers' relaxation of their one-time exclusiveness was similarly to maintain their subscription income. In fact, of the smaller closed unions in cotton manufacturing it may be significant that only the Tapesizers, whose Amalgamation has no full-time officials at all, and only one or two of whose local societies possess them, has been quite exempt from a tendency to dilute its original membership.

Then there is again the pressure arising from collective bargaining's extension. Some of the once-independent closed societies in cotton, like those of the cop-packers and roller-coverers, may well have been partly inspired to affiliate with the larger open Amalgamations by a desire to secure their officials' negotiating assistance. But particularly, a reason why the first primitive cardroom associations chose not to proceed on the direct road towards an exclusive union of cardroom men was the difficulty of establishing their position on such a restricted basis in an industry which had come to be dominated by the then-formidable mule-spinners' associations. Since in response to the Spinners' consolidation the employers had enforced at least area-wide (and sometimes industry-wide) bargaining, the results of which were effectively binding on all other spinning operatives, it was only by converting themselves into a mass organization for the latter that the cardroom unions could tilt the balance of industrial relations in their original membership's favour. While outside cotton, it has again been suggested that the Engineers' establishment, first of special sections for un-apprenticed workers and later (in the Second World War) for women, was at least partly determined by the failure of the old ASE's technique of absorbing smaller craftsmen's associations to give the AEU sufficient strength against the new general unions. In the upshot, the AEU has itself become a predominantly open organization. But the 'craft' AUBTW's recent acceptance into amalgamation of a labourers' union was also a move perhaps not uninfluenced by a desire to increase its strength in relation to its bargaining partners in the building operatives' federation.

Indeed, for a closed union which is under pressure to diversify itself, to open its ranks downwards may sometimes be a more attractive option than a horizontal merger with its like. In such a merger, of course, the partner groups retain their formally-exclusive character. But this is bound to be modified to some extent, because it is much more difficult to maintain mutual exclusions *within* a membership whose original groups are of equal status. Thus the Boilermakers, who already organize several different skills in shipbuilding, and the Woodworkers, who also now include craftsmen of different types, are each now obliged to accept a transferability between these groups which is at least greater than that which they permit between their members' occupations and related skilled trades outside. Moreover, for the minor partner to a potential merger, there is always the further deterrent that its members' special interests may, in the upshot, be subordinated to those of the major participating group.

Thus, had the early cardroom men's associations followed the under-engineers' example in affiliating to the Spinners, they might then have suffered the same neglect as overtook those workers. But in a heterogeneous association of less-skilled spinning workers the cardroom men could hope that their existing strength, reinforced by what they thought their existing membership's superior quality, would give them at least an adequate influence. In just the same way, when negotiations for amalgamation between the closed printing unions broke down, the London Compositors turned quite cheerfully to discuss a merger with the open NATSOPA. Their union appears decided that its special exclusiveness no longer compensates for its smallness relative to other printing unions. In a horizontal 'craft' amalgamation of printers, the preponderance of provincial tradesmen might well make it difficult for London to maintain its obstructions to mobility and its preferential wage-rate. But the Cardroom Amalgamation's experience demonstrates that a vertical alliance of occupational groups is by no means intrinisically incompatible with the maintenance of hierarchical distinctions between them.

V

If closed unions can open up, it is perhaps even more important that open unions may become increasingly closed, as did the original self-actor spinners' associations, or develop what are virtually closed enclaves within their membership, as in the case of the Cardroom Amalgamation's strippers-and-grinders. Moves towards that 'autonomous regulation' of labour conditions usually identified with closed trade unions are, in fact, quite widespread among the members of cotton operatives' associations. Sooner or later the occupational and group solidarity that a stable collective association encourages begins to express itself, not merely in a disciplined bargaining attitude, but in the appearance and elaboration of 'work rules' and 'job controls' which amount to informal attempts to control the supply of labour.

For instance, the rigidity of occupational demarcations in the cotton industry has in recent years been a frequent target of expert or managerial criticism. This rigidity applies not merely to the power of managements to transfer workers to or from jobs which are formally controlled by the closed unions' exclusive entry arrangements (and where it is absolute) but to the general run of machine-minding operations themselves. Despite the basic similarity of most of these jobs—their dependence primarily on a simple manual dexterity combined with an acquired sense of machine-rhythm—it is extremely difficult for a manager to transfer, say a weaver to warping or a cardroom-tenter to ring-spinning and *vice versa*, even though there may be a shortage of work in one department of a mill because of a deficiency of operatives in another. It is even difficult, sometimes, for managers to transfer workers from one machine to another of the same kind.

In the open occupations, these restraints on mobility have not had very much to do with the unions themselves: they are much more comparable with the resistance of workers to transfer between jobs which is a frequent cause of mining disputes, or with the informal practices of output regulation to be found in several other organized trades—especially such piece-working industries as engineering and the docks. They are, nevertheless, the inevitable product of a solidarity which trade unionism itself has helped to create. And beyond them, a union which is unable directly to control entry into its trades may yet develop other, and formal, controls which have an analagous, if less direct, effect on the supply of labour.

That supply (to repeat) has several dimensions, apart from that of numbers. And one of the most important of the cotton unions' activities, historically, has been their persistent campaign to restrict working hours. This was, of course, the principal motive for the mid-nineteenth century general combinations of textile factory operatives and the original *raison d'etre* for the present United Textile Factory Workers' Association. The operatives' legal campaign was conducted as one to protect women and young workers. But while this certainly helped to mobilize outside support for the cotton unions' demands, it would be wrong to regard the tactic—as the Webbs did—as one of 'hiding behind the skirts of the women'. Just as the massive employment of women operatives made it impossible for the early power-loom weavers' unions to restrict the entry of labour, so the women's lesser capacity to resist exploitation made it difficult at first for unions to enforce a reduction of their standard working hours by direct action. On the other hand, the more strongly-organized men could not at that time have long held a working week limited only by union agreement or instruction in face of the desire of employers to work their then-expensive equipment to the uttermost, and of the possibility of replacing men by women in many operations.

But in any case, the legal campaign has been only one wing of the cotton operatives' drive to restrict working hours, which in the 1890s over-rode even their officials' opposition to further reductions. The cotton leaders were criticized at the 1889 TUC for not consulting their members before opposing the Socialist demand for the Eight-Hour Day, and it was a change of front induced in the open Weavers' Amalgamation by district meetings that then led the 'Shorter Hours' movement to spread through Lancashire. While in the present century, normal collective agreement has brought working hours far below those specified as maximal by law.

But in this direction, even more has probably been achieved by straightforward union discipline. The cotton operatives' organizations are quite outstanding among trade unions in their determination that the standard working week shall not be exceeded. In the past, the unions have refused to permit their members to work overtime even when this was volunteered to raise contributions for the support of fellow-members on strike in other mills or districts. And whereas in most other industries, a generation of full employment has recently led to a marked relaxation of union controls over overtime working—so that substantial overtime is the norm rather than the exception in many occupations—overtime was insignificant in the cotton trades even at the peak of their post-war boom. In many cases, the dependence of earnings on the running time of the machines has made the workers themselves anxious to work outside the standard hours—for instance, to get their machines ready for running or to clean them; and union rule books contain many instructions to members as to the 'illegality' of such actions.[1] Even overtime work by men in key occupations is most rigidly restricted, and to exceed standard working hours virtually unknown among the general run of operatives. Over this aspect of labour supply, the restraints of the open cotton unions have thus been more effective than those of such craft amalgamations as the old ASE, whose attempts to control overtime constituted a major historical bone of contention with the engineering employers.

For the biggest cotton unions, then, their special insistence on the limitation of working hours may well have represented a partial

[1] For instance, *Rule* 20 of the Oldham Weavers: '. . . be it hereby understood by the members of this Association that the system of working overtime whether for the purpose of fetching up lost time caused through a breakdown . . . or for any purpose whatever . . . is contrary to the rules and principles of the Association; any member who consents to work overtime forfeits all claim upon the funds of the Association for any case or circumstance that may transpire . . .'

compensation for their inability to control entry itself. But, of course, the cotton operatives' apparently general desire to regulate the supply of labour to the industry had one blind spot—the employment of juveniles. The fact that so many young workers were employed as helpers to piece-working adult operatives, as well as the contribution of juvenile earnings to family income in the cotton towns, made the operatives reluctant to see the minimum age for employment further raised. This applied not merely in the spinning industry, where boys were directly employed by the mule-spinners themselves, but also in weaving, where the ability of weavers to increase their earnings by taking on more looms was partly dependent upon the use of child 'tenters' as assistants. In the early years of the present century the attitude of the British cotton unions to the employment of child labour brought them some odium, not merely in other sections of the British labour movement, but in the International Textile Workers' Federation, of which they were otherwise the mainstay.[1] And the employment of school-children on a 'half-time' basis in the mills of course continued into the inter-War period.

The mule-spinners' desire to employ children was somewhat reduced by the unions' negotiating to transfer responsibility for the payment of their assistants to the employer. But in the manufacturing industry, the operatives' attitude was gradually altered by two other developments. One was a steady technical improvement which reduced the labour requirement of each loom. The other was the growth of attempts in the open union to control the intensity, as opposed to the duration, of the members' efforts. Among the weavers this crystallized in a protracted struggle over the 'more looms' question. Up to late in the nineteenth century the average number of looms supervised by the individual weaver had been rising steadily, and by the 1880s most weavers in the ordinary sections of the trade were managing four. The closed unions had, of course, included the control of machine ratios as a prime objective from their inception. The Rules of the 1882 Tapesizers' Amalgamation, for instance, were even more specific than those of the Spinners and Overlookers already noted:[2] 'No member shall attempt to work more than one machine under any circumstances'. Offending members were to be brought before the Executive and fined on a first offence and, on a second, to be expelled from their association (and thus virtually

[1] It is notable, for instance, that the Burnley Weavers' association, which was one of the centres of the agitation for the Eight-Hour Day, found nothing inconsistent at that time in protesting against the government's 1891 Bill to raise the minimum age for 'half-timers' in mills from ten to eleven as a 'retrograde step'.

[2] See respectively Chapters III, 1, and III, 2—section v in each case.

excluded from employment in 'legal' situations). However, till the 1890s the open weavers' unions seem to have made no attempt to restrict the operatives' acceptance of additional looms, so long as this raised no suspicion of 'driving' by managements or overlookers, or of attempts to cut the standard piece-rates per unit of output.

But by the 1880s the first serious hints of foreign competition had begun to appear. The growth of the British industry slackened, and fear of unemployment seems to have become more marked among cotton operatives. In particular, however, the employers in the coarser sections of the cotton trade began to attempt an intensified use of labour. This undoubtedly played a part in the remarkable growth of unionism among the cardroom operatives. And it is notable that for the latter's strongest-organized group, the strippers-and-grinders, a standard machine-complement per worker was actually specified by the wage-lists the new cardroom unions negotiated. But in the manufacturing industry, the drive to an intensified use of labour was concentrated in the newer mills of North-East Lancashire which were producing coarser cloths for export—and especially, around Burnley, which was also one of the Weavers' weaker districts. Here, certain employers attempted to speed up the natural tendency of weavers' loom-complements to rise by introducing a general system of six-loom working. The result was a struggle that continued for half a century.

The weavers were not able to fully resist the introduction of 'more looms' into the Burnley district itself. But the unions' support of a two weeks' strike there in 1885, to enforce Blackburn List piece-rates, seems at least to have inhibited subsequent attempts to reduce piece-prices per yard of cloth to facilitate 'more looms' working. While in other districts from this time on, the customary ratio of looms per weaver crystallized, for normal cloths and machines, at four.[1] And the rise in average loom-complements appears in fact to have very significantly slackened by the beginning of the present century, and not to have accelerated again until well after the First World War (when 'more looms' became again a central issue of dispute). The consequence, of course, was that technical progress implied a widening difference between the potential and actual work-load of many weavers. So that sporadic attempts in individual firms to raise the loom-complement continued: by 1904 a dispute had already occurred (in Burnley again) over a proposed eight-loom system.

[1] See particularly Wood (op. cit.) p. 152, and Smith (unpublished thesis, loc. cit.) as well as Chapman (*Lancashire Cotton Industry*, p. 46). Between the 1830s and 1880s the average loom-ratio doubled, but between 1886 and 1906 rose only from 3·3 per weaver to 3·44, the continued slight rise in the average being apparently due largely to the raising of smaller loom-complements to the norm.

But it would be a mistake to regard the four-loom convention as simply a 'feather-bedding' device of the weavers, because their unions very soon came also to insist on it as a minimum work-load.[1] In the inter-War period particularly, employers faced with declining trade often reduced machine-complements systematically in an attempt, partly to keep their workers from drifting away, but partly also to extract a higher output from individual machines. The effect was not merely to substantially reduce individual weavers' earnings but also to keep a much larger labour force associated with the industry than even the conventionally-restricted system of loom-working justified. And in the 1930s the Weavers' Amalgamation conducted a campaign against this form of 'under-employment', though it was not until 1952 that it was able to extract a joint declaration against it from the Masters' Federation.

Equally, however, the weavers' attitude on 'more looms' did not embody a resistance to technical progress as such. This is shown by the quite different attitude that they adopted to automatic looms (as opposed to a mere increase in the ratio of normal, or 'Lancashire', looms supervised by the operative). The first automatic looms appeared at the very close of the nineteenth century, while the 'more looms' question was already intermittently active in Burnley. Nevertheless, of automatics '. . . the operatives would do nothing to retard the adoption', although they were '. . . justified in seeing the loom is not a success at the expense of their wages'.[2] The unions accepted from the first a much higher loom-ratio for automatics, and though the local immediately concerned apparently made a half-hearted initial attempt to secure the payment of normal (i.e. Uniform List) piece-rates on their output, from that time on the unions were quite content to negotiate special rates for automatic-loom weaving, which recognized the reduced effort requirement of the new machines and constituted no penalty on a growth in machine-complements as the early equipment was improved. The weavers' four-loom standard for normal, non-automatic equipment thus represented only a convenient basis for a conventional regulation of the supply of labour in terms of effort.

[1] Thus the Darwen Weavers' Rules instruct members to protest '. . . if your employer does not find you full employment', and to consult the union secretary if no improvement resulted.

[2] *CFT*, July 24, 1903. In this century's first decade there were several minor stoppages over the introduction of automatics, but these generally arose from attempts by companies to impose their own wage-lists for them, or weavers' complaints that they were overworked or unable to make agreed earnings. (There is a brief account of the effects of the first introduction of automatic looms in Lancashire in R. Gibson's *Cotton Textile Wages in the United States and Great Britain*, King's Crown Press, Columbia University, 1948, p. 70–5.)

VI

Officially, or unofficially, formally or informally, then, the weavers had by the 1920s gone a long way towards regulating all dimensions of labour supply except that of entry itself. And even here, the Weavers' Nelson district—which includes an unusually large proportion of male operatives—has recently negotiated a 'weaving apprenticeship' with the local Masters' Association. Indeed, it is probably significant that of all the major cotton occupations, it is only those in which the predominance of women makes control of entry impossible that are now without some procedure to that effect. However, at this point it is worth looking again at the development of the strippers-and-grinders entry regulation.[1] The distinctive feature of this, of course, is the requirement that all candidates for the job concerned must have served a year as a boy assistant; this (since candidates might not in fact be accepted for actual training until their late twenties or early thirties) was of purpose designed to restrict the number of potential recruits. But apart from this, there is also the rule that candidates shall only be accepted for actual vacancies and in strict order of their seniority on the district waiting list. And on the other hand there is the establishment of a formal gradation among the cardroom men themselves: whereas a grinder who is unemployed at his regular occupation may perform any other male job about the cardroom (as a blowing-room operative, for instance) no man from another occupation may work, even temporarily, as a grinder. While certain district unions have carried the gradation a stage further, by establishing a fixed proportion of grinders' jobs themselves as posts for 'junior grinders' (or learners).

The grinders' entry system thus includes elements—the learnership period, the graded 'job ladder', the seniority rule—which have in fact become recognizable objectives of not a few open unions outside the cotton trade. For entry to many occupations, the establishment of an agreed 'learner' period has been sought by such unions with some success since the War, and has indeed received some governmental encouragement. On the other hand, the railway and post-office workers' unions—indeed, those of public servants generally—have been very much concerned with the systematic grading of their members: while in manufacturing industry at large, unions of less-skilled workers have sometimes welcomed (or even proposed) the introduction of 'job evaluation' techniques by managements as implying the same results. Granted such a grading, union insistence that vacancies in a higher grade be filled only by promotion from the next lower then implies that, to all grades but the lowest, the supply

[1] See Chapter III, 2, section VII.

of labour is automatically limited. And this restriction becomes absolute if the workers concerned are also able to insist (as the railwaymen generally do) that promotion shall go by seniority—so that for each vacancy that occurs, there is only one candidate. Which brings the arrangement quite close to the traditional entry controls of the mule-spinners and steel-workers.[1]

The seniority rule may even be so applied as to limit entry to the 'job ladder's' lowest grade itself. In private industry, seniority (or 'first in, last out') rules for determining workers' individual liability to dismissal when redundancy occurs have often been opposed by employers' federations as constituting an infringement of 'managerial functions'. Agreements embodying such rules have nevertheless been negotiated, formally or informally, by many individual firms. Their effect is virtually to confine the risk of losing employment to an industry's new entrants, and thus to limit the chance that the trade's reserve of experienced labour will increase as a consequence of fluctuations in demand. And this is much more so when the agreement incorporates—as is quite often the case—an obligation on the employer's part to re-engage, if and when trade recovers and again in order of seniority, the workers so dismissed. The seniority system then amounts to something very much like the prescriptive claim to a job which is implied in the labour control arrangements of many closed unions. Indeed, in some instances, this claim is to all intents and purposes formally recognized. Thus the dyers' and bleachers' agreement with the textile-finishing firms incorporates a list of workers who have been accepted for employment into the trade. These then have an obligation to join the union; but if out of work they also have the right to first offer of any jobs that become available, before workers not yet on the list are accepted.

Several other aims which open unions have particularly pressed tend also to have the incidental effect of limiting the labour supply to the occupations they organize. The obligation generally imposed on employers since the War to pay a guaranteed weekly wage, for instance, by reducing the likelihood that workers will be dismissed

[1] The Spinners' leaders' were in any case (see Chapter IV, 2, section II) unable to persuade their members to adopt the 'principle of graduated progression' in its entirety, implying movement from establishment to establishment *within* the 'skilled' grade. A reason supplementary to those given previously may well have been that this would obstruct the promotion of mule-spinners' sons and nephews who had established claims on particular mills' vacancies by working as assistants to their relatives there. But even the 'patrimonial principle' involved in the latter practice has been adopted by some open unions: the old Great Western Railways had an agreement with the NUR and other unions giving an option on vacancies in its workshops to the sons of employees. And that principle of course applies quite widely, but by convention, to acceptance into port employment.

after very short periods (as was once not uncommon in building) also reduce the pool of experienced labour available to the industry. The more recent development of 'redundancy compensation' has a similar effect, by penalizing the casual dismissal (and hence also, engagement) of workers: it also generally reinforces the seniority rule, since redundancy payments are usually related to the worker's period of employment. And with both these developments, the effect is still more marked when the guarantee or compensation agreement is concluded on an 'industry-wide' basis that involves some central fund, instead of with individual employers.

Thus, the effect of the recent agreement for 'compensation on redundancy' in mining—as to some extent of the similar agreement made by the cotton unions in 1959 under their industry's 'concentration' scheme—is to encourage arrangements for the transfer of operatives from contracting establishments to others, and thus establish a clear difference in the entitlement to jobs in the industry between those already in it and outsiders, as well as to limit the engagement of new labour generally. While the post-war dockers' 'decasualization' scheme, which involved the financing of wage-guarantees from a pooled levy on port employers, had as a necessary corollary the establishment of a jointly-controlled register of dock workers, admittance to which is regulated according to the ports' long-term labour requirements. The post-war scheme for regularizing the employment of merchant seamen has involved similar arrangements. These schemes were, of course, realized by a mixture of collective bargaining and political pressure, so that the unions must still share control at least with the employers. But otherwise, their effect is quite analogous to the entry controls of such closed cotton unions as the Overlookers and Tapesizers.

VII

There are thus several routes by which an originally open union may achieve a control of labour supply to the jobs it organizes—or at least, to some of them. It is not suggested, of course, that in all the instances quoted above this control has been directly, or even consciously, the union's immediate aim. Such things have been sought for more immediate motives—to prevent the exploitation of workers whose ability to resist employers' demands upon them was weak, to achieve some security of employment and earnings for a membership whose condition of life was formerly subject to great uncertainty, to attain 'fair play' in the treatment of individual employees or to reduce their exposure to arbitrary managerial decisions, even—in the case of less formal work-controls like some over job demarcations, machine-complements or output—to establish some equity and cohesion between the members of particular workplace groups. But their implication is identical with that of the more traditional systems of labour restriction—that is, to regulate the supply of labour in terms of numbers, of substitutability, or of the duration and intensity of effort.

All these things are bound up with the appearance, within masses of workers previously little differentiated, of distinct occupational identities, separated by conventions, distinctive (or even preferential) agreements, and a felt or recognized status. Indeed, this tendency within the memberships of open unions generally might well have gone further did it not to some extent conflict with the institutional forms such unions established at an early stage of their development. If this study's earlier suggestion that any organized group of workers would prefer, if it could, to control its conditions by 'autonomous regulation' rather than collective bargaining is sound, then there are many groups (like the dockers) which now possess sufficient solidarity to operate by such methods. But their unions have already acquired professional leaderships committed to and trained in collective bargaining as a pivotal operative technique. And to that, the growth of 'autonomous regulation' (apart from in any case reducing the membership's dependence on officials) might well be prejudicial, since it involves restraints and impositions on employers that would hardly encourage them to be co-operative in bargaining—or might even reduce their capacity to make the cash concessions which have been that bargaining's central and continuing object.

Thus the cotton unions' leaders in the 1890s continued to oppose a new restriction of standard working hours for some time after the movement for it had spread among their membership, on the ground that it would harm the industry's competitive capacity: in spinning particularly, they were at this time involved in disputes preliminary to a major settlement of their bargaining relations with the employers which they did not wish to prejudice further by raising a new issue. While the Weavers' officials rarely objected to 'more looms' systems as such, but concerned themselves solely with their effect on negotiated wage-rates:[1] indeed, when finally an agreement after World War II presented the possibility of bringing the weavers' loom-complement under explicit joint control, many officials became

[1] That the attitude of their rank-and-file was rather different is perhaps suggested by the unofficial *Cotton Factory Times*'s comment on the 1904 incident in Burnley '. . . the eight-loom system may seem all right to the weavers affected, who are in receipt of the preferred wage of 30s a week. But what about the rest of the operatives, of whom in course of time at least 33 per cent. will be thrown out of work?' (*CFT*, January 22, 1904.)

enthusiastic exponents of 'more looms'. Similarly, officials of the Transport Workers' docks group have apparently been on occasion more sympathetic than their rank-and-file to employers' views as to the desirability of admitting more labour to port registers. And leaders of other unions have sometimes accepted employers' reasoning that for promotion or job-security to go by seniority would be bad for efficiency, and resisted their members' preference for the seniority principle.

It is partly for such reasons that many forms of 'autonomous regulation' by workers operate only informally or by custom, independently (in any direct sense) of the unions concerned—or even condemned by their officials as 'restrictive'. Nevertheless, it is fairly clear that the expansionism of open unions—even of those initially organized as recruiting agencies—has tended generally to decline. It is a commonplace to attribute the exhaustion of the British unions' recruiting urge in recent times, and the accompanying stagnation of total union membership in face of just that continuing high employment which in the past encouraged its increase, to the change in their typical official's character, from propagandist organizer to professional negotiator. But it now appears that a change in their memberships' character and status may also have something to do with it. A successful open unionism tends to induce, in the workers it benefits at least, the behaviour characteristics—including an indifference to the organization of other sections—of its opposite.

However, we are here less concerned with the effect of these things on total union membership than on the shape of individual unions. By the time an open union reaches the stage when its membership has developed sectional labour controls of the type described here, it is also likely to have acquired a much greater occupational diversity than had, say, the Oldham Spinners when they began to shed the members they had recruited from minor occupational groups. So that the trend is most likely to involve, not so much the total conversion of open unions to an exclusive form, as the materialization of closed sections within the open unions themselves. One of two things may then happen. The new closed group, though not a majority of the union within which it appears, may be able effectively to dominate the latter's policy. This was the result, outstandingly, of the strippers-and-grinders' success in establishing themselves as a higher-status group within the Cardroom Amalgamation: it was very much the situation of the miners' and steel workers' federations, within which the face-workers and skilled process workers became respectively the most influential element. And this situation is perhaps particularly likely to occur when organization among other grades of worker than the new aristocrats has become so extensive that the latter might fear it would otherwise survive and develop independently of their support, and in despite of their interests. A 'mixed' union of this type is therefore most likely to develop from an open organization which has expanded vertically.

But it is perhaps the alternative course which is most interesting and relevant to recent union experience. Where the new closed section is not merely a minority, but unable to exercise an influence in the union's general direction which is proportionate to its own view of its sectional status and potential strength, then it will tend to break away from the open organization and form an independent union. This was clearly the case with the closed associations of cotton manufacturing operatives—overlookers, twisters, warpdressers and tape-sizers—which emerged from the originally loose collectivity of factory weaving workers. In the cotton unions, however, and for reasons to be considered in another connection,[1] such movements have caused much less friction than those of a similar kind which have embarrassed most of the mass unions which have been formed in more recent times. Thus, on the railways, there is the 'breakaway' National Association of Signalmen, which aims to provide for these now high-status workers an organization analogous to that already achieved by the footplatemen and railway clerks, and separate from the NUR which is formally responsible for the signalmen's organization and representation. In the Mineworkers' Union there have—since its ostensible conversion from a federation into a seemingly-monolithic amalgamation—been breakaway movements of colliery enginemen, of deputies, and of colliery clerks. From the AEU, there are recent breakaways of aircraft mechanics and of tool-room workers. The major post office unions (partly because of a one-time official procedure for recognition by the Postmaster General which gave an unusual facility to minority associations) have been particularly plagued by such secessions. And short of an actual breakaway, many 'unofficial' movements within established unions, such as those of busmen and dockers within the T & GWU, have had their source in sectional dissatisfaction of this type.

Indeed, of all such movements that of dockers is by far the most interesting and illuminating. The dockers were not merely among the most prominently stirred by the New Unionism of the 1890s: they were also one of the original cores of the modern T & GWU itself. In the first great London dock strike, the dockers were helped by the London Stevedores, who had a traditional—and exclusive—organization unique to that port (and possibly derived from the old London guilds of porters and watermen). But as the dockers' own

[1] See Chapter VI, 1, section II.

organization expanded, the stevedores held aloof from its institutional embodiment: though briefly tempted by the transport workers' amalgamation of the 1920s, they withdrew before their absorption in it was completed. Meanwhile the dockers' own status was immensely improved by their ability to mobilize the strength of the new general union in their support. However, the problem of the dockers' minority position within that union was already emerging before the Second World War, when the Scottish dockers formed an independent organization. And in the Second World War itself, the dockers at the same time secured the labour scheme by which they established a near-exclusive position, *and* found themselves overwhelmed numerically by the T & GWU's mass recruitment in other industries. Meanwhile, their status had risen to a point at which it was virtually indistinguishable from that of the London stevedores (in fact the allocation of work between members of the two unions had long ceased to be made on a functional basis, but had become quite arbitrary). While within the ports the dockers were deriving more benefit from their own pressure on local piece-rates and the like than from the T & GWU's central negotiations on their behalf, which seemed inhibited by the union's broader interests. The 1956 breakaway of the Northern dockers, their merger in the London stevedores' union, and the latter's extension to other ports, was a logical consequence of this situation.

The likelihood of such an end-product of open unionism is perhaps evidenced by an American analogy. One of the greatest of the unions that emerged from the United States' wave of mass labour organiztion in the 1930s was the United Automobile Workers. And in this union's consolidation, a key role was assumed by certain workers of recognized skills who formed a small minority among its general membership of machine-hands and assembly operatives: in 1939, indeed, a selective 'strategy' strike of tool-room workers was employed by the UAW to enforce concessions throughout the automobile industry. The skilled workers benefited from the union's earlier successes, in terms not merely of wage increases but of such 'fringe benefits' as pensions. However, they felt themselves increasingly neglected by the union's post-war policy: flat-rate wage increases benefited the lower-paid workers disproportionately, and new fringe benefits took a form which also offered the latter more practical advantage. After the union negotiated its 1955 contracts, which included the 'guaranteed annual wage', there were unofficial strikes amongst the skilled workers which were sometimes led by the union's own specialized 'Skilled Committees'. And afterwards an oppositionist Society of Skilled Trades was formed among these members of the UAW. 'Craft' unions outside the industry also made a rival claim to membership of the skilled grades; while the whole movement reached a climax in 1957–8, when a petition for independent representation of skilled workers in the automobile industry was presented to the National Labour Relations Board with 12,000 signatures.

At any rate, it is sufficiently clear that for British trade unionism, at least, just as for the cotton unions themselves, the division between closed and open organizations should not be envisaged as absolute. Like most categories in the real world, the borderline is blurred by mixed types, and by transfer across it. It would be more accurate to regard the morphology of trade unionism as the product of opposite but also related trends—towards exclusiveness on the one hand and expansion on the other. In many ways the situation has an analogy in the alternative military tactics of the 'wide front' and the 'strong point'. The protection of a 'strong point' may itself sometimes require an extension over a wider front. But on the other hand a 'wide front' which is successfully consolidated tends inevitably to develop potentially-independent strong points within it.

But this raises a general comment on trade unionism's external structure. In that structure, the preceding analysis implies there to be nothing necessarily final. The shape of individual unions is subject to natural pressures to change, as on the one hand new sectionalisms form and crystallize in existing organizations, while existing sectionalisms yield to technical, economic and institutional change on the other. Logically, trade unionism's natural course of structural evolution would appear to lie, first, through the emergence and splitting-off of new occupational or sectional identities from the membership of the great mass unions, and next through regrouping—by way of merger or federation—of the new sectionalisms into alliances for bargaining or other purposes of mutual interest. And such a continuing process would in fact substantially correspond to the reforms envisaged by the earlier of the two major TUC enquiries into union structure. Its 1924 Report recommended that sectional associations be permitted to form within the then-existing unions, and that these associations be then allowed to federate as they thought necessary with others of similar interests. A reform of this kind, moreover, might well have the consequence that it would also counteract the current stagnation of total union membership—since by depriving major unions of their captive sections, it might drive those unions' leaders to recuperate their strength by returning to new recruitment as a major pre-occupation.

But it is partly for just the last reason that such a development in present union structures is also inhibited. On the whole, the separation of new identities from them conflicts with their leaders' views on the requirements of institutional stability. The TUC's second enquiry made no such disturbing recommendations, in its Report of 1946, as did its predecessor of the 1920s. And to form a new union in one of the existing major organization's established 'spheres of influence'—however ineffectively the latter body may have organized the sector concerned—now encounters immense practical difficulties.[1] The major sin in the British trade union calendar is to 'break away'. And while the unions' rank and file may still be stirred by a label that derives its condemnatory associations from the early difficulties of many modern mass unions in establishing themselves against internal personal and political rivalries, and external attempts by employers to encourage secession and division, the main force of the present resistance comes from trade union officialdom itself. The major 'breakaway movements' in recent years have developed despite the opposition to them of both employers *and* the Communist Party's industrial leadership. They have owed such force as they possessed mainly to a strength of feeling among workers who remained trade unionist in principle.

[1] See the instances described by Shirley Lerner, in *Breakaway Unions and the Small Trade Union* (Allen & Unwin, London, 1961).

V

UNION STRUCTURE AND UNION GOVERNMENT

2

Trade Union Democracy

I

The last chapter considered the present-day cotton unions' organization largely for its resemblance to that of others. There remains its difference—the cotton unions' internal structure. We noted earlier that among modern British trade unions a federal system of internal organization is now comparatively rare. But outside Britain (and outside also those countries of the old British Empire where labour organization was heavily influenced by the immigration of British craftsmen who brought their mode of association with them, and by the growth of parallels to the British 'New Unionism') federal forms of union organization not only have had, but still have, a very considerable importance.

In Europe, this arose partly from the fact that trade unionism in several countries was much more the product of *general*, and primarily political, labour movements than it was in Britain, and from the special influence of syndicalism on its growth in those countries. In so far as syndicalist ideas influenced British labour organization, they were largely used to support the advocacy of centralized industrial unions as the best vehicle of 'workers control' of industry. But on the Continent, syndicalism was more identified with the idea of the self-governing workshop, which determined the structure of unions inspired by it—like the pre-Hitlerite German 'Free Labour Union', and the pre-Franco Anarcho-Syndicalist Federation of Labour in Spain.[1] The biggest contemporary instance of this source of federalism is, of course, the French CGT, where the local or sectional unit has a considerable independence of the weak

[1] For some account of these movements, see *Comparative Labour Movements* (Walter Galenson, Ed., Prentice-Hall, New York, 1952).

industrial union centres, to which regional *inter*-union federations have a nearly equal importance—so that the situation is almost as if the British local Trades Councils (with their Regional Trades Council Federations) had retained the position of rivalry to the separate national unions that they briefly held in the 1890s. However, in the United States federalism has been a major strand in union evolution independently of such a political inspiration. Several major American unions still appear essentially federal in structure: and Professor Ulman has shown how much of the earlier history of American unionism was determined by the independence of its local bodies.[1]

The federal method has not been much considered by recent students of union government in Britain.[2] So as the main British example of an important trade union constitutional form—and one alternative to the types now prevalent in this country—it is perhaps worth examining the cotton unions' internal organization rather more closely than hitherto. There would be little point, however, in restricting such an enquiry to their formal structure alone. In every institution, the structure's actual working, in terms of the relationships between its constituents and members, is as important as the formal rules that guide it.

At their peak strength, after World War I, the two hundred or so local associations which then formed the base of the cotton unions' structure must have averaged about 2,000 members apiece. Now, their numbers and memberships are both considerably reduced: at the time of the writer's enquiries, there were about 150 local unions with an average strength of rather over 1,000 each and, in both respects, substantial further reductions will certainly have followed the industry's 1960 'concentration'. The next stage in the structure is the town or district inter-sectional alliance—the Local Textile Trades Federations, which operate in most localities, but which have been mainly supported by the unions on the manufacturing side of the cotton trades. The industry-wide sectional 'Amalgamations' of the separate locals compose what may be thought of as comparable to other national unions. Then there are the federal links between the Amalgamations themselves. The 'Cotton Operatives' Association' has long ceased to unite the Cardroom and Spinners Amalgamations, though their representatives generally consult together before entering any negotiation that affects the spinning trade as a whole; the Northern Counties Textile Trades Federation combines all the

[1] *The Rise of the National Trade Union* (op. cit.).

[2] Thus the PEP study (*British Trade Unionism*, op. cit., 1955 ed. p. 9 et seq.) classifies union constitutions as mostly falling into two types essentially corresponding to what were earlier in this study described as the 'New Model' and 'New Union' forms, quite ignoring the federal one.

unions in the manufacturing industry for bargaining purposes; and the United Textile Factory Workers' Association affiliates *all* the cotton Amalgamations except those of the Tapesizers.

There are, of course, various external affiliations. Many of the local associations belong to Trades Councils together with non-textile unions' branches. Lancashire is actually the main area in which the old-style 'Trades *and Labour* Council' survives—contrary to the TUC's desire to separate political from industrial affiliations in local union affairs. Most of these Councils are in textile or mining towns, where the dominant unions apparently thought their own joint organization—usually the local Textile Trades Federation—sufficiently representative of industrial labour, and saw the general Trades Council primarily as a political body. The cotton unions' affiliation to the TUC is via the Amalgamations (except in the Tapesizers and Warpdressers, which do not belong[1]). The Amalgamations also affiliate to the General Federation of Trades Unions—of which, originally designed as a general national strike fund to compensate for the TUC's weakness as an *industrial* agency, the textile unions are now the main surviving support.[2] Those unions which affiliate to the Labour Party nationally do so through the UTFWA, which supports union M.P's or political candidates, and is also the unions' vehicle of international association.

In this structure of overlapping cross-connections, the key points are the local association itself, and its sectional Amalgamation. Only the local and the Amalgamation have substantial funds of their own—and in particular, their own full-time officials. The inter-sectional federations, local and industry-wide, are serviced by one of their sectional affiliates' officials as a side-line to his main work. It is particularly important, too, that inter-sectional association does not extend to the lowest level of all—the mill. Though at least two and sometimes all Amalgamations will have members in any factory, there is no joint committee of workplace representatives in the cotton unions' structure, like that of shop stewards in engineering establishments or card-stewards on building sites.

The key to the larger Amalgamation's position remains its early

[1] Until quite recently one local union in each of these two small Amalgamations affiliated separately to the TUC, but this has now lapsed, largely on financial grounds.

[2] Other affiliates withdrew as the cost of their subscriptions to the GFTU mounted in proportion to their membership, and the growth of their own funds (and the inter-war decline in demands on them) made them less desirous of outside guarantees. In consequence, the GFTU is now almost an institutional poker-game in which each participant hopes the cost of the annual stake will drive the others to withdraw and leave him controlling the quite substantial kitty that has accumulated.

basic function as a permanent central strike fund for its affiliates. That the present Weavers' Amalgamation was founded on this base is still demonstrated in its provision that the Weavers' delegate assembly must be informed whenever the Amalgamation fund falls below £100,000 and must then take action to safeguard the position.[1] And from this source, other functions and powers of the Amalgamations derive. Thus, most of them have a rule providing that the Amalgamation's Secretary or some other agent[2] may examine its affiliates' records to ascertain whether or not members 'good upon the books' have been properly returned for payments of the monthly Amalgamation levies.[3] On the other hand, a large part of the Amalgamation rule-book will usually be concerned with controlling its power of expenditure, or ensuring that any Amalgamation action has genuine local and mill support. Thus, the Weavers' Central Committee (its E.C.) may only authorize strikes of less than 5,000 members: payment for any larger strike must be approved by a full delegate assembly—which in turn, however, can only do so if 65 per cent. of the workers concerned are members of the union. The Cardroom's E.C. can make no grant to a district without notifying *all* districts in advance, and securing the approval of two-thirds of them at a delegate meeting: a *general* strike of the Amalgamation's members must be submitted to a ballot in which 80 per cent. of them shall support the proposal. The Spinners' Amalgamation applies the same percentage condition to its support of 'individual' strikes (i.e. stoppages of individual mills) as well, and may insist on a second ballot once such a local strike is under way to see 'whether the views of the members have changed'.[4] The Warehousemen require that two-thirds of the members affected must be in favour of strike action.

The Amalgamations' ability to enforce the varying authority their affiliates conceded them for collective bargaining rests largely on their fund. Almost invariably, the rule is that no support from Amalgamation funds be given to a local strike unless it has received the Amalgamation's advance approval. Several rule-books (the Spinners', the Overlookers', the Warehousemen's) provide that Amalgamation assistance shall be conditional on preliminary mill and local negotiation with the employers having been first attempted. Usually it is required that the Amalgamation be given time to conduct its own enquiry into the dispute. And once a dispute has been reported

[1] Amalgamated Weavers' Association, *Rule* 16.

[2] The Spinners' rule is that its EC may depute 'one or more persons unconnected with the district concerned'. It also provides for districts to pay all arrears and meet the costs of enquiry if found in arrears.

[3] Cardroom Amalgamation *Rule* 15.

[4] Spinners' Amalgamation, *Rule* 24, Section 9.

for the Amalgamation's help, the latter is sometimes entitled to assume full power for its conduct. The Spinners' General Secretary is instructed to 'endeavour in a conciliatory manner to effect a settlement' before proceeding further.[1] The Weavers' General Secretary may refuse the technical advice and negotiating assistance which he is usually required to give any local association that demands it, if the dispute has not been authorized by the Amalgamation E.C. or delegate assembly. The Warehousemen and Overlookers, however, impose positive restrictions on their affiliates' power to initiate disputes: no Warehousemen's local 'shall submit proposals for standard rate of wages to either the Local or County Employers' Associations without first submitting same to the Amalgamation Executive.'[2] The Overlookers prohibit any strike within their affiliated districts 'under any pretence whatever' without Amalgamation authority, except for sympathy strikes in support of other textile operatives (which receive automatic Amalgamation assistance).[3]

The Amalgamation's actual bargaining responsibilities are naturally greater where its members' wage-rates are mainly regulated by an industry-wide wage-list. In other cases, the Amalgamation is less concerned with broad wage-policy and more confined to assisting locals in district or mill bargaining, since general wage-movements have, in recent years, commonly been negotiated through one of the inter-Amalgamation federations—the UTFWA and the Northern Counties.

Apart from these bargaining duties, the Amalgamation's main purpose is to act as a vehicle for the formation and pursuit of union policy on trade and general matters, a function which arises partly from its being the channel of local association with the UTFWA, the TUC, and outside bodies of various kinds. There is, of course, an important supplement in the case of those Amalgamations, like the Spinners, which also have central benefit funds; this may somewhat strengthen the Amalgamation's power of scrutiny over district returns and finances. These are mostly unions which control the entry of labour, however; and these also provide the major variant on the usual scheme of Amalgamation powers. In 'closed' unions whose system of entry control assumes the mobility of qualified labour like the Warpdressers, the Amalgamation is much concerned with questions which may arise from the movement of members between districts. Even the Warehousemen, for instance, show their origins as a would-be 'closed' association in their Amalgamation's rules

[1] Spinners' Amalgamation, *Rule* 16, Section 9.
[2] Amalgamated Textile Warehousemen's Association, *Rule* 13.
[3] General Union of Overlookers' Associations, *Rules* 30 and 32.

that no district shall recognize anyone under the age of twenty-one as a clothlooker unless he is paid the full standard rate for the work, or permit its members to accept 'learners' without the local committee's approval, and especially that no member shall seek work in another district without consulting its secretary.

The Overlookers' rules for labour control are particularly extensive. Any member who accepts a 'learner' without the local association's permission or at less than the proper 'poundage' on the learner's earnings is to be expelled; but the local itself must not authorize more than 5 per cent. of learners to its total membership, under penalty of a fine to the General Union (the Amalgamation) for each man accepted in excess. Members offered any job must inform their district secretary. And any vacancies which cannot be filled by a qualified member of the district concerned must be notified to other local associations before a new learner is admitted. No member may apply for work in another district without informing the secretary concerned and verifying that the vacancy is 'legitimate'. But the district must then give *all* 'recognized' overlookers equal opportunity of applying for vacancies (subject to men engaged from outside transferring to the local association), and if the original applicant secured the job in breach of this rule, he must withdraw and may not re-apply. The General Union itself keeps a 'Register Book' of recognized overlooker members, which is published annually; its Executive has a general power to expel any member (subject to his right of appeal to the general delegate meeting), and no local association may accept or recognize an overlooker so expelled. While if a mill has been declared a 'blackshop' in consequence of a dispute, only the General Union can lift the ban on members working there.

But the most interesting development is perhaps that of the Lancashire Amalgamated Tapesizers.[1] The rules of this 'Amalgamation' are even more stringent as regards the training of tapesizers by districts, and particularly their movement between districts, than are those of the Overlookers' General Union. And they are reinforced by fines on individual members for breaches of them (expulsion is reserved for men taking 'improper' learners, or working more than one machine). Moreover, its rule book uniquely includes a detailed demarcation of its local affiliates' boundaries. Up to quite recently it also provided for a central strike fund, to be kept above a minimum figure by regular levy, with the usual sort of rules about its use.[2] But as a result of an inter-district dispute (the details of

[1] It will be recalled that this is the bigger of the two general tapesizers' associations.

[2] Lancashire Amalgamated Tapesizers' Association, *Rules* of 1920.

which, clearly intricate enough in origin, have become so confused by time that it seems impossible to disentagle them) the rules were revised to strengthen further the inter-district code. In the revision the long-disused central strike fund, together with the Amalgamation's formal power to levy money, call a general strike or conduct negotiations, was quite forgotten. *Any* strike called by a district, however, becomes automatically 'official' in the sense that on notification of it to the Amalgamation, all vacancies affected by the dispute become 'illegal' to men from outside the district concerned. So that this Amalgamation's functions in bargaining and disputes (it never developed any political function) have largely withered away. Essentially, it remains as an auxiliary to the tapesizers' highly effective system of entry control, concerned mainly with adjusting inter-district relations.

Rather the same combination of superficial similarity with actual variety appears in the internal constitutions of the different Amalgamations as in their functions and powers. In all the Amalgamations, the governing body is a periodic 'General Council' or 'Representative Meeting'.[1] This assembly of up to about 100 delegates from the affiliated local societies, each of which is represented in some proportion to its size, meets at least quarterly. Then there is a continuing executive council or committee,[2] usually of some ten or a dozen members who must then cease to act as district representatives.

The relation of the Executive to the delegate meeting, however, differs quite widely. The Weavers' E.C. is elected half every half-year by the delegate meeting, which also appoints the principal officers, parliamentary candidates, and delegates to other bodies.[3] But the Cardroom's E.C. is appointed directly by those of its districts with more than 600 members apiece—each such district, however, being represented in diminishing proportion to its strength. And the E.C. is assumed to continue in office except as districts may change their nominees. It has power to interpret the union's rules, and though the Amalgamation's General Secretary is appointed by the delegate meeting, the E.C. examines candidates and makes a recommendation. The Spinners' E.C. is elected, part every six months, by the delegate meeting, but from nominations by districts made on a sliding scale related to their size; 9 of its 15 members must be working

[1] The first term is mainly used in manufacturing Amalgamations, the second by the Spinners and Cardroom: however, the Overlookers call it 'The General Meeting', and the Tapesizers simply 'The Executive'.

[2] This, too, may be called something else—an 'Emergency Committee' in the Tapesizers, for instance.

[3] The Weavers are at present changing their rules to elect the whole E.C. annually. Their delegate meeting also meets monthly.

spinners. However, the Spinners' delegate meeting also appoints a 'Sub-Council' of E.C. members to deal with urgent matters and disputes. These in fact include the full-time officials of the major Provinces, and compose a kind of 'Inner Cabinet'. The Cardroom (which imitated the Spinners' constitution in many ways) similarly provides for two members of its E.C. to be appointed to deal with local disputes, though in its case there is no limit to the inclusion of full-time officials in the E.C. The Overlookers' E.C. is composed by grouping its affiliates into roughly equal 'divisions', each of which nominates one member: but, unlike other Amalgamations, its rules provide that he must be, and continue as, a delegate to the general meeting, which appoints all Amalgamation officers. The Cardroom and Spinners' arrangements seem substantially designed to accommodate the influence which their two major districts of Bolton and Oldham, with their officials, must inevitably possess to an appearance (rather more elaborate in the Spinners' case) of equality between districts.

It is also interesting that in the Overlookers, individual members may complain directly to the Amalgamation E.C. and delegate meeting, with rights of a hearing. The Spinners may only hear such complaints with the local society's sanction. And the Cardroom can only consider complaints from districts themselves. In all Amalgamations, however, the delegate meeting retains control over one essential power: to levy money on the local societies. And the E.C's power to disburse money is often narrowly circumscribed: except as strike pay in disputes properly authorized, for instance, the Weavers' E.C. can make no grant above £100, and the Spinners' and Cardroom rules seem to restrict their Executives' discretion even more narrowly.

II

The Amalgamation's position thus varies considerably, partly with the economic technique of the local unions it affiliates, partly with its specific history. Constitutionally, at least, central authority thus seems highest in the Warehousemen, the last to organize, whose E.C. may visit any local meeting, and '. . . go into any district to organize and to improve existing organizations'.[1] It is certainly least among the Tapesizers. But such variation is certainly much greater among the local societies themselves. One or two of the union 'Provinces' in the spinning trade still have a membership of close to 10,000, and in the past quite a few local unions were around this strength: at the other extreme, some of the autonomous locals have only ten or twenty members. Some of them, again, are virtually small Amalgamations in

[1] Warehousemen's Amalgamation, *Rule* 8.

themselves. Thus, the Oldham Spinners' Province has almost exactly the same rule as the Weavers' Amalgamation about the maintenance of its own fund, and is really quite a centralized union, controlled by an E.C. of branch nominees. Its sub-district (or branch) secretaries are only allowed to retain limited finances in their own hands; the sub-districts' own committees are accountable to the Provincial E.C., although elected by their own members; the latter are only entitled to instruct their representative on the Provincial E.C. itself. The branches all meet on the same night in the month, and though they nominate their own delegates to the Spinners' Amalgamation Representative Meetings, all the delegates from Oldham Province may be required to vote as a block—and must always support the Provincial E.C.'s nomination to the Amalgamation Executive. This centralism no doubt dates from Oldham's ancient attempt—via the 'United Movable Committee'[1]—to make itself the leader of a general spinners' association. By contrast, the Spinners' Bolton Province is much more loosely integrated.

Cardroom Provinces have followed the Oldham, rather than the Bolton model. In the manufacturing industry, however, such 'multi-cell' societies organize only a minority of operatives;[2] the simple town or district association is the usual form. Almost invariably, such a local society's control is shared between the general meeting of members and an elected committee. The frequency of the General Meeting varies immensely—from fortnightly to half-yearly—between societies. The Committee, again, follows no standard pattern in size, composition, or powers. Particularly interesting is the Committee's representational basis. Sometimes it is composed simply of the members the General Meeting prefers: but there is often provision for sectional representation. Thus the Oldham Weavers' Association —which still covers quite a wide area—rules that half the Committee be elected at each half-yearly meeting but that it shall include representatives from several different localities, as well as separate representatives of weavers and other operatives, and that no two Committee members shall come from the same mill. The Darwen

[1] See Chapter III, 1. The Webbs' laudatory reference (*Industrial Democracy*, p. 41) to the 'Cotton Spinners' Parliament' and its provision for 'party meetings' clearly refers to the Oldham 'caucus' and retaliatory attempts by other Provinces to co-ordinate their delegates. But this was to advance or defend local interests, not particular policies or principles. The smaller independent local societies even seemed occasionally to have formed a general front against domination by the big Provinces (see, for instance, Spinners' Amalgamation, *Rules* 20 and 37).

[2] The Overlookers' Amalgamation still has the 'National' and 'United' Associations (see Chapter III, 2) as affiliates; these relics of past rivalries were found convenient by the associated branches to pool the cost of a full-time official, and a similar internal federation was adopted in one or two other districts.

Weavers elect their Committee by general ballot,[1] each member to serve three years; but *they* exclude any member who is not a 'weaver, winder or warper' from election—though other operatives may be admitted to the society.[2] The Oldham and District Cop-Packers' Association (a Cardroom affiliate) has a Committee of representatives from sub-localities, each in turn really composed by a group of 'mill correspondents'. By contrast, the North Lancashire Cardroom Association implicitly opposes mill representation by forbidding committee members to vote in a dispute concerning their own mill: the Rochdale Cardroom Association's rules actually exclude them from the meeting in such a case.

The local Committee commonly has power either to appoint the paid officials, or to submit a panel of candidates to the General Meeting or a ballot of members. It is usually the Committee's responsibility to authorize action in disputes, but cash questions—as in the Amalgamations—are nearly always reserved to the wider assembly of members. Subscriptions and benefits are usually incorporated (as is sometimes the pay of officers) in the Rules, which only the General Meeting can amend. The finance of the local societies is subject to great variation: broadly, of course, 'open' unions have low contributions and benefits, and 'closed' unions high ones, but even within a group there may be quite a range.[3] There is a similar range of reserve funds. Some small closed unions are, in trade union terms, very wealthy: the funds of Tapesizers' locals average up to £60 per member.[4] On the other hand, some Weavers' Associations, in which subs. and benefits are not always as cautiously related as they might be, have had their reserves run very low by recent payments for unemployment—small as these generally are in 'open' associations.

[1] The Weavers' Amalgamation actually has a Rule (28) that all its affiliates' Committees must be elected by ballot of their district members; but some interpret this as a ballot only of those attending the general meeting.

[2] Darwen Weavers', Winders' and Warpers' Association, cf. *Rules* 2 and 6c. Under earlier Rules, members ineligible for election were also exempt from special levies, but this compensation for inferior rights was dropped in the 1934 Rules above. (At time of writing, this local is in process of merger with the Blackburn Weavers).

[3] Generally, subs. in Weavers', Warehouse, and Cardroom unions are now around 1s a week; in the closed unions they are between 2s and 4s a week (plus entry fees sometimes). Strike pay (by rule) is usually about £1 a week in open unions, and up to £4 a week in closed ones. Other kinds of benefit, where paid (unemployment, stoppage, sick, superannuation etc.), are rarely more than half the rate of strike pay; accident (and, of course, funeral) pay is commonly a lump sum.

[4] By contrast, reserves of all trade unions registered with the Registrar of Friendly Societies averaged rather over £9 per member at the time of writing.

The autonomy of local associations rests ultimately on their right to secede.[1] This right has been very rarely exercised; but the Tapesizers' recent rule-book reform was forced by the Great Harwood Society's temporary withdrawal from the Lancashire Amalgamated. Local autonomy is thus quite real, and extends to other questions than those of internal management. The industry-wide wage-lists which now exist for most occupations are, of course, absolutely observed—as minima; even in the Weavers, where the tradition of the Standard Wage is strongest, the district may negotiate alternative systems of payment, or piece-prices for special conditions, which give better earnings than the Standard Lists. On the other hand, Amalgamations have attempted to guide local policy where no uniform wage-list existed. In the Spinners, before the post-war 'Evershed' list was devised, for instance, the Amalgamation occasionally pressed a district to demand some revision in its own price-lists to bring the latter into line with others.[2] And the Overlookers' Amalgamation has persistently encouraged its districts to replace straight 'poundage' rates (based on the weavers' earnings) by a time-based wage. Local support for the various union labour controls—on overtime, for instance, and particularly on entry to closed trades—is also absolute. But beyond these things, even the industrial policy of the district may depart from the Amalgamation's. This especially affects such novel post-war developments as the introduction of so-called 'scientific' wage-systems, 're-deployment', 'work study', shift-work, and so on. Sometimes, these have been blocked by individual locals after their Amalgamation had approved them: but in other cases the position has been reversed, particular districts being ahead of their Amalgamation in their acceptance of such things.

In politics, of course, no local society feels bound by Amalgamation decisions to pursue the same line, say, in the local Labour Party —except perhaps where these concern specific trade interests.[3] And

[1] The right is mildly hedged in some cases; a local Weavers' Association may only withdraw from the Amalgamation on six months' notice, and after two-thirds of its members have voted to do so by ballot. Other Amalgamations merely threaten that special payments may be demanded from a seceding district that later applies to re-affiliate.

[2] A classic case is the 'Fine Counts' dispute of 1906, in which the Amalgamation instructed Oldham to demand an increase in the rates of spinners on certain yarns also spun by Bolton, because the latter was embarrassed by a disparity between the two districts' prices for these grades.

[3] Because of the legal position, political contributions are handled differently from ordinary union subs., which are fixed by the local but include the standard Amalgamation levy. Amalgamations usually levy the political contributors a standard sum of which, however, the local retains a part. But in the Tapesizers (which has no Amalgamation levy or political affiliation) several locals raise their own political funds.

even there, locals have on occasion risked Amalgamation censure by launching an independent action out of impatience with the central body. But in questions of organization, the local association's autonomy is usually limited only by a few Amalgamation rules to preserve good relations with its neighbours—requiring it, for instance, to accept neither members from other societies who have not paid up their subscriptions to the latter, nor the transfer of a mill or group from another district without the latter's consent or (alternatively) the Amalgamation's approval. Thus up to quite recently, the Weavers' Amalgamation was embarrassed by the defects of a particular district's administration: but since the Secretary was supported by his Committee, the Amalgamation was unable to interfere until he retired.[1]

III

There are currently a hundred or so full-time officials in the cotton unions, the majority of whom are district Secretaries. These latter are invariably drawn either directly from the membership, or from more junior officials of the same Amalgamation. (Where the local secretary has an assistant, the latter will customarily succeed him—the Oldham Weavers actually having a rule to this effect.) A candidate is usually required to have a certain period of union membership, sometimes also of service as a lay officer or Committee-member. Most permanent officials must at some stage of appointment undergo the unions' famous process of examination. Usually, this will be conducted by a panel of experienced officials, and will include a quite searching scrutiny of the candidate's knowledge of trade and technical matters, and of his ability to argue and negotiate, and to handle the intricate calculations required for piece-rate fixing.[2]

It would be a mistake, however, to regard the cotton union official as a technician alone, a 'mere calculator' (as the writer has heard him described by officers of other unions). His attitude to the employers' representative or agent whom he meets in negotiations, or accompanies to determine some complicated mill dispute over the correct piece-price or over 'bad work', may often be that of one expert to another—but with something in it of the relationship between professional soldiers in hostile armies. Technical competence is by no means the only quality assessed by the union's selection process, even in the examination itself. And it is quite common for the examination

[1] See 72nd *Annual Report* (1956) of the Amalgamated Weaves' Association, p. 6.

[2] The examination paper described by the Webbs (*Industrial Democracy*, pp. 197–9) is still quite typical.

to select only a group of candidates, from whom the Committee or General Meeting will not necessarily appoint the one with the highest marks.

Most of the present officials appear to have been drawn into trade union activity by Labour views, a generally radical social and political outlook. The system has produced, however, union officers not merely of high technical competence[1] but whose common qualities have made them almost a distinctive type—shrewd, blunt and self-reliant, detached, cautious and reasonable. It is sometimes suggested that the unions' officials transfer quite readily to the service of employers' organizations. The writer has heard of only two or three actual instances—not more than in outside unions.[2] But it *is* significant, for instance, that in some Weavers' districts it is common for local firms to send the local Secretary their piece-prices for new work, not merely for checking but for actual calculation.

A union secretaryship, of course, holds other attractions than those of social interest or class loyalty. The union official is still an important personage in the Lancashire towns; he will commonly be a councillor or a justice, will not infrequently find himself a delegate to major labour conferences or a member of some overseas mission or other. He has some chance of becoming a Member of Parliament or—still more august—the TUC's General Council. And in the inter-War years, particularly, he had a real security by contrast with the irregularities of the operatives's employment. But high pay can hardly be numbered among the job's seductions. Over 1956–7, the writers' enquiries suggested the average pay of local secretaries to be between £12 and £13 a week—not much above the average man operative's earnings at the time: and there is no reason to think this relationship very much changed since. There was quite a range, however; from as little as £8 a week up to about £20. But, even the Secretaries of the big union Provinces in the spinning industry would not get more than the last amount, and the General Secretaries of the Amalgamations themselves then received only up to about £25 a week. And the Secretary's expenses above his salary tend to be very closely scrutinized by lay auditors and committees.

The official's work, on the other hand, is quite exacting and not always entertaining. His duties vary considerably from association

[1] One Weavers' Secretary (now retired) produced his own version of the 'Uniform List'—an elaborate book of many pages—with all the various percentages and allowances to be applied in piece-rate fixing reduced to logarithms.

[2] In earlier days, at least, employers' associations apparently suffered more from the lack of competent and reliable officials than the unions. In 1869, according to R. Smith (unpublished thesis, op. cit.) the North Lancashire Masters' Association had to dismiss its Secretary for embezzlement, and was unable to replace him adequately for three years.

to association; but typically, a local secretary will spend about a day in each week on piece-rate calculations, visit some three mills to settle disputes, and spend ten or eleven hours in his office—some in the evening—with individual members' complaints and problems (often complicated National Insurance questions). He will pass several hours preparing for his local union's committee meeting, perhaps an afternoon and evening receiving contributions, making payments, or checking amounts paid by or to others, and a day in Manchester at Amalgamation meetings or negotiations above the district level. He may also be required to represent his association at two or three outside committees—which may meet in the evening.

As in other unions, only a handful of cotton officials may reach that level at which their life will be largely transformed by their virtual acceptance into a modern aristocracy of power. The remainder will share very much the material and social life of their members. The arrangement has great merits, but the motives that once urged men of character and ability to accept it have lost much of their early force. It is hardly to be wondered that competition for the Secretary's job has been very much on the decline of recent years. Even before the post-war recession in the cotton trade set in, one or two full-time assistants had been recruited from outside the industry.

Union rules frequently emphasize the formal subservience of the official. Many rule-books even specify minutely his duties and obligations, including not only such routine things as to keep accounts, prepare the minutes of Committee and General Meetings, circulate reports and so on, but many provisions which are clearly devised as controls on the Secretary's satisfactory performance. The Spinners' General Secretary is 'to keep a diary of all the business transacted by him . . .'[1] The Oldham Weavers' Secretary is '. . . to make out all calculations of prices . . . and such calculations shall be in the hands of the members within seven days from the time they were left at the office, unless a satisfactory explanation can be given.'[2] It is very usual for the rule-book to specify times between which the secretary must be present at the office or engaged on society business: these hours are, of course, minima—the cotton operatives' usual ban on overtime is reversed for their own officials.

The Secretary's appointment generally continues 'so long as he shall give satisfaction'. In fact, of course, he enjoys a real permanence: the Warehousemen's Amalgamation, for instance, had only two General Secretaries in its first fifty years. But his final dependence on

[1] Spinners' Amalgamation, *Rule* 15, Sec. 4. Such diaries are kept, and published in a summary form in the Report, for several associations.

[2] Oldham Weavers' Association, *Rule* 8 (e).

the membership to which he is responsible is illustrated by the Heywood Weavers' quite recent dismissal of their Secretary, an energetic man who fell foul of a group of members by the methods he used in attempting to restore the position of a society which had previously run down.

Between the various district Secretaries themselves, and between them and the Amalgamation officials, there is little in the way of formal hierarchy. The Tapesizers' Amalgamation has no full-time secretary; and in the Warpdressers' Amalgamation, the secretary also acts as secretary of the Nelson-Colne district. But even the big Amalgamations have a smaller staff than some of their affiliates. The Cardroom's General Secretary has a deputy and a single clerk: its Bolton Province alone has a staff of sixteen. The Weavers' Amalgamation has, besides its General Secretary, an Assistant G.S., another official specially appointed to assist the locals on certain technical questions, and a typist: but the Oldham Weavers' secretary has eight full-time assistants. The once-formidable Spinners' Amalgamation, on the other hand, has always been a one-man show. Its office consists of a single long room, with the General Secretary's desk and a committee-table: the General Secretary answers his own correspondence and opens the door to callers himself. In the spinning operatives' Amalgamations the Presidency is usually held by one of the bigger Provinces' Secretaries, who also handle much of the Amalgamation's work in conciliating disputes. The General Secretaries of the two largest cotton union Amalgamations are customarily nominated to the TUC General Council, a position which in these days translates them to a rather Olympian level—but incidentally removes them for a very large part of the time from the region and from the cotton industry's own affairs. However, officials of quite small unions may enjoy a comparable prestige: the Secretary of the UTFWA has usually been a local weavers' association official, as at present is its sole M.P. And the General Secretary of the tiny Twisters' Amalgamation was recently National Chairman of the Labour Party, and still holds an important position in that Party's National Executive.

Apart from their Secretaries and assistants, some local associations employ a number of full-time 'collectors'. More usually, however, this official is a part-time worker for the union. And it is in such lay officers that some of the most important differences between the unions consist. The spinners have a 'shop club' in every mill. Originally, this system seems to have been confined to the Bolton association, which perhaps derived it from the old hand-mule association of Manchester (which city is now part of this Province). But it has long been generally adopted, and forms an essential part of the Spinners' organization. Under Oldham's Rules, for instance, the shop club's officers handle mill disputes in the first instance, and then have direct access to the Provincial E.C.—although the club is also represented in the Province's local branch. Otherwise, the club is responsible for maintaining the spinners' 'closed shop'. It meets at least monthly, raises its own levy for its expenses, and its secretary is the only recognized channel of communication between the members at the mill and the Provincial officials or E.C.

One of two of the other closed unions also have a 'shop steward' system: the Oldham Cop-packers' 'mill correspondents' have already been referred to. But, otherwise, many of the members of such unions are employed only in twos and threes at individual mills: though where there is an exceptionally large group of members, among the overlookers, for instance, a shop-steward may be appointed informally. The Twisters' many local lay secretaries may handle disputes. The Tapesizers, with typical idiosyncrasy, have, besides their local secretaries (who are often full-time), a number of lay 'work agents'.[1] The shop representative, or the local lay officer who fills his place in the closed unions, will be concerned primarily with disputes and trade regulation: the member is usually himself responsible for paying in his own subscription at the union office or club-house.

But the big open unions have no regular system of mill representation. Several weavers' associations have developed one: and some require that committee-members or other lay officers act as union representative at their own mills. But generally, the Weavers, Warehousemen and Cardroom rely on street or district 'collectors'. It is customary in the cotton unions for lay officers to be paid some small sum in recognition of their work—but this rarely amounts to more than a few shillings a week. The part-time 'collector', however, is paid on commission: and the amount thus earned weekly is large enough to (for instance) have disqualified quite a few operatives from unemployment benefit in post-war recessions. In the past, this system may have been used to avoid exposing individual members to employers' hostility and to the danger of victimization by requiring them to be too obviously active in the mills. But during the last War, the employers conceded the unions' right to collect subscriptions at the workplace: and their attitude was never the whole reason for the open unions' general avoidance of the shop-steward

[1] The title seems to be an abbreviation of 'Out-of-work Agent' which perhaps conveyed the job's original duties. However, this officer will also be responsible for investigating grievances, interviewing employers and so on for perhaps twenty or so tapesizers in his locality, as well as sending regular reports on his trade's state to the union.

system.[1] It is curious, for instance, that the Cardroom, which imitated the Spinners' organization in so many other ways, should not have adopted its shop system—indeed, if several of its district rules are a guide, should have had a certain positive hostility to it.[2] Except that the local society may circulate a periodic Report to the members' homes, the collector provides the main contact between the open union and its rank-and-file member. This difference between the closed and open unions is a major key to the unions' actual government.

IV

All this mainly describes the formal organization of the cotton unions. But it is fairly clear from the last contrast that the 'open' unions—or unions, like most of the Cardroom's affiliates, in which the greater part of membership belongs to open occupations—are much more dependent on paid services. While in the predominantly 'closed' societies, lay members assume much more responsibility. Once this difference is grasped, many other differences fall into pattern. For instance, despite the variation within particular Amalgamations, members' meetings are much more frequent in the closed than in open unions. The Spinners' shop clubs meet monthly: Overlookers' and Tapesizers' lodges generally meet monthly or even fortnightly. On the other hand, the local Weavers', Cardroom and Warehousemen's unions usually hold their general meetings quarterly or half-yearly.

The difference between closed and open unions is similarly reflected in the members' actual attendance at meetings. Recent public concern with low figures of membership participation in union affairs has been largely based on information drawn from a few very large (and therefore largely-open) trade unions: where enquiry has proceeded further it has related the question mainly to such matters as the effect of the union branch's size or its manner of organization.[3] The *character* of the union concerned has been rather neglected. Evidence of the ordinary trade unionist's apathy could in fact, be amply drawn from the record of local Weavers' and Cardroom associations. Enquiries made by the writer among a number of these returned an average attendance of less than 1 per cent. at General Meetings. In only two societies (out of some twenty)

[1] The Spinners' shop representatives, though very long-established, seem only to have been formally recognized by the Master-Spinners' Federation as responsible for the initial handling of mill disputes by an agreement with the Spinners' Amalgamation of November 1946.

[2] See section II, above.

[3] See for instance, the PEP studies (op. cit.) pp. 39–44.

did the attendance exceed that figure: in most of them, in fact, it was little more than the total strength of lay officers, committee members and street collectors. On the other hand, attendance reported at the (much more frequent) meetings of several Overlookers' and Tapesizers' clubs ranged from 20 to 40 per cent. of members. In one Tapesizers' local, where General Meetings were only held half-yearly because its area was particularly extended (it actually had members 100 miles apart), attendance nevertheless did not fall below a fifth and was usually more: but a General Meeting of the Warehousemen's society in the same area's main town was attended by only one member apart from the officers.

Attendance at Spinners' shop clubs in the bigger Provinces was reported as effectively 100 per cent.: moreover, it was not at all unusual for a whole shop to attend also the monthly or quarterly local branch meeting (which basically consists of shop delegates) to, for instance, support their candidate for the branch committee. Members even occasionally availed themselves of their privilege of attending other branches in the Province than their own—at which some Rules permit them to speak, though not to vote. But by comparison with the mule-spinners' own union activity, that of their assistants was imperceptible. The Piecers' (or Assistant Spinners') Associations organized by Spinners' Provinces just did not meet—for lack of interest on the members part.

Quite apart from the closed unions' use of such lay officers as 'shop chairmen' and 'work agents' to handle grievances, it is evident that a greater proportion of lay members must be drawn into their general administration. The size of their local committees, for instance, does not seem to differ much—on the average—from those of open unions. But the average local Twisters' Club has only one-twentieth the membership of the comparable Weavers' Association. In the latter there seems to be about one lay officer or committee member for three to four hundred members: in the Overlookers' and Tapesizers' clubs, some 10 per cent. of the members are office-holders. For a generally similar organization and membership, the ratio of full-time officers tends to be lower in closed unions: compared with the Bolton Cardroom Province's sixteen, for instance, the Oldham Spinners have only three. The larger Cardroom Provinces have a number of full-time secretaries for their own internal branches: in the Spinners' Provinces, the branch officers are lay members.

And one cannot avoid an impression that the relation between the official and the members rather differs between the closed and open unions. In the former, he seems more definitely regarded as the paid, if respected, servant of the union: in the latter he may assume a role of authoritative leadership. Certainly, lay members play a more prominent role at the level of the closed Amalgamations themselves. The Spinners' Executive Council includes a majority of lay members by constitution; but the E.C.'s of all the smaller Amalgamations seem to have some by normal vote. On the other hand, the Weavers' Central Committee consisted, at time of writing, wholly of full-time local Secretaries: the Cardroom Amalgamation's E.C. had only one lay member.

But just as in the Spinners one section of members does not display the high interest in union affairs otherwise characteristic of the organization, in the Cardroom one group of members seem excepted from the general apathy. Nearly all the cardroom unions' full-time officers, as well as a majority of its lay committee-members, have been or are strippers-and-grinders. In some districts there are even unofficial 'grinders' locals' which exist to concert voting and action in the general meeting, and especially, to advance their own candidates for office.

Similar contrasts to these can be found in unions outside the textile trade. The printing craftsmen's 'chapel' corresponds quite closely to the Spinners' shop club. The shop-steward system in general was derived from the old craft unions (where the 'card-steward' formed an integral part of their organization) and was often first adopted by the membership of open unions 'unofficially', against the opposition of their professional leaders.[1] Generally speaking, closed unions tend to have smaller branches,[2] so that a larger proportion of their lay members are drawn into active office. On the other hand, it is not unusual for the big branches of such unions as the NUGMW and the T & GWU to be managed by full-time secretaries. The ratio of full-time officers to members seems generally lower, *ceteris paribus*, in unions dominated by a closed section. The PEP study reported the T & GWU as having 500 to 600 officials for its million and a quarter membership: the AEU, to over 800,000 members, had only 120 full-time officers.[3] And it is fairly clear that the officials' influence in the T & GWU and the

[1] The Seamen's Union has only recently (and partially) accepted the appointment of union representatives on ships, though since most of its membership is at sea this is the only way it could usually handle its own affairs, and though the system operates in ships of other nationalities.

[2] See the PEP studies, *British Trade Unionism* (op. cit.) p. 38, for some analysis of average branch size.

[3] Ibid., p. 120. A more recent study, *Trade Union Officers*, by Clegg, Killick and Adams (Blackwell, 1961), gives slightly different figures, but still suggests the AEU, even allowing (dubiously) for those shop-stewards who are virtually full-time, to have distinctly lower officers-to-membership ratios not merely than the T & GWU itself but also than the similar NUGMW and USDAW (loc. cit., Table 60).

NUGMW—particularly that of the senior members of their hierarchy—is considerably greater than in the AEU. The writer is informed that among the miners attendance at local lodges is considerably higher in the separate colliery deputies' and overmen's associations than in the general locals of the NUM, and that ASLE & F branches are commonly better attended than those of the NUR.

On the other hand, one can also find examples of unions where, just as in the Cardroom Amalgamation, active participation by the members is concentrated in—or even restricted to—a particular section. Many unions have some group of members which constitutes, by reason of its occupational status or a special historical role in the union's growth, a sort of internal aristocracy—the dockers and busmen in the T & GWU, the train-guards and signalmen in the NUR, and so on. And these may also be more active in the union's affairs than its other members: delegates to the NUR's Annual Council, for instance, seem to include a quite disproportionate number of guards and similarly-graded railwaymen. In predominantly-open unions where this 'aristocracy' feels itself subordinated by the growth of other interests, it may—as in the T & GWU and NUR—be a continuing source of internal friction. But in other cases, it may dominate the union's management. Thus, virtually all the AEU's full-time officers are drawn from the apprenticed craftsmen who also provide a majority of its lay officers, although these workers now constitute a minority of the union's membership. The colliery face-workers are less than half the membership of the NUM but the dominate its local committees and its various offices. In the iron and steel workers' union, BISAKTA, the influence of the smelters and similar high-paid steel process workers is apparent. Some such unions formally limit the rights of certain classes of member. Just as the Spinners, for instance, provide that local representation shall be on the basis of spinner-members only, and that even the officers of the Piecers' Associations shall be appointed by the spinners,[1] so the ASLE & F restricts representative rights to footplatemen proper, and bars engine cleaners from office. It is not unusual for former craft unions which have opened their ranks to unapprenticed workers to limit the latters' right to, for instance, hold office. Alternatively, election may require a lengthy period of

[1] The *Rules* of the Assistant Spinners' Association of the Oldham Spinners' Province actually provide that its secretary be a spinner though Rule 4 says: 'Nothing in this rule prevents the *appointment* of a fully financial . . . Assistant Spinner . . . to the position of Checker'. (The checker in spinners' unions is responsible for checking the entry of subscriptions by the branch chairman and secretary on contribution nights.) Piecers are now eligible for selection as delegate to Amalgamation Representative Meetings, or even to its Executive Council: I have not been able to discover that one has ever in fact been so elected.

preliminary membership, so that workers in the union's open occupations (where there is naturally a higher turnover) are less likely to be qualified.

The actual government of a trade union really depends on the relationships between three groups: its full-time officials, that proportion of its lay members which takes an active part in the union's management and the usually more passive majority of the rank-and-file. From this point of view, and to judge by the cotton operatives' organizations, it seems possible to classify unions into three types. First, there is what might be called the 'exclusive democracy'. This is found in unions which have not significantly diluted their closed character, so that the membership consists essentially of workers either already in a closed occupation to which it controls entry, or definitely accepted (as apprentices or learners) for admittance to that occupation. In cotton, the purest examples are the Overlookers' and Tapesizers' unions (the Twisters and Warpdressers have somewhat, and the Warehousemen largely, modified their original quality by expansion). Outside examples are, for instance, the London Typographical Society (whose absorption of the printing-machine managers has not much altered the character it possessed as the old LSC) and certain other printing craft associations, the Patternmakers in engineering, or the independent Deputies' Associations in mining. Such unions are generally marked by a high membership participation in their affairs and management. They usually have relatively few full-time officials. And even more important from the members' viewpoint, the official is very much one of themselves: his specialist qualities are largely an extension of the intimate knowledge of their occupation's conditions and practices which all its members possess in large measure. So that there is also little distinction of status or interest between the members themselves.

The second type may arise from the extension of an originally-closed union to include workers in open occupations, as in the case of the Spinners' recruitment of piecers, the AEU's acceptance of non-craft engineering operatives, or the old iron-smelters' merger with the less-skilled workers' organization. It may equally arise by the emergence from an initially-open union's membership of a dominant and virtually closed section—as in the case of the strippers-and-grinders in the Cardroom Amalgamation, or of the face-workers in the miners' unions. Such unions are 'aristocracies': they would normally be, in fact, largely-vertical unions operating in industries where the higher-grade (or better-paid) wage-earners have secured some control over their own recruitment. This aristocracy's role in the union may have some of the same quality of the 'exclusive democracy'. Its own members will take a relatively large part in the union's affairs, and will provide a disproportionate number of its officers. It is sometimes an associated trait that not merely is there a relative equality between the lay 'aristocrats' and the full-time officers whom they largely provide, but there is little in the way of real hierarchy among the officials themselves: in unions like the Spinners, the NUM or the AEU, local and district organizers display an evident independence towards the central officials. But, on the other hand, another section of the members will be relatively passive. This section's ability to participate in the union's management may be formally restricted: it may even have—as do the spinners' assistants—almost the status of a subject class.

The third type consists of unions which are overwhelmingly open—not merely in the sense that the mass of their members is in open jobs, but also in the sense that no closed group of workers has achieved a dominating influence in these unions' direction. For this reason, perhaps, it is especially evidenced by unions which have expanded horizontally, to cover a variety of occupations, like the two big general unions and possibly the USDAW. In cotton, it is most clearly illustrated by the Weavers. And some of its quality may exist in non-cotton unions whose interests are less diverse than the three giants already mentioned, but which operate—like the Seamen, or the Dyers, Bleachers and Textile Workers—in industries where workers in closed occupations are not numerous or have separate organizations.

At any rate, such unions are marked by a generally low level of membership participation, and by the greatest difference between the members and the professional officials on which they depend. In their case, the full-time officers' expertise necessarily embraces a range of affairs which is quite beyond the ordinary member's experience. And there is often a distinct hierarchy among the officials themselves. The central, and usually dominating role of the General Secretary in the T & GWU, or of the virtual oligarchy of District Secretaries in the NUGMW, is obvious; and in such unions these senior officials may virtually appoint their own successors. The federal structure of the cotton unions prevents a hierarchy appearing among the Weavers' district and Amalgamation secretaries: but the Weavers' district secretary who has an assistant will largely influence the choice of the latter, and thereby help to nominate his successor. And where the district has a sizeable staff—as in Oldham—the secretary proper has a clear authority over it: the Bolton Cardroom's full-time branch secretaries, on the other hand (usually drawn from the 'aristocracy' of grinders), have their own representative on the Province's E.C.

For such reasons—and for want of a better term—unions of this third type might be called 'popular bossdoms'. And thus, in them, the relations which actually exist between the membership and the key officials will depend very much on the latters' style of leadership. Within the general characteristics of cotton union officials as a class, for instance, some of the Weavers' local secretaries behave virtually as straight 'business unionists'; the normally-low interest of their members in union affairs they accept as natural, and they take rank-and-file approval of their arrangements to be implied by the absence of visible objection. One or two, indeed, have assumed an almost dictatorial position. Others, however, attempt to draw their members into union decisions and management—by an emphasis on democratic forms and procedures, by adopting a militant attitude, by devices to increase the members' interest (like organizing social functions) and so on. The effect of the leaders' 'style' is similarly evident in other unions of this type. One has only to consider the apparent switch in the T & GWU from (in trade union terms) a conservative to a radical position that followed the death of Arthur Deakin, and the unforeseen succession of Frank Cousins to that union's General Secretaryship—or to consider again the impact of two such different personalities as Joseph Hallsworth and Bryn Roberts on the unions (respectively the Distributive Workers and the Public Employees) whose major development they supervised. And since such leaders largely choose (or at least mould) the assistants who will inherit their place, a particular 'leadership style' may be transmitted down the line of succession—as Arthur Deakin's, for instance, was modelled on that of Ernest Bevin—so that two unions of essentially the same real governmental type may present very different characters to the outside world.

V

Of course, the three types of governmental actuality, into which the foregoing suggests unions may be divided, are not hard and fast categories into some one of which every union must neatly fit. Just as in our previous classification of trade unionism's external structure into 'closed' and 'open' organizations, unions change their character; so that some may also possess a rather mixed internal quality. Indeed, the most likely reason for such an internal shift—in the relation between a union's leadership and its members—is just that its external form has changed. Thus the Warpdressers, until recently an 'exclusive democracy', are becoming an 'aristocracy' by their recruitment of other, and less-skilled, operatives. The Twisters, whose inclusion of reachers-in (the key workers' assistants) already made their unions potentially 'aristocratic' in type, have become more clearly so by widening their ranks further. The Warehousemen, had their original membership of clothlookers succeeded in establishing a solidly closed organization, would have become an 'exclusive democracy'. Their conversion to an open union, and the merely limited success of the clothlookers themselves in raising their status, makes them a mixture of 'popular bossdom' and 'aristocracy'. The present cardroom unions, on the other hand, built up as mass, open organizations by a dominant handful of full-time organizers, have since produced an internal aristocracy; while their Amalgamation's affiliated societies of cop-packers and roller-coverers are virtually autonomous 'exclusive democracies'. A completely-closed union naturally tends to the latter type of internal control. While a completely-open one equally tends towards 'popular bossdom'. A mixed union, with both closed and open sections, tends to aristocracy; but mixtures differ, and change their balance. Thus, the history of the T & GWU's relations with the dockers might be interpreted as that of an open union which produced a closed aristocracy—an aristocracy whose struggle with the union's popular bossdom led to its attempted breakout and merger in the exclusive democracy of stevedores.

One can equally conceive, of course, that a union's internal character might influence its external form: for instance that an aristocracy might balk at its union's further expansion for fear of becoming submerged, or that a popular bossdom might hesitate to absorb an exclusive democracy lest the latter challenge its control. It is perhaps important, however—since the mere *size* of unions has often been considered a critical factor in their internal democracy[1]—that these three categories also bear only the roughest correspondence to relative memberships.

In general, open unions naturally tend to be bigger than closed ones. And to that extent, the bigger a union, the lower its degree of membership participation is likely to be, and the more likely that it will be dominated by an aristocracy of lay members or by a group of full-time officers. But many other things influence an individual union's size besides the particular external form it has adopted. Its natural opportunities for growth, for instance, will have been indicated partly by the occupations among which it was founded—by the extent of its original field of organization, and the outlets (in the way of allied but unorganized occupations) that field provided. Thus a closed union can still be quite big. The Boilermakers' Society has very few non-apprenticed members, but numbers some 100,000

[1] See, for instance, *The Dockworker*, Liverpool University Social Science Dept., 1954.

nevertheless. And the amalgamation of metal-craft unions which that Society recently canvassed would have about twice that membership. The merger of printing craft unions also recently proposed would have had nearly 100,000 members—of which about 70,000 alone would be compositors. While the AEU, Britain's second largest trade union, is at least an 'aristocracy' in which the aristocrats (the 'Green Card' men of its Section I) number a third of its 900,000 total membership.

On the other hand, the size of not a few predominantly-open unions has been restricted by a relative industrial or local isolation—and particularly by other unions' prior organization of potential recruiting fields. The Warehousemen's Amalgamation, for instance, could never have hoped to become a very big union. But in any case, a union's size is also influenced by the formal internal structure it has historically affected. In organizations which adopted the federal mode of the cotton operatives, the national association is less important to the reality of union government than the local unit—which is to all intents and purposes the union proper. The biggest, currently, of the local cotton unions, the Oldham Cardroom Province, has less than 20,000 members. At the time of the writer's enquiries, the biggest weavers' association had only some 5,000. And it would not be difficult to quote instances from outside cotton, of still smaller unions which nevertheless are both open *and* possessed of all the qualities of popular (or even unpopular) bossdom.

However, the validity of applying this analysis to the cotton unions' actual government does involve one obvious question. It is common knowledge, not only that trade unionism is weak among women, but that their participation in union affairs is relatively lower than that of men. How far is the 'popular bossdom' of the Weavers, or the aristocratic government of the cardroom unions, due to the great majority of their members being women? The Cardroom Amalgamation's membership is 90 per cent female. But it has not one full-time woman official: and all but a dozen of its two to three hundred lay officers and committee members are men.[1] It is also true, however, that (apart from the affiliated societies of cop-packers and roller-coverers) cardroom union officers are overwhelmingly drawn from one particular section of the male membership only. Other men than strippers-and-grinders, such as blowing-room hands, seem

[1] Dr F. Zweig, in *Trade Unions and Productivity* (Oxford, 1951), incidentally reported only 12 out of 260 Cardroom committee members to be women: the number has not changed significantly since he wrote. Nevertheless the ratio seems an improvement on that of the 1930s! A photograph of the Cardroom's officers and committee members assembled for the Amalgamation's Jubilee Dinner in 1936 shows only two women among the three hundred or so workers and officials present.

much under-represented in the Cardroom's active membership and, certainly, in its officialdom. On the other hand, the Weavers have a rather smaller proportion of women members (87 per cent). But two of their 28 local secretaries were, at the time of writing, women; and so are an actual majority of their lay officers.

True, the proportion of women appears to decline the higher up the scale of union office (so that one will find fewer local Weavers' Presidents and Treasurers to be women than collectors and committee members). But no evidence of a higher participation by the generality of members is provided by the attendance records of local weavers' associations with an unusually large proportion of men. Nelson's reported attendance at general meetings was above the average—but was still only 1½ per cent. While Burnley's was less than ½ per cent (and despite its large male membership Burnley has historically been one of the Weavers' weakest districts). An attendance of over 5 per cent.—quite uniquely high among the weavers' unions—was, however, reported of a local association with a woman secretary but only a normally-low ratio of male members. On the other hand, the low attendance at Warehousemen's meetings cannot be attributed to their female membership, because this comprises only a small minority. And the lowest attendance of all—nil!—was reported of certain all-male associations of spinners' piecers and assistants.

In discussion with trade unionists—including women—one will usually find reasons for women's low participation in union management which essentially suppose a natural female inferiority.[1] But the basic reason seems to be the interruption of women's normal working life by marriage. This has three consequences. First, that men, who usually become interested in union affairs after marriage, have in this respect a long head start on women who return to work later. Second, that even a woman who then becomes an interested trade unionist may still find her ability to be actively participant in union management limited by domestic commitments. Both the Weavers' full-time women Secretaries were spinsters: and it is notable that their women lay officers are often older married women whose children have left home. But third, this normal

[1] Witness the following extracts from essays submitted by cotton operatives at a union summer school. *A man:* 'Women elect men officers because of the jealousy of woman to another woman and the natural attraction of woman to man'. (So why don't men always elect women?) *A woman:* 'Women prefer a man at the head; they are easily swayed and lack confidence in the capabilities of one another'. *A man:* 'Women can't count' (this related to a supposed female incapacity for the calculations involved in cotton wage-fixing: a curious comment from a region with a tradition of near-absolute female supremacy in domestic accounting).

interruption of working life—even in the cotton districts, where an unusually high proportion of women work, the woman's average continuous working period seems to be only about four to five years[1]—facilitates the exclusion of women from better-paid jobs. Formally, there is 'equal pay' in cotton. However, even in those occupations where women and men are nominally interchangeable, such as weaving, it will be found in practice that there is a strong tendency for the better-paying types of work to be reserved to men. More usually, however, the better-paid jobs are those of closed occupations. So that women, being confined to open jobs, have the characteristics—including an indifference to active personal responsibility for collective interests they may none the less recognize—of 'unskilled' workers generally, if somewhat exaggerated by other hindrances to their participation in union affairs.

The reason for the differing internal qualities of trade unions—and the basis of the threefold classification of their real government which is here developed—is thus the different characteristics of their members themselves. Workers in closed jobs compose the 'exclusive democracies', as well as the 'aristocracies' of mixed unions. And they are, of course, generally more-skilled, not least because it is often part of their union's purpose to foster and preserve the occupational knowledge that it has monopolized.[2] It is in fact, very common for closed cotton unions like the Tapesizers, and particularly the Overlookers, to have technical lectures at their local meetings, or for these to hear and discuss members' accounts of their experience with new products, processes, and equipment. And both these groups will refuse the final admission—and thus an entry to their trade—of a man accepted as a 'learner' if the members who teach him and the local society involved both conclude that he lacks ability for the work.

To this extent, the members of closed occupations tend to be better-educated, if not more able, than others. But the prime reason for their different quality is their sense of common possession of a trade—an occupation to which they are individually committed, and with the status of which their individual interest is intimately bound-up. They thus possess to an unusual degree that occupational stability which was seen in the history of the early unions to be a condition of spontaneous collective association.[3] And they have, moreover, strong personal interests in their trade's protection and good management.

[1] See F. Zweig (op. cit.).

[2] See Chapter III, 1, for a discussion of the meaning of 'skill' and its connection with trade union organization.

[3] See Chapter II, 2, section VII.

Workers in an open occupation, however, have no such personal identification with it. The attitude to trade unionism of the woman weaver or cardroom tenter who expects to leave work after marriage and may return to some quite different job, of the warehouse or taperoom labourer who may have previously worked on colliery haulage and tomorrow be in an engineering factory—just like the Midland assembly-line hand who becomes a bus-conductor, or the bricklayer's mate who switches to a chemical plant—thus reflects the consequences of an obviously lesser occupational stability.[1] Such workers may be trade unionists in a general way, in the sense that they regard union membership as a necessary insurance or an appropriate demonstration of class or group solidarity. But they lack the 'skilled' worker's fixed interest in the welfare of a particular trade, and are thus more inclined to leave its management to professional union officers.

VI

It is, at any rate, in a union's actual practice, which its formal rules may or may not reflect, that its internal character is revealed. And so far as its government is concerned, this includes things—like the relationship between its principal official and its Committee—which are not always known. Nevertheless, the actual quality of a union's democracy will have some effect on the formal rules themselves. Thus, it seems possible that the threefold classification of 'real' union governments which is indicated here bears some correspondence to the typology of *formal* union constitutions which was suggested in an earlier discussion of trade unionism's institutional evolution.

It has been shown that the federal structure typified by the cotton unions permits the most varying degrees of actual membership participation or domination by officials. And the primitive constitutional forms that survive in some small or purely local non-cotton unions are probably not inconsistent with any type of real government, though they are now mostly identified with closed and exclusive democracies, like that of the London compositors. But the constitutional form evolved by certain modern mass organizations from the 'New Unions' is clearly adapted to a popular bossdom. And the constitution typical of the craft unions' modern descendants

[1] It may be a subsidiary explanation of differences between the cardroom and weavers' unions that the opportunity of alternative work was always greater in the South-East Lancs. spinning area than in the Northern weaving districts. While the general diversification of the region's industry since the 1930s may also have contributed to a reduced membership interest in the open unions—if it was ever *normally* much higher than it is now.

was originally identified with an exclusive democracy, which has in several cases become an aristocracy by opening its ranks to a sort of 'second-class citizen'. So a union's internal character will be at least partially reflected in its constitutional development: it is significant, for instance, that the Spinners alone among the cotton Amalgamations formally insist on a lay majority among their Executive Councillors, and that they have the most elaborate requirements of membership consent to strikes. This emphasis on democratic forms (of course, only for the spinners themselves) may well reflect a determination to control what might otherwise have been an exceptionally powerful officialdom.

True, such forms may be adapted to a practice rather different from their intention; a provision that officials be elected, for instance, may readily be converted to a system of nomination.[1] Similarly, the cotton unions' appointment of officials by examination may, as a matter of practice, merely confirm a Secretary's assistant to succeed him, or alternatively provide only a qualifying test of several candidates for election. Or again, the power of a formally-supreme representative body will depend very much on the actual procedure of its meetings. A mass conference which primarily discusses an Executive Report, and in which the leadership thus has a debating initiative, will be a rather different thing from a smallish representative council which gives its own motions priority of discussion.

But certainly, the relationships between union leaders, active lay members, and the rest of the membership do affect more obvious matters of organization. The Spinners' general adoption of the 'shop club' system, for instance, is probably not unconnected with the members' desire to retain, within the large Provinces partly forced on them by external developments, as much as possible of their unions' management in their own hands. On the other hand, the Cardroom's reluctance to emulate the Spinners in this one respect may perhaps be attributed to a combination of the early officials' unwillingness to provide a channel through which they might be subjected to pressure from the mills, and the strippers-and-grinders' realization that workplace union organization would automatically encourage a representation of other operatives in the union's running that might overwhelm their own influence. Similarly, the insistence of all the closed unions in cotton manufacturing except the Warpdressers on small local units, by contrast to the big

[1] See H. A. Clegg's *General Union* (op. cit.) for a description of the way the NUGMW's formal requirement of election to all full-time posts has been in fact converted to a system by which junior officials are virtually appointed by the union's oligarchy of District Secretaries, and election effectively dispensed with for all higher offices short of the General Secretaryship itself.

local associations of Weavers, may be partly due to their members' desire to manage things for themselves. And the Warpdressers' exception is explained by considerations of economic policy imposed by their special exclusive technique that, among other factors which were earlier suggested to have historically influenced the different unions' size, were in their case overwhelming. It seems at any rate significant that—since the post-war contraction of the cotton industry began, the Weavers have merged five (out of an original thirty-three) local associations into others, while the Overlookers and Tapesizers have made no such adaptation to declining membership; and even the Twisters (whose local organization is most fragmented) have only wound up three small societies. The same insistence on small local branches seems quite generally characteristic of closed unions outside cotton; some craft (or like the AEU, ex-craft) societies even have rules limiting the size of branches.[1]

Indeed, it does not seem unreasonable to say that even a union's external policy is affected by its internal character. The principle on which the Weavers' 'Uniform List' of wages is based, for instance, involves such an expertise in its application that this inevitably became dependent on professional officers. The Twisters, on the other hand, have resisted attempts to standardize their traditional local wage-lists, which remain uninformed by any such common technical principle as that of the 'Uniform List'. Similarly, the Tapesizers rely largely on mill bargaining, and were only recently persuaded to press for even a general minimum rate. In the Twisters' case, it certainly seems that this apparent convervatism derived from the members' reluctance to see wage-fixing removed from their lay-managed locals' direct control. And one could suggest other analogies, both inside and outside the cotton trades. The strippers-and-grinders' exclusion from the post-war standardization of cardroom wage-rates, for instance, may perhaps be paralleled in the development of miners' wage-fixing. The NUM was able several years ago to conclude a major agreement with the National Coal Board on a standard wage-structure for day-wage workers in the mines. But it has apparently found it singularly difficult to devise a similarly-acceptable standard wage-system for its own aristocrats, the coal-face workers who have hitherto had a close hand in fixing their own piece-rates at the pit itself. Is the difficulty altogether attributable to merely technical problems?

There is one item of union policy which is certainly influenced by

[1] PEP (*British Trade Unionism*, pp. 39–42) noted that union voting and attendance was usually higher in small branches. It may be, however, that branch size is itself as much a reflection of a union's level of membership participation as these more obvious things.

the differing internal characters of particular organizations—their attitude to union membership itself. In this discussion, trade unions have been classified largely by reference to the extent of membership participation in their management. In itself, this says nothing final about the 'degree of democracy' in trade unions, because democracy can be defined in terms, not of participation, but of consent. However, it does by implication run counter to one view of that desideratum. Some think the first requirement of democracy in trade unions is that their members be free to lapse. Indeed, one recent student has gone further, suggesting the unions' main function is to provide services to its members, so that bureaucracy is inevitable because it is the most efficient way to fulfil that function, but is also tolerable provided it is kept efficient by the threat of dissatisfied union members leaving.[1]

As regards the inevitability of bureaucracy—if by that is meant more than a necessity to employ full-time agents—we have already noted that whether even those unions which were classed as 'popular bossdoms' could also be termed bureaucratic depended largely on their officials' 'leadership style'. Some local Weavers' Secretaries certainly behave on the assumption that they, in general, know best, and that their actions meet their members' approval unless the latter give some positive and substantial signs of discontent. But we have noted that others are much concerned at the seeming 'apathy' of their members, and go out of their way in attempts to stir their interest, consult them, and generally to thrust responsibility upon them. While still other local cotton union officials, in similar circumstances, believe the presentation of an obviously-militant stance which will rally their members' support and activity more important than mere 'office' efficiency.

This is not to say that there has been *no* significant trend to bureaucracy in union government. But in that case, fluctuations in membership clearly reflect too many other things than particular membership discontents for the latter to exert an effective pressure on union leaders via individual lapsings alone. Neglect of what a section of members considers to be its interest *may* lead individuals to lapse their membership—as the Under-Engineers decayed within the Oldham Spinners' Union. A union's membership *may* fall because of its officials' administrative incompetence: one could quote instances from the history of several local cotton unions.[2] Or it may dissolve,

[1] See Allen (op. cit.).

[2] The unions' usual method of selection may make this seem unlikely. However, officials grow old; and it has happened that a local committee has been both too miserly to pension off a secretary who was past his job, and too kindly to dismiss him. While men in office sometimes acquire vices which destroy the capacities that gained it them.

where the union is new and not yet firmly established, from frustration at its ineffectiveness—as the early cardroom unions apparently declined when their attempted imitation of the Spinners' successful technique met with failure.

Otherwise, however, the membership of unions is clearly affected by large general causes[1]—the level of economic prosperity and employment, the public attitude towards labour organization and social movements—which overwhelm the gradual nibblings of individual dissatisfaction or disillusionment. While in those unions which are perhaps most open to a charge of 'bureaucracy', the very occupational instability which makes for a passive membership also involves a high membership turnover that swamps such voiceless protests as individual lapsings may represent. But particularly, and in any event, to put the freedom to lapse as a prime test of union democracy is unsatisfactory mainly because a tendency to compulsory membership seems an automatic extension of the collective discipline trade unionism itself implies.

Compulsory union membership, we noted, takes two principal forms. One is the 'closed shop' proper, which implies that employers can only engage workers who are either members of the union concerned or whom that union has agreed in advance to accept. The closed shop is (appropriately enough) a necessary device of closed unionism. All the closed cotton unions, as well as the closed sections within open organizations, apply this condition of employment to the occupations they control, commonly imposing by rule (though it is now hardly ever necessary in practice) penalties—up to expulsion from the trade—on men who work with 'illegal' operatives, or instruct 'illegal' learners. The other form of compulsory membership is the 'union shop', in which an employer may engage (broadly) whom he thinks fit, but each worker is then required to join the union and to maintain his membership thereof while his engagement continues. This practice is, of course, identified with open unionism. And most open unions will, in fact, when they feel strong enough, attempt to impose it by one means or another.

Thus, as the nineteenth-century power-loom weavers' unions consolidated themselves, they abandoned their early tolerance of non-unionists. Local weavers' associations continued to pay strike benefit to non-members, on strategic occasions, up to just before the First World War. But as early as the 1860s strikes against non-unionists occurred in the strongly-organized North East Lancashire districts. And after the forming of the present Weavers' Amalgamation, such pressures increased, working up to a regular campaign in the early years of this century. The great 1912 stoppage,

[1] Witness, the union membership graphs of Chapter III, 1.

when 160,000 weaving workers 'frightened the country almost out of its wits'[1] by facing a two weeks' lock-out rather than withdraw their support of a mill strike against non-unionists, was the climax of this movement. But though the employers' associations have always resisted the union shop, attempts to enforce it have continued up to the present day. It now exists in not a few weaving sheds; in the Oldham district, it is effectively imposed by the local weavers' association rule requiring members to instruct and assist no new workers who do not join the union; an agreement on certain working arrangements that the employers proposed to the Weavers' Amalgamation itself in 1958 broke down on the latter's insistence that the workers concerned be required to have union membership. A rather similar historical course of events has occurred in the Cardroom Amalgamation which, although it, too, has failed to overcome the objections of the spinning employers' federation to the union shop, at least extracted from that federation—after a mill dispute in 1935—a statement that it '. . . *preferred* that employees in cotton spinning mills should be members of a trade union . . . (and) to remove any doubt on this point . . . (would) circularise the members of the Federation to this effect'.[2] In the cotton unions indeed, the principle of the union shop has been extended from the workplace to the home. It is very common for local associations' rules to impress on operatives the desirability of ensuring that working members of their families should also be trade unionists, sometimes making this a condition of candidature for union office, or even of acceptance into a closed union. This use of the family as a lever to re-inforce union strength was, in fact, and in the conditions of the cotton towns, a not unimportant factor in the unions' final consolidation.

But it is also apparent that the 'union shop' has, in many cases, only been preliminary to the 'closed shop' proper—a point connected with an earlier proposition as to the mutability of external union forms, and the tendency of initially-open unions to develop essentially exclusive practices and produce closed sections. Thus the early self-actor spinners' and male cardroom hands' societies in North Lancashire apparently began by demanding, not absolute regulation of entry, but only that all workers the employer engaged should join their unions.[3] But one of the Cardroom Amalgamation's two major

[1] Dangerfield, *The Strange Death of Liberal England* (Constable, London, 1936) p. 278.

[2] *Agreement* of Cotton Spinning Industry Conciliation Board of November 12, 1935. Author's italics.

[3] Smith (unpublished thesis, op. cit.) quotes a letter received by the North Lancashire employers' association in 1867 from their cardroom overlookers' 'Mutual Improvement Society' complaining of this interference with their engagement of hands.

contributions to the pre-War I wave of industrial unrest, the lock-out of 100,000 spinning workers in 1910, arose—by contrast with the great weaving dispute referred to above—from a stripper-and-grinder's refusal (which the Amalgamation supported) to do work he regarded as not proper to his occupation. This cause identified his section of the Cardroom Amalgamation, at least, with exclusive unionism, and in turn implied insistence on a closed shop for his occupation. And in any case, from the union shop to the closed shop there exists a convenient and logical intermediate step: this is the 'preferential shop', providing that no one at present a non-member shall be engaged while unemployed union members are available. And this, even one or two local weavers' associations have in practice operated, although the Weavers' ultimate inability to fully control labour supply to its memberships' jobs has prevented it going further.

Nevertheless, the demand for a closed shop seems a logical implication of those attempts to control the supply of labour which the previous Chapter suggested any organized occupational group will evolve. While it is again important that these attempts have developed to a large extent informally, as occupational identities crystallized, and sometimes without the support of the unions involved. (So that if the 'closed shop' proper is not more general in other employments than cotton, this may be attributed either to the comparative recency of trade unionism in many trades or to the disruption of occupational stabilities—and solidarities—by technical or economic change.) It is, however, in just the groups which have been most successful in these attempts—and among which, therefore, compulsion to union membership is most stringent—that participation in union management is highest.

But if pressure towards the 'closed shop' has often come, so to speak, from below, it is equally true that the (preliminary?) drive towards the 'union shop' has also emanated, not mainly from the officials (to whom compulsory union membership has been sometimes suggested to give an arbitrary power over their members) but from the members themselves. Both the Weavers' and Cardroom Amalgamations, for instance, were obliged to restrain mill sentiment against non-unionists in the early years of this century by announcing that they would not support workplace strikes on that issue unless 85 per cent of the operatives concerned were already union members. And outside the cotton trade, a perfect illustration of the main source of pressure for compulsory unionism occurred just after the unofficial London dock strike of 1952, when several thousand dockers stopped again—and again unofficially—to compel certain lorry-drivers to join the very union (the T & GWU) against the policy and instructions of which they had just been striking.

Again, all this is not to say that compulsory membership has not been used by an officialdom or by a group within a union to impose itself or its policy on objecting workers—as it clearly was so used, for instance, by the Spinners' aristocracy of 'minders' in relation to their piecers' attempts to form independent associations.[1] But certainly, compulsory membership seems far from being at all widely regarded by workers as an infringement of their freedom. One might put the point in rather a high-flown way, perhaps, by saying that wage-earners see freedom in terms of collective advancement, to which individual refusals to subscribe are a threat.[2] Though it is also important—witness, the piecers' case again—that this does not necessarily justify compulsion to join a *particular* union.

VII

Since a pressure towards compulsory membership, under one form or another, seems inherent in trade unionism, it follows that its internal democracy is important. And though, again, this Chapter's earlier analysis implies no formal definition of 'democracy' in the trade union context, it does suggest some things that may be relevant to it. For instance, one of the most significant indices of a union's inner democracy is clearly the extent to which its members not merely are *able* to take a hand in what it does on their behalf, but in fact do so. On the same analysis, however, a large proportion of trade unionists will not wish an active participation in their organization's management. So that a second test of union democracy would well be the degree to which such 'passive' members are also able to identify their leadership's policy and actions with their own interest. In practice, of course, the degree of this identification is difficult to measure, but one indication of it would certainly be the willingness of individual members or groups to join or stay in one union *rather than another*.

However, it has also been suggested here that the difference between those unions with a high 'membership participation' in their management, and those whose members' attitude to the latter was overwhelmingly passive, consisted largely in the degree of conscious sectional solidarity amongst a union's members themselves—and that the growth of such distinct solidarities might be as much a consequence

[1] See Chapter III, 2, section I.

[2] Thus, the contrastingly hostile attitude of some salary-earners' organizations to compulsory membership may arise because their constituents still see their advancement as mainly an individual affair, which a requirement to conform to collective interests may jeopardize. The professions, however, have generally had no such inhibitions!

as a cause of trade unionism itself. So that—and since British trade unionism has in any case taken a shape which is primarily one of organized sectional interests—union democracy particularly implies a freedom of interest groups to form within it and to associate as suits them best. Which brings us back to the preceding Chapter's discussion of the shape of trade unions. The question of trade union democracy involves both (what have here been called) the external and internal structures of trade unions.

But this implies a certain dilemma. In this study's Introductory, *two* sets of trade union problems were noted, of which those of union government comprised only one. On the other hand, there is the necessity of common policy between different interest groups. Common policy seems often relatively easy to achieve where what is at issue is a broad political programme or attitude. The well-known difference in attendance between union meetings on questions immediate to a particular membership's pockets, and those where political resolutions are passed, suggests that such things as the latter are usually regarded by the union's rank-and-file as affecting only a secondary area of union activity, in which they are content to leave decisions to the officers and the interested lay minority (which no doubt explains why they have been occasionally prepared to acquiesce in their union's domination by a group whose political views the generality of them certainly did not share). Common policy, however, is much more difficult of attainment when it affects the unions' sphere of direct action—wages, and the regulation of employment. A major recent example, of course, is provided by the 1945–51 Labour government's experiment in 'wage-restraint' by agreement with the TUC. But the difficulty of co-ordinating the action of separate labour interests arises when these are much less diverse than those embraced by the TUC as a whole. In the cotton industry, for instance, it has not been unknown in recent years for one union's members to be unemployed or on short-time because another union has been unwilling to accept new entrants for key vacancies, or the transfer of labour to a process which was short-handed. Outside cotton, there is again a major recent instance in the strike-wave of early 1955, when three great stoppages—of newspaper printing, on the railways, and in the docks—all arose from what were essentially inter-union disputes.

Whether these two needs—for internal democracy and for common external policies—can ever be fully reconciled is doubtful. On our earlier analysis, again, the most democratic unions—in terms of such things as their high degree of 'membership participation' or their small dependence on full-time officers—are the most exclusive, closed organizations. But this is so just because their members share an undiluted sectional interest, with the preservation of which they identify their association. So that such unions tend inevitably to a narrow view of what is relevant to their policies: they are, for instance, the source of those most stubborn of inter-union conflicts, the 'demarcation' disputes. In cotton, this quality of the 'exclusive democracy' is perhaps particularly evident in the closed unions' attitude towards technical and methodological improvement—on which, in the post-War period, the trade's chances of any enduring rehabilitation depended. So that one could cite, for instance, the tapesizers' generally hostile attitude towards new chemical 'mixes' and mixing devices, or the twisters' attempt to impose penal wage-rates on the new knotting machines. On the other hand, the least democratic unions, in terms of their membership's participation in union management or of its identification of the union with a shared and homogeneous interest, are the 'popular bossdoms.' But just because of their officials' relative detachment from their members, and of the diversity of interests which their leaderships must reconcile, these unions often tend to be the most progressive and experimental in trade questions, and to display a broader (or what it has recently become fashionable to call more 'responsible') outlook on the general policy of trade unionism.[1]

Thus, the Weavers, of all the cotton Amalgamations, appear to have been least affected by internal parochialism. The Spinners' and Cardroom Provinces, for instance, usually appoint their officials only from their own local members—some even having rules that this be done.[2] But a local weavers' association may appoint its Secretary from any other district. In fact, a large proportion of the Weavers' Secretaries are drawn from the traditionally-militant Nelson area (where the local Committee at one time ran 'calculation classes' to instruct members in the intricacies of the weaving wage-system): while several others have come from the Oldham union, whose system of full-time collectors provided a preliminary training. So that the Weavers' officials tend to have a broader view of their members' interest than those of other unions. The Weavers have certainly been the most ready to adapt themselves to the cotton industry's post-War circumstances and needs. The 'C.M.C. Wage-System' which the Weavers' Amalgamation negotiated in 1949, despite certain deficiencies and its rather slow adoption at the mill level (for which managements must be held equally responsible with

[1] This point, as it turns out, is an old one! Nearly a century ago, Jevons remarked: 'It is in the Trades Societies which combine many grades of workmen and several branches of industry that we naturally find the most enlightened policy.' (*A Lecture on Trades' Societies*, 1868.)

[2] e.g. *Rules* 10 and 12 of the Oldham Spinners' Association.

their operatives), represented a radical break with the historical forms of wage-fixing, and was perhaps the most thoroughgoing attempt to rationalize its wage-structure that any British industry has recently undertaken. The CMC system was specifically designed as an aid to productivity: but other cotton unions, by and large, accepted only adaptations of their traditional wage-systems—if that. The Weavers have similarly been the most advanced in their acceptance of shift-working, new equipment, and 'redeployment': they are alone among the cotton unions in having a special officer to advise local societies on the application of new working methods or payment systems. And the Weavers took the initiative in sending local officials to courses on time-and-motion study arranged first with commercial consultants, and later by the Cotton Board. In a broader way, the Weavers' Amalgamation has been again unique among cotton unions in arranging occasional week-end schools for its members, and in sending operatives to an annual summer course.[1]

Again, one could draw analogies from trade unionism at large. The post-War Labour government's attempt to secure 'wage-restraint', for instance, may or may not have been well-advised. It was certainly motivated to general economic ends which the trade union movement enthusiastically approved, and depended on that movement's voluntary co-operation. But if the final break-up of that policy could be traced to any one union, it was that most exclusive of democracies, the LSC—whose successful strike of September 1950 to increase the London printer's differential over his provincial colleagues initiated a succession of major wage-advances. The most solid supporters of 'wage-restraint', however, were undoubtedly the two great general unions—or, at least, their exceptionally powerful officials. Trade unions have often been criticized in recent years for a lack of effective democracy. They have been equally urged to display 'responsibility' towards a general interest. But in trade unions, are 'democracy' and 'responsibility' compatible?

At any rate, in the light of all this one can at least doubt whether the typical solution of this century to trade unionism's structural problems—the merger of separate interests into yet larger, and relatively centralized, mass organizations—remains adequate. Its original adequacy, whether derived from the amalgamation of craft or of unskilled workers' unions, is not at issue. When the great

[1] Its isolation in this respect was broken only recently, when the Overlookers' Amalgamation also sent a few nominees to the same course. The Overlookers generally seem more positive than other closed cotton unions—possibly because their members stand on the whole to benefit from new technical development, which increases the maintenance requirements of weaving equipment. However, there *are* limits: the Overlookers have refused to permit AEU textile-machinery fitters to do their work when trained overlookers were particularly scarce.

amalgamated unions that at present dominate the labour scene were first formed, their memberships were generally smaller, their leaderships were often necessarily different in character, separate sectional identities were much less formed inside them, and their external policy less complicated by considerations of its general impact on the economy. It is not merely that such unions have since become very big (it is questionable whether, beyond a certain size, a further growth of membership *alone* makes much difference to a union's internal character). It is rather that the elaboration and consolidating of their official hierarchy has opened some unions to a charge of bureaucracy, that their memberships have often become too heterogeneous to retain the sense of obvious common interest which union democracy apparently requires, and yet that these unions are too powerful individually for common policy to be effectively achieved between them.

True, the TUC still envisages joint arrangements between unions as a prelude to new mergers on 'industrial' lines.[1] But it does not seem that much progress can now be made in that direction—although the TUC has recently revived attempts to stimulate it. The multiple interests of several very large unions—the AEU and the two general unions, for example, are represented in practically every industry—make it virtually impossible to produce a single union for each (or even any) major industry by merger alone, without that involving the amalgamation of nearly *all* sizeable unions. No doubt there are still some small unions whose inability to achieve either a viable base of mass membership or a restrictive employment control will drive them to accept a bigger organization's embrace; the very big unions, however, are too big to merge with each other. The two general unions, for instance, have closely parallel organizing and bargaining interests. But an amalgamation of them would involve a radical disturbance of their established hierarchies; and even were that acceptable, their leaderships might well doubt their own power to control the enormous and diverse membership of the combined organization. In any case, it has been shown that recent moves towards new major amalgamations have certainly not always been inspired by a desire for 'closer unity' in general, but rather to enable particular groups to present a more effective rivalry to other unions which operate in the same industries. While the TUC's encouragement of union mergers neglects their possible implications for internal democracy—with which that body (in the protracted affair of the ETU's disputed leadership) has recently confirmed its limited capacity to concern itself.

T.U.C. policy on union structure and inter-union relations now

[1] *Final Report*, 'Trade Union Structure and Closer Unity,' TUC, 1946.

seems, in fact, largely conditioned by its need to avoid treading on any of its major affiliates' toes. It cannot propose the formation of new unions in any sector where *some* members are claimed by its existing affiliates, however desirable (for instance, in nursing or the catering trades) the latters' relative failure to organize there might make that; it certainly cannot support a particular membership's secession from existing unions to form a new one. In the trade union world, all marriages are apparently blessed, however bigamous or unnatural; but all births are now illegitimate. As an alternative to this programme of yet larger, and relatively centralized, mergers it is perhaps worth re-considering the possibilities of the federal organization that the cotton unions still typify.

VI

TRADE UNION POLICY

1

Union Organization and Leadership

I

The cotton unions' federal form has several advantages by comparison with more centralized structures. Many of these arise from the cotton unions' foundation upon the autonomous local society. The reality of this local autonomy has been shown to extend not merely to such things as the rules by which the local unions are conducted, their subscriptions, benefits and so on, but to actual industrial policy. Thus one or two local Weavers' associations for some time refused, not merely to give positive support to the new weavers' wage-system already noted or to the 'redeployment' of labour in general, but actually to countenance their introduction into their area. On the other hand, although the Cardroom Amalgamation collectively refused until 1955–6 to accept both shift-working and wage-systems based on 'work-measurement' (which have generally been advocated since the War as an aid to efficient use of labour by managements as well as an incentive to productivity for operatives) one of its biggest Provinces—largely under its Secretary's influence—made several agreements with mills in its district providing for such new methods of work. If in fact, a local society feels so keenly about an issue that it is prepared to risk depriving itself of Amalgamation support in local negotiations and Amalgamation cash in disputes, it may assert its independence. While in the last analysis, there is always the right of secession. That this has been so little exercised is certainly not explained by the minor constitutional precautions with which some Amalgamations hedge it. It remains a fact: in the case of the Great Harwood Tapesizers' dispute with other districts of the Lancashire Amalgamated, for instance, the local society chose to remain divorced from its Amalgamation for several years.

The local union's autonomy imparts an intimacy to the relationship between the union official and the members, even in societies which might be regarded as 'popular bossdoms', which is often lacking in unions of more centralized constitutional types. This intimacy was perhaps somewhat damaged by the spread of the telephone—which made it possible for full-time officials to deal directly with managements if they wished to, instead of visiting the mill where a dispute arose. But the Weavers' local secretary, for instance, still remains his members' man, not the agent of some distant central or regional body. Whereas in some other unions the local organizer is obliged to manage his affairs with a main eye to the attitude of superior officials in the union hierarchy, the local cotton official must first look downwards to his members' desires and reactions. It is not merely that he is appointed and paid by the local society or its committee (we have illustrated the emphasis that local cotton union rules often put upon the formal 'employee' status of the Secretary). The limits to his assumption of the members' acquiescence are much narrower. If he exceeds them, he will soon be made aware of the fact by complaining members' visits to his office and by reports of union collectors or mill representatives. And that it is personally dangerous for him to exceed them has again been quite recently illustrated by the case of the Heywood Weavers' Secretary already referred to. Moreover, local autonomy necessarily enforces, even in unions where the generality of members is inactive, much more responsibility on lay committee-members than in the case of the branches of centralized national unions. In the smaller closed Amalgamations, of course, local management is often entirely in lay members' hands: and since in their members' case wages and working conditions are often effectively determined at the local or mill level, the full-time official not infrequently appears in the role of a friendly adviser from the Amalgamation rather than as an instrument of external policy.

On the other hand, the relative equality between the hundred or so local officials, and between them and the handful of full-time Amalgamation Secretaries, makes for plain speaking and direct dealing. And this, combined with the simplicity of the Amalgamation's own organization and the participation of lay delegates from the locals in the frequent Amalgamation meetings, all mean that local opinion and situations have a more direct and effective impact on central policy, while opinion in one locality is at the same time more immediately aware of conditions and feeling in other districts, than in unions where communication may be distorted or muffled in its passage through successive tiers of representation or an elaborate official hierarchy. In a sense, the institutional super-structure which has been a main product of the past century's trade union development is minimized by the cotton unions' federal organization.

This has also permitted a high degree of flexibility in the local unions' government and structure. Despite the general similarity of the different cotton operatives' associations, the detailed variety amongst them—in such matters as size, internal organization, the arrangement of committees and lay offices—illustrates their basic unit's adaptability to local circumstances, traditions and preferences. While—beyond one or two Amalgamation rules requiring that affiliated societies shall have properly elected committees—nothing prevents the local union from revising its organization as it pleases, or from experiment with new arrangements. And we saw too that a similar flexibility characterizes the relationship between the Amalgamation proper and the local union—so that in the Tapesizers even the original function of the Amalgamation as a central strike fund has now disappeared, and it remains essentially as an inter-district committee to prevent disputes arising from the movement of members and to deal with such few 'industry-wide' negotiations as their local unions are interested in, while on the other hand the Cardroom Amalgamation has itself now acquired a membership apart from that of its affiliated societies. The critical level of decision and action may thus shift from the local union to the central Amalgamation, or from that to a still broader federation like the UTFWA and back again, without this involving any constitutional upheaval.

These advantages, however, mainly concern the cotton unions' *formal* organization. And in the previous Chapter that was distinguished from the *effective* government of trade unions—which was roughly divided into three types, according to the extent to which it was dominated by full-time officials or by a particular section of the membership. But this was not to say that the power of a 'popular bossdom' or an 'aristocracy' within a union was absolute. Generally, however, the checks on that power do not consist primarily in opposition through the union's formal machinery so much as in certain extra-constitutional pressures. These pressures include those of inter-union competition: they also include the threat of 'unofficial movements' and 'breakaways' like those already referred to. And one of the less obvious merits of the cotton unions' system is that it has permitted pressures of this kind to operate, as some insurance that no substantial membership interest will be neglected, with little of the friction—and hence without the labels—by which they are identified in union structures of more heavily institutionalized types.

Thus, if the chance of *individual* lapses from membership is a relatively minor influence on union leaderships in general, competition for members *between* unions has been a much more effective pressure. And this is particularly true for the 'popular bossdoms' because—from the nature of their memberships, again—unions of this type are also those which are most likely to develop jurisdictional overlaps. A mere decline in membership is one thing: but a decline accompanied by the growth of a rival organization—which carries the possibility of dislodgement from established negotiating positions—is quite another. The implicit competition between the Weavers and unions like the Warehousemen for other operatives than weavers proper has been in the past a significant stimulus to the union leaders' care for such 'fringe' memberships. Similarly, in 'open' or 'mixed' unions outside the textile industries, the possibility of members drifting imperceptibly into another organization—still more, perhaps of a rival union's making greater headway among an as yet unorganized group—has been an important extra-constitutional pressure on union leaderships, which tended to keep them watchful to their more passive membership's desires.

But this possibility has been very greatly reduced, in recent years, by inter-union jurisdictional agreements, and by the TUC's own elaboration of a code of inter-union behaviour based essentially on the recognition of established 'organizing rights.'[1] True, the National Union of Public Employees has built itself up partly by a skilful, if risky, exploitation of the gaps between other unions' 'spheres of influence'. But on the other hand, in the major case where a state of formal inter-union rivalry still persists—among the railwaymen—actual membership competition appears negligible. Competition for members is much more difficult to suppress, however, when the organizations concerned are themselves federal bodies. And this is not merely because recruitment policy is a local matter, so that occupational overlaps between the federal organizations themselves tend to become more complex, but because of competition within the federation itself.

The fact that the exact geographical area of each local society within a cotton Amalgamation was not determined centrally but by local arrangement,[2] based largely on priority of organization in particular mills, thus encouraged an alertness on each local union's part to its attractiveness to workers as yet unorganized. Today, the Rules of the Amalgamations usually recognize their affiliates' vested 'membership rights'—requiring a worker moving to a new district

[1] See Shirley Lerner, op. cit., for a discussion of the interpretational development of the TUC's 'Bridlington Agreement'.

[2] Except—as usual—in the Tapesizers.

to transfer to the local society, but frowning on transfers of allegiance for other reasons.[1] But some unions have permitted members to retain their original district membership on moving if they so preferred.[2] And in the case of open unions it is not always easy to control transfers of membership by workers employed or living near the frontier between two locals. Moreover, the Amalgamations themselves have occasionally turned a blind eye to the transfer of members who might otherwise have lapsed because of inefficiency in their original local's administration. All this has exercised a certain pressure on local union leaderships.

Of course, other things being equal, competition for members is likely to be more important in new and expanding occupations and industries. But even where the possibility of new recruitment is negligible, the presence in the same trade of other unions, with alternative 'leadership styles' or combinations of sectional interest, may still serve as a stimulus to union leaders. The comparison between the Weavers' and Cardroom's agreements for winders in the neighbouring localities where they organize such workers—and between both these unions and the NUGMW's arrangements for doublers—has been some insurance against neglect of these operatives by any one of the unions to which they form only a subsidiary membership. And again, the effect is multiplied within a federal structure. The radicalism of the far North-Eastern cotton towns (Nelson itself was once popularly known as 'Little Moscow') may be variously explained: most reasonably, perhaps, by the immigration into this then rapidly-expanding district of victimized Socialist textile workers from the Yorkshire wool trades in the 1890s. But in the Weavers' Amalgamation, the relative aggressiveness of the local unions there has certainly exercised a continuing influence on other weaving districts. And generally, the mere contiguity of the different local cotton unions often subjects them to continual comparison with their neighbours. If one local Secretary's members are not employed in the same mill as another's, they often drink in the same pubs or shop in the same markets. This relative sensitivity of union officers and committees to membership sentiment has its drawbacks: in recent trade recessions, for instance, some Weavers' associations have been driven to raise their unemployment benefits against their officers' better judgement, so as to emulate neighbours who were better stocked or more profligate with funds. But at least, such experiences oblige them to take more pains with their members' instruction thereafter.

[1] For instance, Weavers' Amalgamation, *Rule* 7. And compare Spinners' Amalgamation, *Rules* 8 and 40.

[2] Cf. North Lancs. Cardroom Association, *Rule* 44.

In a sense, the cotton operatives' organization makes inter-union competition much more pervasive an influence on union policy. But just because this pressure operates—whether within or between Amalgamations—on a largely local basis, it is also too dispersed to damage inter-union relations. Charges of 'poaching' between cotton unions are almost unknown: they have never, for instance, been involved in cases before the TUC Disputes Committee. And certainly, competition has never hardened into the persistent mutual antagonism that characterizes relationships between certain non-textile unions.

II

At the extreme, of course, competition between unions has occasionally extended to the point of encouraging wholesale secessions from one of the parties to another. The existence of the independent Stevedores' Association has obviously been an important factor in the dockers' rebellions within the T & GWU. And in such affairs, there is always the chance that a union may balance the anathema it will incur by accepting a 'breakaway' membership from another against the accession of strength and numbers it might receive thereby, and choose the latter—as indeed happened, not merely in the case of the Northern dockers, but in that of the old cotton mill engineers' union, which recently achieved some small notoriety by embracing what the AEU considered a secession from itself.[1]

However, since 'voting with the feet' in trade unions generally takes a collective, rather than an individual form, even without the stimulus of an established rival organization the risk of such movements is an important extra-constitutional safeguard that those who may dominate a union's active government will not presume too far on the acquiescence of its more passive membership. Here again, however, the protective hardening of trade unionism's institutional structure in general has increased at the same time the obstacles that any secessionist movement will encounter and the tensions by which it will be accompanied. And by contrast, perhaps one of the most important qualities of the cotton operatives' federal organization has been its apparent flexibility to new interest groupings. In the modern textile unions' early development, it was shown how the first closed unions in cotton manufacturing seem to have split off from the early power-loom weavers' associations, and how several such small societies in the spinning industry left the Spinners to join the Cardroom or Warehousemen. This process was, of course, important mainly at a stage when the progress of collective association was still engendering distinct occupational identities among the

[1] See *TUC Reports* (National Engineers' Association).

cotton operatives. And it might be thought that this relative freedom to associate—and disassociate—would have since suffered from the rigidity which now affects union jurisdictions in general. But it too remains quite real.

Thus, the Amalgamated Society of Textile Workers and Kindred Trades, a Staffordshire silk workers' union, in 1950, decided that it was dwarfed by other unions which, though having no greater strength in the silk and narrow fabrics industry itself, brought the prestige of their great outside memberships into joint negotiations. The union's E.C. therefore recommended its 6,000 members, in their own interest, to merge with a bigger organization. But rather than those most obviously available—the two great general unions, and the big National Union of Dyers, Bleachers and Textile Workers—it chose to affiliate to the Weavers' Amalgamation. From six years' experience, however, the Staffordshire union decided that such a merger had after all little to offer it, because the bigger body's centre of interest naturally lay outside the silk trade. The union—to the Weavers' regret but with no ill-feeling on their part—then resumed its independence. This would have been quite impossible had it joined one of the big non-cotton unions.

The cotton unions' structure thus permits very much the elasticity of sectional alliance and regrouping that was envisaged in the TUC's 1924 recommendations for the reform of union organization at large—which were both more enterprising and less careful of existing vested interests than any made since. Secessions from existing unions seem, in fact, never to have been accompanied in cotton by the bitterness with which more centralized bodies have looked upon 'breakaways'. Even the small group of 'non-political' weavers' societies which was formed in North-East Lancashire between 1889 and 1906, apparently in reaction to the special domination of the established local unions by militant socialists, seem to have received a relative toleration.[1] They observed agreements made by local Weavers' Amalgamation affiliates, whose officials in turn negotiated with managements on the assumption that the result would apply to the 'non-political' societies' membership. Three of these societies were in the 1920s re-absorbed into regular unions, after the TUC had sponsored 'conciliation meetings'. And the last

[1] Three of these, Blackburn, Nelson and Preston, are shown in the *Main Chart* of Chapter III, 1, as 'Oppositionist Unions'. A fourth, Clitheroe, was linked with these in a federation of 'Weavers' Protection Societies'. Another independent association, of women weavers, existed in Manchester until quite recently: this was apparently a Catholic organization. Catholicism also seems to have been an influence in the North-Eastern secessions: the district was predominantly Nonconformist, and Methodists seem to have taken a leading part in local labour affairs.

of them merged peaceably with the Blackburn Weavers' Association in 1949. But up to that time it had belonged separately to the Northern Counties Textile Trades Association; and the Weavers' Amalgamation had already accepted it as an independent affiliate.

Secession from the cotton unions has thus rarely incurred the stigma of 'splitting'. But the 'breakaway' is often only the last stage of an 'unofficial movement'. And it is well known that in such demonstrations as unofficial strikes, workers who generally play a passive role in their union's affairs may display a surprising solidarity. The Cardroom Amalgamation's conclusion in 1949 of the 'Aronson' agreement, merging the separate area wage-lists that formerly existed for preparatory operatives, was greeted—to the apparent surprise of the local union officials—by a remarkably solid strike of cardroom women at Werneth Mill in the Oldham district, because the new standard scales had reversed the differentials amongst themselves to which they were accustomed. (Significantly enough, the area wage-lists for strippers-and-grinders had been excepted from the merger.) And what improvements in status the piecers gained within the Spinners' unions mainly followed on a threat of unofficial strikes or breakaways.[1] Similarly, one may perhaps speculate (for instance) how far Mr. Cousins' choice of a militant posture for his General Secretaryship of the T & GWU was determined by his predecessors' failure to contain such demonstrations by suppression.

But if the cotton unions are not without experience of such affairs, it seems equally true that their structure has provided poor soil for internal 'unofficial movements' of the systematic sort that have affected the engineers' and transport workers' unions since the First World War. There is an interesting contrast here between the cotton unions' Local Textile Trades Federations and those more universal inter-union bodies, the local Trades Councils. The latters' gradual recession from the prominence they enjoyed in late nineteenth-century trade unionism has been accompanied by persistent friction with the leaderships of the national unions. This has happened because the transfer of control from the locality to central union executives turned opponents of the officials' policy outwards, from their own now powerless union branches to the accessible inter-union bodies. If they were unable to change their own union's policy, they might at least then influence that of others. The Trades Councils, like the Joint Shop-Stewards' Committees in several industries, thus provided a natural platform for radical and 'militant' criticism of official union policy, and one from which

[1] See Chapter III, 2. Also 'Trade Unions, Differentials, and the Levelling of Wages' (loc. cit.) for some discussion of effects on piecers' relative wages.

would-be rivals to established leaders could advertise themselves. While for organized oppositionist fractions, the Joint Shop-Stewards' Committees at the workplace and the Trades Councils in the locality could be seen as offering the basis of an alternative system of labour organization to that of the national unions, cutting across the latters' structure and particularly adapted to mobilize class, rather than sectional, labour sentiment. Such fractions might be rarely able to gain the leadership of a national union: but a command of the *inter*-union bodies might still enable them to influence, and at critical moments dominate, industrial events themselves.

In defence, the national union leaderships were obliged to retaliate through the TUC.[1] The Trades Councils have been largely deprived of industrial functions, and rebuked for assuming political ones; while those that still retain the old form of a joint 'Trades Council and Labour Party' have been pressed to abandon it. In the inter-War period, of course, when the Trades Councils were an especial taget of the left-wing 'Minorities Movement', they were instructed to exclude Communists from office. The TUC still prescribes 'Model Rules' for them, keeps a register for 'recognized' Councils, warns them repeatedly against undesirable associations with outside bodies, and 're-organises' Councils that misbehave (one of the latest to have incurred this fate was the historic London Trades Council). The Local Textile Trades Federations have had no such troubled experience. They receded gracefully as their original main functions of organizing joint recruiting campaigns and sympathetic action in local strikes dwindled in importance. They still occasionally provide a useful service in bringing the help of one local union's official to another that lacks a full-time negotiator. But otherwise they are content to concern themselves with such necessary but minor tasks as concerting the holiday arrangements of a district's various mills.

The reason for this difference is that the Local Textile Trades Federations are composed of much the same people as those who determine the cotton Amalgamations' policies—the delegates (officials and lay members) of the local unions. So that no division between the central leadership and an active rank-and-file element arose. Similarly (and apart from a very brief outburst at the end of the First World War) the Spinners' shop clubs have never provided a basis for an unofficial 'shop-steward movement' because the shop clubs themselves control the local society—or in the bigger provinces, the branches which in turn nominate the provincial E.Cs. There was

[1] A rather similar conflict between the national union and the local *inter*-union organization seems to have occurred in the earlier growth of US trade unionism. See Ulman, *The Rise of the National Union* (op. cit.).

apparently a militant 'rank-and-file' group in the Oldham Cardroom Province about the end of World War I, perhaps influenced by the engineering shop stewards who are strong in the district (though this union was by then the biggest of the local cotton associations anyway). And it is possible that the unofficial 'grinders' locals' already referred to emerged from this movement. If so, they have since changed their original character significantly, having become rather an instrument of the strippers-and-grinders' 'aristocracy' than an oppositionist group. Similarly, the militant North-East Lancashire weaving unions have sometimes been led by impatience at what they regarded as the political caution of the majority in their own and other Amalgamations, in face of cotton trade depressions, into independent protests which have embarrassed the federal leadership.[1] But before World War I, *ad hoc* rank-and-file committees once or twice opposed, not the *caution* of union leaders, but the militancy of their industrial policy. And in general, systematic 'unofficial movements' have never been significant in the cotton unions because the critics of current policy have rarely been driven to extra-constitutional action—or have rarely felt it offered a better hope of success than the normal union procedure. There is nothing, save the necessity of securing enough members' votes, to prevent the critics replacing the existing local committeemen and Amalgamation delegates.

But this introduces one other advantage of the cotton unions' structure. Phenomena like inter-union competition, breakaways and unofficial movements do not destroy the difference, amongst unions generally, between the three effective governmental types. In the 'exclusive democracy' or the 'aristocracy', union government involves a high active participation, respectively by the membership at large and by a dominant section of it. But in the 'popular bossdom' —as for the inferior membership of an aristocratic union—democracy is more negative in character. Here, union government assumes only the members' consent; of this, however, it is by the extent or possibility of these extra-constitutional pressures that the effective limits are most indicated. Curiously enough, however, it is this quality that also makes the 'popular bossdom' particularly sensitive to penetration by any determined and systematically-organized group. Generally, inertia favours such a union's existing leaders. They are known, while their opponents are not: they occupy not merely the key-points in the union's administration but the main platforms from which the members may be addressed. An organized fraction,

[1] A history of the 1931 'Cotton Weavers' Delegation' to London is contained in a pamphlet written by Z. Hutchinson of Nelson, one of the participants, which is in the AWA's possession. A somewhat similar incident occurred in the first post-War II recession.

however, can somewhat offset these advantages by providing a ready-made leadership for the occasional demonstration of rank-and-file protest. And once both publicity and a platform have thus been secured, the low participation of members in union elections only facilitates the capture of union office by fraction methods.

Thus, in general, Communists have only achieved much power in British unions where they were able to identify themselves with historical—and often local—militancies specific to particular industries.[1] This has been so in the mines: and similarly, it is only in the traditionally-radical North-East that there has been any significant Communist influence in the cotton unions. But it was the T & GWU that sent the only Communist to have held a seat on the TUC General Council (except by accident), and just after the War had a sizeable Communist group on its own E.C., which had also appointed Communists to several important full-time posts. So that it is perhaps significant that what has here been suggested to be the T & GWU's nearest analogue in the cotton unions, the Weavers, should have the only three full-time officials who to the writer's knowledge are currently Communist: and that one of them should have raised a sizeable minority vote for his nomination to the Amalgamation's General Secretaryship at the last contest for that office.[2] And it is possibly just the relative vulnerability of unions whose very working implies a normally-low membership participation that explains why the trade union campaign against Communists that opened in 1949 should have found the then-leader of the T & GWU at its head. Unions of other types could afford to be more tolerant because they are naturally—and other things being equal—less susceptible to Communist tactics. In an 'exclusive democracy', or even an 'aristocracy', the effectiveness of fraction methods is normally diluted by a higher membership participation and a lower liability to rank-and-file protest movements.

If, however, the cotton unions' federal system avoids driving radical opposition into systematically-unconstitutional channels, it also makes it especially difficult for an organized fraction to secure control of a whole Amalgamation. In some more centralized unions, to capture two or three national offices would suffice to give such a

[1] So that the recent situation of the ETU seems—circumstances peculier to that union apart—explicable as being the one case in which Communists were able to exploit an association with the engineering industries' tradition of shop-steward militancy to the critical point of capturing the key union offices.

[2] One other, the Burnley Weavers' Secretary, was for a time a member of the Communist Party's Executive—until that body expressed an apparent disappointment in the cotton operatives' reaction to the post-war recessions by deleting them from the industries regarded as worthy of representation! The third is in Nelson, again.

fraction a dominating position. But in the cotton unions (as to a large extent in the Miners, who have been able to have both Communist General Secretaries and highly respectable policies) that would be of little use unless the fraction were able *independently* to control a majority of the Amalgamation's local affiliates—in which case it could hardly be regarded as a mere fraction any longer. Similarly, a mere change of personality in some leading office can make no such difference to an Amalgamation's character as it might in many outside unions. General policy must be the joint product of local opinions.

III

The dispersal of power over many local and sectional units improves the cotton unions' democracy. Whether it has helped or hindered the formation of common policies is another question. In one sense, it has certainly advanced that aim, because the different forms of federation which are available to the individual society make it possible for particular groups to support one front of common policy without supporting another that might otherwise have deterred them from any common association at all. Thus, the Cardroom Amalgamation affiliates to the Labour Party, to which some 90 per cent of its members pay a political levy. But this has not driven the United Roller-Coverers' Association from its membership of the Cardroom, although its Secretary is currently a Conservative and a bare dozen only of its 300 members pay the Cardroom's political levy. In effect, all that happens is that the Roller-Coverers make no contribution to the UTFWA (through which go the political links of the unions) while still supporting the Cardroom's industrial activity. On the other hand, the fact that the Lancashire Tapesizers' Amalgamation itself has no political affiliation does not prevent two or three local tapesizers' clubs from having their own political fund and supporting the Labour Party. In the industrial field itself, the Jacquard Gaiters' Union, a small society originally of specialist loom overlookers and confined to the Bolton district, has never joined the Overlookers' Amalgamation, considering its interests too distinct from those of that body's members. But it *has* joined the Northern Counties Textile Trades Association to participate in industry-wide wage-movements.

But in any case, common policy often seems easier to achieve between a number of small organizations than a few big ones. The smaller units have, other things being equal, a greater need of outside help, and to secure that, are prepared to concede more to outside opinion. The numerous local weavers' associations, for instance, which do not differ greatly in size, have clearly found it easier to arrive at a uniform wage-policy than have either the Cardroom or Spinners' Amalgamations, in each of which the two big Provinces of Bolton and Oldham not only confront each other but outnumber the memberships of other affiliates. Similarly, the Northern Counties Textile Trades Federation has for over half a century united the several Amalgamations in cotton-manufacturing for general wage-movements. The Spinners' and Cardroom Amalgamations in spinning, however, found it impossible to maintain an agreeable formal alliance between themselves alone.

But if some cotton unions are big to each other, they are small by comparison with several outside unions. And in the wider field, it is again interesting that the cotton workers should have been such faithful supporters of the General Federation of Trade Unions. Had that body succeeded in its original intent to become a common strike fund for the British trade union movement, it would have inevitably given the latter a central authority with much the same standing in relation to the separate national unions as the major cotton Amalgamations have with their local affiliates. It would, in effect, have made the British TUC Scandinavian. And it was, in part, just this reluctance to accept a closer external supervision that led the great non-cotton unions to withhold or withdraw their support.

Of course, common policy appears relatively easy to attain *inside* a single big organization where the power of decision is formally centralized. But in this case, the mere acquiescence of its central representative body, and the discipline its institutional form imposes on its members, may mislead its leaders both as to the support their programme commands and their ultimate ability to impose it. As in the T & GWU's experience of 'wage-restraint', the policy's attempted application may then provoke such growing internal friction as will not merely make it ineffective but endanger the cohesion of the union itself. In a federal organization, central policy must from the first rely on the persuasion that it accords with the final interest of the groups concerned.

By the nineteenth century's end, with their major groupings firmly established, a certain mutual recognition of sectional interests, and of those they shared in common, enabled the cotton unions to present very much the appearance of a common front to the outside world—so that in the TUC, for instance, the 'cotton men', despite the diversity of organizations they represented, appeared very much as a single block. And this identity was founded, not merely in a common trade interest, but in their officials' and members' sharing of certain traditional techniques, by then highly developed and effective. But all this was changed as the situation of the British cotton trade itself began to fall back from that of world dominance. And the great weakness of the cotton unions in recent years has been, not their lack of central *disciplinary* power—which is not essential to authoritative leadership—but rather the inadequacy of their means for developing *new* common policies and for expounding and publicizing them amongst their members.

Perhaps the most common self-criticism that one encounters from members of the cotton unions themselves is of excessive sectionalism—and such criticism has been persistent since the 1920s. The effects of this operate at several levels. In the district association itself, reluctance to surrender local independence has often been carried to the point of endangering the association's ability to maintain a viable existence. Jewkes and Gray noted after the inter-War slumps that many smaller spinners' unions were still unwilling to merge into larger units, although their diminished membership (and thus income) made it difficult for them to maintain an adequate service to members, much less to provide a full-time official.[1] Similarly several Weavers' locals now have less than 1,000 members, which makes it virtually impossible to pay an adequate salary to their Secretaries. The more intimate a society's control by lay members, the greater the likelihood of short-sighted management. And many cotton unions are peculiarly exposed to the democratic vice that their desire to bestow largesse on their members is not sufficiently moderated by their reluctance to tax their constituents and to finance the necessary administration. Smaller societies' benefits are often excessive in relation to their contributions: and this has been an obstacle to a better grouping of local units, because better-off locals are often unwilling to accept responsibility for their less provident neighbours. But as long ago as 1910 a scheme of the Spinners' E.C. for a centralized benefit fund, with standard local contributions to provide minimum benefits over the range then covered haphazardly by Spinners' locals, fell through.[2] It was only quite recently that the unions began to provide reasonably for their officials' retirement, and that on an initiative (in 1943) from the then Chairman of UTFWA. The Weavers' Amalgamation General Council was wise enough to resist a proposal that its own superannuation scheme be submitted to a district ballot: it was symptomatic both of the need for such a scheme and the likely attitude of the members to it that on its subsequent introduction seven out of the seventy-odd officials covered should have promptly retired. Similarly, local unions are often unwilling to provide their officers with cars, thus compelling them to spend a deal of time in buses and trains that might be saved

[1] *Wages and Labour in the Cotton Spinning Industry* (op. cit.) p. 160.

[2] The *Manchester Guardian* for November 6, 1911 carried a report of the experience.

for the unions' own work. But the downfall of the former Heywood Weavers' secretary is said to have begun with his extracting a car allowance from his Committee.

Many such democratic pettinesses could be avoided if the Amalgamations themselves could do more to educate their members in good administration and the need for it. But the resources, even of the major Amalgamations, are barely adequate to the prime functions of collective bargaining which have been entrusted to them. And they have become less so with the growth of the TUC General Council's responsibilities: the Secretaries of the two biggest cotton Amalgamations have usually played a prominent role in that body, and now spend a large part of their time on its affairs.[1] The Amalgamation's own officers would usually be unable to deal with all requests for negotiating assistance, or with the local disputes referred to it, were it not for the help of senior local officials; and the latter commonly take part in central negotiations. The arrangement works admirably when the issue is of a kind within the officials' experience, and to which their high traditional techniques can be applied. But it seems much less adequate to new problems of the sort raised by much of the past generation's development in industrial relations. The Weavers' post-war 'CMC Wage System', for instance, was based on a scheme prepared by industrial consultants, who used an ingenious mathematical technique to reconcile certain traditional wage-differentials with the need to relate operatives' earnings and work-loads more equitably. It was also presented in a mathematical form derived from the 'incentive wage-systems' of contemporary 'scientific management' practitioners, and superficially alien to the established cotton wage-lists' principles.[2] This form, however, incidentally concealed an important departure from the traditional system. It was an effect of the Weavers' old 'Uniform List' that the operatives' earnings rose automatically—and quite apart from any consequential increase in machine-complements—as technical improvement raised their output. And this effect the new 'CMC

[1] The Cardroom's General Secretary, for instance, has for some time been the British Workers' Delegate to the ILO, as well as Chairman of the TUC's Social Insurance Committee. The Weavers' General Secretary was until recently Chairman of the British Productivity Council.

[2] The CMC System relates earnings to a percentage of 'attained efficiency'. The traditional Uniform List provides for a payment per yard of standard cloth produced, to which various additions are made for variations from standard conditions. It took the present writer nearly two days of mathematics to discover that the CMC System was also based on a similar payment per yard of cloth produced, to which similar major additions were made for variations from standard conditions. The essential difference between the two systems of payment was a method of adjusting the standard price per yard (together with the operative's work-load) 'scientifically'.

System' largely eliminated. Now this was arguably a desirable result: but it does not appear that its likelihood ever became clear, at least in the open discussions that preceded the Weavers' Amalgamation's acceptance of the new system.[1]

On the other hand, the CMC Wage System was introduced as of an urgency that the Weavers' Amalgamation accepted, and after elaborate enquiries supervised by a government-appointed commission whose report—to which Weavers' representatives subscribed—concluded that 'The Uniform List must go'. Six years after their Amalgamation signed the agreement, however, 90 per cent. of weavers were still paid on the traditional system.[2] The Weavers' Amalgamation was thus lacking in resources both to deal with an unfamiliar expertise, and to persuade its affiliates to press a novel policy: and the Weavers have been one of the more forward-looking groups. That the Amalgamations should be staffed on shoestring budgets is, however, only partly attributable to the unwillingness of their rank-and-file to pay for more adequate central services. Spread over the membership of a major Amalgamation, the cost of one or two additional officers would be insignificant. It is fairly clear that a critical factor has been the attitude of the local Secretaries to anything likely to raise the standing of their Amalgamation's officials in relation to themselves.

A similar problem, however, has affected the possibilities of co-ordination between the Amalgamations themselves. The cotton unions' constitutional system, combined with their (at least, preliminary) selection of full-time officials by examination, has produced officials of a remarkably high type, with qualities going far beyond those of mere 'calculators' (as the writer has heard them described by outside trade unionists). They are generally men not merely very well-versed in trade and technical matters, but occupying prominent positions in local political and social life, and individually shrewd, blunt and self-reliant, balanced and reasonable. And despite the differing relationships between official and members in individual unions, there is little doubt—as the part played by the officials in the cotton unions' reorganization of the 1880s indicates—that had the various officers of the major Amalgamations acted as a group, they could have radically affected the cotton operatives' response to their

[1] The point is, for instance, not brought out in the 'History and Mathematics of the CMC System', an explanatory pamphlet issued by the Weavers' Amalgamation in 1950.

[2] 'Plan for Cotton' (UTFWA, 1957), Appendix I, Table VIII. The last published figure is for 1955, but the writer has no evidence that the CMC System had extended much further before the 1960 'concentration' of the industry scrapped most of the old-style looms. Indeed, in 1955 the number of weavers on it had actually fallen.

twentieth-century situation. Yet it was perhaps just in the broadest area of the unions' federal activity—where they are dealing with problems of the cotton trade as a whole—that the problem of relations between the officials has been most important.

IV

In the British cotton trade's economic debacle of the 1920s, and the long inter-War doldrums into which that merged, internal disunity in face of the trade's problems was by far its most commonly attributed vice; though whether other industries, exposed to a crisis similarly acute, would have displayed any greater measure of accord is an open question. At any rate, reported an independent research organization in 1934: 'The industry is rent by acute sectionalism . . . Numerous sound ideas for partial reforms have been put forward since the war but have broken down (partly) through lack of agreement in the industry and internal, often personal, dissensions . . .'[1] While even the *Encyclopaedia Britannica* noted '. . . a lack of co-ordination, with each section considering the others guilty of unfair practice, and each anxious to exact the maximum return for its services without regard for the possible consequences to the general interest'.[2] So that if the cotton operatives were affected by the same vice, they might fairly claim that it was less in consequence of any internal defects of their own organizations than by contagion from their employers.

But the unions represented the common interests of the operatives, while the employers were still avowedly in competition with each other. Yet it is at the level of the cotton trade as a whole that sectionalism has had its most damaging impact on the cotton operatives' affairs. And though this was, perhaps, particularly evident in the inter-War period, it in fact became pretty apparent in the years of general trade union growth and labour militancy that preceded the First World War. By then it had already become customary for a change in the wage-rates of any important group of operatives to be followed by other sections. Even before the Weavers' Uniform List of 1892, alterations in Blackburn wages had generally set a pattern for the manufacturing trade as a whole. Similarly, the level of the Oldham Spinners' Wage-list had before the 1890s become critical to wage-rates in the spinning industry at large. But by the early years of this century, it had also become virtually impossible for wage-movements in one of the two industries not to be mirrored in the other.

Nevertheless, formal 'industry-wide' bargaining developed

[1] *Report on the British Cotton Industry*, of PEP Industries Group (PEP, London, 1934) p. 5.

[2] *Encyclopaedia Britannica;* Fourteenth Edition, on 'Cotton'.

separately for the spinning and weaving trades, extending its area with the consolidation of the employers' organizations and the gradual replacement of surviving local and specialist wage-lists by—or their merger into—the major spinning and weaving agreements. And in the spinning trade particularly, its practice was greatly hampered by inter-union disagreement. In 1908, for instance, the Cardroom Amalgamation's rejection of a wage-cut which the Spinners had accepted led to the whole spinning industry being locked out for several weeks. And in 1913 the Spinners withdrew independently from that industry's revised 'Brooklands' Agreement on negotiating procedure. But although a new procedure agreement was negotiated within a year or so, the two spinning unions were again divided in 1918 when the Cardroom held aloof from the other cotton unions' protests against proposed changes in a war-time system of 'work-sharing' and special unemployment compensation, while on the other hand the Spinners' Amalgamation carried its opposition to the point of a (then illegal) strike.

However, the weakness in inter-union co-ordination was still more important in the relations between the two industries. Thus, the two spinning Amalgamations' acceptance in 1910 of a five-year standstill of wage-rates prejudiced the prospect of wage-advance for the manufacturing unions—which were unable to secure any increase for three years from 1912. And from 1915 to 1918 the weaving operatives were unable to improve on wage-advances previously-accepted by the spinning unions—although these amounted to only about half the war-time increase in living costs, and cotton profits were then still kept at comfortable levels by scarcity. Only in World War I's last year was a synchronizing of wage-movements achieved. And in December 1918, a week's strike of the combined industries forced real wage-rates nearly back to their pre-war level.

After this success, the unions formally recognized their interdependence by presenting their 1919 demand for a 44-hour working week (it had previously been fixed at 55½ hours by the 1901 Factory Act) and for further wage-increases through the UTFWA. And the consequent general strike of cotton operatives within a day or two secured a compromise agreement, that included a reduction of working hours to 48. But that was repudiated by the Spinners' delegate meeting (which is by rule required to approve all general agreements). And the Spinners' refusal to return to work extended the stoppage for nearly a fortnight as a lock-out—in which the employers were able to take the position that the dispute was essentially one between the unions.[1] After this, the Spinners demanded a stronger voice in

[1] In the upshot the stoppage ended with a limited additional concession on wages.

centralized negotiations than was secured them by their merely numerical representation on the UTFWA's 'Legislative Council'. And it was agreed to handle such matters through the necessarily clumsy method of combined meetings of all the Amalgamations' Executive Committees instead.

In the following year, however—1920—the major groups made separate claims for wage-increases, the Cardroom outbidding the Spinners and Weavers—though the unions' strike-threats necessarily secured only standard advances (except for certain higher- and lower-paid men[1]). But just afterwards the post-war boom broke. The 1920 agreement had been dated for one year only: and on its expiry the unions were unable, despite a three weeks' strike, to hold their gain from it in face of the employers' concerted demand for a wage-reduction. Some Amalgamations were dissatisfied with the result, and in February 1922, the Cardroom resolved not to submit to joint negotiations through the UTFWA thereafter. Almost immediately, the employers demanded a further wage reduction, and notices of another stoppage were served. But the Cardroom Amalgamation made an independent (if tentative) agreement to accept a substantial wage-cut. The other unions tried for better terms, but the Cardroom's concession made it pointless to carry their objection to the point of a strike and they were obliged to accept the same reduction. Thus, the brief negotiating unity the major unions had achieved at World War I's end failed the test of the great post-war crisis.

Disunity between the Amalgamations was also a factor in the events that culminated in the great four-week stoppage of the weaving industry in 1932, which was to be the last real mass strike by British workers for twenty-five years.[2] For several years after 1922, the level of standard wage-rates was held—though the unions had frequent notice of their now exposed position from local reports of employers' departures from agreed conditions. And this warning was confirmed by the Masters' Associations issuing, in 1928, proposals for improving trade of which the most definite was an increase in the working week with less pay.[3] The onset of the second inter-War slump in 1929 persuaded many employers who had previously hesitated that matters should be forced to an issue. The Master Spinners decided to enforce acceptance of a wage-cut on the unions by a lock-out. The three weeks' stoppage was ended

[1] One of the demands of the Oldham-centred Cardroom 'ginger group' referred to in section ii had been for a £5 general minimum weekly wage.

[2] That is, up to the engineering and shipbuilding strike of 1957—which though much shorter, naturally involved greater numbers of workpeople.

[3] In the *Reports on the State of Trade* of the Federation of Master Cotton Spinners and the Cotton Spinners & Manufacturers' Association for the year 1927.

by the Prime Minister's persuading both sides to accept arbitration. But divisions between the unions had already become apparent. The spinning and weaving groups had been negotiating separately with the employers; and when the arbitrators awarded a reduction, there was a movement among the Weavers (accompanied by several local stoppages) to withdraw from the inter-union bodies, as well as for an independent wage-claim to recover their lost ground. The Weavers actually took a ballot which returned a large majority for striking, but their General Council decided the number of abstentions did not justify action on it.

At this time the Weavers were themselves becoming the main target of employers' attempts to reduce costs. In concession to employers' pressure, their Amalgamation had accepted an experimental scheme for 'more looms per weaver' in certain Burnley mills. But at the end of 1930 the manufacturers announced their intention to extend the scheme, and introduce new piece-rates based on it, despite the Weavers' objections. So on New Year's Day of 1931 the Weavers called out the 'Burnley Experiment' mills; and the employers retaliated by a general lock-out of weaving operatives. In the previous month, however, registered unemployment in the cotton industry had reached a peak of 47 per cent., and the Weavers' rank-and-file now resisted any proposals (including an initiative from the then-Labour Government) that their leaders re-open negotiations on the 'more looms' issue. The determination with which the operatives met the lock-out was, in fact, probably explained by their fear that 'more looms per weaver' would increase unemployment. (Their leaders' concern had been more with the very real risk that individual firms would apply 'more-looms' piece-rates to the workers on normal four-loom complements: they had demanded a 'fall-back wage' as a condition of the system's acceptance). On the other side, however, the success of the Weavers' resistance may be attributed partly to divisions that developed among the employers as soon as the Weavers' obstinacy became plain: many firms were not particularly anxious (or able) to adopt 'more looms', and had first seen the issue merely as good ground on which to isolate and challenge the biggest union Amalgamation. At any rate, in the stoppage's fourth week the employers called off the lock-out.

How far the Weavers had the sympathy of other cotton unions in their struggle of early 1931 is uncertain.[1] Despite the apparent

[1] A. Whewell, in a useful but unpublished thesis on these disputes for a Manchester University B.A. (Hons.) 1950, quotes some evidence against contemporary Press suggestions that other cotton unions did not approve the Weavers' attitude. But it is fairly clear from the next year's events that other unions' militancy was less pronounced than the Weavers'.

solidity of that demonstration, their Amalgamation was unable to prevent a piecemeal spread of 'more looms' working to other districts—so that in the following year the manufacturers' Association was to use 'unfair competition' from firms operating it as a leadering argument for a general wage-reduction. And in the upshot the Amalgamation, having spent[1] 'at a conservative estimate' £700,000 within four years in strike pay for disputes connected with 'more looms', was obliged to negotiate an agreement to facilitate the system's introduction in spite of the leadership's unresolved doubts about the consequence. But this came only as part-settlement of the climactic conflict of 1932. And meanwhile the employers' pressure was temporarily switched to the cotton trade's other branch.

At the end of 1931 the employers' federation in the spinning industry demanded that the unions there negotiate a longer working week and, when the unions refused, terminated their agreements —thus leaving individual mills free to make local deals on the matter. But the spinning unions took no direct and general retaliatory action. The Master Spinners' tactic was then repeated by the manufacturing employers, when the Northern Counties Federation in early 1932 rejected their demand that the weaving unions negotiate on an unspecified wage-cut whilst accepting in advance that a reduction was necessary. The Weavers, however, took the renunciation of collective agreements as a blow to the principle of collective bargaining, and accused the manufacturers' association of giving 'impetus to this movement of guerrilla warfare' that breaches of agreement by individual firms had already launched.[2] But despite the Weavers' anger, opinion in the smaller manufacturing Amalgamations was against strike action; and the unions finally agreed to negotiate on definite proposals from the employers for a general wage-reduction —the Northern Counties Federation had already denied its competence to discuss certain selective adjustments to the wage-rates of particular operatives which the employers had additionally demanded.

But in the Burnley district—the focus of the previous year's conflict—employers cut wages without waiting for the negotiations. And here the Weavers struck independently—a decision that '. . . strained the relations of the various textile (workers') organisations almost to breaking point.'[3] But the Burnley Weavers were supported by the Warehousemen's and Twisters' unions, the Weavers expelled members who accepted work in the firms concerned, and the district

[1] Amalgamated Weavers' Association, *Report* for 1933.
[2] *Ibid.* For instance, many firms were covertly cutting wage-rates by levying 'contributions to capital' from their workers.
[3] *Ibid.*

strike continued until after four weeks it merged in a general stoppage. The central negotiations, in fact, finally broke down on the employers' failure to guarantee re-instatement of the Burnley strikers.[1] It was this, and the lack of assurance about employers' observance of future collective agreements, that finally persuaded the Northern Counties Federation to call out all the manufacturing industry's operatives.

The weaving unions' strike at least succeeded, after a month's general stoppage, to the extent that the final wage-cut was only about half that first demanded by the manufacturers' association—and that it produced (by the so-called 'Midland' Agreement) not only an improved conciliation system but a joint understanding that later led to legislative enforcement of the weavers' wage-lists. By now, not a few weaving employers were disturbed at the implications to themselves of a widespread non-observance of collective agreements. But the manufacturing settlement was immediately adopted by the spinning employers as the model for a notice of wage-reduction to their own workers. The Cardroom Amalgamation's E.C. accepted the cut with only a slight amendment; the Spinners' delegates rejected it, but ballots showed insufficient rank-and-file support to continue the resulting stoppage, which had meanwhile briefly involved some 130,000 spinning operatives. It was, in any case, then too late for effectual resistance on the latters' part.

It is perhaps significant that the Weavers' Central Committee should have concluded its account of 1932's events: 'It is extremely difficult to maintain an equanimity, but yet it is essential that bickerings amongst ourselves should not be allowed to predominate . . . all officials should be pulling their weight against the economic and industrial storms confronting us.' At any rate, at almost every stage of their great inter-War conflicts, the cotton operatives' position was clearly weakened by open disunity or, at best, a lack of co-ordination between the separate Amalgamations. And one could continue the recital into the cotton workers' wage-history from the Second World War on, if there the effects have not been so grave. Since 1939, wage-rate increases in the two industries have been almost identical. Yet at the UTFWA's 1952 Conference, for instance, a resolution demanding closer co-operation in negotiations was supported by the statement that the two spinning Amalgamations'

[1] The *Ministry of Labour Gazette* for 1932 commented (p. 360) '. . . although one isolated issue may appear to be the immediate cause of the stoppage it is clear that it has arisen from the virtual breakdown of the system of collective negotiations in this section of the cotton industry. For the past three years there has not been a single subject on which it has been found possible to reach general agreement.'

previous acceptance of an unusual 'once-for-all' bonus on 1951 earnings (in partial settlement of the larger increase in standard rates that the unions first demanded) had virtually imposed the same settlement on the manufacturing operatives despite their objection to it. While in reply, the Cardroom's General Secretary referred matters back to the negotiations of 1939 (when a 'cost-of-living' adjustment was arranged that was carried over the early war years). The unions had then agreed to evade the employers' desire to keep wage-bargaining divided by maintaining a liaison. But the weaving unions had modified their claim without consulting the spinning operatives' negotiators. And so on.[1] The effects of inadequate policy co-ordination moreover, overflow into other aspects of the operatives' employment. The Weavers', for instance, have been prepared to work Saturday mornings on a two-shift system provided it is paid at extra rates. The spinning unions opposed Saturday working altogether. But it is impossible to have different shift arrangements for the various departments of a 'combined' mill. However, perhaps the greatest failing of common policy in the cotton unions has been in confronting the industry's renewed decline since 1952.

V

The British cotton trade's contraction was resumed, after World War II, in circumstances quite different from those of the inter-war period. In the first place, the decline of the 1950s followed several years of intensive pressure to modernize the industry's methods and equipment. After the United States' entry into the war, the cotton industry (till then treated as an earner of essential foreign exchange) was 'concentrated', under government direction, to release labour and resources for war production. But the post-war Labour government was faced on the one hand with a critical need to restore the depleted balance of foreign payments, and on the other with an equally urgent domestic demand for the metal products and coal that might otherwise have been readily sold abroad. It saw in the world shortage of textiles, and the disorganization of European and Oriental textile industries, an opportunity to rehabilitate the cotton industry as a major export trade. The wartime Cotton Control Board was given peacetime legal standing as a joint body to promote the industry's development. The industry was

[1] There is some note of War and post-War cotton wage-movements, with particular reference to their relation with wage-differentials, in 'Trade Unions, Differentials, etc . . .' (loc. cit.). See also Miss G. Evans, 'Wage Rates and Earnings in the Cotton Industry, 1946 to 1951" (*Manchester School*, September 1953).

subjected to propaganda, advice and inducement to raise its productivity. Spinning concerns that would re-group into units officially considered large enough to be economical were offered subsidies for re-equipment. Enterprises that might compete with the cotton trade for labour were for a while prevented from expanding or establishing themselves in the cotton area by building controls. Under the auspices of the Cotton Board or other publicly-supported bodies, surveys were made of the trade's equipment and joint missions sent to the United States and other countries to compare their textile techniques. And as part of this drive to re-construct what had become during the inter-War years one of the British economy's most depressed sectors, there were those official enquiries into cotton wage-systems and working methods already referred to.

The effect of all this is not easy to assess. A careful estimate of post-War changes in the cotton worker's productivity put this as showing no change up to 1951 (the peak of the post-War expansion) in the spinning section, and increasing by 2 per cent. yearly in the weaving industry.[1] Over the same period, the present writer estimated that labour *utilization* (i.e. the ratio between machine-hours and worker-hours) was declining by 1 per cent. each year in spinning, and rising by 1 per cent. annually in weaving.[2] Together the two estimates suggest that re-equipment barely balanced the effect of that dilution of the labour force with inexperienced workers which was necessary to restore its strength to near its pre-war figure, and that the principal gain in the cotton trade's efficiency was attributable to the 'more looms per weaver' movement—which the Weavers' Amalgamation (thanks partly to the Labour government's persuasion) now supported. This movement, the 'CMC Weaving Wage System' was designed to encourage: and it would account for the manufacturing industry's advance in labour productivity and utilization compared with spinning. And yet re-equipment was quite extensive: even before the new 'concentration' of 1960 eliminated much of the older plant, at least one-sixth of spinning capacity had been installed since the War; and new capital expenditure seems to have been of the same order in manufacturing.[3]

[1] K. S. Lomax, 'Recent Productivity Change in the British Cotton Industry', *Bulletin, Oxford Institute of Statistics*, April 1953.

[2] In 'Measuring Unemployment', *Journal*, Royal Statistical Society. Series A, Part I, 1955. It is, of course, difficult to calculate the effect of technical improvement since 1951, because labour productivity and utilization have both been intermittently affected by under-employment. An increase in average productivity should certainly have followed the 1960 'concentration', however.

[3] The Chairman of the Cotton Board estimated (*Manchester Guardian*, March 26, 1952) that £60 million had been spent on all re-equipment since the war: a statement by the FMCSA a few months later put the spinners' expenditure at

However, such averages conceal an important tendency for the differences in efficiency between mills to widen. It was noted by several observers at the peak of the post-war recovery, that in both spinning and weaving a great range of efficiencies existed, and that the gap between older and newer techniques in operation was widening.[1] A similar differentiation marked the industry's attempts to capture and consolidate new markets. 'The future of the industry,' wrote one observer, 'lay in its own power to a much greater extent than it did before the war . . . it has not taken advantage of its greater potentialities.'[2] Thus, if the response of the unions to the post-war modernization drive was uneven, so was that of the employers. In each of the four years up to 1951, the reported profits[3] of cotton companies exceeded those of any year since the fantastic boom of 1919–20. But some firms continued to run down their old (often paid-off) plant, accumulating reserves and spending little on managerial re-organization. While others chose to re-invest a large part of their profits in new equipment, acquiring a proportionate interest in methodological improvement. This division represents a quite natural divergence in the reaction of firms to future uncertainty. But it was a fact of some importance to union policy, because it implied that many employers were substituting labour for the more permanent expenses of new capital equipment or (since the latter usually involves an increased ratio of staff to operatives) of managerial improvement.

The second difference from the industry's inter-War experience was that the new post-War contraction took place in a situation of high employment in the economy at large. At root, its source was a resumption of the foreign competition which had already reduced the proportion of cotton products exported from over four-fifths in 1913 to less than one-third in 1951, and was to make Britain a net importer of cotton goods by 1958—but which now came almost as much from high-wage European as from low-wage Oriental industries. The decline, however, was now complicated by several other factors which had before the war been either insignificant or

£30 million. However, the Post-War Committee of the war-time Cotton Board had estimated firms' investment requirements at about £75 million (at post-war prices) in the first five post-war years.

[1] See, for instance, the *Reports* of the 'Productivity Missions' to the United States on Cotton Spinning (March 1950) and on Cotton Manufacturing (June 1950). E. Devons, in a paper to the 1949 Cotton Board Conference, 'The Future of Prices and Costs in the Cotton Industry', commented on the wide range of actual spinning costs for similar counts.

[2] B. Vitkovitch in 'The U.K. Cotton Industry, 1937-54', *Journal of Industrial Economics, July 1955.*

[3] Estimated from Frederick W. Tattersall's 'Cotton Trade Review' (Annual).

concealed by the export market's overwhelming importance. A growing use of continuous synthetic filaments instead of spun yarn and an accelerated substitution of ring- for mule-spindles increased the recession's impact on the spinning industry. And superimposed on it were fluctuations attributable to the enlarged importance of the home market for textiles, and to the cotton industry's own structure. The fact that consumers may postpone clothing purchases made textiles peculiarly sensitive to fluctuations in real wages and to the competition of such new mass luxuries as TV.[1] While, given the 'horizontal' specialization of textile firms, any swing in the final demand for cotton products was greatly amplified by the speculative accumulation or unloading of semi-finished stocks at the different stages of production—so that in the first post-war recession of 1952, for instance, active employment fell by 49 per cent. in cotton spinning and 26 per cent. in cotton weaving, as against 17 per cent. in textile finishing and a cut of only some 6 per cent. in consumers' demand. And a similar 'acceleration' in the incidence of under-employment from the final stage of production to those nearer the raw material certainly appeared in the 1954 recession.[2] It follows that employment in the spinning industry increased disproportionately in the boom to 1951, and again from 1952 to 1954: again, an implication which might have been thought of some relevance to trade union policy.

Thirdly, of course, the Lancashire cotton trade's renewed withdrawal of the 1950's was covered by much greater government support than its inter-war retreats. In particular, as a systematic attempt to eliminate surplus and obsolescent capacity the 1960 'concentration scheme' went very much further than the so-called 'Spindles Act' of the 1930s. Under the Cotton Industry Bill of 1959, the government proposed to pay two-thirds of the cost of eliminating surplus plant in each of the trade's main sections—spinning, doubling, weaving, and finishing—subject to firms in the section concerned having registered a minimum proportion (which amounted to about a quarter) of its capacity for scrapping by March of 1960. The Cotton Board was authorized to raise a statutory levy on cotton firms to finance the residual cost of the scrapping programme: in point of fact the plant actually registered amounted to nearly half

[1] The initial slump of 1951–52 was attributable to a fall in home market sales, in turn associated with a temporary fall in average real income, and with the first boom in TV sales. See 'The Slump in the Cotton Industry, 1952' (*Bulletin, Oxford Institute of Statistics*, April 1954) by Mr Roland Smith and the present writer.

[2] For a detailed examination of this 'accelerator' effect, see the present writer's 'Unemployment in Textiles: a Note and Some Conclusions' (*Bulletin, Oxford Institute of Statistics*, October 1953).

of the capacity in spinning and over two-fifths of that in weaving, and the Board finally estimated the total distributed in compensation to the firms involved to be some £16½ million. But beyond this, the government also undertook to pay one quarter of the cost of re-equipment carried out by the firms remaining in the trade, up to a total grant (for scrapping and modernization together) of £30 million within the following five years. While during the period of the 'concentration', the British cotton trade received some further protection from the agreement (negotiated with government assistance) of producers in Hong Kong, India and Pakistan to restrict exports to the United Kingdom for a period—then, to 1962—and thus to temporarily limit foreign competition in the British home market.

These measures were justified as enabling the British cotton industry to put itself in order to stand independently, on a narrower but sounder base of economic competition. How widespread was the desire to take advantage of that opportunity amongst firms is, of course, another question: in early 1961 the total expenditure proposed by them for the re-equipment subsidy amounted to only £20 million.[1] But if the textile trade represents perhaps the extreme case of public assistance to the re-organization of private enterprise, in other respects the cotton industry's experience was only unique in that it was the first to be affected by a major recession since the British government became committed to 'full employment'. In so far as foreign competition was largely due to the diffusion of modern textile techniques to less advanced economies, it could be expected to overtake any industry whose trade was based on the advantage of an early technological start. Other industries are affected by technical change. The share of output devoted to durable consumers' goods rises as living standards rise, so that an increasing sector of employment is liable to disproportionate reactions from marginal changes and shifts in general consumption. And in any 'horizontally-organized' sequence of production and distribution, fluctuations in its final demand are likely to be greatly amplified at the early stages of the process.

In kind, then, if not in degree, practically all the phenomena that affect the cotton operatives' employment prospects are to be found in other industries than theirs. If, for instance, the cotton trade was the great mass-production industry of the nineteenth century, car and motor vehicle manufacture has been the typical mass-production industry of the twentieth. The British motor industry's output curve still has the apparent dynamism of the early cotton trade's. But its

[1] According to Sir Alfred Roberts in a lecture 'The Effects of the Concentration Scheme on Labour' to the Textile Institute, February 7, 1961.

remarkable post-war rise was at least half-based on exports, in which British motor firms had a temporary advantage but which have recently encountered accelerating foreign competition. Meanwhile the car trade in general has taken on a distinct cyclical pattern—with three recession in the decade from 1950. And as in the cotton case, demand cycles are complicated and magnified by the motor industry's own structure. So that the cotton unions' problems in the post-war period may not prove untypical of those other unions may come to confront.

VI

At any rate, the cotton operatives have at least experienced a pretty full range of the problems brought to trade unions since the war by that 'guided', 'mixed' and 'full employment' economy in the creation of which their own movement's pressure has played a major part. To the cotton unions' attitude in the first phase of their post-war experience—that of the Government-stimulated modernization drive—several references have already been made. In the second phase—of renewed contraction—they made no obvious withdrawal from such co-operation to modernization and 're-deployment' as they had already extended. Rather the reverse, indeed: acceptance of shift-working, for instance, widened after the first post-war recession. The Weavers in 1955 began to make conditional agreements with individual firms for three-shift working. The other major cotton union, the Cardroom Amalgamation, still rejected that—at least, until 1960, when it consented to the introduction of night shifts in spinning rooms proper: though this was partly to facilitate the re-employment of redundant mule spinners, and did not affect its key membership of cardroom men. And the UTFWA was never entrusted with shift negotiations. But at least the Cardroom Amalgamation in 1956 formally agreed to the introduction of double *day*-shifts and wage-systems based on 'work measurement', of a kind that it had also earlier refused.

Beyond this, however, the unions reacted in a way which was strongly conditioned by their memories of the inter-war recessions. They were faced with no such demands for industry-wide reductions in wage-rates as accompanied the inter-war slumps, because wages and prices generally were rising. Instead, they continued to make combined wage demands: but whereas up to 1951 wage-rates in the cotton industry had risen rather faster than the national average, the unions since seem to have been satisfied if cotton wage-rates kept pace with the cost-of-living, rather than the general level of wages.[1] The unions also attempted to maintain the operatives' hourly earnings in line with their wage-rates. The revised piece-rate systems introduced after the war usually included a 'fall-back' around 80 per cent. of 'target' earnings. And the Weavers, particularly, secured a pronouncement from the Manufacturers' Association against the system of 'under-employment' (scaling down the individual weaver's machine-complement, and therefore his or her earning power) which had in the inter-war slumps reduced the earnings of some weavers for full-time work to less than the public unemployment benefit.[2] But, with the exception of one or two closed societies—which were in any case generally able somewhat to offset the labour surplus by tightening their entry controls—the unions made no attempt to keep up the operatives' *weekly* wages. To the contrary, in fact: they supported systems of short-time working which effectively shared out the available employment (and thus earnings) among the operatives remaining on the payrolls.[3] And it was not until 1958 that the unions also demanded the compensation of operatives for actual redundancy.

The unions were undoubtedly correct to maintain a willingness to co-operate in modernization after the post-war recession's onset. The direct effect of re-equipment and re-deployment was often labour-saving. But the long-run prospects of employment and high wages in the industry depended on its efficiency in competing with other textile producers and other products. Indeed, the unions might well have gone further in discriminating between employers who were prepared to modernize and those who were not. The Weavers' Amalgamation would only accept, for instance, double-shift working in re-equipped, or at least substantially redeployed, mills.[4] But such measures were negative, in the sense that they merely reduced *obstacles*

[1] From 1951 to mid-1959, for instance, wage-rates in the cotton industry rose by about 30 per cent., against a national average increase of over 50 per cent. (Calculated from Table 4 of 'An Index of Wage-Rates by Industries', by Ely Devons and R. C. Ogley, *Manchester School*, May 1958). Over the same period, the general level of consumers' retail prices also rose by about a third. (Earnings generally rose more than rates, with modernization—particularly in the 1960 'concentration', however.)

[2] *Joint Circular* of the Weavers' Amalgamation and the Cotton Spinners & Manufacturers' Association to their affiliates, May 14, 1952.

[3] See the joint statement of the Weavers and the Master Manufacturers, *ibid.* The 'Guaranteed Week' agreements made by the cotton industries (in common with others) after the lapsing of war-time labour controls include a 'State of Trade' clause which permits employers to contract out of the obligation to pay a full weekly wage if trade is bad.

[4] Although negotiations for a central agreement on three-shift working broke down in 1955 on the additional Weavers' demand that a 'union shop' be imposed on night-shift workers—a demand the Weavers' pressed because night-shifts

to modernization from the labour side. They offered no positive inducement to it, nor imposed any special penalty on backward firms.

The unions were similarly correct to attempt to keep the operatives' hourly earnings up at least to the level indicated by current cotton wage-rates. Again, they might well have gone further in this direction. The traditional wage-systems had, in effect, operated so as to give a considerable incentive to managerial efficiency. The disputes that most pre-occupied local Spinners' and Weavers' Secretaries were (and continue to be) concerned with 'bad work' —that is, a claim that poor material, bad maintenance, or some other managerial deficiency prevented the operatives from earning the normal yield of the standard piece-rates ruling in their occupation. Since this average level of earnings rose steadily with technical improvement, the effect was a persistent pressure on individual managements to keep up with the general progress.

This feature of the traditional cotton wage-systems, incidentally, helps to explain why so much freedom for local action remained in cotton's apparently quite centralized wage-fixing procedures. It also partly explains the cotton unions' relative lack of interest in the modern fad of 'joint consultation'. Because of the bearing that managerial arrangements had on earnings, the unions had never accepted that exclusion from intervening in 'managerial functions' for which, in other industries, joint consultation was designed to compensate. Local cotton unions have secured the dismissal of inefficient overlookers or supervisors. And at least one local Weavers' Association has actually arranged the replacement of a mill manager, under threat of a strike. The principle that wage-rates themselves should be a stimulant to managerial efficiency was, moreover, explicitly provided for in the former Oldham Spinners' Wage-list by a 'speed clause', which reduced piece-prices to employers who introduced more modern (and so faster) machinery.[1] And this clause was incorporated in the uniform 'Evershed List' for mule-spinning introduced in 1949.

---

might require the recruitment of men from outside the industry—they also remained willing to negotiate three-shift working with individual firms on that condition.

[1] The 'speed clause' of the Oldham List is discussed in some detail by Jewkes and Gray (*Wages and Labour in the Cotton-Spinning Industry*', op. cit., Appendix V). The 'speed clause' was, however, perhaps not quite so unique as they suggest. Several of the nineteenth century mule-spinning lists (like those of Preston and Blackburn) included a clause providing compensation to operatives whose machines were abnormally slow. The Oldham List's innovation seems to have been that the critical speed was fixed above, instead of below, the then current average.

It would not have been illogical, in the industry's post-war circumstances, to have taken matters a stage further, and converted the traditional piece-price lists wholly into standard time-rates—or at least into 'standard earnings' lists—which would have given a still greater stimulus to labour-saving techniques. It was, indeed, the major justification of the Weavers' 'CMC System' that it tended in that direction—though the case for it was not, so far as the writer is aware, put in those terms. A time-rate or 'standard earnings' system would not have deprived the local unions of industrial functions. But it *would* have made them responsible mainly for preventing the over-loading of operatives at the standard wage—in other words, for fixing 'a fair day's work' rather than 'a fair day's pay'. It would thus have demanded a substantial adaptation of their officials' technique.

On the other hand, the unions' acceptance of a lag in wage-rates themselves behind the national movement cannot be justified as an aid to the cotton trade's recuperation. This tendency implied that the labour of cotton operatives became relatively cheaper than that of engineers and technicians, and thus also cheaper relative to the cost of modern textile machinery and management. Its affect was therefore to impose a penalty on modernization, and to offer a virtual subsidy to the technologically backward employer. True, the unions were not often well-placed, after the recession, to force up wages by direct action. But several of their claims since 1951 have been taken to arbitration, where *this* argument for them was not put, so far as the writer knows (at least, until quite recently). And in one or two years they did not press claims at all, although nearly all other unions were then participating in the 'annual wage-round' that became a recognized feature of British wage-movements after 1950. In any case, a principal restraint on the cotton unions' wage-demands was the extent of short-time working (rather than full and open unemployment, which remained statistically negligible).[1] And for this they were themselves partly responsible.

It is in their traditional approval of systematic 'work-sharing' to meet bad trade that the cotton unions' policy was perhaps most defective. Short-time working had three effects. First, that it permitted unmodernized firms to hang on to labour which—because in such firms labour forms a large proportion of costs—it would have put them out of business to employ full-time. It thus also limited the ability of modernized firms which had been prevented by labour

[1] In the worst post-war month of May 1952, registered 'wholly unemployed' operatives were 8 per cent. of cotton employees, against 37 per cent. on short-time. In May 1955, after the second recession's onset, less than 1 per cent. were wholly unemployed but some 10 per cent. on short-time.

shortage from exploiting new equipment fully (for instance, via shift working) before the recession, to take advantage of the latter to appropriate the unmodernized mills' labour surplus by offering it employment.[1] Secondly, however, repeated short-time working involved reduced earnings and insecurity that drove the more mobile operatives to seek other work. These were inevitably the younger and more adaptable workers. And many of them quitted the industry altogether, leaving it dependent on a labour force increasingly and disproportionately aged. Yet it became a commonplace that in each brief recovery since 1952 (or even during the recessions themselves) some mills were unable to put their remaining employees on full-time because of a lack of workers in some key process. Analysis of the effect of such things on the age and sex composition of the cotton trade's employees shows clearly how the industry repelled its most valuable operatives. When its total recorded labour force fell by 21 per cent. from 1951 to 1956, for instance, the number of adult cotton workers aged under forty fell by 32 per cent.—and that those who withdrew were not inexperienced operatives is suggested by a lesser decline in the number of juveniles. Over the same time the proportion of married women in the labour force rose from 62 to 66 per cent.; and it is likely these figures understate the increased reliance of the industry on these immobile workers because from 1952 on there was probably some persisting unregistered unemployment of married female operatives who thus constituted virtually its sole labour reserve.[2] After the 1960 'concentration' an unexpected shortage of male labour developed, and it became a commonplace that experienced operatives who had left the mills for other jobs which were often unskilled and arduous would refuse to return despite the offer of higher wages. The effect of these trends on productivity, and on the adaptability of the labour force—to say nothing of the average militancy of the unions' own membership—is obvious. But thirdly, the practice of systematic 'work-sharing' largely concealed the extent to which employment in the cotton districts had declined, and thus materially weakened their case for the government-promoted alternative work

[1] Cotton employers are generally reluctant to compete openly for labour with each other through wages. In December 1950 the Master Cotton Spinners' Federation 'blackballed' six member firms for paying 'bonuses' above the standard rates. Similarly, an agreement for evening shift-work in weaving included a clause against 'poaching' other firms' labour to run it.

[2] See 'Measuring Unemployment' (loc. cit.). A more detailed examination of the recession's qualitative impact on the work-force is contained in 'Cotton's Labour Force' *Textile Mercury*, weeks of July 17, 1953 (Part 1) and April 2, 1954 (Part 2), also by the present writer.

which might have helped to restore the unions' own bargaining position.[1]

VII

In their attitude to 'work-sharing', particularly, the cotton unions' policy was not untypical of recent trade union response to similar situations. But in several ways it worked against the long-run interest of their own members—by effectively (if unintentionally) favouring the less-advanced firms, and by encouraging both a maldistribution of the labour force, and a deterioration in its quality and general balance. Once the post-war world shortage of textiles had been made up, cotton operatives could only be offered full employment at the going national level of wages by a compact and modernized industry capable of effective competition. To that, union action itself could best have contributed by deterring employers from engaging labour merely as a substitute for modern plant or managerial technique. And of the methods by which that could be achieved, the most effective would perhaps have been an adequate penalty on the *dismissal* or *under*-employment of workers. In effect, that suggests that union policy should have aimed to make labour an overhead cost—a condition which would both discriminate heavily against backward firms (because labour forms a higher proportion of their total expenses) and offer more security to young recruits to the labour force.

In fact, several ways of realizing this increased security presented themselves to the cotton unions. Some Tapesizers' locals, for instance, have recently refused to accept new entrants unless their would-be employer guaranteed them salaried status. In textile finishing, an agreement of 1949 between the machine calico printers' union and the cartel provided a virtual guarantee of employment to all operatives on a jointly-recognized list. In 1952, the UTFWA's Legislative Council discussed a suggestion to levy employers in good times so as to make up or pay operatives' wages in bad.[2] In 1953, the Cardroom's General Secretary proposed an assurance of 'work or maintenance' to cotton operatives to restore recruitment.[3] In 1954 a Fabian Society Report recommended the offer of an 'Annual Guaranteed Wage' to the cotton unions in exchange for further

[1] An incidental implication of these comments is that to pay public unemployment benefit for short-time working (a five-day week firm could actually get its workers two days' benefit by stopping on one day only) virtually subsidizes the retention of labour by less efficient firms.

[2] The proposal was made by an article 'Decasualisation for Cotton?' in the *Textile Weekly*, May 30, 1952.

[3] First *Quarterly Report* of the Cardroom Amalgamation for 1953.

co-operation in the industry's modernization.[1] Indeed, the Weavers themselves had thirty years' before proposed a scheme to guarantee the operatives against unemployment, short-time and under-employment.[2] The unions' own final proposal of 1958 for 'compensation on redundancy', however, would not have done the trick even had it been accepted. Since it proposed that compensation be paid from a fund raised by a levy on the wage-bill, and made no provision for payments if the fund were exhausted, it was virtually equivalent only to a small (0·25 per cent.) increase in wages. By proposing that redundancy payments be financed by *general* levy, it penalized the progressive employer by requiring him to subsidize the unsuccessful firm. It provided in any case no compensation for workers dismissed with less than five years' service (which exceeded the normal period of continuous employment for many operatives). And since it was accompanied by no guarantee to weekly earnings whilst employed, it would not have prevented employers postponing redundancy (or encouraging workers to leave voluntarily, and thus uncompensated) by short-time working. So that it involved no deterrent to the unnecessary engagement of labour in the first place.

The unions' demand, in fact, proposed a humanitarian measure, not an economic strategy. It was rather designed . . . 'to obtain reasonable treatment for long-service employees . . . who suddenly find themselves face to face with unemployment'.[3] But it followed very much the lines of the 'redundancy compensation' agreements made by other unions after the British Motor Corporation strike of 1956, and supported by the Ministry of Labour.[4] Indeed, since under the original operatives' scheme, the employers would presumably have reckoned the minor increase in the wage-bill involved as a factor to offset against other wage-claims, the scheme really amounted to a small redistribution of wages in favour of long-service employees: so it is hard to see why the employers should have twice rejected it. Nor, in fact, did the agreement for 'Compensation for Redundant Operatives' at last imposed on them as a condition of

[1] John Murray, *Plan for Cotton* (Fabian Research Series, No. 181).

[2] In April 1923. Negotiations broke down on the employers' counter-proposal to increase the suggested operatives' contribution to the guarantee fund. The previous year, the cotton unions had supported a GFTU draft Bill to legalize 'supplementary unemployment benefit' schemes in individual industries—anticipating their American advent by thirty years.

[3] Spinners' Amalgamation *Report of Council* for quarter ending July 31, 1958.

[4] 'Positive Employment Policies', *Ministry of Labour and National Service* (HMSO, 1958). However, the cotton employers' reply to their unions' original demand was that '. . . protection against the consequences of unemployment is a matter for the State' (*Manchester Guardian* report, November 29, 1958) which makes the government's seeming support of private schemes like that then proposed look less than disinterested!

the government's financing the 1960 'concentration' provide any more penalty on inefficient employers. Rather the reverse: since it was financed by a compulsory levy on the industry it effectively obliged those firms which continued to offer work to cotton operatives largely to meet the humanitarian obligations of those which did not—preferring to take full advantage of the government-financed scrapping payments and withdraw from the trade. (Even so, the operatives' compensation scheme represented a good bargain from the employers' viewpoint. The scheme was limited to workers over twenty-one with five years' service, and was otherwise based on age. Since the theoretically-possible payments to the 34,000 workers benefiting ranged from a few pounds at the minimum to about £500 at the maximum, and probably averaged not more than some £100, the firms' total expenditure was a fraction of the subsidies offered by the government). And the scheme was in any case restricted to operatives displaced by the 1960 'concentration' itself, or by the government-subsidized re-equipment associated with it.

For an effective and permanent guarantee to wages and employment it would have been well worth the unions' while to offer—if the employers' associations refused, then to individual employers—further union concessions to efficient management by way of trade. And one of the most useful might well have been a greater adaptability of labour. A greater freedom to switch operatives to other processes would have been a material consideration to a plant with the elaborately-interdependent production sequences of modern equipments. It would also have minimized the total labour requirements of firms, and thus made guaranteed wages and employment more acceptable. And it would have involved a widening and flexibility of the major occupations that might well have made them more secure and more attractive to recruits than the rather narrowly restricted jobs provided by the conventional inter-worker demarcations. But on this side, the proposal of one post-War commission that the modern ring-spindles might be worked by men, and so by ex-mule spinners,[1] was virtually ignored by the spinners' unions for fifteen years—until, in fact, the 1960 'concentration' (which naturally affected the older types of spinning plant most drastically) made half the mule-spinning operatives redundant at one stroke. But by then, it was too late for the employment of men on ring-frames—

[1] *Report* of the (Evershed) Commission to Review the Wage Arrangements, Methods of Organisation of Work, etc., in the Cotton Spinning Industry (HMSO, 1945) para. 63. It has been noted that, by contrast to the extraordinary utilization of equipment achieved by the mule-spinners, the employment of girls on what is still essentially the 'gang' system has rarely achieved the full technical potentiality of the ring-frame.

which in principle offers considerable productive possibilities—to have been sufficiently explored to offer the displaced mule-spinners much of an alternative: and in the face of general redundancy, only night-shift work (on which women ring-spinners are prohibited from employment) was open to them. It is hardly surprising that the skill of most of the mule-spinners displaced should have been lost to the industry. However, this shortsightedness was not confined to the spinners' unions. Another post-war proposal for a general apprenticeship to manufacturing occupations, for instance, received a similar neglect: ultimately, it would have forced the closed unions in the weaving trade to merge their sectional controls of entry.

In essence, of course, these comments imply that the unions' best tactic in face of their post-War situation would have been to adapt their wage-policy to restrict entry to the cotton trade *as a whole*, but to relax sectional restrictions on entry into particular occupations and on mobility between them. And since, to some large extent, the cotton trade's recession was due to its failure to maintain its one-time technical leadership, such a union policy might have helped as much to forestall the trade's decline as to counteract it once it became apparent. The argument thus also implies a broad proposition on trade union policy in a 'mixed' economy. Summarily, trade unions cannot by themselves ensure general full employment—by 'work-sharing', restraints on labour mobility, or similar devices. Still less can they ensure high wages by such means. But unions *can* do a great deal to promote security and high wages in individual jobs—as well as high productivity and living standards in general—by encouraging the use of labour-saving equipments and methods. Union policy should reward well-equipped and well-organized employers and punish backward ones, because the difference between such employers lies not merely in their competitive efficiency but in their respective ratios of labour to other costs—and thus also in the unions' prospect of extracting concessions from them. Union policy should therefore oblige employers to engage labour only if they can offer it security of employment and income. And it should insist on wages which are standard to all concerns, high enough to continually threaten the less efficient with bankruptcy, and guaranteed at a level that makes labour effectively a standing charge—so that backward enterprises cannot get out of trouble by subjecting their workers to under-employment and reduced earnings. On the other hand, unions should also encourage progressive concerns by conceding them a flexible use of labour and encouraging adaptability in the labour force. If the *general* level of employment is maintained by government action, the unions' main responsibility towards the use of labour is to protect workers against exploitation by overwork, bad conditions, or under-payment for their skill and qualifications.

Could the unions, through such methods, have much affected the post-War situation, either of the cotton operatives or the cotton trade? They could certainly have done something to iron out the short-term economic fluctuations, due to the cotton trade's structure and to swings in home consumers' demand for textiles, to which their members became subject in the 1950s. The unions' willingness to accept both a relative lowering in the price of cotton labour *and* further reductions in its earnings by repeated under-employment helped to make labour itself an item of trade speculation. But could they have put off the long-run decline? A large contraction in the British cotton trade was probably inevitable in the 1920s: there was little that Lancashire could do to surmount barriers set up by the determination of other countries to create textile industries of their own. But, in an industrial revolution, an early start has potential advantages, as well as disadvantages. These include the accumulation of skills, and a superior capacity to evolve and master new products and techniques. And in a world not merely of fast-rising populations, but of disproportionately-rising textile consumption because of advancing standards of life, demand for higher quality and novelty also increases.

But a remarkable feature of the British cotton trade's inter-War crisis was its relapse from a position of industrial advancement to one of technological backwardness. Notoriously, there is the much faster adoption by other countries of the ring-spinning and automatic weaving processes when these proved their superiority to the earlier Lancashire techniques.[1] But this technological lag does not seem to have been much made up in the post-War years. Still newer machines have come predominantly from the USA and from Western Europe. Since 1920, the cotton trade has had in the Shirley Institute what is certainly the biggest joint research organization of any British industry, and probably the world's most advanced centre of textile research. But its former director recently complained that, although all the techniques for a complete revolution of cotton processing were available, limitation of the Institute's finance (it is largely dependent on contributions from the industry) had compelled it to concentrate on detailed technical improvements —while the great majority of cotton firms were in any case uninterested in the application of science.[2] And even a minor device

[1] By contrast, the ring-spindle's technical ancestor, the early nineteenth-century 'throstle' (in turn derived from Arkwright's water-frame), was rapidly abandoned by Lancashire as the self-actor mule was perfected.

[2] Dr F. C. Toy, reported by A. Whewell in 'Technical Development in Cotton' (*The New Scientist*, January 17, 1957).

that substantially improved one weaving preparatory process had, after five years on the market, been adopted by only five per cent. of manufacturing firms.[1] Similarly, British exploitation of the novel man-made fibres fell behind. Whereas the British textile industry was rather ahead of its rivals in the development of rayon, its use of the newer synthetic fibres was below the world average.[2] And most startling, perhaps, is the failure of textiles to hold their share of the expanding domestic consumers' market, not merely in proportionate but in absolute terms. Whereas, in general, textile consumption rises with living standards (so that it is about 50 per cent. more per head in the USA than the UK)[3] by 1955 the average Britisher's clothing expenditure was about 9 per cent. less, in real terms, than in the 1930s.[4]

Said one commentator on the British cotton trade between the Wars '. . . invention seems to have run dry since the end of the nineteenth century. Even the prolonged and severe depression since 1921 has failed to rouse employers to strike out on new lines. Is it mere coincidence, it may be asked, that trades unionism has been equally conservative in the maintenance of a long-accustomed policy? . . . It is at least an open question whether, if the cotton unions had pursued a more militant policy, and applied a stronger and more persistent pressure for higher wages, the Lancashire genius would not have speedily supplied at least a modest measure of their desires'.[5] But another inter-war comment on the unions' policy was that '. . . the immobility of labour has been accentuated by the general system of short-time working, which has been steadily adhered to since 1921 . . .'[6] An immediate post-War student, comparing the condition of cotton operatives in Britain and North America, attributed the Lancashire unions' failure to do much more than maintain real wages since the 1920s to attitudes which had hampered modernization and limited the operatives' long-run employment prospects: 'It would be better for the welfare of the workers and the community as a whole if the unions would allow managements considerable flexibility in re-organizing job assignments and classifications . . .

[1] *Manchester Guardian*, February 13, 1957. Report of address to Bolton Textile Institute by Dr F. C. Toy (the reference is to the Shirley Automatic Size-box).

[2] According to the *Financial Times*' 'Survey of the British Chemical Industry' (October 1952) pure synthetics made up 1 per cent. of total world consumption of textile fibres in 1951, but only ½ per cent. of British consumption.

[3] Food and Agriculture Organization, *Bulletin 22* (Rome, 1952).

[4] Mark Abrams, in the *Financial Times*, October 1, 1955.

[5] Rowe, on 'The Policy of High Wages', to the International Association for Social Progress, 1931.

[6] J. Jewkes and H. Campion, 'The Mobility of Labour in the Cotton Industry', *The Economic Journal*, March 1928.

hand-in-hand with technological improvements'. The unions' failure to do so had been due to a tendency of particular groups to 'press privileged bargaining positions at the expense of the less well organised' and to 'concern themselves with maintaining their *own* status—which does not serve the best interest of *all* workers'.[1] With little modification, comments of this kind might still be made.

[1] Gibson, 'Cotton Textile Wages in the United States and Great Britain', op. cit.

VI

TRADE UNION POLICY

2

Change in Trade Unions

I

The great weakness of the cotton unions since the 1920s has thus been their lack of a common drive—of effectively concerted policy in relation to their industry, and particularly to their own place in it. Which leads back to our earlier discussion of the unions' structure. Not, one should hasten to add, that this failing of effective common policy is specifically a product of the cotton unions' federal organization. Outside the textile trades—and quite apart from the obstacle presented, to the formulation of *national* economic and industrial policies through the TUC, by the concentration of union power in certain great, and relatively centralized, organizations—this same concentration also inhibits the agreement of effective programmes to deal with many contemporary labour issues that arise at the level of individual industries. And this is paradoxical enough, because the amalgamations that produced these concentrations were often advocated very largely on the ground that they would enable or promote concerted policy and action at the industrial level. Had the growth and merger of major unions followed the natural grouping of employers by 'industry' or product market, that might very well have been the case. But because the expansion in fact followed the lines of opportunity and least resistance, multi-unionism at the industrial (and even workplace) level was its inevitable concomitant. So that conflicts of policy at this level have been almost equally inevitable. Thus, the unions in the motor industry, confronted with a situation in many ways similar to that of the cotton operatives, have been unable to evolve an agreed policy to meet the displacement of labour by technological and structural change—or by the sharp fluctuations in activity now characteristic of their trade—because of active disagreement between the AEU, the 'craft', and the 'general' unions.

However, policy considerations like those set forth in the previous Chapter's conclusion were familiar to not a few of the cotton unions' leaders. They are not only more than usually well-versed in the technical and economic situation of their trades, but include men very conversant with external trends and controversies, and are often widely-travelled. Since the war the Cotton Board's Annual Conference has provided a forum for the examination of the textile industry's problems, which many of the union officials have regularly attended. But it is nevertheless notable that the UTFWA's Legislative Council—which includes that Association's M.P. and the General Secretaries of all the union Amalgamations, as well as the Presidents and senior executive members of the larger ones—should for several years past have organized for itself an annual private seminar, which outside experts were invited to join, and at which many of these general problems of trade union policy have been discussed. So far as the writer knows, it is quite unprecedented for the professional leadership of a major union grouping to thus recognize its own use for instruction[1], and the arrangement argues at least a large willingness to examine new ideas. But just the same, it was partly at this level of leadership that the difficulty lay.

One obstacle to the cotton unions' adoption of a radical and concerted industrial policy was the problem of formulating it in detail, and of adapting its practice to a moving industrial situation. None of the Amalgamations has any staff for research and for specialized enquiry—and if any *one* had, it is most unlikely that the others would be willing to accept its implied leadership. A second obstacle was the difficulty of persuading the many independent local officials to a programme that would require a large change in their own techniques. Their own Amalgamations have often been unable to do so where smaller changes in union practice were at issue than those indicated by the post-war situation. And attempts by the Amalgamation officials alone to press a strong line might provoke the local Secretaries' jealousy of their standing. While the third obstacle was the problem of persuading the union memberships themselves. Short-time working, for instance, is a practice deeply-rooted in the cotton trade's history, and one that appeals to the operatives as a fair way to deal out the misfortunes of trade. And to force wage-guarantees from marginal firms, or to relax labour restrictions on efficient ones, would awaken individual fears of losing a job—even

[1] The Amalgamated Society of Woodworkers has recently started an annual summer school for its full-time officials. But in this case, the National Officers themselves play the role of instructors, the 'students' being mainly local organizers.

if it increased the individual's job chances in general. Such feelings and fears run deep; and the sectional and local officials are too sensitive to their own final dependence on the members to go radically against them.

In each case, there was a need for some body of a standing apart from local and sectional interests, but able to consider and speak for no interest but that of cotton workers as a whole—and to appeal to the operatives from that vantage point. And there was a need for a central organization for research, policy preparation, publicity, and union education. For these things, the obvious agency was the UTFWA. And a practical need in any case existed for a pooled, specialist service to assist the unions in preparing sectional economic claims, or particularly in dealing with the application of new managerial and mechanical techniques. But the UTFWA has no staff or office of its own, its secretarial duty being customarily performed on a distinctly part-time basis by one of the Weavers' local officials. It provides no educational services to the unions' members or local officers—a deficiency which has not been significantly made up by the individual Amalgamations themselves. To prepare a recent major statement of proposals for the cotton trade's reorganization, the unions were obliged to rely on outside assistance, distinguished though it was.[1] And since the demise just before the Second World War of the *Cotton Factory Times*, which had for more than half a century provided an unofficial (if by no means unauthoritative) weekly view of the cotton operatives' condition and a public platform for their opinions, the unions have lacked any common vehicle of information and publicity.[2] It would not have been hard for their leaders to persuade the membership to finance a small full-time staff for the UTFWA. But that would have meant elevating that federation's Secretary above themselves.

If the UTFWA had been made a forcible federal agency, however, it would still have lacked a channel through which a common opinion could be shaped and made effective at the workplace itself. The absence of a shop organization in most cotton unions (outside the Spinners) has encouraged sectional isolation within the mill itself. Equally, it would be almost inevitable that the appointment of mill representatives for the different groups of operatives would lead to closer interchange and co-operation amongst them. And

[1] 'Plan for Cotton' (op. cit.) was, of course, drafted by Mr Harold Wilson, M.P., former President of the Board of Trade in the post-war Labour Government.

[2] The *Cotton Factory Times* was produced weekly from 1885 by a radical printer and publisher in Ashton-under-Lyne, W. H. Andrews. Local unions circulate reports to their members, but not usually more often than quarterly. And they are mostly short formal reports of the union's finances and affairs, with at best an accompanying open letter from the Secretary.

again there were sound practical arguments for such a system, apart from its relevance to fundamental union policy. The membership of the open unions might well be increased by inter-union co-operation at the workplace. With a quarter of cotton workers still unorganized, the unions could do quite a lot to stave off the impact of the cotton trade's decline on their own strength and finances. Moreover, the early solidarity of the cotton operatives was promoted, especially in the North-Eastern towns that depended almost wholly on cotton manufacture, by an identification with the community outside the mill. But since the 1920s this communal identity has been increasingly diluted by local industrial diversification, so that the case for a stronger association at the workplace itself has grown in inverse proportion. And for the cotton operative, the need for some formal unity at the workplace is the greater because he or she is often tied by the machine's persistence and isolated by its clatter, and so lacks the chances of informal meeting and discussion during working hours that workers in other trades often have.

Particularly, however, the efficiency of the unions is impaired by their lack of mill representatives. Local Secretaries whose unions have them consider that the job constitutes a stimulus to active interest in union affairs as well as a training for higher union office, and that when they are available a higher proportion of disputes are settled at the mill itself. This does not mean that there are less disputes referred to the union office: complaints which would otherwise remain unspoken are often raised just because a mill representative is there to take them up in the first instance. But those reported to the union are better prepared. On the other hand, unions without shop representatives have less control over working conditions, because the secretary is not informed of many things that happen at the mill.[1] And lest this be thought wholly encouraging to managerial initiative, be it also said that managers have themselves complained that innovation is hindered by the absence of a procedure for workplace consultation.[2] Nor does there seem to have been any great practical difficulty in the unions' all adopting mill representatives. But again, the fear of union officials that workplace representation would subject them to greater rank-and-file pressure, perhaps inspired by ideas or movements external to their own Amalgamation or local union, must be reckoned a major obstruction to the system's general use.

[1] Mr L. C. Tippett of Shirley Institute, in a paper to the 1954 Cotton Board Conference, 'Productivity in the Cotton Industry', stated that changes made by managements were often not challenged by the unions because they did not know of them.

[2] 1947 Cotton Board Conference, discussion *Report.*

The cotton unions' structure is thus weak at its very top, and at its base. But in this it resembles the trade union movement at large, and for not dissimilar reasons. At the top, British trade unionism has clearly been hampered in the post-war period by the relatively limited authority of the TUC—and particularly by the latter's virtual inability to guide the economic policies of its affiliated national unions. While at the bottom, it has suffered from the relative failure of the national unions to absorb the largely spontaneous growth of workplace union organization into their institutional framework. This organization they now generally recognize, of necessity; but it was in the first place largely thrust on them by unofficial pressure and is even now not usually fully integrated in their structures—so that in many unions where the workplace represents the only significant area of lay activity, the formal source of executive powers is still the anachronistic local branch. In each case—at top and at bottom—the key to the situation is the reluctance of powerful union leaderships either to accept greater central guidance or to expose themselves to greater rank-and-file pressure. The difference to the cotton unions is simply in the level at which this reluctance is most effective. And this in turn reflects the level at which the process of 'institutionalization' principally concentrated internal union authority. So that whereas the merely federal cotton unions have needed an effective central leadership to unite local and sectional interests in relation to the cotton trade as a whole, trade unionism outside might well benefit from a decentralization of the national unions that would at the same time reduce the power of individual union leaderships in relation to the TUC, and shift their locus closer to the workplace. And for such a move—particularly if it were accompanied by a strengthening of the trade union movement's central apparatus for policy formulation and communication—the cotton unions' structure seems at least to indicate a possible direction.

II

But all this raises one last problem in trade union evolution. Why have the cotton unions changed so little in the last half-century? The 'Main Chart' of Chapter III, 1, shows that no new local unions or Amalgamations were formed after 1910. But the broader cotton workers' federations—the UTFWA and the Northern Counties—were also then already in existence. And the internal organization of the local unions, Amalgamations and Federations has since changed in no significant respect. Indeed, the only present difference from the unions' structure as it stood before the First World War is that the number of local associations has fallen with dwindling union membership.

This stagnation is doubly startling. The cotton unions' structure perhaps worked admirably when the cotton trade itself was still expanding. Then, the strongest group of the moment could push ahead, and other sections use its success to lever themselves forward. It is the long economic decline of this century that has most exposed the unions' weaker points. Yet it was just in the phase of industrial advance that their structure developed most rapidly: while the cotton trade's retreat put an almost complete stop to change in the cotton unions. In fact—and this is perhaps most surprising of all—the cotton unions' structural evolution effectively ceased at just about the time when the movements that have largely moulded the structure of contemporary trade unionism outside the cotton trade were getting under way. The great mergers into (would-be) 'general' or 'industrial' unions, the rise of the shop-stewards' movement, the re-organization of the TUC—all these came between 1910 and the early 1920s. Yet they inspired no similar reconstruction in the cotton unions. And neither, substantially, did anything that has happened since—in particular, the cotton trade's period of government-stimulated re-development after World War II.

It is not that all reformist spirit among the cotton workers evaporated so soon after this century's opening. It is fairly clear, for instance, that the present Northern Counties Textile Trades Federation was originally envisaged as a kind of 'super-Amalgamation' of the manufacturing unions. Its Objects of 1906 included the organization of 'a system of local education in the principles of federation',[1] it was to be equally represented with the Amalgamation concerned in the settlement of local disputes where its help was called for—indeed Amalgamations were '. . . to be discouraged (from) embarking on strikes on their own initiative . . . on the ground that when one section is withdrawn it not only punishes the employer but other operatives as well'[2]—and the Federation could only support a local dispute after a *general* meeting of all the operatives who might become involved. The Federation, in fact, followed an earlier scheme for closer unity between the manufacturing Amalgamations, which had broken down ten years before on the objection of some unions to a proposal (among others) that the new body have its own full-time officials.[3] This idea was dropped in the Northern Counties Federation. But the Federation was still prevented by Rule from

[1] *Objects* of Northern Counties Textile Trades Federation.
[2] *Rule* 9e of Northern Counties Textile Trades Federation.
[3] *CFT*, September 25 and October 23, 1896. See also some notes in the Webb Collection.

accumulating its own funds, which effectively limited its function to that of a joint negotiating committee. However, proposals for a general re-grouping, to include both spinning and manufacturing unions, continued to be canvassed for several years, until in 1920 the UTFWA's Annual Meeting instructed its Council to prepare a scheme for a 'Cotton Workers' Federation'. But three years' discussion failed to produce general agreement between the Amalgamations. And in 1923 the scheme was dropped. In 1928 the UTFWA's annual meeting passed a new resolution for 'closer unity'; but again its Council was unable to formulate an agreed scheme. And when, over the next year, the TUC's General Council, under instruction from its Congress to stimulate further mergers of trade unions, approached the cotton workers' societies, only the Weavers' Amalgamation replied—and that pessimistically.[1]

The Weavers had in fact been the most persistent supporters of schemes for an effective industrial federation (as opposed to the still largely-political UTFWA): indeed, a fear that any such body would be dominated by the Weavers' relative numbers and militancy partly accounts for the reluctance of other groups to join one. But the Weavers' Amalgamation had no more success in reforming itself. Like the Spinners' Amalgamation several years before, it failed in 1919 to persuade its district associations to accept a scheme for standard contributions and benefits. In 1932, shaken by their great battles of the preceding three years, the Weavers' delegate meeting ordered their Committee '. . . to take immediate steps to submit a complete scheme of re-organisation . . . for this Amalgamation, with the object of making it a centralised trade union'.[2] But when, by return of the following year, they received a detailed proposal for a 'National Union of Weavers and Allied Workers' the delegates had second thoughts and rejected it. Even a moderate revival of the scheme in 1939, as one for a centralized drive to strengthen local union organization, was not prolonged after the one organizer in consequence temporarily appointed to the Weavers' Amalgamation himself became a local Secretary.

And as for further schemes to re-organize the cotton unions as a whole—the TUC's General Council was in 1946 '. . . satisfied that there is no industry in the country in which it is more essential to secure the greatest possible unification of the administrative and economic policy of the unions'.[3] But its recommendations, that 'with the utmost speed' the cotton unions form an effective industrial federation and then proceed to make each of their Amalgamations

[1] See TUC *Annual Report*, 1929.

[2] *Resolution* of Weavers' Amalgamation General Council, October 15, 1932.

[3] TUC *Final Report* on 'Trade Union Structure and Closer Unity', p. 48.

a centralized body, with an ultimate view to merging into two such unions only (one for spinning, one for manufacturing) were ignored. While the Communist Party, which for some years after the War considered the cotton unions a sufficiently hopeful field to include one of their officers in its Executive, barely achieved notice with an (eminently sensible) wartime proposal to give the UTFWA power to co-ordinate the unions' industrial activity and make it the vehicle of their TUC affiliation.[1] Nor was the unions' interest in such schemes revived even by the then President of the Board of Trade, Sir Stafford Cripps, calling in 1947 a special meeting of the various unions' committee-members to discuss the difficulties that their disparate policies had created for the post-War Labour Government. After the great state-supported 'concentration' of the cotton trades in 1960, the UTFWA's annual conference instructed its Legislative Council to propose methods of achieving 'closer unity' in the new situation. But although delegates had urged actual fusion, not merely of the cotton Amalgamations themselves but with outside unions of related interests, it soon became clear that the Council itself was not prepared even to consider anything so radical. At the next year's conference, the UTFWA's Secretary was obliged to report that, although a special committee had been set up, 'we have made very little progress'. For the manufacturing unions, the Northern Counties Federation had apparently made the—hardly revolutionary—proposals that the spinning unions' locals should join the Local Textile Trades Federations, and that the General Secretaries of the three biggest cotton operatives' Amalgamations should meet quarterly to discuss common policy and tactics. But even these moderate suggestions the two spinning Amalgamations had not yet met to consider—a languor that seems to have owed much to the at least unhurried attitude of the Cardroom. Inevitably, the continued decline of the Spinners' Amalgamation will provoke suggestions of its merger in the former association. The attitude of the Cardroom's leadership to any proposals tending in that direction is very likely not unaffected by the possible effect, on the strippers-and-grinders' aristocratic domination of the Cardroom Amalgamation, of an injection into the latter of the residual but still more aristocratic mule-spinners.

For half a century—and in contrast to its previous steady evolution—the cotton unions' structure has thus resisted very considerable pressures towards change. But perhaps one should look more closely

[1] 'Towards a greater Trade Union Movement', *Communist Party of Great Britain*, August 1944. (Up to 1943, many district cotton unions affiliated separately to the TUC. It was only in 1943–4 that the Amalgamations became generally recognized as their agent in this respect.)

at *other* unions' degree of change in recent years. If the past century's national trade union revolution came mainly after 1910, it was also largely completed by 1930. The half-dozen amalgamated organizations that now command half trade unionism's total membership were then already in existence—with the sole exception of USDAW, which only waited on the merger of the small Shop Assistants' Union into the much bigger Distributive Workers. And subsequent minor amalgamations of other unions have not greatly affected trade unionism's general structure. Nor has the internal organization of unions much changed: the shop steward system was then established, if it has since received a wider 'official' acceptance. The then new TUC General Council was arguably at the height of its influence at the time of the General Strike. The unions' relations with the Labour Party were already defined in a way since essentially unaffected by such things as the 1927 Trades Disputes Act and its repeal in 1945. Their main structure of collective bargaining and conciliation was established by the 1920s, and has since been merely extended. It is, indeed, doubtful whether even the proportion of trade unionists among employees as a whole is now significantly above what it was at the inter-War membership peak of 1920. Movements for internal union reform, radical or otherwise, in fact subsided in the 1930s, and major experiments like that of the abortive 'Triple Alliance' ceased.

The domestic history of the last generation's trade unionism is thus one of consolidating established lines, not of novel advance. And yet, again, this period has been one in which the unions' external environment has changed most dramatically. There is not merely an almost uninterrupted high employment, but a government committal to maintain that condition. There are the extensive nationalizations, and the 'Welfare State'. And there is the acceptance of trade unionism as almost an official 'estate of the realm'. Such things represent an immense political victory of the labour movement, which has in turn produced a major economic modification. Why should this coincide with a relative stagnation in union development? It is perhaps instructive, here, to consider the recent history of *political* action in the cotton unions.

III

In their long crisis since the 1920s, the cotton unions have vacillated between two programmes towards their industry. For one, there was in fact a long tradition already established. Throughout the nineteenth century, the cotton operatives repeatedly attempted to induce employers to regulate output collectively in face of trade depressions.

The handloom weavers' proposals of 1810, and the Oldham Spinners' more successful proposition of 1846, were frequently revived by the modern unions.[1] In the negotiations that preceded their 'Great Strike' of 1878, the Weavers' First Amalgamation offered to accept a wage-reduction if the mills were worked only four days a week, on the ground that . . . 'over-production is the sole cause of narrow margins and low prices'. Next year, the Oldham Master-Spinners were actually persuaded to work short-time instead of cutting spinners' wages. And in 1885, the Oldham spinners' union met their employers' demand for a 10 per cent. wage-reduction by offering a 5 per cent. cut in rates if the employers would repeat the earlier arrangement to reduce output—although the limited companies which had meanwhile increased in importance now refused to operate it.[2]

But if the employers were not usually willing to submit their own policy to negotiation, after the great spinning disputes of 1891–3 they accepted the unions as equally interested in the general prosperity of the trade, and particularly as equal partners in pushing trade interests politically. One clause of the famous Brooklands Agreement provided for a joint committee to deal with . . . 'the opening of new markets abroad, the alteration of restrictive foreign tariffs, and other similar matters which may benefit or injure the Cotton Trade . . . All the Associations (i.e. employer and union) uniting to bring the whole of their influence to bear in furthering the general interests of the Cotton Industry in this Country'.[3] And in the First World War the unions made a further advance by securing an equal voice with the employers on the Cotton Control Board, a body (to allocate scarce raw cotton) then '. . . unique among war controls in the degree to which it assumed the character and elicited the response of a representative trade organisation'.[4] The unions, in fact, were made solely responsible for administering the wartime scheme of state supplementary unemployment benefit then introduced especially for cotton operatives—including its payment to non-unionists!

[1] See Chapters II, 1 and II, 2, section v (each), for the earlier references.

[2] According to R. Smith (unpublished thesis, op. cit.).

[3] Brooklands Agreement, 1893, Clause 10. Under Clause 11, the Committee was to meet when either the masters *or* workers were '. . . of the opinion that questions affecting the general interests . . . should be discussed'—a proviso that in fact proved of some embarrassment to the spinning unions later. In the 1952 slump the Cardroom Amalgamation's Secretary met an employer's proposal to call the joint committee by requesting a special meeting of the Cotton Board instead, because the latter has no power to discuss wages.

[4] H. D. Henderson, *The Cotton Control Board* (Clarendon Press, Oxford, 1922), p. 12.

One union policy was thus to attempt to secure 'joint control' of the cotton trade with the organized employers. And in 1928 the unions joined the 'Joint Committee of Cotton Trade Organisations', set up two or three years before on the Master-Spinners' initiative. This Committee (apart from appointing a secretarial and statistical bureau that was later to form the nucleus of the modern Cotton Board's staff) had a hand in most of the inter-War attempts to 'rationalise' the cotton trade, which included some amalgamation of companies under pressure from the banks, the attempted promotion of minimum-price agreements, the formation of a specialized Export Association to compete in Eastern markets, and the purchase and scrapping of some redundant spinning capacity by the legally authorized Spindles Board.[1] In particular, the Joint Committee focused a persistent agitation for the Government to negotiate or enforce discrimination in favour of Lancashire products overseas, and for legislation to support general 'rationalisation' of the trade through a collective agency. The unions objected to some of the employers' moves in this direction—particularly those which condemned operatives to permanent redundancy, with their machines but unlike them without compensation. But they also advanced their own demand for a statutory Board to control the cotton trade and license producers. This combined pressure achieved a fruition in the Act of 1939, which established a representative Cotton Board with legal powers to father schemes for eliminating surplus plant, regulating prices, and promoting sales. However, World War II's outbreak prevented the Board from operating in that form, though it continued as an advisory body and its staff administered much of the war-time controls. And in re-establishing the Board, the post-war Labour government reduced its scope because it believed that '. . . powers of compulsion within an industry . . . should be reserved to the government with the sanction of Parliament'.[2]

In fact, of the 'Development Councils' originally envisaged by the Labour Party as a method of engineering a collective influence in private industry without transfer of ownership, the Cotton Board was the only major one to be successfully established under the 1947 Industrial Organization and Development Act. Nevertheless, both employers and unions continued to hanker after direct (and more autonomous) forms of trade regulation. Attempts at minimum price-fixing had been rather unsuccessful in the 1930s; but these were renewed more effectively by the post-war Yarn Spinners'

[1] See a recent account by Sir Raymond Streat, the Cotton Board's former Chairman, in 'The Cotton Industry in Contraction' (*District Bank Review*, September 1958).

[2] Sir Stafford Cripps, at a meeting in Manchester, September 8, 1945.

Association. And to such moves the unions were at least not hostile. The spinning unions avoided giving an unqualified support to the YSA: but their reports contain quite frequent, if guarded references to '. . . the value of the Yarn Spinners' Association Scheme . . .'[1] While the Weavers reacted to the Monopolies Commission's condemnation, in 1953, of minimum-price arrangements in textile finishing with a statement that '. . . there is room for some form of price-fixing mechanism within textile industries', thus implying a desire to see such arrangements extended to the weaving trade.[2] And when the YSA's minimum price scheme was finally declared illegal by the Restrictive Practices Court in 1958, the Operative Spinners protested that '. . . the human consequences have been ignored'.[3]

The unions' second line of policy, however, advocated the nationalization of the cotton industry. To this demand, they came rather late, and in a way which could hardly be attributed to any doctrinaire inspiration of their leadership. The Burnley Weavers' adoption in 1892 of '. . . the ultimate object, the Socialization of the means of production, distribution and exchange . . .'[4] indicated no general return by the cotton operatives to their political radicalism of the early nineteenth century. And for several years their leaders were among the strongest opponents the Socialists had in the TUC. However, they seem to have had no objection of principle to public ownership as such. Shackleton, the one-time Liberal Weavers' official, thought nationalization might be an appropriate treatment of the 'trusts' to which various troubles of the cotton trade were, at the time of its 1902 recession, vaguely attributed.[5] While one of the last acts of Mawdsley the Spinners' leader, a former fellow-Tory candidate for Parliament with Winston Churchill, was to send a message of support to the Social Democratic Federation's candidate in the Dewsbury by-election of 1902. But up to this time the unions, despite the importance that political action always played in their affairs, conceived that technique as largely concerned with securing a favourable governmental attitude, first to factory legislation, and second to cotton trade interests at large. And to both these aims—since they could each command substantial non-labour support—the Socialist idea of independent working-class representation seemed damaging.

[1] Spinners' Amalgamation, *Annual Report* for 1955.

[2] Weavers' Amalgamation, Memorandum of May 28, 1954, 'Monopolies and Restrictive Practices Commission Report on the Process of Calico Printing'.

[3] Spinners' Amalgamation, *Quarterly Report* for January 1959.

[4] *Rules* of Burnley Weavers' Association.

[5] David Shackleton's answer to a question at a public meeting on his candidature for Parliament, quoted by F. Bealey (loc. cit.).

Union leaders in those days generally took the political colour of their districts. So that several leading Weavers' officials came from the North-East Lancashire valleys where the strength of Methodism predisposed them to the Liberal view. But if Lancashire elsewhere was predominantly Tory, this reflected not only the greater strength of Catholicism there, but the Conservative Party's historical association with factory reform. And the Spinners' leaders' active support of Toryism was to some extent attributable to a belief that the Conservative Party would take a stronger line to open the Indian and Oriental markets for British textiles.[1] However, Birtwistle, the Secretary of the old North-East Lancashire Weavers' Amalgamation itself, said of the 1885 trade slump that '. . . if our future government does not turn their attention more to trade and less to party political strife, we shall without doubt go from bad to worse, until all the capital in this country will be in the hands of a few and almost everybody out of work. Nor will this system of government ever be set aside until working men sink party politics and go in for men who will look to the interests of Trade, irrespective of Liberals, Radicals, Conservatives or Tories.'[2] And four years later the UTFWA actually selected two Parliamentary candidates, its then Secretary Mawdsley to stand as a Tory, and the weaver Holmes to stand as a Liberal (though the scheme to promote them broke down on disagreement over details).

Thus the modern cotton unions' original political attitude was fundamentally opportunistic (so that in this respect, as in several others, they anticipated the position of modern American unionism). And if the UTFWA's affiliation to the Labour Representation Committee in 1903 was the latter body's biggest gain to that date, the change was due to no conversion of principle. There is some evidence of a growing disappointment with the cotton unions' formerly successful tactic of offering a conditional support to both major parties. 'It is plainly a waste of time,' said Mawdsley to the operatives in 1893, 'to bring forward certain Bills and then go home and vote for men who will oppose them.'[3] Nevertheless, in 1900 the Weavers' Amalgamation had rejected independent labour representation, and only its Nelson and Colne locals took part in the meeting that inaugurated the LRC. But in late 1901 the Weavers were restrained by legal injunction from picketing in a Blackburn strike, and on terms which apparently gave the employers access to all documents in the union office. The Weavers' delegate meeting

[1] See R. Smith, unpublished thesis (op. cit.).

[2] *Annual Report* of the 'North-East Lancashire Amalgamation of Weavers, etc.' for 1885.

[3] UTFWA *Annual Report*.

thereupon instructed its committee '. . . to secure direct representation in Parliament': and it was the Weavers' change of front that carried the other major Amalgamations, through the UFTWA, along the same line.

IV

The cotton unions were thus pushed into their early association with the Labour Party, not by the adoption of Socialist convictions but by an extension of the legal attack to which the Taff Vale judgement had exposed trade unionism at large. And at the 1906 election, Lancashire provided the biggest group of Labour M.P.'s. But the cotton workers still remained among Labour's more moderate adherents. From 1918 to 1920 the Weavers' delegates to the TUC were the leading spokesmen against 'direct action'—the use, then hotly advocated, of industrial pressure for such political purposes as the nationalization of the mines. It was only after their own bitter experience of the 1920s and early '30s that the cotton unions themselves approached the Labour Party and TUC with a demand to socialize the cotton trade. However, this programme they then maintained, and confirmed in 1943 with the UTFWA's proposals for post-war reconstruction.[1]

The unions' committal to nationalization in fact came hard on the heels of their 1934 proposal for a representative *joint* Control Board. Yet it seems oddly incompatible with that more traditional demand for 'joint control' with the employers, on which it was superimposed. And indeed, both the TUC and the Labour Party found it somewhat embarrassing as the War's end brought Labour close to power. Labour members of the wartime Coalition had been associated with governmental plans for cotton which assumed its continued private ownership.[2] The post-war Labour government was unwilling to add to its legislative commitment of fuel, power, steel and transport nationalization—still less to risk disturbing a supposedly-key export trade. The unions agreed, if largely by implication, to postpone indefinitely their demand for socialization in return for the promise of other measures to rehabilitate the cotton trades.

[1] *Report* of the Legislative Council on 'Ways and Means of improving The Economic Stability of the Cotton Textile Industry', UTFWA, 1943. For the proposals for nationalization previously formulated by the TUC at the cotton unions' request, see TUC *Annual Report*, 1935.

[2] For instance, Dr Dalton's 'guidance' of September 1944, to the Cotton Board on lines of post-war development was welcomed by the Board's Chairman as indicating that '. . . with one or two exceptions for special cases, the government would rely in most industries for the immediate post-war years on employers and trade unions to solve the post-war problems' (in a speech at Leeds, November 28, 1944).

But the 1952 textile slump stimulated them to a renewed interest in statutory reform. The 'Plan' they adopted in 1957, after some years' discussion, envisaged the admixture, to a private enterprise induced or compelled to rationalize itself under a legally-authorized joint body, of a selective government participation through the purchase of controlling shares in key firms, the direct ownership of certain plant, and similar measures.

The cotton unions' 1957 Plan would by now be of largely historical interest did it not provide an unusual insight into the motivation of union political action in general. In one sense—perhaps inevitably, in view of its draftsmanship—it was a not untypical product of the so-called 'Socialist new thinking' that followed the Labour Party's 1951 defeat. But certain key items gave the unions' 1957 Plan a special aspect. On the one hand, it favoured the retention of minimum price agreements, modified to give all sections of the trade a voice in the prices to be fixed.[1] The government was also to give 'The home market additional stability by Government purchases in times of erratic commercial demand . . . and by . . . long-run guaranteed orders for a range of standard specifications'.[2] Particularly, it was to secure restriction of imports coming '. . . on the basis of unfair competition', if necessary by setting up a Government Imports Commission.[3] Such a Plan, drafted by a man who might be in a government expected to implement these proposals, could hardly be put without hedging: minimum prices, for instance, were to be subjected to Board of Trade approval and review—a proviso that a body associated with the Labour Party could hardly fail to include. But these proposals' combined intention was fairly clear. While on the other hand, the Plan contained no programme of positive action by the unions themselves, either in their economic policy or in their organization. It merely reaffirmed the conditional concessions they had already made to 're-deployment' and to shift-working. For the latter, however, spinning and weaving unions offered different terms—a disagreement which consorted oddly with their stated common desire to encourage '. . . vertical grouping(s) which hold out hope of reduced costs . . .'[4] The only novelty in industrial relations the plan suggested was that 'The establishment of effective Mill Production Committees should be a condition for any State Assistance' (presumably to individual

[1] 'Plan for Cotton' (UTFWA, op. cit.) para. 65. The weavers had felt themselves 'squeezed' between the spinners' and finishers' cartels.

[2] 'Plan for Cotton', para. 150 (xvi).

[3] 'Plan for Cotton', para. 118. This repeated a proposal put forward by the Parliamentary Labour Party for the UTFWA in 1955.

[4] 'Plan for Cotton', paras. 59 and 47–50.

employers).[1] In this, the unions accepted the resurrection of a demand made by Sir Stafford Cripps in 1945. They did not explain their own subsequent failure to appoint workshop representatives, or indicate any intention to reform that deficiency.

The cotton operatives had a very special claim to government help in this period of renewed contraction, because many of them had been 'steered' into or kept in the trade by the government's post-war restraints on the development of rival industries in the textile region, as well as by official promises of permanent full employment in textiles.[2] But the public responsibility was to the cotton workers as individuals—to ensure alternative work, and compensation for the hardships of re-adjustment or premature redundancy; an obligation fulfilled (at least in principle) by the 'compensation for redundant operatives' condition of the 1960 'concentration' scheme, by public encouragement of the entry of new local industries, and above all (since this permitted most of the workers displaced in 1960, for instance, to find other jobs) by the general maintenance of full employment. With this last condition, however, a public obligation to maintain indefinitely industries which could no longer compete effectively in product or labour markets would inevitably conflict: to the cotton *industry*, the limit of state liability was thus to provide it with such temporary cover as was needed for it to re-organize itself to meet its altered situation after 1951. But in the absence of positive action by the unions themselves, their 1957 demands for government action suggest a veiled proposal for a protected, subsidized, and continuing industrial monopoly.

Nor was the lack of a programme for union action accidental. In the 1930s, the unions had seen the first task of the Control Board they then demanded as '. . . to ensure that agreements reached as a result of collective bargaining are enforced . . .'[3] And if by the 1950s, they had moved some way from the inter-War position, when in cotton . . .'almost nobody seriously contemplated change so far as

[1] 'Plan for Cotton'. This phrase appears only in the 'Summary of Recommendations'. The main paragraph (60) it purports to embody refers only to the industry's backwardness '. . . in consultation at the mill level'. And its Interim Conclusion states only that: 'Joint consultation . . . should be actively pressed by both sides of industry'. The idea of compulsion appears to have been an afterthought—whether designed to hasten or defer the process is not clear. The proposal for workplace representation had in any case been made—as one for Works Councils—as far back as the TUC's report on cotton of 1935 (loc. cit.).

[2] See, for instance, the speech of the Parliamentary Secretary to the Board of Trade, to the Lancashire Industrial Development Association on January 4, 1950 —'Diversification of industry in Lancashire has been carried far enough'.

[3] Speech of the then Weavers' Secretary, Andrew Naesmith, to the 1934 TUC.

he himself was concerned . . .'[1] and the trade became protectionist because that transferred the onus for action to the government, the unions were still essentially defensive—but in an institutional sense. The justification for a substantial cotton industry's continued existence in Britain was assumed by their Plan. Had this also included a statement of the unions' own intention systematically to penalize inefficient employers and encourage efficient ones so that a nucleus of firms could ultimately survive without public support, and to revise their own practice and organization for that purpose, the Plan would have had a different implication. But without such an intention, the unions' political demands of 1957 appear in essence designed to *avoid* change on their own part, not to supplement it.

This attitude to political action explains the seeming incongruity of the unions' previous simultaneous advocacy of 'joint control' in private enterprise *and* of socialization. Essentially, the union leaders' interest was not one of principle, but of preserving an environment in which they could continue their accustomed methods. If that could be done by combination with the employers alone, so much the better. If not, then the state must step in—or excuse their own relative inflexibility by its failure to do so.

V

Our broad conclusion, then, is that—since the early years of this century at any rate—the unions' political programmes have been at least heavily conditioned, less by a desire to reform industry or society as such than by one to create an environment favourable to their own established forms of organization and action. This is not to deny that trade unions—as the main permanent associations of people who as individuals were relatively powerless in social and political affairs—have been a major vehicle of great social movements: still less, that the continuing inspiration of many union leaders is social and altruistic. What it *does* say is that where these things have implications that conflict with the unions' own established institutional forms, it is rarely the latter that yield. In the contemporary context, in effect—and despite its superficially radical attachments—trade union political action is fundamentally conservative. So that of the three classic techniques of trade unionism—'autonomous regulation', collective bargaining, and political pressure—the last has become as much a method of avoiding modification in the former two as an alternative route to collective improvement.

But in this, the cotton unions did not differ from others. For

[1] Sir Raymond Streat (loc. cit.).

instance, the key industries in Labour's post-war nationalization programme—mines, railways and steel—although their selection was covered theoretically by describing them as 'basic', were also ones whose inter-War experience cast great doubt on their future possibilities for successful collective bargaining. When that fear proved unfounded in steel, the union leadership there notably cooled in its attitude to the industry's socialization. While in other cases, the unions rejected proposals for new forms of management in public undertakings, with direct 'workers' participation', because these would involve them in a 'dual responsibility'—in effect, would compromise their ability to continue their collective bargaining and labour control practices unmodified.[1] They thus perpetuated, in the new national enterprises, managerial systems and labour relations not dissimilar to those of private corporations. In the mines, repeated internal pressures to re-organize the unions were reinforced by the severest external criticism. 'The miners', said the TUC, 'are in favour of the nationalisation of the mines: they cannot consistently afford to decline the responsibilities for nationalising their present form of trade union organisation.'[2] And the old MFGB was finally induced to convert itself into the 'National Union' of Mineworkers; but the change was more nominal than real, since the NUM's new 'areas' were essentially the old district unions with their autonomy little disturbed.[3] On this study's earlier argument, it is doubtful whether the Miners should have gone much further towards formal centralization. But in the case of the railways the continuance of active rivalry and the absence of effective federal arrangements between the various unions have been a recurrent handicap to the nationalized transport service. Had the railways remained under private ownership and exposed to the full competition of other forms of transport, such things could hardly have continued. In the light of them, reform by nationalization appears almost as a protection to unreformed trade union leadership.

Similarly, the unions at large demanded full employment. But that they were not prepared to modify their sectional bargaining practice to make full employment easier to maintain suggests that their leadership saw this aim rather as one to create favourable conditions for 'free collective bargaining' itself than as having

[1] See the TUC's *Interim Report on 'Post-War Reconstruction'*, 1944, where the argument against direct workers' representation in management is set out.

[2] TUC *Interim Report*, 'Trade Union Structure and Closer Unity', 1944.

[3] A most interesting light on the character of the NUM was thrown by a recent strike in the Lancashire field caused by a 'jurisdiction' conflict between two 'areas' of the NUM itself. But see G. Baldwin, 'Structural Reform in the British Miners' Union' (*Quarterly Journal of Economics*, Harvard, November 1953), for a brief history of the Miners' recent reorganization.

priority over the latter. Indeed, Mr Arthur Deakin, the most prominent union leader at the time of the Labour government's experiment in 'wage restraint', declared he would accept the abolition of the individual worker's free choice of a job rather than have a 'National Wages Policy'.[1]

To be surprised that union form and practice have responded so little to major changes in their economic and political circumstance is therefore to misconceive the essence of union aims. After the 1920s, trade unionism crystallized around two familiar forms: that of the 'closed' sectional union, and that of the professional specialist in sectional collective bargaining. To sharply swing the balance towards the latter type was, at the level of union leadership, a main effect of the expansion in this century's second decade. But for either form, the critical concern in social and economic reform has been to make its environment more responsive to its traditional technique. And the active interest of union leadership in such reform has generally ceased at the point where further environmental change would involve significant institutional changes in the unions themselves.

But this permits an answer to our starting question—why did the cotton unions change so little after 1910? The change *after* that date in outside unionism was attributable neither to political and economic circumstances, nor to the social and ideological impact of the general labour movement with which that change was historically associated. The critical factor was the new mass membership these things brought to the unions, which disturbed their existing institutionalism. Just as in the mid-nineteenth-century case, of the effects of exclusive unionism's consolidation, the change then cut itself—for two reasons. To some extent, because of the emergence of fresh sectional identities (and hence separatisms) among trade unionism's new recruits. In this study's earlier chapters it was shown how the self-actor spinners of Oldham, as they consolidated their control over entry to their occupation, lost interest in the minor groups (like the under-engineers, roller-coverers and others) that their union had initially recruited to reinforce its strength. By parallel, the relative failure of British trade unionism to expand substantially beyond the area it captured in the great wave of trade union growth from 1908 to 1920 may well be thought attributable just to the success of the 'New Unions' themselves, to the consequent crystallization of occupational identities within them, and to a tendency of organized occupations to become both closed—and thus

[1] Roberts (*National Wages Policy in War and Peace*, Allen & Unwin, London, 1958, p. 56) identifies this as a comment on the Miners' 1947 demand for preference in wage-increases.

proportionately less interested in the organizing of others. Total trade union membership reached a higher point after the Second World War than the peak of 1920; but as a proportion of the employed population it may actually have been smaller. And although the majority of British employees are still non-unionists, the hesitant upward creep of trade union membership in the 1950s has hardly kept pace—and this in a period of continuing high employment—with the growth of the working population itself.

But the second reason for the cessation of change was the unions' re-establishment of stable institutional forms, now centred on the professional negotiator. And here the political successes of the unions were of a kind that limited the union leaderships' need of further development. One of the mysteries of recent British industrial relations, for instance, is why the system of legal wage-boards, initiated just before the First World War to protect certain then unorganized and 'sweated' groups, should have since extended to cover nearly a third of all wage-earners despite (indeed, along with) the growth of unionism. And an explanation seems to be that, while providing the union officials with a similitude to normal collective bargaining, it permitted them to avoid that task of mass recruitment in difficult sectors for which they had ceased to be fitted.[1]

The cotton unions, like those of the miners, did not change substantially after 1910 because most of these things had happened to them already: especially the critical extension of membership to the mass of operatives via 'open' unionism, but also the subsequent crystallization of internal sectionalisms, the emergence of the full-time bargainer to a dominant position of leadership—and even the use of political action as protective device for established practice (the 1934 Act that made weaving wage-agreements legally enforceable was only an extension of much earlier legislation).

Thus, the prospects of future change in British trade unionism would seem linked to those of a new and spontaneous growth of membership. If the great events that have befallen the cotton operatives since 1910 have induced so little change in their organization and practice, no other nearly-foreseeable political or economic upheaval seems likely to induce a new wave of change in other unions. This study's historical discussion divided British union development into three phases. The general labour movement that brought a new influx of workers into organization in the 1830s and '40s sets the dividing line between the limited but 'natural' unionism of the preceding century, and the 'institutional' but largely 'closed' unionism of the nineteenth century's second half. The dividing

[1] See 'The Legal Minimum Wage, Employers and Trade Unions', by B. McCormick and the present writer (*Manchester School*, September 1957).

line between this middle phase, and the modern one of 'institutional' but (at first, at least) predominantly 'open' unionism, is the similar movement and influx of 1890 to 1920. Of any future movement of the same kind, the only possible source would seem to be those many non-manual and salaried employees who have not yet been touched by collective organization. And their outlook is perhaps as distinct from that of the manual wage-earner as was once that of the skilled from the unskilled worker.[1] If trade unionism in one respect now stands again much where it stood towards the nineteenth century's end—as representing a minority of workers, in relatively organized sectional interests only secondarily concerned for the welfare of employed people in general—those unorganized now include perhaps less of the under-paid and exploited than of the better-educated, with some historical sense of status.

But so far, at least, the spread of combination among the fast-growing 'salariat' has been persistent rather than explosive. And, with one or two consititutional idiosyncrasies, it has taken forms not dissimilar to those of wage-earners' organization. The proliferation of so-called 'professional associations' essentially reproduces the closed unionism of certain manual workers. The big 'white-collar' unions of civil servants, local government employees and so on display no great difference in organization or economic practice from the mass organizations of operatives. The non-manual unions have, of course, been less militant in an industrial sense—but their characteristic reluctance to resort to the strike-weapon seems (to judge by the recent schoolmasters' strikes, for instance) gradually dissipating. Neither the gradual growth of 'middle-class' unionism, nor the imminence of a majority of salaried workers among employees, thus appear likely in themselves to bring about any dramatic change in trade unionism's general character.

It is, perhaps, rather the indirect effects of these developments that may be more far-reaching. Conflicts of sectional interest between employed people themselves were a major determinant of the cotton unions' evolution. Similarly, the growth of 'white-collared' organization has certainly received a recent stimulus from the relative economic gains of manual wage-earners—which to many at least of the salaried appeared to have been increasingly at their own expense. By reaction, the emergence of powerful bargaining organizations of non-manual employees may in turn compel the still dominant manual workers' unions to revise their own programmes and approaches. Particularly, however, the continuing reluctance of salaried people and their organizations to assume the same

[1] See D. Lockwood's *The Black-Coated Worker* (Allen & Unwin, London, 1958).

political associations as wage-earning trade unionists will inevitably reduce the latter's political influence, and restrict their ability to protect accustomed union methods by its use. The declining political power of the manual worker may thus also oblige his organizations to consider new techniques of industrial and economic action. While for those who are interested in such a change, there remains one further hope. This study of the textile unions confirms the central role of the professional officer in union organization and policy. And after all, there are only a few thousand of him to persuade.

VII

APPENDIX

1

The Growth of Employers' Organizations—and its effects on Trade Union Development

It would be hard to say whether collective organization in the cotton industry truly began first among workers or employers. Indeed, its roots may very well go back to a time before separate classes of employers and employees could be clearly distinguished: which would support the implication of this study's early chapters, that purposive collective association (particularly of labour) is not a by-product of industrial capitalism—and thus in a sense an artificial or contrived imposition on a supposed state of natural competitiveness—but the result of a separate and continuing impulse to associate, the expression of which was only interrupted and modified by the economic revolution.

At any rate, the first report of a combination of employers as such antedates by two years the first evidence of trade union activity. In the 1745 Jacobite Rebellion, the Young Pretender's men came through Manchester on their march south, and '. . . took a large sum of money out of the town'.[1] The city's manufacturers agreed to recompense themselves by forcing a wage-reduction on their weavers. So it is perhaps not impossible that the smallware-weavers' combination that apparently began to adopt regular rules in 1747 was first stirred up by some resistance of the weavers to being thus obliged to bear reparation for the Scots of the 'Forty-Five. And from then on there is repeated, if intermittent, evidence of association among the handloom weavers' employers. The Manchester merchants were certainly combined to deal with the striking checkweavers in 1758; some committee or group of masters was presumably party to the weavers' wage-list of 1769, and certainly to the fine-weavers' agreement of 1792; several early nineteenth-century attempts at joint regulation of wages by groups of Lancashire weaving employers have been noted elsewhere in this study.[2] Similarly, the Scottish handloom weavers' unsuccessful attempt at a wage-list in 1780 was apparently opposed by a combination of Glasgow manufacturers, which survived to resist the Scots weavers' outburst of 1787,

[1] According to a checkweavers' statement of the origins of their 1758 strike, quoted by Chapman (op. cit., p. 206).

[2] See Chapters II, 1 and II, 2.

was revived to fight their action for legal wage-rates in 1812, and presumably revived again to make the regular collective agreements of the 1830s.

The employers' associations of the early factory industry seem to have been of a rather different kind. The early handloom masters, like their employees, may have inherited some tradition of collective association from a preceding age of public and corporate regulation. The master-spinners' alliances, however, seem to have been conceived purely as a counter to trade unionism. The first such combination to be reported thus appears several years after the first operative spinners' societies—the association of Manchester factory owners in 1803 to raise a fighting fund to defeat the mule-spinners' demands. If that body was ephemeral, a succeeding organization that fought the great 1818 strike of factory-operatives had by then already been in existence for several years (at this time, of course, combinations of employers were nominally as illegal as those of workers, but there is no evidence that they were much reminded of the fact). But it was just the peak of the early spinning unions' activity, in the 1820s, that called forth the strongest alliances of employers. So that the Glasgow masters' association was formed in 1823 with the deliberate intent of challenging the particularly formidable local union's hold on the Scottish factory industry—an intent which it apparently fulfilled. In Lancashire about the same time master-spinners' associations were formed in several major towns—Bolton, Oldham, Ashton, Preston; while the Spinners' Grand Union of 1829–30 provoked, and was defeated by, the most impressive of all the early employers' combinations.

The central purpose of all these early factory-masters' associations seems to have been to defeat the selective, or 'rolling strike' tactics of the hand-mule unions by widening the battle front. Thus, one of the Glasgow association's first acts was to turn a strike at one mill into a general lock-out of the district. Similarly, in the great Manchester strike of fine-spinners in 1829, the employers locked out the coarse-spinners when they refused to stop contributing to their comrades' support. The method was to be repeated in more modern conflicts; and there is some evidence that early factory-employers' associations also attempted another modern tactic, of forcing disputes to the point of a stoppage in slumps so as to exhaust the unions' resources (Engels even suggested[1] that the Plug Plot, the great general strike of 1842, was deliberately provoked by the employers to anticipate a revival of union strength in the economic recovery then merely expected). This attempt may account for the tendency, already noted, of the old spinning unionism's active phases, which were at first confined to booms, later to spread into periods of depression.

But it seems doubtful that the early employers' combinations possessed sufficient cohesion to endure for long without the cementing pressure of union aggression. There is, in fact, much to suggest that conflicts of interest between different groups and firms prevented their associations attaining any stability. The support of some larger-scale manufacturers for the handloom weavers' minimum-wage petitions was partly directed by fear of

[1] In *The Condition of the English Working Class in 1844*, p. 231–2 (1892 Edition).

competition from 'small masters'. In the late 1820s, certain groups of factory-employers even opposed other spinning firms' attempts—which caused the so-called 'long-wheel' strikes—to scale-off piece rates for bigger and faster machines because this would aid competitors with more recent equipment. Employers' alliances had to be held together by legal bonds which imposed substantial fines on non-complying firms, or by threats of 'cut-throat competition' against them: the Manchester factory-masters' association was unable even to agree on a chairman from their own ranks, and chose an outsider. Firms were accused of contributing to strikes against their rivals, or of harbouring strike-leaders whom the latter had dismissed.[1]

Thus the early employers' associations appear to have generally disintegrated as the early cotton unions' activity itself subsided in the 1830s or '40s—though several, no doubt, were never formally disbanded. Only the Preston association, which was re-formed during the 1836–7 spinners' strike there, seems to have maintained an intermittent activity in disputes over the next decade; and this district was then the most advanced centre of the factory industry, where the newer operatives were already moving into trade unionism. The effect of the latter movement's spread in the mid-1840s, however, is evidenced by the several district wage-lists for power-loom weaving that were drawn up about this time by local *ad hoc* committees of employers—for Ashton and Burnley in 1843, Stockport in 1844, and Oldham in 1846. And it was, in fact, the rise of the new power-loom weavers' combinations, and the rash of consequential disputes about the mid-century, that induced the critical event in the development of the modern cotton employers' organization, the formation of the Blackburn Association in 1852.[2] It is apparent from the memoir of one of its leading members that the Association's prime purpose was to reduce the frequent interference in production from labour disputes by agreeing a regular wage-list with the district's operatives.[3] But in the same year as the Blackburn List's agreement, the great Preston strike of 1853–4 broke out, and the employers of other districts combined to form a defence fund for the Preston masters which (among other things) financed the import of Irish and Scottish 'blacklegs'. Other weavers' strikes promoted further steps in employers' organization. When the weavers' First Amalgamation met its initiation test in the Padiham strike of 1859—and although it was the Blackburn employers' association that actually settled the stoppage in the end—the newly-combined (and always more aggressive) Burnley employers

[1] We have already referred (see Chapter II, 2) to the Rochdale flannel-weavers' agreement, whereby the employers concerned subscribed to strikes against non-participating firms. It was no doubt such incidents that account for the proposal of Nassau senior reported by the Webbs (*History*, p. 147) that employers be prosecuted for encouraging combinations of workers.

[2] There is an account of the development of cotton employers' organization in the second half of the nineteenth century in Chapman's 'A Historical sketch of the Masters' Associations in the Cotton Industry', *Proceedings*, Manchester Statistical Society, 1901. But see particularly R. Smith (unpublished thesis, op. cit.).

[3] See Eccles Shorrock (op. cit.).

formed 'The Lancashire Master Spinners' and Manufacturers' Defence Society', which Preston and other districts joined. The consolidation of this alliance was apparently postponed by the subsiding of union activity during the Cotton Famine. But during a mill strike in Preston in 1866 the employers there received ample notice of more labour trouble to come when trade revived; so they approached the Blackburn association to propose a joint organization. The resulting body was shortly joined by Burnley, the federation of these three employers' districts (as the North and North-East Lancashire Spinners' and Manufacturers' Association)[1] then controlling most of the plant in the North Lancashire cotton area. Within a few years the new body federated several other districts and moved its office to Manchester; it is the direct ancestor of the present weaving industry association, United Kingdom Textile Manufacturers' Association (formerly the CSMA).

At this time, of course, many firms in North Lancashire were still 'vertical' concerns, combining spinning and weaving. But in the rising specialist spinning centres of South Lancashire, active employers' organization waited on the revival of spinners' trade unionism by the new self-actor operatives. It was not until 1866 that a new employers' association was formed in Oldham, which was to play the central role in the later development of employers' organization in the spinning industry. The original motive of the Oldham Association's establishment was to fight the local mule-spinners' demand that a ten per cent. cut in wages made during the Cotton Famine be restored. The association was actually a federation of four neighbouring districts, but decided its policy by firms voting on their spindleage, and was felt to be controlled by the larger concerns. A separate association was formed in the Ashton district (where several firms had preserved a 'vertical' structure), but in several towns the spinning employers remained quite unassociated. And the 'Egyptian' firms of the second biggest spinning centre, Bolton, which had meanwhile also revived their own organization, repelled several advances by the Oldham employers for a united front.

Thus the divisions of interest that had afflicted the early employers' combinations re-appeared in their modern successors. These frictions were particularly marked between the big North Lancashire Association and the Oldham group. The former had adopted an entirely different form of organization, in which each firm had one vote, and firms were excluded from committees on mill or local disputes in which they were directly concerned. The North Lancashire Association's conciliatory attitude to the unions after the Great Strike of 1878, and particularly its acceptance of a

[1] There seems some doubt about the actual date of the North Lancashire Association's formation. Eccles Shorrock himself gives 1872, Wood 1876, and Smith 1866 and 1868. The initial 1866 federation of Preston and Blackburn was actually called the 'United Association of Spinners and Manufacturers of the Preston and East Lancashire Districts', possibly changing its title when joined by Burnley. But there was a break in the Association's continuity between 1869 and 1872 because its paid secretary absconded with the funds—an accident that could apparently overtake early employers' associations as well as unions—and it was re-organized afterwards.

central conciliation procedure three years later, were resented by other districts. The Oldham Masters' Association had at first refused even to recognize the unions. But having been compelled to end the 1885 Oldham lock-out with a compromise, it concluded that it could not face both the now re-organized Operative Spinners' Amalgamation *and* the newly-formed Cardroom Amalgamation by itself. Moreover, the Bolton employers' renewed rejection of the Oldham Association's proposal for a joint organization made the Oldham firms afraid that their town's becoming a cockpit of spinning labour disputes would encourage trade competition from firms outside the district. So when in 1888 the spinners' union advanced a new wage-demand, the Oldham Masters sent deputations out to canvass support from other centres, and set up a new body, the United Cotton Spinners' Association; and this consisted, not in a federation of local associations, but in a tightly-centralized combination of individual firms. In this enterprise they were joined by the Ashton employers; and in 1892 (the year when the Weavers' Amalgamation negotiated its 'Uniform List' with the North Lancashire employers who now dominated the manufacturing industry) the 'vertical' Ashton firms also took a leading part in forming the similarly-centralized United Cotton Manufacturers' Association. This body recruited members, not merely in the south-east, but also in Preston and the north-eastern towns, and was thus in direct rivalry with the established North Lancashire Association.

At the same time, however, the Ashton employers themselves were widening their own local association, merging four neighbouring districts into a single combination of spinning and weaving firms. And this move, though helped by the new United Cotton Spinners' Association, was by implication at variance with the latter body's tendency, since it strengthened the independent local organization as an alternative form. In the upshot, the Oldham employers themselves became dissatisfied with the UCSA's effectiveness. The Bolton association still refused proposals that it join a separate federal body, but instead set about widening its own organization. So in 1891, anticipating new labour conflicts, the Oldham and Ashton employers set up the Federation of Master Cotton Spinners' Associations, with a constitution more designed to reassure those employers who had been unwilling to join the UCSA for fear of domination by the Oldham 'Limiteds'.[1] And in the great Stalybridge and 'Brooklands' lock-outs of 1891–3, the UCSA slipped into the background.

After the Brooklands Agreement had put conciliation in the spinning industry on to much the same footing as that achieved by the Weavers twelve years before, the UCSA converted itself into the Cotton Employers' Parliamentary Association (it had been one criticism against the North Lancashire Masters' organization that it had not put up a sufficient fight against the legislative compaigns of the United Textile Factory Workers' Association). However, the reformed organization expired before the First World War, achieving little success in this secondary attempt to make itself

[1] The Federation was to be governed by a committee of associated districts: these were represented in proportion to their subscribed spindleage, but all policy decisions required a 75 per cent. vote.

a political agency for all cotton employers—partly because most of them preferred to use their industrial federations and other bodies even for this purpose, partly because of disagreements on the actual policies to be advocated. Meanwhile the UCSA's intended partner organization for the weaving trade, the United Cotton Manufacturers' Association, likewise failed to become a serious rival to the old North Lancashire Association in industrial matters, and met a similar fate. In between the Stalybridge and Brooklands lock-outs the newly-constituted Master-Spinners' Federation had actually approached both the Bolton group and the North Lancashire Association to join in a single combination of cotton employers with the UCMA for the purpose of imposing a general wage-reduction. But though the North Lancashire Association's spinning members ran short-time during the Brooklands conflict 'in sympathy' with the stopped firms of the south-east, the Association rejected the proposed united employers' organization as likely to provoke disputes.

Thus the organization of cotton employers—though it came many years before the great federations of engineering and building employers—on the whole followed on that of operatives. But the conflicts of interest on the employers' side assume, even in this brief account of their associations' development, even more complexity than appeared in the history of the trade unions. Among the cotton workers, the main divisions of interest were between different occupational groups, and conflicts between localities were in general reconciled by the unions' consistent use of a federal organization. But among the employers, conflicts of interest between different sections of the cotton trade were complicated by differences between localities, between larger and smaller firms, and between firms of different structures. In the end, local differences were eased by the main employers' associations adopting the same federal form as the union Amalgamations. And by the First World War, the divisions among employers were to be further reduced by the more important independent districts' affiliation to the major federations—the Bolton master-spinners joining the Federation of Master Cotton Spinners' Associations, and the Ashton group affiliating to the Cotton Spinners' and Manufacturers' Association as well. But up to 1906, when the weaving unions federated together, there were still four separate major—and in some respects, rival—employers' organizations for the cotton industry, as well as one or two non-federated local associations. And that the Federation should later have come to represent the spinning employers, and the Association those in weaving, was largely due to the accident that the spinning interests of the Association's member firms gradually withered away. While to the present day the cotton employers have no general federation equivalent to the operatives' UTFWA.[1]

Of course, the existence or otherwise of an employers' association is usually less important to the bargaining strength and general influence of

[1] The writer understands that a link beween the two (spinning and manufacturing) associations, already separately consolidated in 1961, is at present under discussion. Should this produce a single federation with its own officials, the employers will for the first time have a distinct lead in central organization.

firms than is a trade union to workers. The cotton employers, and the company directors that succeeded the original private entrepreneurs, were themselves generally men of wealth, able to exercise political and social pressure as individuals. The mere fact that they were relatively few made it easier for them to combine informally if they thought it necessary: so that the gap in the history of cotton employers' organization in the 1840s, for instance, was to some extent filled by *ad hoc* associations to oppose the operatives' demand for a shorter legal work-day. And the employers had, in any case, other channels of organized influence open to them. As early as 1794 the Manchester merchants and manufacturers formed 'The Commercial Society' which later, as the Manchester Chamber of Commerce, was to become as important a platform for cotton trade interests as the Masters' Associations proper. In the 1870s quite a few cotton firms belonged to the Associated Employers of Labour, which seems to have recruited many textile and engineering concerns in Lancashire and Yorkshire, though it was too heterogeneous to become very effective. The Chamber of Commerce itself took a hand in industrial relations after the 1881 establishment of the 'Joint Standing Committee' in cotton manufacturing, and set up a Conciliation Court of its own; but though this was used to some extent by other industries, it achieved little success in an attempt to induce those cotton employers who were not party to the Weavers' Agreement to use this conciliation procedure instead.

The cotton masters' organization have traditionally assumed a wider role than employers' associations in other industries, which are usually more narrowly specialized to labour questions. Nevertheless, and particularly since the Second World War, there has been a certain tendency for textile firms to form associations apart from the main employers' federations (to which they often also belonged) for various 'trade' purposes—like the Condenser Spinners' & Manufacturers', the Rayon Weavers', the Yarn Doublers', and the Rayon Spinners' & Doublers' Associations to represent specialist interests, and the Yarn Spinners' Association for trade co-operation and price-fixing. Since the 1960 'concentration' several of these bodies have again merged in the major employers' federations—so that the old Master Spinners' Federation is now renamed the British (Cotton & Allied) Spinners' & Doublers' Association. But that the employers' organizations' significance to their affiliates remains less than is that of the unions to *their* members is sufficiently indicated by the very different standing of their respective officials. The union secretary—despite the union rules that circumscribe his formal status[1]—is always something more than a paid official, standing rather in a role of industrial and political leadership to the operatives, of whom he is taken as the public and symbolic representative. The employers' secretary has much more the actual position of a professional agent—as is for instance suggested by the fact that nearly half of the thirty-odd local masters' organizations affiliated to the FMCSA and the CSMA (as they were up to 1961) share their official—who sometimes acts for spinning, weaving and other employers' organizations impartially—with another local association. And employers' organizations have often

[1] See Chapter V, 2, section III, for instances.

retained a local accountant or solicitor to act as their secretary—or even acquired an ex-union official—rather than finding him among the ranks of employers or managers themselves.

Nevertheless, the employers' associations have usually been able to command a high degree of discipline from their members. Partly, no doubt, this arises from their relatively long history, which was also conditioned by many great industrial disputes. In the days when the present associations' ancestors were formed, they were in any case perhaps less inhibited about their fundamental purpose, of countering the bargaining strength the unions gave their workers, than have been recently-founded associations in other industries; so that their constitutions usually included disciplinary clauses. Thus the spinning employers' associations commonly imposed a special fine or levy on mills that continued (even with permission) to run in disputes. And the old North Lancashire Association refused assistance (either from the dispute fund which its subscriptions were mainly intended to accumulate or from its officers) to firms that paid above or below the agreed standard wage-rates—unless they had first applied to its committee for permission to do so and received it. So recently as 1950, certain firms were expelled from their association for paying unauthorized bonuses on wages.

The actual attitude of cotton employers' associations to trade unionism appears to have varied. On the whole, the manufacturing employers' organization appears historically to have been more conciliating than that of the master-spinners. Perhaps this appearance simply arises because it is older: certainly, even some of the local weavers' associations that formed quite late (like those at Bury and Ashton) encountered bitter hostility—and their leaders, victimization—from their district employers. But the weaving firms are themselves generally smaller than those in spinning, which may have made them less willing to stand up to labour troubles—and the North Lancashire Association's rules in any case gave its smaller members a greater influence than did the spinning employers' procedures.[1]

[1] It has been suggested (see F. Bealey, loc. cit., and Beatrice Webb's *My Apprenticeship*, Penguin Edition, Vol. I, p. 191) that there was more identity of interest between the weaving employers and workers because of the different and closer personal relations in the manufacturing industry's smaller firms and in the more isolated weaving towns. But the spinning trade's adoption of joint stock company organization made it possible for many operatives—those with high occupational or family earnings—to become shareholders, which might have been expected to give a more material foundation for conciliatory labour relationships. While the co-operative weaving mills, of which there were several in the nineteenth century (Ward describes the initiation of one such enterprise, and Beatrice Webb refers to others in her letters from Bacup thirty years later), seem to have died out in the twentieth. Many writers have commented on the fair-mindedness with which in the two or three decades up to the First World War cotton employers and operatives viewed each others' claims, and particularly on the friendly relations which then existed between their respective officials, contrasting these things with the situation of other industries. But it is unlikely that these things were due to any special social qualities of the cotton districts: familiarity is as likely to breed contempt as tolerance. And a generation before, weaving labour conflicts sometimes culminated in violence: in the great 1878 strike, martial law was actually proclaimed in Blackburn!

Particularly, weaving firms are mostly longer established than those in spinning, where the formation of joint stock companies largely transformed the industry during the late nineteenth century. And in general, it seems to have been the newly-developing centres where the employers were most aggressive in their attitude to the unions—Preston in the 1850s and '60s, in the following decades Oldham and the Ashton district (where the automatic loom was first adopted), and so on. At any rate, and although the spinning unions could hardly be regarded as naturally more aggressive than those in weaving, the spinning unions have twice withdrawn from agreed conciliation procedures similar to those in the weaving trade because in their case they thought them to work too slowly or disadvantageously—once in 1905, when they cancelled the Brooklands Agreement, and again in 1935, when they abrogated the Conciliation Board appointed for spinning in conclusion of the great 1932 disputes.

On the other hand, cotton employers have rarely been so extreme in their attitude to trade unionism as have some in more monopolized industries. A cartel or monopoly often seems to swing sharply according to the solidarity of its employees. When the latters' unions are new and weak, it is most determined in its opposition to them. But once it is clear that the unions are established, the employing body may move to a quite opposite attitude, of accommodation to collective organization among its workers. There is something of this, given the now remote historical circumstances, in the relation between the old north-east coast 'Hostmen' and their miners' combinations. But it is clearer in the case of the cartellized textile finishing firms, which having first strongly opposed their dyers' unionization, then conceded recognition to it on what were—particularly for the 1890s—quite extraordinarily favourable terms.[1] The cotton employers, by contrast, have always refused to recognize formally anything in the nature of a 'union shop'—having, for instance, quite recently refused to conclude a general agreement for three-shift working in manufacturing which they themselves desired because the Weavers' insisted on union membership for night-shift workers (who would mostly have had to be new recruits) as a condition of it.

Although the cotton employers' associations were first formed in defence against trade unionism, it seems indisputable that their mere existence was in some ways helpful to labour organization. This was particularly so for the 'open' Weavers' Amalgamations, because of their reliance on collective bargaining. The North Lancashire Association's rule that all members firms must pay no more nor less than the agreed standard rates was partly designed to maintain a united front against the Weavers, and partly to reduce the numerous mill disputes arising from discrepancies in piece-prices. And one of the Association's first moves was to set up (though in the result unsuccessfully) a sub-committee to draft a standard wage-list for the three employers' organizations that formed it in 1866. But the main aim of the Weavers themselves was to establish standard wage-rates: and they were certainly interested in reducing the risk of local stoppages that might drain their meagre strike-reserves. To this extent the interest of the

[1] See Chapter IV, 2, section II—and IV for the miners' reference.

unions and organized employers coincided—though in a perhaps rather paradoxical way. The main area of conflict between them concerned the general level of wages; and they both usually wished to reduce other disputatious claims on their resources to be the better-equipped for that central arena. Once the unions were accepted, therefore—but only then—the employers' organization itself became an assistance to them in dealing with many minor complaints and in generally organizing their procedures. Thus the practice of local employers' associations, once federated, of automatically referring disputes which could not be settled locally to their central organization, also ensured that the union Amalgamation itself should be brought in whenever any issue of principle was raised. While the 'Mill Rules' that the manufacturing employers' Association and the weaving unions agreed in 1908 (as part of a general revision of the old 'Weavers' Complaints' procedure) constituted a detailed recognition of the unions' standing in the workplace itself. Even the *threat* to refer unsatisfied mill complaints to a local joint meeting (as the Joint Rules provided) remained an important practical lever in the manufacturing unions' hands against employers who did not want their troubles aired amongst their rivals.

Similarly, the concern of organized employers at the infractions of agreed rates and conditions by individual concerns in the 1930s led their Association to combine with the Weavers' Amalgamation in demanding legal enforcement of collective agreements. While one of the Weavers' weakest areas was always Burnley, where the presence of many small (so-called 'commission' or 'room-and-power') firms made the organization of employers themselves less complete than elsewhere. The Cardroom Amalgamation, too—again, once it had surmounted the critical step of achieving recognition—was able to use the existing spinning employers' associations as a lever to consolidate itself. The 'closed' unions, because of their emphasis on 'autonomous regulation', had less to gain from organization on the employers' side. But it has been shown that the Weavers' willingness to associate the closed unions in manufacturing with the joint procedure for 'Weavers' Complaints' was of some help to their consolidation; and certainly the Weavers' sponsorship of the weak Warehousemen's Amalgamation in the latter's early central negotiations appears critical to its survival as a 'mixed' union.

Even the Spinners' control of labour supply may have received an unforeseen reinforcement from their recognition by employers' organizations. Once that was achieved, the masters' associations themselves became generally unwilling to involve themselves in expensive local disputes by supporting individual managements' attempts to challenge the Spinners' labour regulations and conventions. And this unwillingness was later re-inforced because the Spinners' system in fact proved to be extraordinarily efficient—largely because of certain accidental qualities that only became apparent when it had been widely accepted and established. These were that by providing the mule-team as a group with (more or less) straight piece-rates, but permitting the mule-spinner himself to pay the team's other members only time-wages out of their joint earnings, it in effect put the team's controlling workman on a steeply progressive scale of 'payment by results'; while the inability of the mule-spinner who lost his job to transfer to other mills because that would break the latters' own promotion ladders gave him an interest in his own firm's competitive efficiency. (Things which obliged the spinners' unions themselves to restrain their members from increasing output by such 'unfair' means as cleaning and adjusting their machines outside regular working hours.)[1] And granted that the Spinners had been pressed by the development of employers' organizations into at least *area*-wide collective bargaining, they also found their resources conserved and organization strengthened by the procedure that they then developed with the masters' associations—of settling mill wage-grievances by joint 'deputations' of union and employers' officials to determine the exact application of the standard agreements to the actual conditions of the workplace in dispute. In one sense, of course—and this is quite as true of the manufacturing industry—the reduction in small local disputes by such procedures merely concentrated industrial conflict into a number of great strikes or lock-outs: indeed, by permitting both sides to accumulate reserves for such affairs it may well have made them the more inevitable. But at least these great disputes confronted the parties to them with obvious and unavoidable decisions of principle and policy. Whereas (and as the histories of the great craft industries and of mining more recently both suggest) few industrial organizations have shown themselves capable of developing a coherent and flexible policy in dealing with many scattered stoppages forced on them by separate local incidents and situations.

However, the help given to trade union development by the existence of employers' organization in cotton can best be regarded as an indirect consequence of the growth of trade unionism itself. This is shown by the fact that the primary purpose of all the successful voluntary combinations of cotton firms (apart, of course, from actual financial mergers) has been to deal with labour problems. If, for instance, the Weavers in pressing for a standard scale of wages had been able to exploit a natural tendency on their employers' part towards cartels or other anti-competitive devices, one might expect the latter to be reflected in other directions. But in fact no attempts at mutual price-regulation (and other costs were certainly more important than those of labour) were made by manufacturing firms before the inter-War period, and even those then proposed broke down on the unwillingness of sufficient weaving concerns to submit to them. In no

[1] Since the war, several attempts have been made by industrial consultants and 'efficiency experts' to improve the working arrangements at mule-frames: the writer understands that these alternative systems have generally produced lower outputs than the methods developed by the spinners themselves. One very old spinner has described an almost mythical character of his youth, a 'man in white trousers' whose almost supernatural power to extract more than the normal output from his frames was signified by his commonly exceeding that norm by as much as 5 per cent! It is perhaps an open question, whether the incidental efficiency of the mule-spinners' labour system explains, not merely why no other country was able to develop a substantially-competitive spinning industry before the ring-frame was perfected, but also the long survival of the mule-frame in Lancashire despite the ring's marked technical advantages.

section of the cotton industry, in fact, did even standard wage-rates appear before active workers' combinations. On the other hand, since organization among employers has appeared primarily as a response to that of workers and as a defence against the latter, its effectiveness has also largely depended on the extent to which the pressure of trade unionism has submerged divisions between employing interests. We have seen that the growth of the manufacturing employers' association was much less disturbed by internal conflicts of interest (although these certainly existed)[1] than has that of the master-spinners. It now seems probable that this was because the weaving operatives' organization was historically much more extensive and better co-ordinated than that of the spinning workers—amongst whom trade unionism was first intensively concentrated only in a single exclusive group that for long itself had rival centres of leadership. In particular, the Weavers' persistent pressure to widen the coverage of their major agreements—the Second Amalgamation fought major strikes in Burnley and Ashton between 1885 and 1887 to bring the district wage-rates into line with Blackburn and the north-east—made even those employers' districts which were critical of the old North Lancashire Association's then-conciliatory attitude feel the advantage of joining it in the hope of strengthening resistance to general wage-advances, rather than putting up an isolated fight to maintain advantageous local wage-rates.

But there is an apparent interdependence between the growth of trade unions and of employers' organization. Perhaps the effect of the latter can best be expressed as really being to concentrate employers' resistance to trade unionism about a particular stage in union development—so that before the employers accord it recognition, unionism's growth is more difficult, and afterwards easier, than it would otherwise have been. Since this effect depends on the extent of employers' organization itself, and the possibility of such organization is in turn affected by the structure of the industry concerned, it would partly explain the different experiences of trade unions in monopolized trades as against those where there are many small and competing firms.

One final aspect of the relation between the cotton employers and operatives is perhaps of some interest. It has often been argued that trade unionism is an inevitable product of the worker's separation from ownership of the tools of production—of the divorce of labour from capital. From which it would seem to follow that the sharper that divorce, and the less the employee's chance of rising to the status of employer, the more aggressive would be the labour organizations that developed. Of the degree of 'social mobility' in the textile regions in the early nineteenth century the Hammonds noted that 'The Industrial Revolution put a new ladder within

[1] As late as the 1930s, when the manufacturers' association supported the Burnley employers in a great stoppage to impose higher loom complements on the Weavers, the resultant agreement was subsequently revised to give wage differentials on 'more looms' systems that substantially reduced the latters' cost advantages. This revision favoured employers with old mills and equipment, showing that differences on the employers' side which were precisely analogous to those in spinning (between the South-East and North Lancs. firms) had existed over the whole forty years' history of disputes over 'more looms'.

the reach of diligence and worth . . . the cotton industry offered to the English workman the prospect that the revolutionary armies had offered the French peasant'.[1] Just before the First World War, it was still true that in cotton manufacturing (where the private business was the main form of economic organization) the great majority of employers had started as operatives, while in cotton spinning (where the joint stock company dominated) most members of boards of directors, as well as a probable majority of factory managers, were drawn from the same source.[2] From the late nineteenth century to the 1920s, moreover, shareholding in cotton companies was widely spread amongst the operatives (for whom it was a common form of family savings)—so much so that some have attributed to it both an alleged reluctance to press wage-claims *and* some extensive opposition that appeared among the cotton workers in the 1890s to the Eight-Hour Day.[3] But such employee shareholding certainly declined in the inter-War slumps. And a recent study has shown that the proportion of directors and managers in the contemporary cotton industry who have risen from the ranks has since become negligible.[4] It is at least curious that the collective militancy of the textile factory workers should have been highest just in the period of highest social mobility within their trade—and that the apparent decline in social mobility during the present century (at least so far as the textile districts are concerned) should have coincided with a patent falling-off in the aggressiveness of the cotton unions.

[1] *The Bleak Age*, p. 47.

[2] See Chapman and Marquis: 'The Recruiting of the Employing Classes from the ranks of Wage Earners in the Cotton Industry'. *Journal*, Royal Statistical Society, 1912.

[3] See Smith (op. cit.) and Beatrice Webb's letters from Bacup, again.

[4] See R. V. Clement's *Managers: A Study of their Careers in Industry* (Allen & Unwin, London, 1958).

VII

APPENDIX

2

A Chronology of the Cotton Unions

The following sequence of what seem to be significant incidents in the history of the cotton operatives' organization is divided, for convenience, into periods corresponding to the main stages of the British cotton industry's own evolution which are suggested in Chapter I, 2, section v. However, it will be seen that these stages also coincide with different phases of union development. Thus, the first period covers the rise of the early handloom weavers' societies, and closes with the first appearance of collective organization among workshop spinning operatives. The second and longest period, of the Factory Revolution, embraces the growth and collapse of handworkers' protest movements and the rise of the first substantial factory workers' organizations. The period of industrial consolidation sees the emergence of trade unions of a modern type, followed—in the phase of decelerating industrial growth—by the completion of their organizational structure and economic practice. While the last period, of industrial contraction, is one of relative organizational rigidity and declining membership. Otherwise, this Chronology includes also a number of events—particularly in connection with the development of wage-systems, working conditions and union political activity—which are not specifically referred to in the main text.

FIRST PERIOD: GROWTH OF CAPITALIST DOMESTIC INDUSTRY

1736 Manchester Act exempts Lancashire textile producers from general prohibition of 'calico' manufacture.

1730–40 Kay's 'fly-shuttle' invented, improved handlooms introduced, simple warping and winding machines, first attempts at 'spinning by rollers'.

1740s Riots against fly-shuttle.

1745 Manchester merchants combine to impose wage-reduction on handloom weavers.

1747 Manchester smallware weavers' society probably already in existence.
1753 Attack on 'cotton reel' machine.
1754 Manchester smallware weavers arrested for 'combination'.
1755 Smallware weavers' society re-organized.
1756 Outbreak of Seven Years' War.
1757 Smallware weavers demand increased piece-prices.
1758 Strike of several thousand check-weavers around Manchester for wage-increases, regulation of entry to trade and recognition of weavers' 'box-society'; Oldham fustian-weavers' and Manchester silk-weavers' combinations.
1759–60 Check-weavers' and smallware weavers' leaders tried for 'combination'. Minor weavers' strikes in outlying districts.
1764–69 Hargreaves' spinning-jenny, Arkwright's spinning system, Kay's loom improvements.
1768–69 Riots in North Lancashire, partly connected with spinning-jenny's introduction. Collectively-agreed wage-list for certain weaving branches.
1770–79 Improved carding engines available, construction of water-powered factories. Crompton perfects spinning-mule.
1779 Lancashire riots, smashing of 'patent machines'—and jenny-spinners' Petition for control of machinery. Handloom weavers' 'Address' demands legal wage-enforcement. Move to Lancashire weavers' federation. New Act against combinations.
1780 Scottish weavers' federation to secure wage-list.
1781 Oldham weavers' manifesto demands 'regulation of the trade'. Smallware weavers' strike to enforce wage-list.
1783–85 Release of Arkwright's spinning patents. Steampower successfully applied to spinning. Attempts at automatic spinning-mule and powered loom.
1785 Stockport spinners' combination (probably of domestic or workshop operatives) for standard piece-prices.
1787–88 Scottish weavers' federation against wage-reductions.

SECOND PERIOD: THE FACTORY REVOLUTION

1790 First Manchester power-loom factory burnt by handloom weavers.
1791 'General spirit of combination'.
1792 Stockport and Manchester mule-spinners' unions formed. Domestic fine-weavers' collective agreement. Peak of handloom weavers' prosperity.
1793 French War begins. Anti-'Democrat' measures. Long-term decline in handloom wages begins.
1793–95 Friendly Societies legalized—hundreds formed in Lancashire.
1794 'Commercial Society' (later: Chamber of Commerce) formed in Manchester.

1795 Whitbread's Minimum-wage Bill rejected. Manchester mule-spinners' union re-organized—spinners' strikes for wage-increases.

1796 Oldham mule-spinners' union.

1798 Fine-weavers' agreements become ineffective.

1799 'Association of Weavers', Lancs. federation of handloom societies. 23,000 signatures to weavers' Petition for legal wage and apprenticeship enforcement. New Anti-combination Act.

1800 Association of Weavers disbanded formally. Cotton Arbitration Act, for settlement of piece-price disputes.

1801 Weavers' Petition for improved Arbitration Act.

1801–02 Successful strikes by Manchester spinners. Stockport spinners arrested for 'combination'.

1803 Manchester master-spinners raise defence fund against spinners' unions. Weavers' collective appeals under Arbitration Act ruled illegal.

1804 Arbitration Act amended to prevent collective appeals. Weavers' movement to re-form open federation, deputations for legal minimum wage to Ministers.

1807 Handloom weavers' 'Monster Petition' for legal wage—130,000 signatures.

1808 Unsuccessful employers' attempts at collective regulation of weavers' wages. Weavers' Monster Petition rejected by Parliament. Great weavers' strike for direct wage-increase leads to 'most brutal industrial conflict in British history'.

1809 New Weavers' Petition.

1810 Glasgow spinners' union appears: lock-out and violence in Glasgow. Spinners now organized throughout major cotton districts. Lancs. federation's 'Assembly' organizes 'rolling strike': defeated by four months' general lock-out of 30,000 operatives, and Manchester union temporarily collapses.

1810–11 Weavers' societies propose joint 'regulation of the trade' to employers.

1811 Spinners arrested for combination. 53,000 signatures to Manchester and Bolton weavers' legal wage petitions. 30,000 from Scotland. Scottish weavers' legal action for wage-lists under Elizabethan statutes.

1811–12 Radicalism and Luddism among Lancashire weavers: 'steam looms' attacked in Stockport and other towns.

1812 National links between regional weavers' federations. 40,000 Scottish handloom workers strike to enforce legal wage-list: leaders arrested after three weeks.

1813 Parliament repeals Elizabethan statutes.

1813–14 First known district wage-list for mule-spinning in Bolton. Stockport mule-spinners' collective agreement. Preston spinners' union re-formed. Temporary recovery in handloom wages.

1815 Peace—and mass unemployment.

1816 Disunity in weavers' leadership. Movement for political reform: only 20,000 sign new legal wages petition. 38 weavers arrested in Manchester for Reform agitation.

1817 'Blanketeers' March' for Reform, supported largely by handloom weavers. Lancashire spinners resume links outside county. Manchester master-spinners' defence association revived. Scottish operatives tried for administering unlawful oaths, on evidence of provocateur.

1818 Spinners take lead in 'Philanthropic Society'—general trades union. Manchester master-spinners' organize short-time to defeat spinners' demands for increased wages and reduced hours. Spinners' strike involves 20,000 for two months. Regional strike-wave spreads through other trades, drawing in handloom weavers organized by 'Associated Weavers'. First reported strike of power-loom weavers. Spinners' and handloom weavers' leaders arrested. Repression of trade unions follows.

1819 Lancashire hand-weavers' Petition to enforce minimum wages. Further employers' attempt at weaving wage-regulation. Reform agitation, and Peterloo. 'Short-Time Act' prohibits employment of children under 9 in spinning, limits juvenile hours to 12 daily.

1819–20 Handloom weavers' strikes outside Lancashire, especially Glasgow.

1821 Bolton spinners' strike against new wage-list.

1822 Efficient power-loom marketed. Substantial growth of power-loom weaving follows.

1822–23 Re-formed spinners' federation supports Bolton wage-campaign—leads to district lock-out and arrest of Bolton leaders.

1823 Glasgow employers' alliance against spinners' union. Master-spinners' associations formed in several Lancashire districts about this time.

1824 Repeal of Combination Acts. Handloom weavers' federation publicly re-formed, in association with Scottish federation. Glasgow weavers arrested for organizing 'boycott'. Four months' general lock-out of Glasgow spinners; Lancashire spinners' federation supports six months' strike at Hyde; several smaller strikes in other districts.

1825 Spinners and weavers both represented in committee against re-enactment of Combination Laws. Further legal reduction of juvenile working hours in spinning factories. Chorley spinners' strike.

1825–30 Efficient self-actor spinning mules marketed.

1825–26 Severe slump, and particularly sharp fall in handloom wages. Further weaving employers' attempt at collective wage-regulation. Oldham spinners' mill strikes involve violence, after wage-reduction.

1826 Lancashire weavers smash power-looms, attack factories, in general outbreak: Lancashire handloom workers' organization virtually destroyed after arrests and transportations. Spinners associated with Manchester attempt at general trades union. Glasgow spinners' organization recovered, and enforcing own wage-list after series of mill disputes.

1827–28 Various small spinners' strikes in Lancashire.

1829 Six months' Stockport spinners' strike against wage-reductions. Six months' general strike of Manchester spinners (against employer-imposed wage-list) defeated. Lancashire spinners initiate 'Grand General Union of the U.K.'. Weavers' attacks on handloom 'factories' and steam-looms.

1830 Spinners' strikes in Bolton and other districts, 'rolling strike' in Manchester. Manchester spinners initiate National Association for the Protection of Labour: several unions of power-loom weavers, overlookers and other new factory operatives affiliate. Ashton master-spinners' combination to impose new wage-list; Grand Union calls county strike—defeated after ten weeks' stoppage of 20,000 workers. Henry Hunt elected at Preston as first and only working-class M.P. in unreformed Parliament.

1830–32 Spinners' Grand Union and NAPL disintegrate. Manchester spinners diverted to Ten-Hour agitation.

1831 Attempt to re-form hand-weavers' federation fails, but minor spinners' strike in Ashton.

1832 Reform Act. Cobbett and Fielden elected for Oldham.

1833 Lancashire spinners' federation revives. Spinners associated with Society For National Regeneration's campaign for shorter working day. Legal hours of young factory operatives reduced to 8 per day: unpopularity with spinners stimulates wider 'Ten-Hour' movement.

1833–36 Renewed boom in power-loom installation.

1834 Oldham spinners' strike for 8-hour day. Attempts to revive Manchester spinners' union. First known district wage-list for power-loom weaving in Oldham. Glasgow and Paisley handloom weavers' collective agreement for annual piece-price review.

1834–35 Last cotton handloom-weavers' legal-wage Petitions.

1834–37 Power-loom weavers' unions formed in Glasgow, Oldham, Preston. Introduction of new Poor Law in North disrupted by popular agitation.

1836 Preston spinners' unsuccessful three months' strike for wage-increases stimulates introduction of self-actor mule.

1837 Oldham spinners' strike against wage-cuts defeated—union disintegrates. Other Lancashire spinners' unions collapse or enfeebled, but factory and local 'short-time' committees maintain campaign for Ten-Hour Day and Manchester union re-organized. Glasgow spinners' strike defeated by employers' combination.

1838 Glasgow spinners' trial invokes national demonstrations of solidarity: but leaders transported. Scottish spinners' unionism virtually disappears.

1839–40 Lancashire union lodges recruited to Chartism.

1840 Hand-workers' riots in Colne, factory-weavers strike in Wigan. First attempt at federation of power-loom weavers' unions, to support Stockport strike.

1842 'Plug Plot'—Chartist general strike of whole N.W. England manufacturing districts—develops from strikes of Ashton spinners and Stalybridge weavers against wage-reductions. Independent strikes in other districts.

THIRD PERIOD: CONSOLIDATION OF MECHANIZED COTTON INDUSTRY

1842 Lancashire spinners' federation, including self-actor spinners, re-formed from Bolton; promotes 'Short Time Committee' to support Oastler's campaign for legal reduction in working day.

1842–46 Attempts at Manchester power-loom union.

1843 Oldham spinners' union re-formed, with own district federation.

1843–46 District wage-lists for Bolton spinners, and for power-loom weavers in several towns.

1844 'Half-time' system for young factory operatives introduced by law, together with Factory Inspectors. Spinners' mill strikes in Manchester.

1845 Spinners' and power-loom weavers' unions send observers to 'United Trades for the Protection of Labour'.

1846 Mill strikes against wage-reductions. Oldham master-spinners agree to reduce output instead of wage-cut. Bolton spinners' federation renounces Chartism.

1847 Ten-Hour Act secured: provides maximum 60-hour working week for women and juveniles in textile factories. Chartist Parliamentary candidate defeated at Stockport.

1847–50 Spinners' federation collapses after withdrawal of major district unions. Frequent mill strikes by spinners against evasion of Ten-Hour Act.

1848–52 Many local strikes in North Lancashire for wage-increases, particularly of powerloom weavers. Repeated mill strikes of Blackburn and Darwen weavers on piece-rate issues.

1850 on Permanent local Weavers' Associations formed in North Lancashire.

1852 Blackburn employers' association formed, meets weavers' representatives to propose standard wage-list.

1853 Agreed Blackburn 'Standard' List ('The Cotton Operatives' Charter') promulgates standard rates for weavers, spinners and other factory operatives, and includes dispute-conciliation procedure. New Lancashire spinners' federation formed to recover 1846 wages. Widespread strikes in Lancashire.

1853 Thirty weeks' Preston strike/lock-out of 20,000 operatives follows weavers' demand for wage-increase. Weavers supported by existing informal federation of Lancashire power-loom unions. Defence Fund organized by Lancashire cotton employers to support Preston Masters' Association.

1854 Blackburn Weavers' Association formed, with branches in neighbouring towns.

1857 –58 Bolton cardroom union attempts general cardroom operatives' federation.

1858 North Lancashire Power Loom Weavers' Association formed (the 'First Amalgamation').

1859 –60 'First Amalgamation' appoints Secretary Thos. Birtwistle by examination.

1858 –66 Various local unions of skilled manufacturing workers—overlookers, tapesizers, twisters—formed, mostly in North Lancashire.

1859 Twenty-nine week strike of Padiham weavers for standard wage-rates, with support of First Amalgamation. Burnley and Preston employers organize 'Master Spinners' & Manufacturers' Defence Association'.

1859 –69 Agreed district wage-lists for spinning and weaving generally adopted—mostly on Blackburn List principle.

1860 Frequent local strikes. Attempt to re-organize spinners' federation. New attempt at cardroom workers' federation.

1961 Independent Bolton self-actor spinners' union formed.

1862 –63 American Civil War causes the Cotton Famine. 250,000 operatives unemployed.

1866 Demands for wage-increases (or restoration of cuts made in Cotton Famine) accompanied by mill strikes, lead to formation of North Lancashire employers' federation and Oldham Master Spinners' Association.

1866 –67 Unions of 6,000 spinners, 11,000 power-loom weavers represented at United Kingdom Conference of Organized Trades.

1867 Textile Unions' delegate meeting to promote 8-Hour Bill. Manchester Trades Council calls first TUC. Second Reform Act extends manhood suffrage.

1868 Oldham spinners' union appoints full-time secretary.

1869 Seven months' strike of Preston operatives against wage-cuts. First Oldham Spinning List for self-actors.

1870 Present Spinners' Amalgamation formed. Oldham and Bolton spinners' unions re-organized. New wave of union organization among weavers begins, followed by other manufacturing operatives—new local union development concentrated particularly in South-East Lancashire.

1871 Factory Acts Reform Committee fails to secure 8-hour day, but legal textile factory hours reduced by one per week—'one o'clock Saturday' introduced.

1872 Oldham Spinners' unsuccessful strike for 'twelve o'clock Saturday'. Cotton unions form Factory Acts Reform Association for 54-hour week. Oldham Spinning list Revised.

1873 First cardroom men's district wage-list, in Blackburn.

1874 Liberal government replaced by Tories. New Factory Act concedes 56½-hour week. Partial Amalgamation of overlookers' unions.

1875 Oldham Master Spinners' Association attempts concerted reduction of output to meet depression, but frustrated by rival group of new Limited Companies. Oldham spinners' strike against wage-reductions. Several strikes of cardroom men in S.E. Lancs.

1876 Revised Oldham Spinning List includes 'speed clause' and specifies piecers' wages. Spinners' strikes against wage-reduction in Blackburn district.

1877 Bolton spinners' strike against wage-cut exhausts Spinners' Amalgamation funds.

1878 'Great Strike' of 100,000 North Lancashire operatives against wage-reduction, defeated after nearly two months. Re-organization of Weavers' First Amalgamation. Spinners' Amalgamation appoints permanent secretary by examination.

1878–79 Bolton Spinners' List becomes ineffective after failure of revision negotiations. Piece-rates introduced for women cardroom workers in S.E. Lancs. Installation of ring-spinning plant becoming significant.

FOURTH PERIOD: SLOWING INDUSTRIAL GROWTH AND INCREASING FOREIGN COMPETITION

1880 30,000 Blackburn operatives stopped by weavers' strike for return of 1878 wage-cuts. 'Northern Counties' Weavers' Association' formed to co-ordinate First Amalgamation and non-affiliated weavers' unions. North Lancs. Tapesizers' Amalgamation formed. Oldham spinners form 'Provincial' organization. Further unsuccessful attempt at cardroom operatives' federation.

1881 North Lancs. employers' association and Weavers' First Amalgamation agree on joint conciliation procedure. Six months' 'unorganized' strike of Oldham doublers.

1882 Oldham Spinners form 'United Movable Committee' to organize coarse-spinning districts.

1883 Factory Acts Reform Association revived.

1883–84 Failure of 6 weeks' Blackburn weavers' strike on wage-revisions.

1884 Present Weavers' (the 'second') Amalgamation formed. Spinners' Amalgamation re-organized.

1885 Spinners' Amalgamation survives three months' lock-out of Oldham district on wage-reduction. Oldham cardroom union forms 'Provincial' Federation. Two weeks' strike of Burnley weavers for Blackburn wage-rates leads to opening of negotiations for uniform weaving list. Present Overlookers' Amalgamation formed.

1886 Cardroom Amalgamation formed. Northern Counties' Factory Acts Reform Association for better legal enforcement.

1886 –87 Second Weavers' Amalgamation survives twenty weeks' strike of Ashton district weavers for higher wage-rates.

1887 New Bolton Spinning List. N. Lancs. List for 'fancy' weaving.

1887 –88 Weavers' Amalgamation supports local strikes against underpayment, including 22 weeks' strike at Barnoldswick.

1888 Ineffective cardroom strike in N.E. Lancs. Cardroom Amalgamation appoints full-time secretary.

1889 Oldham cardroom strike/partial lock-out lasts 17 weeks.

1889 –90 Factory Act Reform alliance re-organized as United Textile Factory Workers' Association. Organizes campaign for 48-hour Bill and more factory regulation. 200,000 signatures to 'Monster Petition' against 'steaming'.

1890 Oldham cardroom wage-list agreed. Twisters' Amalgamation formed.

1891 New Factory Act includes 'piecework particulars' clause (requiring employers to provide details of work and piece-prices); Birtwistle appointed Inspector to enforce. Federation of Master Cotton Spinners formed. Spinners' and Cardroom Amalgamations form ineffective alliance ('Cotton Workers' Association').

1891 –92 'Stalybridge' Lock-out involves 100,000 spinning operatives for three weeks, after 17 weeks' mill strike on 'bad work' (i.e. inferior working conditions). Piecers attempt 'breakaway' organization from spinners' unions.

1892 'Uniform List' of weaving wage-rates agreed.

1893 20 weeks' 'Brooklands' Lock-out of 100,000 spinning workers on wage-reduction. 'Brooklands Agreement' provides conciliation procedure for spinning industry.

1894 Warpdressers' Amalgamation formed, and first warehousemen's local union. International Textile Workers' Association formed to meet employers' argument that low-wage European competition prevented wage-increases: Manchester conference attended by French, Belgian, Danish, and Austrian delegates (German unions joined later).

1895 Warehousemen's Amalgamation formed (originally as the 'Clothlookers' Amalgamation').

1896 Attempt at general amalgamation of manufacturing unions fails.

1898 Weavers' Amalgamation demands legal enforcement of Uniform List.

1900 Nelson and Colne Weavers' Associations attend first meeting of Labour Representation Committee.

1901 New Factory Act introduces 'twelve o'clock Saturday'. Injunction against Weavers in Blackburn strike leads Weavers' Amalgamation to demand independent Labour representation in Parliament.

1901 –02 Petition of 70,000 women textile operatives for women's suffrage.

1902 Weavers' official David Shackleton elected unopposed as LRC candidate in Clitheroe bye-election.

1903 United Textile Factory Workers' Association joins LRC. 'Universal List' for male cardroom hands agreed. Automatic looms introduced at Hyde; dispute on wage-rates. Weavers' First Amalgamation finally absorbed in Second.

1902–06 Weavers' Amalgamation campaign against 'slate system'.

1906 Northern Counties Textile Trades Federation formed as association of manufacturing unions. UTFWA concludes agreement for 11½ days' holiday per year. Joint Labour/Women's candidate at Wigan in 1906 election—several Labour M.P.s returned from Lancashire.

1907 Local strikes against employment of non-unionists. 'Universal List' for female cardroom hands agreed. Blackburn County Court case on dismissal of weavers leads to negotiated revision of 'Mill Rules'.

1908 Seven weeks' general lock-out of spinning trade after Cardroom's refusal of wage-reduction. Second attempt at piecers' 'breakaway' from spinners. Manufacturing industry conciliation procedure revised as 'Joint Rules'.

1909–10 Uniform Lists agreed for various types of specialized weaving.

1910 Lock-out of 100,000 spinning operatives over male cardroom hands' skill-status and interpretation of Brooklands Agreement. Spinning unions agree to 5-year 'standstill' of wage-rates. Injunction against political expenditure from Weavers' funds.

1911–12 160,000 manufacturing operatives locked-out for two weeks on Weavers' support of strike for 'union shop'.

1911–14 Many minor disputes, general unrest.

1912 Major cotton unions become 'approved societies' for new unemployment insurance.

1913 New T.U. Act legalizes 'political' expenditure. Unions temporarily withdraw from Brooklands Agreement. Universal List for Ring-Spinning agreed. Historical peak of U.K. cotton goods output.

1914 First World War leads to widespread unemployment in cotton.

1917 Cotton Control Board, with union representatives.

1918 Illegal strike of Spinners' Amalgamation for improvement of special war-time unemployment compensation scheme. Armistice followed by successful one-week general strike of cotton trades for wage-increases.

1919 Brief general strike of cotton operatives achieves reduction of working week from 55½ to 48 hours. Spinners' rejection of agreement leads to two weeks' lock-out.

1919–21 First standard wage-lists for winders. Warehousemen's general agreement for 'odd hands'.

1920 Plan for 'Cotton Workers' Federation' (super-Amalgamation of all cotton unions) fails.

1920–21 Cotton unions' peak membership (about half-million).

LAST PERIOD: CONTRACTION OF THE COTTON INDUSTRY

1921 Major slump follows collapse of post-war speculative boom. Three weeks' strike of 375,000 cotton operatives against wage-reductions. Masters' federations agree on systematic short-time to reduce output. 'Half-time' system of juvenile employment abolished.

1922 Further wage-reductions lead to strike-notices, unions withdraw after Cardroom's acceptance.

1925 Weavers' Amalgamation draws up 'Weavers' Charter', demanding guaranteed minimum wage, payment for under-employment, etc.

1926 Cotton unions involved in General Strike, make substantial grants to Miners.

1928 Unions join 'Joint Committee of Cotton Trade Organizations' with employers' associations, to demand trade protection and legal support for 'rationalization' measures. Masters' associations propose wage-reductions and longer hours.

1929 New slump. Three weeks' lock-out of spinning industry ended by arbitration award of general wage-cuts. Local weaving strikes in protest. 'Burnley experiment' for 'more looms-per-worker', with Weavers' consent.

1930–31 Registered unemployment in cotton reaches 47 per cent. Failure of negotiations for permanent 'more-looms' wage-systems. Burnley firms continue 'more-looms' working, and Master Manufacturers announce new piece-rates to be based on this. Weavers' Amalgamation strikes 'Burnley experiment' mills.

1931 General lock-out of 110,000 weaving trade operatives called off after nearly 7 weeks. Master Spinners suspend collective agreements after unions' rejection of longer working hours and wage-rate reductions.

1932 Master Manufacturers demand wage-reductions, suspend collective agreements. Burnley weavers' strike against wage-cuts. Breakdown of general negotiations leads to 4 weeks' strike of 150,000 weaving workers. Strike ended by conciliation in 'Midland Agreement', including wage-cuts and rates for 'more looms'. Master Spinners demand similar wage-cuts—accepted after week's stoppage of spinning industry. Conciliation Agreement restores 48-hour week.

1934 'Undercutting' of List rates leads to successful joint demand of Weavers and Master Manufacturers for legal enforcement of Uniform List (including 'more-looms' rates). Unions demand Cotton Control Board.

1935 Master Spinners 'recommend' union membership after mill disputes on non-unionists. Spinning unions withdraw from Conciliation Committee. Unions demand nationalization of cotton industry.

1935–37 Uniform Weaving List revised.

1936 'Spindles Act' provides legal support for reduction of excess capacity.

1937 Joint Committee of Cotton Trade Organizations' proposals for 'rationalization' of cotton industry.

1939 Cotton Industry Re-Organization Act provides for 'rationalization' schemes under legal Cotton Board. Holidays with pay agreement. Outbreak of Second World War. 'Cost-of-Living' agreement for war-time wage-adjustment. Cotton Board set up as war-time control agency, with union representation.

1941–42 Application of war-time labour controls to cotton industry leads to Guaranteed Wage agreement (but not applying to 'bad trade' in peacetime version).

1943 Cotton unions re-affirm nationalization as post-war programme.

1944 Coalition government rejects nationalization in immediate post-war period. Cotton Board sets up joint committee on post-war problems.

1945–46 Labour Government's 'working party' on cotton industry re-organization. 'Evershed' and 'Hughes' Commissions to review cotton wage-systems.

1946 UTFWA makes agreement for general 45-hour week.

1946–47 Drive for 'modernization', including re-equipment of mills, re-deployment of labour. Partial and conditional union acceptance of double-shift working. Government subsidy to spinning re-equipment.

1948 Permanent Cotton Board legally established as a 'Development Council', with union representation.

1949 'Evershed', 'Aronson', and 'CMC' agreements for revision of cotton wage systems. 'Indian Summer' of cotton trade follows devaluation of £.

1951–52 Sharp slump, intermittent recession continuing after. Part of N.E. Lancs. scheduled as a 'Development Area' for special assistance to provide alternative employment.

1955 Weaving unions accept 3-shift working conditionally.

1957 UTFWA'S 'Plan for Cotton' (the 'Wilson Plan') proposes 'mixed economy' for cotton industry, with state participation and support.

1958 Unions demand compensation for redundancy, rejected by employers. U.K. cotton goods imports exceed exports.

1959 Government scheme for organized contraction of cotton industry, with £30 million subsidy towards buying-out excess plant and re-equipment, makes compensation for displaced operatives a condition.

1960 'Concentration' reduces cotton trades' capacity by third to half: 37,000 operatives apply for 'redundancy compensation'. Spinning unions accept limited 3-shift working. Standard week reduced to 42½ hours.

INDEX

In principle, this Index does not include general subjects to the extent that these appear sufficiently indicated by the Chapter and Section headings of the CONTENTS (pp. 5–9) and are covered in those Sections, nor does it refer to the *Chronology* of the APPENDIX, Part 2 (pp. 383–94) unless the events, etc., concerned are not referred to in the main text.[1]

Personal names in italics (thus: *Wadsworth*) indicate references to other authors.

Words italicized in other references (thus: Amalgamated *Weavers'* Association) indicate alternative or related references in this Index.

Page numbers in heavy type (thus: 84, **86,** 95) indicate that the reference continues on the following page(s).

A

[1] The help of Dr. P. Wexler and the Computer Section of Manchester University in compiling this Index has been appreciated.

B

D

Y

Z

For Product Safety Concerns and Information please contact our EU representative GPSR@taylorandfrancis.com
Taylor & Francis Verlag GmbH, Kaufingerstraße 24, 80331 München, Germany

www.ingramcontent.com/pod-product-compliance
Ingram Content Group UK Ltd.
Pitfield, Milton Keynes, MK11 3LW, UK
UKHW020023200926
475702UK00014B/2036
9781032255064